.... Draper

For
B. A. W.
this work by the Editor

The Letters of
Ruth Draper

Self-Portrait of an Actress,
1920–1956

Edited by Dorothy Warren
With a Foreword by Sir John Gielgud

Southern Illinois University Press
Carbondale and Edwardsville

Acknowledgment is made to the following publishers and individuals for permission to reprint copyright material:
Mrs. Russel Crouse. Letter of Russel Crouse to May Seymour Eckert, Museum of the City of New York. Courtesy of the museum.
Brooks Atkinson. Review originally published in *The New York Times*.
Norris Darrell. Letter of Learned Hand.
Edward Downes. Letter of Olin Downes to R. D.
Sir Oliver Franks. Letter to R. D.
Miss Helen Hayes. Letter to R. D.
Christopher H. Phillips. Quotation from the journal of his mother, Mrs. William Phillips.
Faber & Faber, London, and the Oxford University Press, New York. The drawing of Lauro de Bosis that appeared as the frontispiece to *The Story of My Death* (London and New York, 1933) and quoted portions of *The Story of My Death*.
Malvina Hoffman, *Yesterday Is Tomorrow*. © 1965 by Malvina Hoffman. Used by permission of Crown Publishers, Inc.
Harcourt Brace Jovanovich, Inc. Anne Morrow Lindbergh, *Locked Rooms and Open Doors* (New York, 1974) and *The Flower and the Nettle* (New York, 1976).
Harper and Row Publishers, Inc. Hamilton Fish Armstrong, *Those Days* (New York, 1963).
Houghton Mifflin Co. *John Jay Chapman and His Letters*, ed. by M.A. de Wolfe Howe (Boston, 1937); *Henry Adams and His Friends*, ed by Harold Dean Cater (Boston, 1947); *Letters of Henry Adams*, vol. II, ed. by Worthington Chauncey Ford (Boston, 1938)
Alfred A. Knopf, Inc. Arthur Rubinstein, *My Young Years*. Copyright © 1973 by Aniela Rubinstein, Eva Rubinstein Coffin, Alina Anna Rubinstein, and John Arthur Rubinstein.
Erich Linder, Agenzia Litteraria Internazionale, Milan & Baron Cecil Anrep. Bernard Berenson, *Sunset and Twilight (Diaries 1947–1958)* (New York, 1963).
Iris Origo. Article in Cornhill Magazine, Issue No. 1014, winter 1957/58.
The New Yorker. Janet Flanner, "Paris Journal 1944–1965" (Atheneum) Originally in *The New Yorker.*
Random House, New York, and Heinemann Educational Books, Inc., London.
Ronald Hayman, *John Gielgud* (New York and London, © 1971) by Ronald Hayman.
Anne Morrow Lindbergh, *The Most Unforgettable Character I've Met: Edward Sheldon*. Originally appeared in *Reader's Digest.* Copyright © 1947 by The Reader's Digest Association, Inc.
Compton Russell Ltd. *Freya Stark's Letters*, 1935–1939. © Freya Stark 1976.
St. Martin's Press. Sir John Wheeler-Bennett, *Friends, Enemies and Sovereigns* (New York, 1976); Joyce Grenfell, *Joyce Grenfell Requests the Pleasure* (New York, 1977).
Charles Scribner's Sons. Eric Woollencott Barnes, *The Man Who Lived Twice* (New York, 1956).
The Viking Press Inc., and Hamish Hamilton Ltd. Harold Acton, *Memoirs of an Aesthete 1939–1969* (New York, 1971, and London, 1970) © Harold Acton 1970.
A. P. Watt & Son for permission to quote from *The Journal of Arnold Bennett*. London, 1932–1933.

First published 1979 by Charles Scribner's Sons
Paperback edition published 1999 by Southern Illinois University Press
Printed in the United States of America
02 01 00 99   4 3 2 1

Library of Congress Cataloging-in-Publication Data
Draper, Ruth, 1884–1956.
    The letters of Ruth Draper : self-portrait of an actress, 1920–1956 / edited by Dorothy Warren ; with a foreword by Sir John Gielgud.
        p.   cm.
    Originally published: New York : Scribner, c1979.
    Discography: p.
    Includes bibliographical references and index.
    1. Draper, Ruth, 1884–1956. 2. Actors—United States Correspondence. I. Warren, Dorothy, 1905– . II. Title.
PN2287.D549A4 1999
792'.028'092
[B]—DC21   99-25456
ISBN 0-8093-2188-2 (pbk. : alk. paper)   CIP

The paper used in this publication meets the minimum requirements of American National Standard for Information Sciences—Permanence of Paper for Printed Library Materials, ANSI Z39.48-1984. ∞

Note to the Reader

The Letters of Ruth Draper, which I edited under the name Neilla Warren, has long been out of print. Now reprinted in paperback, the book presents one aspect of a rounded portrait of Ruth Draper, a fiercely private person and reticent stage professional.

The Letters of Ruth Draper tells what she thought about herself, her life, and her career. *The World of Ruth Draper*, published concurrently, is in large part, a distillation of the memories and experience of her family and close friends—those who knew her best.

Dorothy Warren
February 1999

Errata

Several errors crept into the first printing of this volume. They are corrected as follows:

Page	Line	
2	19	*For* hecperhaps, *read* her perhaps.
7	6	*Replace the semicolon with a comma.*
18	8	*For* July 7, 1920, *read* July 5, 1920.
47	19	*For* 1919–1920, *read* 1918–1919.
60	22	*For* October 29, 1923, *read* Sunday, October 28, 1923.
66	35	*For* Duchess—, *read* Duchess—[Grand Duchess Cyril].
75	13	*For* yo, *read* you.
75	28	*For* Kenneth Terry Martin, *read* David Terry Martin.
77	31	*For* Tues 20th, *read* Tuesday 25th.
97	18	*The dog was not a gift from Lauro.*
106	18	*For* old town, *read* old tower.
107	13	*For* youngest son, *read* second son.
107	17	*For* Cortesi, *read* Cortese.
109	24	*For* Matteotti, *read* Matteotti [July 10, 1924].
109	28–29	*For* he had applied for the semi-official appointment as, *read* the Italy-America Society approached him to be.
109	33	*For* June 1930, *read* October 15, 1930.
110	3	*For* Olympic Prize for Poetry, *read* Olympic Prize for Dramatic Poetry.
110	12	*For* League, *read* Institute.
110	28	*For* December 1st, *read* November 25th.
110	35	*For* a friend, *read* a friend [Ruth Draper].
110	35	*For* three members, *read* two members.
111	14	*For* to sign, *read* to write.
111	28	*For* had signed, *read* had written.
114	4	*For* another letter (250 letters), *read* a compilation of all letters.
117	36	*For* tried, and acquitted, *read* neither acquitted nor found guilty.
119	15	*For* Milan in 1948, *read* Turin in 1948.

119	16	*For* July 11th, *read* July 13th.
119	17–19	*Omit text from* On the plane *to* the French police.
119	31	*For* [Paris], *read* [From Hotel Lancaster, Paris].
126	6	*For* October 6th, *read* October7th.
126	32	*For* the 5th, *read* Tuesday, October 6th.
134	8	*For* To Bernard Berenson, *read* To Bernard Berenson with Edith Wharton at Hyères.
139	35	*For* put out by Salvemini, *read* edited by Salvemini.
149	25	*For* born, *read* borne.
189	6–7	*For* but, apparently, at Clivedon, *read* but with Ronald and Nancy Tree at Ditchley Park.
191	29	*The performance on March 29 was not at Kunstring.*
191	31	*The performance on March 31 was not at Kunstring.*
191	3	*The performance on April 2 was not at Kunstring.*
232	28	*Omit* "shadow cabinet."
238	9	*For* January 1947 she, *read* January 1947 (except for December 1942) she.
249	34	*For* shaken aout, *read* shaken about.

Contents

Acknowledgments

The mere mention of Ruth Draper's name has, without exception, opened a wealth of cooperation and of memories—joyful, incredulous, laughing memories, always delightful, endlessly fascinating. The biographical portions of this book are a mosaic of memories.

The Editor's most grateful thanks are due, above all, to the heirs of the Estate of Ruth Draper for their enthusiastic approval of this undertaking and for the necessary legal permission to publish her letters; for their considerable consultation, thanks are due most particularly to William Draper Carter, Ruth Dana Carter, Paul Draper, Penelope Draper Buchanan, and Mrs. George Draper. They have reviewed the significant portions, if not all, of the manuscript and have not requested substantive changes of any kind.

Thanks are due also to the nephews of Lauro de Bosis, Alessandro Cortese-de Bosis and Arturo Vivante, for permission to quote various letters of their uncle, and for reviewing and approving that portion of the manuscript.

The Editor and heirs alike are infinitely grateful to Sir John Gielgud for his warm and personal Foreword, and for his so evident pleasure in writing it.

To Ruth Draper's friends and professional associates, who gave of their recollections and special insights in many hours of engrossing talk, the Editor remains deeply obligated: Miss Aileen Tone with whom, initially, this work was discussed, Mrs. W. A. Burnham (Alice Boit), Mrs. Lawrence White (Laura Chanler), Mrs. Reginald P. Grenfell (Joyce Phipps), Mrs. Nelson Dean Jay, Mrs. Louis Graves, Mrs. Felix Salmond, Mrs. Clarke K. Oler (Wendy Salmond), Mrs. Arthur O. Choate (Eloise Weld), Mrs. C. Haven Ladd (Phyllis Howe), Mrs. Eva Rubinstein, Miss Viola Peters, Miss Gulburg G. Groneng, Mr. Neville Rogers, Mrs. Janos Scholz, Mr. Paul E. Wilson, Mrs. R. McAneny Loud.

Mr. Charles Bowden, Miss Draper's manager, was extremely helpful, as was Richard Barr and her stage managers, Barnet Owens and Gerald O'Brien, and her dresser, Wilhelmina Reavis. Mr. Richard Mohr provided factual information and his special knowledge of Miss Draper's recording sessions for RCA. Harriet Marple's brother and niece, William E. Marple and Miss Harriet B. Marple, were generous in recollections of Ruth Draper's great friend, as were her godson, Richard M. Sheble, and Mrs. Sheble. In the study of Edward B. Sheldon his niece, Georgiana MacArthur Hansen, became an invaluable resource, Miss Helen Hayes was considerate and helpful, and Dr. Loren K. Ruff, then completing his biography of Sheldon, was unbelievably generous in sharing material and the fruits of his own research.

Without the kindness of many individuals and libraries, both in providing access to collections and in granting permission to publish, this narrative-in-letters could not have been possible. The Editor's debt of gratitude is measureless: to Her Majesty Queen Elizabeth II for gracious permission to quote excerpts from the diary of Queen Mary, from a letter written by Queen Mary's Lady-in-Waiting, Lady Cynthia Colville, and from letters of Ruth Draper to Sir Alan Lascelles, then Private Secretary to King George VI; to the Rt. Hon. Sir Martin Charteris, Private Secretary to the Queen, for his extraordinary generosity of time and helpfulness; and to John Alsop for letters to his mother, Corinne Robinson Alsop; to Charles Burlingham for two letters to his father, C. C. Burlingham; to Mr. and Mrs. Charles L. Hoffman and the Malvina Hoffman Properties for letters to Malvina Hoffman; to Mrs. Harley Merica and the Library of the Performing Arts of the New York Public Library for letters to Harley Merica; to Mrs. Perry D. Trafford for a letter to Aileen Tone; and the following libraries and their curators of manuscript collections: to The New-York Historical Society, which has custody of the bulk of Miss Draper's papers, and particularly to James Gregory, Librarian, for his interest, advice, and encouragement from the first proposal of this work; and to Thomas J. Dunnings, Jr., Curator of Manuscripts, who has taken endless pains to further the Editor's research and to the Curator of the Museum for the 1896 drawing of Ruth Draper; to the Butler Library of Columbia University in the City of New York for a letter to John Erskine; to the Fondazione Giorgio Cini for a letter to Eleonora Duse; to the Library of Colby College, Waterville, Maine, for all letters to Grace M. Martin; to the Houghton Library of Harvard University, for a letter to Corinne Roosevelt Robinson, for access to the de Bosis papers, and to its Edward B. Sheldon Memorial Theatre Collection for letters to Theodore Sheldon, Jr., and to Mary Sheldon MacArthur; and to the Harvard University Center for Renaissance Studies for letters to Bernard Berenson as well as to Baron Cecil Anrep for permission to publish them; to the Humanities Research Center of the University of Texas at Austin for two letters to Arnold Bennett, two to Stark Young, and one to J. L. Garvin; to the Theatre Collection of the Museum of the City of New York for access to its files on Ruth Draper and for perission to publish the J. S. Sargent drawings and photographs "in character"; to the Franklin D. Roosevelt Library at Hyde Park, New York, and to Franklin D. Roosevelt, Jr., for a letter to Mrs. Franklin D. Roosevelt; to the Schelling Archive for a letter to Mrs. Ernest Schelling, and to the Sterling Library of Yale University for letters to William Adams Delano; Station WFMT, Chicago, for a cassette of a Studs Terkel interview; to the BBC, London, for a broadcast of 16 March 1946; and to the New York Academy of Medicine for a presentation address of May 1948. Most appreciative thanks are due, also, to those librarians who provided material of great value to the whole but which, for a variety of reasons, it was not possible to include: Bodleian Library, Oxford University,

England; Dumbarton Oaks Collection, Washington, D. C.; Harvard Law School Library, Mrs. James H. Chadbourn, Curator of MSS and Archives, for letters to Judge Learned Hand; the Huntington Library, San Marino, California, William Ingoldsby, Assistant Curator of Literary MSS; the Massachusetts Historical Society, Boston, Stephen T. Riley, Director, for review of the Henry Adams correspondence, 1913–14; the Newberry Library, Chicago, Diana Haskell, Curator, Modern MSS; Princeton University Library, William Seymour Theatre Collection; Trinity College Library, Cambridge University, England, letters to Lady (James) Frazer; Beinecke Library, Yale University, Donald Gallup, Curator, Collection of American Literature; the British Library, London.

Grateful acknowledgment is made to Mildred S. MacPherson for translations and knowledgeable advice throughout the construction of this book and for endless, most patient listening; to Helen Wormser for translations and research; to Suzanne Pettit and to Christine Schutt whose enthusiasm, sensibility, and special skills advanced completion of this MS by many months; and, finally, gratitude in full measure to Elinor Parker of Charles Scribner's Sons, the most congenial and least meddlesome of editors, who thoroughly comprehended the realization of this enterprise.

N.W.

Foreword

The curtained stage was empty save for a few pieces of essential furniture: a sofa, a couple of chairs, and perhaps a table. Ruth Draper walked on, a tall, dark-eyed lady, elegant in her simple brown dress, beautifully cut, and looked out over the auditorium with grave composure. Her authority and concentration were absolute. How swiftly she transformed that stage into her own extraordinary world, transporting us at her immediate bidding to other places, other countries—a boudoir, a garden, a church, a customs shed—London or New York, Rome or Paris, the coast of Maine—creating in each of those imagined settings a single dominant personality, and then seeming to surround herself, as she needed them, with an attendant crowd of minor characters, children, animals, servants, husbands, lovers. Her wit and imagination never failed to enthrall one, never palled with repetition, however often one had seen some of her most famous monologues. How did she set about composing these extraordinary sketches, so marvellously observed and minutely executed? How did she rehearse and develop them over the years? She once told me that she never even wrote them down until quite late in her career, and that she could shorten or lengthen them while she was playing as she felt the reactions of her audience demanded. Her diction was impeccable, her mastery of all kinds of different accents inimitable. Her gestures and the deployment of her head, body, and feet exactly varied according to each of the women she portrayed. So too her use of external properties—the fan, the shawl, hat, or lorgnette chosen with such perfect selectivity. The telephone she used so effectively in *The Italian Lesson* was imaginary, however, as were many other concrete objects which a lesser artist would have found necessary to complete illusion. I only saw her once appear in full costume—elaborate wig and wide skirts—as a Spanish lady of the Court of the Velasquez period, and this was the only occasion on which I found her less than completely successful.

I can never forget her snobbish wife in *Three Women and Mr. Clifford*, lolling back in her limousine, her whole body jerking with the vehicle whenever the traffic hindered its smooth progress, or the moving curve of her arm when, as the mistress in the last episode of the same sketch, she leaned over the back of the armchair to embrace her lover.

Of course she was admired in London long before I saw her first, but I remember being intrigued as a very young man by the poster she then used for the few public recitals she gave (I think at the Wigmore Hall) in addition to performances at private parties—the famous charcoal sketch that John Sargent drew of her with a shawl draped over her head.

I met her first at one of Lady Colefax's luncheon parties in Chelsea some forty years ago. Sibyl Colefax has been often disparaged in recent memoirs (and even during her own lifetime) as a snob and a lion-hunter, but I was extremely fond of her, and grateful for the wonderful opportunity she gave to young artists like me of meeting many brilliant literary, political, and theatrical figures of the time whom we should never have had the good fortune to encounter without her hospitable invitations.

After that first meeting I always went to see Ruth Draper after enjoying one of her performances, and found her immensely sympathetic and delightful, though the trenchant, acid wit that often sharpened many of her stage creations was not in the least evident in talking to her in private life.

I cherish in particular three occasions connected with her. The first was an evening in New York when, at the end of a dinner party, she invited a small group of us back to her flat, and there, in front of the fire, as we all sat around in chairs and on the floor, she acted several of her scenes for us. How fascinating to observe her at such close quarters in such intimate surroundings!

The second was a summer afternoon in London. The great singer Kathleen Ferrier was dying of an incurable disease, and some friends of hers, Ruth Draper amongst them, had taken a beautiful ground-floor flat looking out onto a very pretty garden, so that she might recuperate there after several weeks in hospital. I was invited to go to see her, and found Ruth standing beside her bed. We all tried to behave quite naturally, talking and laughing as best we could, while Miss Ferrier, radiantly beautiful as she sat up to greet us, in a little pink jacket edged with white fur, held Ruth's hand and waved gallantly to us all as we bade her farewell.

On the third occasion, I had taken an American friend who had never seen her to one of her last performances at the St. James' Theatre in London, and when we went round to her dressing-room afterwards she was standing on a white drugget, looking much smaller than I remembered her, greatly aged and a little deaf. Yet only a few moments before we had marvelled at her final sketch—one I had never seen before—in which she played a temperamental Polish actress full of fire and emotion and speaking at a tremendous pace in an amazing mixture of languages.

During one of her last London seasons she made a few television versions of some of her sketches. These have never been shown, I believe, and I only hope they are somewhere in the archives, preserved to be seen one day by a generation that never had the privilege of knowing what a consummate artist she was.

My friend the late Hugh Beaumont, for whom she made the films, told me that on the last day of shooting she was asked which sketch she proposed to give next day. She answered promptly, "I shall do *The Debutante!*" Everyone looked somewhat dismayed—for she was then no longer young—but on the following day she arrived, flung a great scarf of pink tulle around her throat, and gave such an inspired performance that the whole studio burst into spontaneous applause.

I have always felt that Ruth Draper was (with Martha Graham) the greatest individual performer that America has ever given us, and I count myself infinitely fortunate to have known her a little as a woman as well as having been given so much joy by the extraordinary and unique subtleties of her art.

John Gielgud
London, 23 April 1978

An Introduction to Ruth Draper

RUTH DRAPER and Her Company of Characters—so she was billed and so she was acclaimed: the greatest character actress of her time. For thirty-seven years she performed alone, on a bare stage, with a few shawls, an odd hat or coat, and perhaps a chair or table. The nearly sixty character sketches carried in her memory were solely of her own imagining and ranged through a wide variety of types, emotions, and stories. What was her essential quality, she who was so many, so easily?

Ruth Draper had an extraordinary personal genius. If one could separate the woman, the self, from the brilliant artist of the theatre, still she remained unique. With an inborn gift, such as Nijinsky had, to *personify* rather than merely to impersonate, she possessed the ability instantly to *become* the character and personality that she held in her imagination. This ability she never lost and at 70 could truthfully say: "I see the world always through the eyes of a child." It is this quality of the child that was at the core of her genius and of her self.

First to consider the self:

Unexpectedly naïve, there was a point beyond which she did not mature but kept forever the purity and innocence of youth: the freshness, the eagerness, the wonder—which isolated her from much of the reality of the everyday world. She was not a worldly person; but she was armed with a concentrated intense vision and enough shrewdness, if she cared to use it, to protect herself against encroachment. Although she spoke easily of her work, she did not talk of herself or of her own affairs, even in the family, only to a very few, very special friends. Essentially a private person, she held tightly the initiative and independence of her life. She had common sense. She held strong views on moral values. Her wit was acute and perceptive.

Ruth Draper's devotion to her family was complete and close. Primarily an artist, her work came first but her relationship with her seven brothers and sisters was continually warmed by mutual interest and concern, by her need to communicate with them and about them within the family. No matter how distantly she traveled, letters to and from home were a constant and vital link.

Friendship played an important role: hers was warm, outgoing, and compassionate. Never a snob, her criterion was the quality of the person, the integrity of character, the "realness." She made friends with a London "barrow man," a long-time admirer, who sold secondhand books from a barrow, or pushcart. There were two good seats for him at a performance and he took her "by tube and tram to Walworth for tea and cake and a special treat of flan with my lady and to see some of my little treasures." Some days after this she had tea at St. James's Palace with Lord and Lady Clarendon where the King and Queen were guests. Both occasions she enjoyed and appreciated, each in its own context, and if she juxtaposed them in her mind at all it was only to relish them the more. As, inevitably, the range and scope of her friendships grew, she delightedly savored every turn of the scene; never a lion-hunter, she nonetheless immensely enjoyed her opportunities to appraise the lions. And no matter how casual the encounter she found interest and pleasure. In February 1955 she wrote her sister, describing "a touching letter from a perfect stranger I smiled at in the National Gallery in Washington. I was on my way out and just said—'how beautiful it is—I hate to go!' I paused a moment and must have said I was on my way to my matinee. I had lunched in the Cafeteria before starting and she evidently saw me there. Such little incidents are precious. She had a nice face so I smiled—a refined and charming person, tired, but moved by the lovely things in the rooms where the tiny objects are—ivory, gold things and bronzes."

With her close friends—the friends of her heart—there was no limit to her appreciation, her active concern, her generosity, and her participation in their lives. She enjoyed equally what she found and what she could give in return; no effort was too great, and she took pride in remembering special "treats" she thought would give pleasure. In her attitude there was no shade of difference to any, however situated.

Sir Sydney Cockerell spoke of her as humane and civilized. Isabella Massey wrote: "Never can a personality of such forcefulness have been more universally beloved!" Air Chief Marshall Sir William Elliot wrote in the London *Times* a few days after her death:

> Nothing can repair the loss of her friendship. Memories remain—her beauty . . . her joy in all that is fine and noble in mind and body, and her revulsion from any form of injustice or intolerance; her culture and her artistry. . . . She was sophisticated yet simple, a woman of the world who was a saint, and so the most delightful company. Surely no one ever gave so much pleasure to so many with so little to-do. . . . Her day was always the morning with the freshness of dawn.

Open-handedly generous to others, Ruth Draper was thrifty, almost stingy in her personal expenditures. Characteristic of her generation and background, thrift was ever present in daily life; there is constant reference to the "costly postage," or her "costly bed" in a very good hotel. She was better suited with the inexpensive, the hotel or pension native to the area rather than the deluxe, the "Grand" hotel, and her ingrained simplicity of taste and perspective on herself reinforced this continuing preference. Always well turned out, she bought good clothes—being a professional woman and socially much in the public eye—clothes of the best material, of fine design and workmanship, but never "showy," never expensive beyond their value. Ruth Draper delighted in her success and "the dollars rolling in" because it brought her comfort—living simply, and in no great style—but above all because it enabled her to help "the less successful earners in the family," as well as to meet an emergency or smooth the rockier passages of those she loved—or perhaps had never met. Always it was done with tact, sensibility, and proportion, often anonymously. Paul Kochanski, the Polish violinist, received $5000 to buy a Guarnerius to enhance his brilliant talent. The purchase of a mink coat for herself was accompanied by the purchase of a fur coat for a friend with more limited resources. A cheque to Aileen Tone was received as "a sudden élan du coeur." Wealth beyond her own needs embarrassed her and in her Puritan conscience was acceptable only as it enabled her to help others.

As a child Ruth's individual qualities were early recognized even by her brothers and sisters. Delicate and forlorn looking with great brown eyes, she was somewhat apart from the four elder ones—observant, quiet, busy in her own mind. Before she was nine years of age she was "pretending": the little Jewish tailor who came to the house, the seamstress who also came several times a year. Both were the models for "another self" in which she would spend a long afternoon, sewing, sniffling, talking to herself, complaining about the light; completely oblivious to the children's games going on around her, she was self-sufficient in her imaginary world. In this way began the natural expression of her genius.

More rounded personifications followed: her life-long friend Alice Boit, then a next-door neighbor at Islesboro, remembers going to the Drapers', where she found Ruth "with her hair tied up, on her knees on the kitchen floor, scrubbing away for all she was worth." Asked why she was doing *that*, she paused not a moment in her labors as she told a long tale of being a "widow with all these children" and how hard she had to work to feed them! On another occasion, asked to join in some small expedition, Ruth, busy with other things, responded by instantly becoming another person for whom such an outing was quite inappropriate. With such complete spontaneity could an entirely unpremeditated character be summoned into play. So intrinsically a part of her was this gift that as she grew the character of the "pretending" grew also, but without ever losing its true quality: "the child's ability to *become* what he imagines he is—to believe it himself—and believe that you think so, too." But this was never to become a way of life obscuring the real person. It was fun; it was an unarguable way of making her point; often it was a sort of protective coloration as her life broadened and she grew in fame and stature as an actress. In this context she might assume a personal role as a defense, an armor for her deep sense of insecurity, for she held always a very poor opinion of herself as a person. This self-evaluation, certainly, her solidly New England background, probably, were at the root of her sense of inferiority. She was super-sensitive, and the most trifling remark might be received as a personal hurt, even an attack. Her emotions were ever at the surface. But when her insecurity could not meet the test, Ruth Draper reacted in one of two ways: either she withdrew completely, almost into a state of non-existence, or she became the diva—the important actress. The diva often appeared in the greenroom and sometimes appeared socially among friends, occasionally with a cutting remark, quite oblivious of hurt to others. The self-effacement occurred in the company of writers or musicians, actors or scientists, those eminent in a special field, any one of whom she regarded as more significant, more worthwhile of accomplishment than herself. Developing slowly and late, it would seem that her inner self never kept pace with her public position, however certainly she grew in competent professionalism. Her success was accepted with gratitude and humility, but always with wonder—for rarely was she satisfied with her own performance.

The monologue is a special form of acting, a dramatic composition for a single performer evoking other characters upon the stage. Over the years of theatre history there have been many practitioners: Cecilia Loftus in England, Beatrice Herford in the United States, George Grossmith, Charles Mathew, back to Albert Smith—the list is long and the variations many. Most could be considered "platform entertainers" and the usual vehicle was farce or comedy, mimicry or the dramatic reading. But no one, before Ruth Draper, had such mastery, such range, or such complete independence of all aids; none were exclusively their own playwright. She was the greatest exponent of this form of theatre art—and its supreme individualist. Brooks Atkinson called hers "an inscrutable art, . . . for all art that travels the full range of emotions from comedy to tragedy, carrying truth on its back, is not to be presumptuously explained." She would say: "Diseuse, recitalist, monologuist—I am not any of these, I am a character actress," and she regarded her sketches as character dramas. Determined that she would be on a *stage,* she intensely disliked performing on a platform, whether in a college hall or a hotel ballroom, and possibly felt her theatrical image to be diminished if she regularly, even for a season, accepted less than a theatre. As far as the actual performance went, she could work anywhere, but whatever the psychological effect may have been—on audience or on performer—the *theatre's stage* was where she felt herself to belong.

Ruth Draper began her career, she said, because for her it was so natural and so easy. Natural it surely was, and easy because it was her natural instrument of expression—yet effort she gave to it, hard, concentrated, and relentlessly self-critical effort. "This urgent active driving thing—my work" was the force of her genius, peremptory, overriding, not to be denied, and in its exercise she found her enduring satisfaction, her sense of life and awareness. Uncompetitive, even withdrawn among her peers of the theatre, she was, beyond doubt, what the Germans call *theatermensch,* a being of the theatre, whose inmost soul comes to full and vivid flowering only when performing.

Except for two sketches (*County Kerry* and *Three Generations*), none were based on her observation of actual incidents or people and none were in any sense autobiographical. Never did she put anyone she knew or had seen into a sketch, all her characters being purely fabrications. She did not mimic or impersonate, for true acting is neither of these. She simply imagined a character and *became* it—the voice, gestures, and dialogue springing directly from her conception: "I just *feel* the person I depict." All her life, alert as a chipmunk, she must, unconsciously, have been registering gesture, speech, accent, physical mannerism, the essence of character and personality, storing them away in her subconscious, in her muscles and sinews and bones, above all in her emotions, ready to draw upon when a story with its character suggested itself. Her people were drawn cleanly with sure strokes but, however sharply penetrating of human foibles, never cruelly or with acid. She claimed not particularly to think of this, but as she "saw a little of the ridiculous, of the pitiful, in everyone," her characters were "made up of many parts, as human beings are," and there was no malice, no scorn, no hate—only understanding and compassion, tenderness or amusement. Each character emerged from its depiction in the round, with integrity intact, having suffered no indignity and having in no way offended anyone's sensibility. The most ridiculous or most humble was somehow ennobled; the poignant or tragic reached a plane of quiet intensity, a great depth of meaning. Beyond doubt, this quality stemmed directly from her own reserve and ingrained good taste—her own civilized self. Learned Hand was to say after her death: "She seemed to have lived countless lives and remembered them all; she had to have the whole creation of her people, as though she must transmute her own being into another's."

Ruth Draper's aural memory was quick and true; she must have had perfect pitch and it never failed her. As she was completely given over to *being* the person she portrayed, her gestures flowed spontaneously and naturally. She was amazed, rehearsing in her one attempt to play with other actors, to hear Marie Tempest, in a tone of desperation, say to the Director: "What shall I do with my hands, Willie, what shall I do with my hands?" And she thought, "How funny to ask such a question for surely the use of the hands should be an unconscious expression of the character in action—surely the whole body should act." She never thought of, or practiced, gestures yet was a superb master of mime, with a hand-mime quiet, economical, and sure. She could "sit on a beach and play with the sand" until the audience felt it between their fingers.

Ruth Draper was blessed with extraordinary health and vitality, which she felt to be the most important gift any artist could have, great vitality being essential if the actor is to project across the footlights. Particularly in her form of acting, projection of the character was indispensable, for it had to be strong enough to fire the imagination of the audience into supplying all that was not there: the more than 300 different supporting characters she evoked onto the stages with her, the scenes, the churches, the rooms—all before a plain neutral or brown velvet curtain—and the costumes suggested only by a shawl or a hat, sweater or coat. She said, "I must get the audience up onto the stage and into the scene with me—they contribute in proportion exactly what the performer contributes, and when they give their *whole* imagination, their concentration and thought and creative ability, something happens—it's a mixture. The audience is not right in giving me the credit—it is something in them—their capacity to create is stirred and that is why they enjoy it." Because what the audience gave back became part of the play, whenever she faced an audience that did not share—did not respond—she would nearly explode with frustration, feeling it less than a whole performance. But with an intelligent and responsive audience she could reach the heights, and reveled in it, fully aware that this participation carried them all back, through Shakespeare, to the Greeks.

Never fully written down, her dramas were available instantly at the summons of her will. The fluidity of the changing, inspired dialogue and gesture was part of her stage genius. If she tried to write she never liked what she had written, and it was only in the last two or three years of her life that she made recordings or was filmed. With none of the results was she satisfied. She said that if she ever saw herself in performance she was sure she would never act again; and it made her acutely uncomfortable to see others in solo performance, for there she saw herself.

Her stage gifts were so dazzling that few realized her skill as a dramatist. Thornton Wilder, Robert Emmet Sherwood, Alexander Woollcott, Brooks Atkinson, all testified to this, with Wilder and Sherwood in 1954 proposing her for membership in the American Institute of Arts and Letters—as a playwright! To their dismay, the Institute's definition of a playwright was too rigid to permit her election.

Ruth Draper died in 1956. The on-stage image fades, and though some of us have memories of her vital genius and vivid personality, these too will fade. But here we have her letters covering the entire span of her thirty-seven years on the stages of the world. These carry a clear narrative line through the pattern of her career—which was her life—through her growth in character, and through the personal drama of her art. In her passion for writing letters—for truly it was a passion—Ruth Draper has, perhaps, spontaneously and unaware, with never a thought of publication, achieved her early dream of becoming a writer. *This* achievement can be held securely within the covers of a book.

N.W.

Editorial Notes

"Selection" of Ruth Draper's letters was made, primarily, by her family and friends, who routinely disposed of many, as she did of theirs. However, more than a thousand letters have been made available from which to choose those that advance and sustain her narrative; it has remained for the Editor only to set up the warp through which to weave the strands of her own telling.

The greatest affinity, the moments of most poignant, sympathetic response, lay in her work abroad, where, except for the years of World War II, she spent nearly half her adult life. It was these months, in Great Britain—particularly London—in Italy, and in Paris, on the long tours of the 1930s, that held the deepest professional experience, the real fulfillment and satisfaction of her career. Because nearly all these letters were written from abroad to her sisters and friends at home, it follows quite appropriately that this aspect of her life is the more fully covered.

While no attempt has been made to chronicle in detail Ruth Draper's professional engagements, which would be tedious indeed, indications of her constant activity are implicit in the letters. They were written wherever she had a free moment, written straight off, at great speed, in an almost unchangingly clean, legible, and characteristic hand, with rarely a correction or addition and almost never a misspelling.

There are some omissions, aside from repetitious passages: almost all the purely family references, in which her letters abound, are family trivia or far too personal to be included. Many close relatives, or their children, are still living, and the various worries and comments regarding health, finances, or the conduct of life should be of little interest to the general reader, as should some of her references to friends, for Ruth Draper was ever concerned and involved and wanting to help. She never gossiped.

Salutations and closing expressions of affection have, in general, been omitted. As the greater number of these letters were written to a very few people, the recurrent greeting and phrases become monotonous, add little to the letters, and distract from the easy flow of her narrative.

Political comments are infrequent, but where they refer to opinions of others—who might not have wished to be quoted publicly—they have been omitted. Ruth Draper had little interest in politics as such, being aroused only when she saw injustice.

These omissions are not indicated in all cases, but additions or explanations are meticulously bracketed. Although many of the letters were dated only by the day of the week, performance schedules and engagement books have served to fix quite accurately all but a few. Punctuation remains as written except for a bit of tidying up in the interest of clarity.

All statements of fact or interpretation are based on Ruth Draper's own letters, papers, and records, on letters and memoranda of family and friends, and on their conversations with the Editor.

Finally, too-evident scholarship—particularly footnotes—seems uncongenial to Ruth Draper's eager pursuit of life and beauty. Therefore items such as chronology, family connections, persons perhaps not well known to today's reader, and similar information have all been placed separately, or with brief biographical notes in the Index, except where they could agreeably be set in brackets into the context.

Genealogy

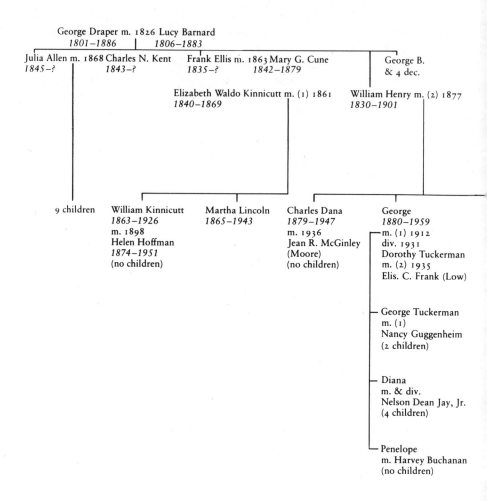

George Draper m. 1826 Lucy Barnard
1801–1886   *1806–1883*

Julia Allen m. 1868 Charles N. Kent   Frank Ellis m. 1863 Mary G. Cune   George B.
1845–?   *1843–?*   *1835–?*   *1842–1879*   & 4 dec.

Elizabeth Waldo Kinnicutt m. (1) 1861   William Henry m. (2) 1877
1840–1869   *1830–1901*

9 children

William Kinnicutt
1863–1926
m. 1898
Helen Hoffman
1874–1951
(no children)

Martha Lincoln
1865–1943

Charles Dana
1879–1947
m. 1936
Jean R. McGinley
(Moore)
(no children)

George
1880–1959
m. (1) 1912
div. 1931
Dorothy Tuckerman
m. (2) 1935
Elis. C. Frank (Low)

George Tuckerman
m. (1)
Nancy Guggenheim
(2 children)

Diana
m. & div.
Nelson Dean Jay, Jr.
(4 children)

Penelope
m. Harvey Buchanan
(no children)

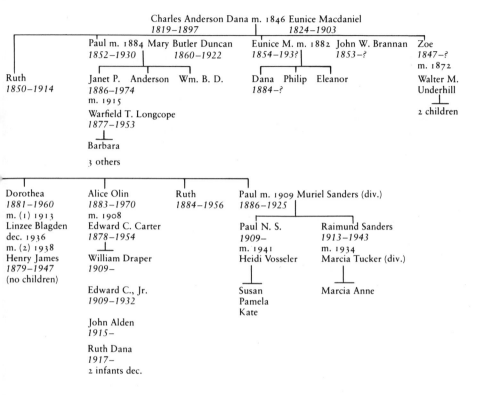

Charles Anderson Dana m. 1846 Eunice Macdaniel
1819–1897 | *1824–1903*

Paul m. 1884 Mary Butler Duncan   Eunice M. m. 1882 John W. Brannan   Zoe
1852–1930 | *1860–1922*   *1854–193?* | *1853–?*   *1847–?*
                                       m. 1872

Ruth   Janet P.   Anderson   Wm. B. D.   Dana   Philip   Eleanor   Walter M.
1850–1914   *1886–1974*   *1884–?*   Underhill
             m. 1915

             Warfield T. Longcope   2 children
             1877–1953

             Barbara

             3 others

Dorothea   Alice Olin   Ruth   Paul m. 1909 Muriel Sanders (div.)
1881–1960   *1883–1970*   *1884–1956*   *1886–1925* |
m. (1) 1913   m. 1908
Linzee Blagden   Edward C. Carter   Paul N. S.   Raimund Sanders
dec. 1936   *1878–1954*   *1909–*   *1913–1943*
m. (2) 1938   m. 1941   m. 1934
Henry James   William Draper   Heidi Vosseler   Marcia Tucker (div.)
1879–1947   *1909–*
(no children)

             Edward C., Jr.   Susan   Marcia Anne
             1909–1932   Pamela
                                                Kate
             John Alden
             1915–

             Ruth Dana
             1917–
             2 infants dec.

Life is too wonderful,
too full, too short
and strength too limited
to contain its wonder.

Ruth Draper
May 1, 1953

Prologue   1884 –1919

What I had as a child I've never lost—
the child's ability to *pretend:* to *be*
what he imagines he is.

Ruth Draper
1955

Ruth Draper was born in New York on the second of December 1884.

She grew up in the New England Victorian tradition in a large but closely knit, individalistic family; the pattern of life was established, intellectual, broadly cultivated, liberal in thinking yet conservative in standards. Among eight children Ruth was seventh, with four brothers and three sisters. She was a shy child, tightly reserved, and so frail, so "rickety" in appearance that goat's milk was regularly fetched from a Harlem farm to strengthen her.

When Ruth Draper died at 72 her name was up in electric lights on Broadway; she had become a legend of the theatre on the stages of all the continents, and a legend in friendship and warm response wherever she touched the lives of others. Her stamina was beyond believing.

Ruth Draper lived her life in two worlds. First was the cultured, close though cosmopolitan world in which she grew up—the sheltered social world of Henry Adams and Henry James, of Edith Wharton, of Henry L. Higginson and M. A. de Wolfe Howe, where The Stage was held a world apart, and not really admissible, even in the 1920s. But The Stage became her other world where she achieved acceptance, recognition, and greatness, a world in which she took great pride. Some of the elder, the more conservative of those who knew hecperhaps felt she had made a personal transition in crossing the footlights, but though she was *in* the Theatre she was yet not *of* it—for no matter where she walked outside her own social world she still remained firmly within it. In some extraordinary way she fused—not bridged but fused—her two worlds, within herself, into one incredibly brilliant whole. So it was on her own terms as a person that her audiences had to accept her and it was to their hearts they held her—for thirty-seven years—bywhich time their grandchildren discovered her and brought their grandparents to share their newfound delight. As her audiences responded, enchanted, no less was she enchanted with them, and in the British Isles this enchantment flowered into a mutual love affair across the footlights, for always there was some special magic between them.

Harold Acton has written of "the very special art [of] that Protean diseuse, Ruth Draper . . . each performance was a transformation, for she was demure, stiff, even shy in casual intercourse. . . . Behind the prim spinsterish facade lurked the Henry James heroine with smouldering eyes."

With almost no formal school education, but the spark lit by a remarkable German governess, Ruth's hunger was so compelling, her curiosity so wide, that she was quite literally nourished and developed by voracious reading, by an eager, questing observation of everything that came before her eyes, and by acute listening to all the sounds, all the speech, and all the music of her worlds. From this grew the art of her monologues, and so she came to occupy a unique position, peculiarly her own, in the creative world. Pre-eminently civilized, dignified, distinguished, she was at the same time unaffected, unimpressed, and had true simplicity.

Pain and sorrow there were, and great grief, but happiness, delight, and triumph came in abundance as she rapturously responded to every moment of joy and beauty. Looking at the tapestry of her life, she was continually amazed, so incredulous always that just two years before her death she could write of her career: "My wonderful life goes miraculously on." She never lost the wonder of it.

Her roots were in New England. Her grandfather, Charles A. Dana, born in New Hampshire, worked his way through Harvard, became immersed in Emersonian intellectualism, and participated in the five years of the Brook Farm experiment at Concord, Massachusetts. Here he met Eunice Macdaniel, who had come north with her mother, brother, and sister from an old Maryland family. Dana and Eunice were married in New York in March 1846 and for a short while kept secret their marriage because Eunice, who had long cherished the dream of a stage career, had entered a school of drama in New York. Her stay was brief, however, for with the sudden end of Brook Farm, Dana entered his long career in journalism which culminated during the last thirty years of his life as Editor and part owner of the *New York Sun* and as the outstanding exponent of liberal, independent journalism.

A daughter of Eunice and Charles Dana, Ruth Dana, though twenty years younger than he, became the second wife of Doctor William Henry Draper.

William H. Draper was born in Brattleboro of old Vermont stock. He graduated from Columbia College in 1851, and took his degree in medicine four years later. He became an eminent practitioner, Professor of Clinical Medicine at the College of Physicians and Surgeons, beloved, respected, and greatly influential; dignified and handsome, he was a man of rare graces of mind and heart. He married Elizabeth Kinnicutt of Worcester, Massachusetts, but their two children, Martha Lincoln Draper and William Kinnicutt Draper, were very young when their mother died. After eight years, in 1877, Dr. Draper married Ruth Dana, a musician, as he was, with wide interests in the arts and with a strong social conscience. Two years later Charles Dana Draper was born, then George, Dorothea, Alice, Ruth in 1884, and Paul. Ruth and Paul were born in the big brownstone house at 19 East 47th Street, where Dr. Draper had his office on the first floor, with a large schoolroom and nursery on the top floor.

Both Will and George became doctors, George a pioneer in psychosomatic medicine. Martha, the very much older sister, who never married, was as responsible in the family as she was to be responsible in public education and in the Red Cross in two wars. Charles, who became head of the family, combined a successful career in Wall Street with a long and constructive support of Boys' Clubs. Dorothea was to be a founder of the Schola Cantorum and for many years a leader in the administration of the Bellevue Hospital School of Nursing and in many other philanthropic and civic activities. Alice, the only one of the sisters to attend college, accompanied her husband around the world in his YMCA and War Relief work for several nations, filling her own vital role in associated causes, hospitals, and Play Schools. Ruth and Paul were the artists of the family. All led independent, diverse, and valuable lives. Their mother, a brilliant woman with a strong dominant personality, said that she respected each child's individuality as a trust and saw that it was fostered and educated. In their very young years she took them all to England and Europe for summer holidays, thus early indoctrinating Ruth with her love of travel, although in her childhood she was woefully seasick. More than sixty years later she wrote from a cold, wet winter London to her sister Dorothea: "I find 'Valentine's Beef Juice' marvellous! I remember it with *horror* at sea when I was six and Mother administered it to keep me alive!"

Music was a daily force in all their lives. Dr. Draper sang and played both piano and organ (by which he had financed his medical education); Mrs. Draper also was a fine musician. When Paderewski first came to New York in 1891, staying at the Hotel Windsor on the corner of Fifth Avenue and 47th Street, he was recommended to Dr. Draper for the removal of a felon on his finger. Hearing Mrs. Draper playing upstairs, he asked to be presented and their mutual interests led to a close family friendship. Charles and George told of roller-skating home from school to see the curtains blowing out of the open windows and hearing their mother and Paderewski giving full rein to their talents on the two concert grand pianos in the drawing room. She did much to foster Paderewski's early concert career in New York and often held series of concerts in her own house.

Mrs. Draper built a large, comfortable, wide-verandahed house at Dark Harbor, Islesboro, facing the western view across Penobscot Bay to the Camden Hills. There, in 1897, began Ruth's great love of the sea, the Maine coast, of sailing and swimming. Eventually she came to own the Islesboro house, which held some of her happiest childhood memories and most cherished associations. It became her haven, her spiritual home, her fountain of youth. A summer without Islesboro brought pangs of loneliness and nostalgia.

The Draper home was full of music, gaiety, fun, and strict discipline, the whole family gathering at the breakfast table and the parents always present at the lunch table. With the Dana grandparents at 25 East 60th Street, the families of uncles, aunts, and cousins nearby, it was a close, congenial, and diverse group. Ruth's particular playmate was her brother Paul, two years younger than she. Both were imaginative and creative; their artists temperaments and sympathetic humor and responsiveness binding them closely, with his gaiety a foil for her more serious mind. After one year at Harvard Paul turned to music, learning to use his pleasant tenor voice with great sensitivity and skill in German Lieder.

Ruth's innate gift for impersonation, her detached observation, her incredibly accurate aural memory for voices, inflections, and nuances would have been extraordinary in a much older person, but by the time she was eight all these were manifest and set her apart. Fraulein, the tailor, the seamstress, a Channel crossing—all were enacted with wit and sympathy to the delight of the nursery and, later, to the astonished amusement of the elder members of the family and their friends.

Hamilton Fish Armstrong remembers Ruth "in her little fur toque" in Grace Episcopal Church, where "the Draper family sat directly in front of us; ranged according to age, they filled their pew even more snugly than we did ours. Ruth already used, without guile but not without effect, the lambent eyes which would so perturb later audiences. When Noel [Armstrong] was home for the holidays her head would turn by imperceptible degrees until she could just glimpse him out of the corner of one eye. She would retrieve herself with a jerk, but in a moment, involuntarily, the head would begin turning again. His reply was to crack his knuckles nervously. . . ." Later, about 1906, he speaks of his Sunday School teachers, who "were two soft and warm-hearted young girls, Dorothea and Ruth Draper."

When she was ten Ruth followed her sister to Miss Spence's School for one year and returned briefly in the autumn of 1896. Aileen Tone, six years her senior and later to become an intimate friend, recorded this memory: "Then came a morning when, in the very middle of the school singing class with (dry as dust) Frank Damrosch beating his rigid measure, the door opened and Ruth Draper appeared! She couldn't have been more than eleven years old—a thin, straight little figure—thin, pale face—and wonderful eyes—I've never seen such eyes. Her hair had been cut tight to her head— after a typhoid fever—and she looked like a little boy. She wore a stiffly starched white shirtwaist and a skirt of plaid wool—a big pattern—with 'bretelles' going over her shoulders. She looked about the room in a quiet way, not shy, not in the least self-conscious, and then walked slowly to a vacant chair. She was grave and simple and observant and with a look of cool appraisal, not unkind but very keen! No more singing for me that morning, I was absorbed in watching the fascinating child." But to Ruth school was uncongenial and the ordered lessons difficult to follow, so Mrs. Draper found Hannah Henrietta Hefter: German, energetic, small, and a natural educator who, as governess, opened Ruth's mind and eyes to the stimulation of learning and seeing, to books and paintings, a stimulation that never lessened.

When Dr. Draper died in 1901, Mrs. Draper moved to a house at 18 West 8th Street, where Ruth lived until her mother's death in 1914. It was here that she spent her active debutante years of 1902–3, in the Junior League activities, entering a varied social round, among an ever-widening circle of friends. Five feet four inches in height, she now became dynamic, vital, full of energy.

Already she had begun to give her monologues before a wider audience, in private homes and for charity. She had seen Beatrice Herford perform, and always acknowledged her debt to this master of comedy. In 1912, after seeing *The Yellow Jacket* on a stage with no scenery and few props, she began to understand the power of illusion. But it was Paderewski, in 1910, who spoke seriously to Ruth. He knew that Mrs. Draper, although having the same talent as Ruth, strongly opposed a professional career for her daughter. He spoke about the development of her talent, for he saw bigger things, wider horizons: "You must do this professionally. Perhaps you should go to Paris to study. Mind you, I am not advising this. You may not need training. *You* must make the decision. It must come from you, from inside." So, quietly, without confiding in anyone, she was working up a repertoire, rehearsing alone before a mirror in her bedroom (a practice she continued for the rest of her life), developing her technique, polishing, perfecting. She never did take a lesson in acting or in elocution. Her gift was innate. Henry Adams wrote from Washington in 1911: "The most vital [visitor] was Ruth Draper. . . . She is a little genius and quite fascinates me."

During the years 1910 through 1913 Ruth Draper recorded thirty to thirty-five engagements each year, all near New York. Then, in June 1913, she began in London, at the houses of the great London hostesses (it was several years before she could spell *Duchess* without a *t*) and often for charities. H.R.H. Princess Christian of Schleswig-Holstein (Princess Helena, the third daughter of Queen Victoria) asked her to recite privately for a small group of guests. Delighted with the performance, she repeated the invitation twice more—the third party including King George V and Queen Mary with a large group of Royal relatives, among them the Connaught and Battenberg families. Obviously, this was a special occasion requiring special preparation. Henry Adams wrote from Paris to Anna Lodge on May 15, 1913: "We have had various passers-by, the last and most vivacious being Ruth Draper who has been staying with Looly Hooper for a week, to get a dress for to act before the Queen who has sent for her through the Princess Christian. She has rushed my Social Secretaries about like wild gazelles but goes today, so that I shall probably pass only a part of my time at Worth's henceforward. The two lovely dresses I have made for her are of course too good for Queens, but what could I do?"

In her diary for Friday, May 16, 1913, Queen Mary noted: "We went to tea at Schomburg House and heard a little American lady Miss Draper recite too delightfully."

This capped the success of her first London "season," private though it was.

During these years Henry James was counted her "friend and counsellor in London." She asked his opinion about her pursuit either of her dramatic or of her writing abilities, and received the oft quoted reply, with all its

Jamesian pauses, "No, my dear young friend—you have made—my dear young friend you have woven—my dear young friend you have woven yourself a magic carpet—stand on it!" He spoke often of "her strange brilliant impersonations." Like Henry Adams, he found Ruth Draper's talent and personality fascinating and took great pleasure in going about London with her; even, to her astonishment and embarrassment, taking her into the Athenæum to see the library and its special books—she who had been brought up never to raise her eyes to the windows of a gentlemen's club!

During the following winter at home she made the first of many White House appearances; her engagements began to include schools and clubs and she went further afield, though still mainly in the East. Her record for 1914 shows double the number of recitals and, again in London, she was booked for many more evening parties.

In the years 1912 to 1914 Paul Draper, who was studying Lieder with Raimund von Zur Mühlen in London, lived with his wife Muriel and their two small sons at 19 Edith Grove, on the far edge of Chelsea. Here, usually after a concert, came many great musicians to a supper party, to relax and to make music together far, far into the morning hours. Arthur Rubinstein remembers these nights as the "supreme musical euphoria of my life." Eugène Ysaye came with Jacques Thibaud, and Lionel Tertis, Pablo Casals, Félix Salmond, Pierre Monteux, Paul Kochanski and Karol Szymanowski, Désiré Defauw, Harold Bauer, Alfred Cortot, Pedro Morales, Barrère, the London String Quartet. Almost every musician visiting London was brought to Edith Grove. These were the glorious prewar London seasons of opera, concerts, and the Russian Ballet of Sergei Diaghilev. Ruth Draper was a part of this scene, sometimes visiting at Edith Grove. All this came to an end in the summer of 1914, and for Paul Draper it ended precipitately at the Derby of that June. He had wagered a large amount in a last desperate gamble to recover recent losses. An inveterate gambler, usually lucky (he had won handsomely on an Irish Sweepstakes), he had in this way financed Edith Grove, the box parties, the Savoy Grill suppers, and his voice lessons. Not only was every last penny suddenly and irretrievably gone, but he had substantial debts, those to his bookmaker being the most alarming. A mortgage on the house having proved insufficient, Ruth provided crucial help from her own small resources. But her anxiety was to continue, for his gambling and chronic periodic drinking made disaster inevitable.

Her final month in London, although full of anxiety, held much of interest and satisfaction. Ruth called on Princess Victoria of Schleswig-Holstein at Schomburg House but declined another invitation to perform there. Among a dozen private engagements was a party at 10 Downing Street where, after dining, uniquely, in the Cabinet Room, she performed for the Prime Minister, H. H. Asquith, and his guests. She was ever mindful of the people and events of history and this room held many such memories—which she touched, herself, in setting down her list of "sketches" at the desk of William Pitt.

She saw Henry James frequently and John Singer Sargent, who had drawn her the previous year before seeing her act, now made two portrait drawings to stand in stead of the earlier one, which he felt to be unworthy. The drawings were "in character": the Dalmatian Peasant and the Scotch Immigrant, Lesley MacGregor.

Early in July she sailed for home in the S.S. *Lusitania*—looking forward to a quiet summer gardening and telling her mother of her months abroad, of her "dear Uncle Henry" Adams, of their many friends in London, as well as of her own new friends.

World War I began on August 4th.

On August 16th Mrs. Draper died. Nearly a year later, Ruth wrote to her mother's great friend Mrs. Yates Thompson, in London, whose own mother had recently died:

Sweet Briar Farm, Geneseo, N.Y.
June 4 [1915]

It must indeed be a comfort to realize that your mother has been spared the agony of these times. I feel it constantly in thinking of Mother, for with youth and strength it is all crushing enough. I know you have thought of me in my great loneliness and your love and admiration for Mother is a real support. I believe you can understand what life without her, after our close companionship, must be, and the only comfort I have is the wonderful sense of her spirit in me. The unfailing strength of that possession helps in the conflict against things in me which are consuming and hurtful. How I should love to be near you now, talking of Mother. She was happy that we were friends and the thought that I saw you in London these past two years gave her a sort of confidence and pleasure, I know. She loved your letters so and I really can't tell you how I value your friendship for her sake. Thank you a thousand times for writing.

And now I have much to tell you of my strange winter, the long wonderful journey that is almost over. I think I wrote you of our having moved to a nice little house uptown, near Will [Draper]. After I had things running nicely for Charles and Martha, I took old Christine (the Scotch maid we've had for years) and started on January 18th for a tour of the States. I felt very strongly that I must go on with my work and that I must find new fields among strangers. You will understand all the possible good of such a journey. The effort to do my best work, the effort to get the best from each experience, the people, the places, was all helpful. I could never have been content just to wander idly in search of change and impressions and I have been grateful beyond words for my work and its success. I have been gone not quite five months and have recited thirty-eight times. Really wonderful luck, considering I knew practically no one to start with, and it was only by word being passed along that I secured the engagements and ventured to give a few "on my own". I went to Pittsburgh, Cincinnati, Chicago, St. Louis, Kansas City, Colorado Springs, and then for three weeks to a ranch in New Mexico where Robert Munro-Ferguson and his beautiful wife—great friends of mine—live. That was a rare and wonderful experience and there I recited to an audience of 200 or so miners, in the grocery store of the rough little town [Tyrone, N.M.], with two counters serving for a platform and the Sheriff with pistols on his hip, keeping order! It was a huge success.

I went to the Grand Canyon, a stupendous and overwhelming sight, and then to California for six weeks where I wandered slowly up the coast, reciting frequently.

I have done many benefits so I don't feel utterly useless in these times when one longs so to help. Christine and I knit twenty pairs of socks on our travels!

For the next years of World War I Ruth Draper toured across the country with a steadily growing list of engagements and for a variety of War Relief Benefits. However, friends were urging her to go on the stage and she was, herself, somewhat ambivalent. So in May 1916 she canceled twelve scheduled engagements to take the very small part of the lady's maid in Cyril Harcourt's A Lady's Name, starring Marie Tempest with Daisy Belmore and Beryl Mercer. It ran for only six weeks in Atlantic City, Montreal, and New York. But she was no happier with this than she had been with the sketch Henry James wrote for her in 1913 and which she never attempted to perform (see Bibliography). In 1917 she made one more try: on February 6th she staged her own production for one matinee at the Comedy Theatre in New York with three one-act plays, appearing herself in Strindberg's The Stronger, in a three-character pantomime of her own devising, and in her own sketch The Actress (which was to become one of the most popular and brilliant of her character sketches). Only The Actress got good notices—the program as a whole was dismissed by the critics as "ill-advised, singularly misguided and tedious." She now knew for certain that she would perform only in work which she herself had conceived and written. Except for a role in one or two all-star benefits in later years she never again appeared in any work but her own.

With her three brothers serving overseas and her sister Martha on a vital Red Cross mission, Ruth sought more active participation. She worked during July and August of 1918 at the International Arms and Fuse Factory in

Bloomfield, New Jersey, and, on October 12th, sailed in the S.S. *Baltic* for England to entertain at hospitals and army camps on the staff of the YMCA. On November 12th, the day after the Armistice, she crossed to France. There she met Miss Harriet Marple, who was assigned with her to entertain American troops in France.

From Columbus, Ohio, and five years younger than Ruth, Harriet Marple was a small, handsome woman of vital personality, strong, decisive, and stylish. She and Ruth quickly developed a close friendship, intensified by the sharing of war-time experiences.

Early in the war, probably in 1916, after training in Canada, Harriet had gone to France and was nursing at the American Hospital at the time of the Armistice. Now she turned to music, for she had studied singing since childhood. For the next four months they gave programs daily—often several times a day—staying in Neufchâteau, Nancy, Chaumont, Châtillon-sur-Seine (81st Division), Tonnerre (36th Division), Semur (78th Division), Montigny-sur-Aube, Aignay-le-Duc (6th Division), and were at the Hotel Majestic in Paris to see a few days of the Peace Conference in February 1919, where Ruth performed for the delegates.

To Martha Draper

January 6 [1919]
Châtillon-sur-Seine [France]

Happy New Year!
I'm in the most lovely panelled room, with a fire, and a bed that was made for Heaven. One window looks on a little court with a well dated 1672, and moss-grown cobble stones; another looks on a walled garden of cabbages, spinach, etc., and red roofs and yellow walls and tall spruce trees and green and brown branches of fruit trees. Never have I been so cosily fixed or had such hot coffee and toast. The landlady is a treasure and comes in every morning with fagots for the fire and darling pewter pots of hot water. Then I make my breakfast and eat it before the fire, and return to bed to read and write until about eleven. Then I walk and go to get orders at the office and then go to lunch with my friends. One is the baker's family—grandfather and mother, mother and four beautiful children and the cat, and we sit about the table and eat such food! So wholesome and hot and tasty, and we talk and have such a happy time. Another is an old fabricant de voitures and his wife, a perfect father and mother of "Louise", only they have no children. There they make a great deal of me—insist on my having a little bon vin, wonderful Bordeaux, to réchauffer l'estomac. He wears a black velvet vest and a plaid tie, knotted, and Miguette the cat sits beside the bottle of wine on the red and white checked oilcloth table cover. Another is Mme. François, who was a butcher, she has a voice like a man and is eloquent

about the war and life and the prices of food. The other day she was in bed, in the kitchen, with rheumatism, but we all eat together—it was spotlessly clean—her daughter cooked and she directed every turning of the spoon. We had Entrecôte cooked out of doors on a brazier, so that there was no smoke in the kitchen, and it was marvellous, a purée of potatoes such as I never tasted, cheese, and a marron confiture and thick cream with our coffee (the daughter having a cow). Today I go to a new lady in a house with beautiful panelled walls, and I'm going to see the woman who is a famous cook and try and persuade her to feed me now and then. It is so interesting being with the people and changing each day, and not going to the hotel. I've been very lucky.

George Lewis turned up yesterday and he is taking me to tea this afternoon with the noble family of the region and, as they have never seen an American lady, I am quite excited.

The place is full of officers and men attending school in various branches and there is an enormous district to cover. This week we have two, and sometimes three performances a night so you need not think I am idle, with all my dissertation on food! Harriet Marple lost her voice completely (the long, cold damp rides at night are very strenuous on a voice) so I have been working this week with four Privates who sing together, and a cellist. I am the only woman, sometimes with 300–600 men, and it's very amusing. I am amazed at the success of my things. We rarely get officers, though I've been twice to the club here and given them informal recitals. There is nothing to do and the poor souls are pretty desperate. Of course that's the chief reason of my success with the men—they have so little, but they're very quick and we have great fun. The Quartette and I start off every night in a shaky old car, generally without lights, but so far we've come through all right.

To Martha Draper

February 28 [1919]
St. Mihiel [France]

I am overwhelmed by the look of this country; all my delight in the charm and beauty of the little towns of the past three months is turned here to a dumb sadness, and anger and distress. One [w]rings one'[s] hands and sobs inside, so to speak, in a sort of desperation, knowing there is *nothing* to do about it. I've been in dug-outs and trenches, and seen the wreckage and horror and the hideous silence of it all. Now it's all over—*why* need it have been! And now the Spring is coming—and it makes it all so cruel—and the patient, weary, gallant people trying to clear the ground and move into their shattered homes and begin again, is just too much, that's all.

By this time both Ruth Draper and Harriet Marple were exhausted, but after a three-week leave in the south of France they put in another strenuous two months entertaining American troops in Germany. After returning to Paris in June, Ruth Draper visited the Walter Gays at Le Brèau and made a tour through the entire French war-zone, visiting the battlefields. Her war service ended in a very different role in YWCA Camp I at St. Nazaire, where she spent July processing through the French brides of American soldiers. She was in charge of baggage, medical records, English lessons, and orientation. In August she returned to England.

On August 26th Ruth left with Harriet Marple for Ireland on a holiday she always remembered as a special delight. By train and bicycle they covered a great part of the country, visited Irish friends, "met the Gogartys, Yeats, AE and Stephens and other charming Dublin people and heard brilliant talk and delighted in it all. And the beauty!" From taking shelter in a roadside cottage grew her monologue of the old Irish woman, *In County Kerry.*

Seymour Leslie recalls his mother telling of two American girls with bicycles, who appeared at the door of Castle Leslie, Glaslough, asking to stay the night. Lady Leslie (Leone Jerome), amused and intrigued, said of course they might. Ruth and Harriet stayed for three nights and returned a few days later for another two, Ruth enchanting everyone with her monologues and her joy in Ireland and its people. Lady Leslie often saw Ruth thereafter in London, dining or visiting her in one of her Chelsea houses—to Ruth's great delight: "dear Lady Leslie—I *love* her."

To Martha Draper

October 11 [1919]
Hans Crescent Hotel
[London]

We got back from Ireland day before yesterday and have been straightening out trunks and clothes, and collecting mail, etc. Harriet has gone to visit relatives and hopes to sail with Alice [Carter] on the 30th. I am going to the de Glehns' for Sunday and next week to Cis Dawnay.

Miss [Viola] Tree wants me to give three matinees in November, to do, for half the program—before my monos [monologues], a one-act play of Rupert Brooke called *Lithuania,* a "grand guignol" little horror. I am making up my mind over Sunday whether or not to accept. I find no beauty and little merit in the piece and the lines miserably poor, but it is intensely dramatic. She thinks I could do it well. All the parts would be taken by very good people. Of course, I am torn as usual. I don't want to, but the sense of the opportunity haunts me; the fear of failure, and the fear of what success might lead to, are equally painful! I long for Mr. James to counsel me.

I am eager for work, but of course I must be patient, things aren't going yet. If I felt sure of it at home I would come, but the chances for it are as strong here, I think, and I think I can live as cheaply.

Harriet Marple sailed for home and Ruth settled down in rooms at 122 Ebury Street: "I'm most comfortably fixed in my lodging house and amused by the life—so far." She again recited at charity benefits and at private parties, notably at the London house of Lord and Lady Curzon before the King and Queen of Spain.

King Alfonso, very much taken with Ruth, spoke his admiration in Spanish. When she replied in French he switched to German, was answered in Italian, but pressed on in English. She then responded in a *torrent* of language—made-up and incomprehensible. His Majesty was somewhat baffled.

Her sister Alice Carter's twin boys, now at Dragon School, Oxford, spent their Christmas holidays with "Aunt Scrub," who administered hot baths to remove a three months' incrustation of rugby mud from young knees, and provided well-starched Eton collars, before setting off on visits to Hever Castle and other "great houses" for a festive round, and to have Christmas with the Spender Clays in Surrey.

Ruth now was 35, and the years of discovery and experiment were over. Her months with the troops had been a catalyst. Until this time she had, by and large, performed for friends or groups not far removed from her own experience. Now she had met all comers—battle-hardened men from very different backgrounds, from all walks of life—met them, enjoyed their diversity, appreciated their qualities, and found she could amuse them, move them, and hold them in her audiences. With her own increasing maturity, she knew she had reached a turning point and that the time had come to move onto a wider stage. The amateur, the charming young woman who recited those amusing and touching monologues, determined to become the serious professional: a character actress of the legitimate theatre. With a repertoire of nearly thirty sketches, Ruth Draper booked Æolian Hall in London for a matinee on January 29, 1920.

1920 –1927

Je suis seule. Seule, moi.

Ruth Draper to Lugné-Poe
June 28, 1921

ÆOLIAN HALL, LONDON, JANUARY 29, 1920

For two hours yesterday afternoon Miss Ruth Draper kept a large audience at the Æolian Hall smiling and laughing, now and then feeling a little lump in the throat. . . . Her observation is almost wickedly keen, her expression of it is pointed and polished till it is as clear and bright as a diamond.

The Times, 30th January, 1920

Miss Draper sees intensely, understands piercingly, and can express clean-ly. . . . At the bottom of it all lies sympathy. She can jest because she under-stands.

The Observer, 1st February, 1920

The decisive step had been taken: Ruth Draper was "on stage," a profes-sional in the Theatre. And yet, uniquely independent, she could perform her monologues anywhere, without costume, scenery, stage crew, or orchestra. Even without a theatre. All Ruth Draper needed was an audience; but now the theatre, rather than the drawing room, was where she stood. The psychological difference was tremendous—and compelling.

To Mr. J. L. Garvin
Editor of
The Observer,
London

February 9 [1920]
On board S.S. Lapland
Red Star Line

Dear Mr. Garvin,

I want to thank you for the wonderful notice you gave me. I have a strong suspicion that the "middle aged penman" was yourself and not the unin-formed critic which I asked you to send, to see how my things affected a "critic"! I was very pleased—something much deeper than pleased—by the "write up" and shall treasure it, not only for its significance, but as a mark of your opinion which I felt long before you said a word to me—just from the way you listened at Hever [Castle].

I am on my way home, but only for a short time. I feel I must follow up this success and I plan to return in May to give several recitals, stay through the season, and then "do" the summer places, and the big towns in the North in October.

I wish I might have seen you again. I would like to be better equipped with wise and helpful views and interpretations; those of us who speed back and forth across the sea should carry balm and stimulants and magic, wis-dom and understanding to our native lands and the foreign shores. But, as I draw near the port, my mind will be taken up in battling with the cruel law which makes me pay 60% on necessities of life—bought and paid for in England, with *English* money! It is irritating.

Again many thanks for the help you have given me by your and the "Observer's" recognition.

> Very sincerely yours,
> Ruth Draper

ÆOLIAN HALL, LONDON, MAY 27, 1920
(for a total of five performances)
[Ruth Draper] is a hit of the season, who moves her audiences at the Æolian Hall to enthusiasm and drawing-rooms to admiration. It is to be hoped that Miss Draper will return again and again to tell us that this is London and the season by adding her living touch to both.

> *The Observer,* 6th June, 1920

There is something almost uncanny in the insight and penetration distinguishing some of her delineations, while not less remarkable is the versatility which enables her to undertake the most widely contrasted impersonations with uniform success. She was altogether admirable.

> *The Westminster Gazette,* 28th May, 1920

The art of Miss Draper stands alone. . . . To hold an audience enthralled for nearly two hours with this brand of dramatic art, without the aid of properties, music or scenery, is indeed a triumph. There is no doubt that her listeners would cheerfully have allowed Miss Draper to continue indefinitely.

> *The Jewish Chronicle,* 18th June, 1920

To Harriet Marple

> June 1, 1920
> 120 Ebury Street
> [London]

I was very lucky in finding a [sunny top-floor] room next to my old abode, a lovely big double room in front and I am *so* comfortably fixed. I bought some chintz and have covered my trunk and bag, a chair and a cushion, and made a frill for the mantel shelf, and new muslin curtains. I've got a rose tree and ferns and I'm going to get a tea set. I've a lovely pink silk cover on my bed and altogether am delightfully fixed for one guinea a week. I shall keep the room until I return to America for I'll be glad of a pied-à-terre.

My first recital [May 27] was a great success and again I got splendid notices from all the papers. Financially I did not do as well as in January, but there's an awful lot going on, and they say no shows are more than covering expenses. I did more than that and my manager can't see why I'm not delighted. They treat me like an old favorite at the Hall—it's killing.

I've been here nearly three weeks now and haven't accomplished a thing. I mean to get working at something—singing or Spanish or Greek! I've seen a lot of people but had no gaiety, no dances or parties, and don't foresee any. I've been to some splendid plays and had two heavenly (I mean the country was heavenly) week-ends in the country, and have two nice ones ahead. The time flies. Everyone seems glad to see me and I get great comfort from two or three friends and have had moments of being almost happy. London is so charming now, I wish you were here. You would have loved the Barrie play "Mary Rose"—the most hauntingly sad thing I've ever seen, but very lovely.

Thank you for saying what you did about Paul's singing and of your pleasure in your visit. You don't know how glad I am that you came before I left and that you liked my people and my friends. Your friendship means a very great deal to me, and surely what we have borne together makes a bond deeper than words can express.

I hope you will get some happiness out of your summer. All I can say is that resignation and philosophy about keep pace with suffering and my delight in life and beauty keeps my hand steady on the helm that is trembling with the surge of the waters. If you knew what it *felt* like to steer a boat in a high wind you'd know what I meant. It exactly describes the situation. . . .

Well I must go and pack now. I'm so cozy here in bed, a vision in pink. I do enjoy having my nice things again—it's dreadful to confess to taking comfort in chiffon!

To Martha Draper

June 24 [1920]
120 Ebury Street
[London] SW1

One wonders greatly about the British public—they are *childlike* in its best sense, completely concentrated, attentive, warm hearted, generous and sincere, almost simple in their absorbed delight. The Coliseum [after Æolian Hall] will be a different and greater test. Personally, I fear greatly but the managers are quite sanguine and bent on my making a great success. Wish you could see me in huge gold letters over the door. I'm to get 100 pounds a week but am beginning to think that is very little, for I have engagements at 40 guineas every day now.

My last recital [at Æolian Hall] is this afternoon and I anticipate a big crowd and a warm farewell. I do wish you could see me in my moments of triumph. I'll have to tell you because I know it will give you pleasure, Barie dear, that everyone says I look beautiful and admire my clothes greatly and say that no one has ever had such a success.

Unsigned cable to the family cable address in New York

July 5, 1920:
London

COLISEUM CARRIED AWAY

To Martha Draper

[July 7, 1920]
[London]

It's an immense place and an immense sensation I can assure you. The Coliseum is a wonderful institution—quite unique in its way and the audience exceptionally intelligent and well behaved. One has the sense of feeling, through that mass, all the finest, most endearing qualities of a human being: generous, sensitive, intelligent, kind, and one feels them near and friendly in spite of the vastness. The acoustics are wonderful. I go slowly but quite without effort, and I'm told every word is heard throughout the house. The managers seem delighted and quite satisfied. It's all spotlessly clean and very orderly and luxurious. I have a lovely room, and a dresser named "Mrs. Lizzy", and the door man, Dennis, is like a childhood's friend, and all the stagehands are dears, and I feel quite at home and it's all most dignified and proper. You meet no one, just do your turn, dress, and go home.

My friends come, of course, and that's great fun. Nora [Phipps], Hoyty [Wiborg], Mrs. Starr, and Vera Gainsford have been with me continually so far, and tonight Mary Filley is bringing a bunch of Generals! The audience is full of friends, too. Nora tells me a lot of smart people were there the first night. Prince Paul of Serbia, who is very keen, brought a party and so on. Tonight I have a party after my show and again on Saturday and two next week. I refused two as I did not think I should do too many. I get letters and wires and flowers and it's all very exciting and amusing and I try and realize how wonderful it is and how happy it should make me. I wish you all could look in on me.

I had a charming letter from Compton McKenzie, who had heard me and was enthusiastic, saying that there never was anything like it except in his character of Sylvia Scarlett, whom he conceived as doing just such things. Isn't that amusing? So he wants to meet me and talk about it. I've never read the book. Evidently he describes just what I do.

To Harriet Marple

July 9 [1920]
120 Ebury Street
[London] SW1

Life has been pretty much of a rush and my correspondence keeps me sitting up in bed 'till about 11:30 every morning, and if I don't get thro' then, there isn't another moment in the day. All my five recitals were a great success, and for three weeks I had a job every day, nearly, except Saturday and Sunday when I always went away. I've had to get a new dress—at Lucile's and it is quite lovely—pale grey, very soft satin, with a silver lace petticoat, dainty and graceful as you know she makes things look. I think you'd approve. I've been feeling rather tired, London when it's hot is very relaxing, so I went to the Dr. and got a tonic and I take my beloved malted milk between meals and at night and have gained a few pounds and feel better.

Well, last Monday [July 5] began the Coliseum and I wish you were with me now. You'd die laughing as I do when I see my name in electric lights over the door and on posters everywhere. I was really very nervous and scared, for me, and you can't imagine the sensation of coming out before 2500 people and facing that vast space and dazzling light. The acoustics are marvellous and one doesn't have to strain the voice an atom. I did The French Dressmaker, Three Generations [in a Court of Domestic Relations], and Vive la France (in costume) with the Orchestra playing the "Sambre et Meuse" as an overture, and then coming in pianissimo with drum beats when I see the troops and then crescendo and a final burst as I cry out at the end and exit. I never was so excited and moved in my life, as I felt them getting it, and heard the great wave of applause! It goes wonderfully every time and the others surprisingly well. I do [Showing] the Garden now and with great success. The audience is very attentive and intelligent and kind. Entirely different from what you would expect from a vaudeville audience—imagine daring to do these at home! All my friends come and visit me in my room and it's all terribly amusing, and I often long for you (and others!) to see me and laugh with me over it all.

There are many moments of loneliness and weariness, however. I have to dine at seven, which means alone in little restaurants, and I get quite blue at times, thinking how strangely I have been captured and am being led by the demands of this gift—so against my desires and longings—and furious with myself for my ingratitude for what should fill my life with happiness. To think I have arrived at a place most women would have to pay for, and I've not paid in the smallest coin! And without effort or ambition or struggle of any kind—but then perhaps it's not always in direct ways that life asks a tribute. God knows I've paid and am paying, and it looks as if I'd always pay until the force of life is spent, and I'm "nodding by the fire". No word comes from the mountains [N.C.] and nothing appears to take its place—no one really interests me and tho' I get a surfeit of praise and admiration I seem not to touch a spark, except for passing moments, and I see it veiled by a strange awe and embarrassment and then go out.

I have determined not to let the worry and distress about Paul affect me, as for so many years it has. There is nothing to do but steel oneself and be prepared for the new troubles that are bound to come. It's so queer that when I am on the top of the wave—like in 1914—the tragedy of his life should be like an undertow. But I am stronger now, and there are other currents to test my resistance and I *know* that I can swim and the sparkle on the waves, and the spray and the salt and the sun keep me laughing most of the time. Don't think me over pessimistic, but there are complications that are troubling—money, and the children who may suffer.

I've taken passage the end of October. God knows why—I might as well stay on here. It's cheaper and I've a wonderful place here now. If I can gather new material this summer I shall gladly return to work at home, but without it I shall feel unworthy to face the public there. And I *must* work, for I see it is the only way to make me realize that I have something worth living for, and that gradually it will help me to renounce the desire for another life; and to see that I must find my love and my desire, my vision and fulfilment, right in the little brain cell that produces these silly old things that seem to move men and women to laughter and to tears.

During the years immediately after the War—1920–1926—there is frequent mention in letters to Harriet Marple of a romantic attachment that began in France in February 1919. Obviously, Harriet Marple knew all about it, for the actual name never appears, only an occasional reference by the initials N.C., which probably stood for North Carolina, for she admits, rather self-consciously on several occasions, to being drawn to that State and its mountains. To Harriet Marple she poured out her longings—their longings, apparently—for romance and marriage. There is absolutely no evidence of a proposal and engagement, merely a certain starry-eyed interest, infrequent and somewhat casual meetings, and a warm but desultory correspondence. However, these stirrings of heart and fancy over the years do make evident the emotional substance of a vital young woman eager for all that life might hold for her. This quality of romantic naïveté, apparent for many years, was not uncommon in young women of her generation and upbringing.

To Martha Draper

July 13 [1920]
120 Ebury Street
[London]

Thank you for your nice cable. It all goes splendidly. An adorable French Clown [the great Grock] and I shared the honours last week and appear to be carrying the show this week too! (I fear the other items are all rather poor!) The Clown is a gem and my things go surprisingly well. It's a great sensation and interesting to see the way the technique is developing to suit the huge scale—the acoustics are marvellous and my voice *feels* as if it would burst the walls! I hear nothing but good reports from everyone—stage hands, managers, friends, and strangers. I'm not at all tired by it—feel much better than I did the fortnight before. As a matter of fact, it makes for a very regular life and I don't try to do other things every spare minute.

Dear Mrs. Phipps is still a bit staggered by my name in electric lights, but I don't feel that it changes me, my manners or morals in the slightest—it just amuses me.

To be "top of the Bill" in vaudeville meant just what it said: recognition of top quality in professionalism. But to "top the Bill" with the "adorable French Clown," Grock, one of the truly great performers of all time, was an extraordinary achievement for Ruth Draper so early in her career.

Between their acts beginning July 12th, Jean Cocteau's Le Boeuf sur le Toit, *subtitled* The Nothing-Doing Bar, *made its English debut, with an English cast.*

Mrs. Phipps and her family, life-long and close friends, are mentioned frequently in Ruth Draper's letters from England. Mrs. William Wilton Phipps, born an American, Jessie Percy Butler Duncan, had lived at 1 Fifth Avenue, near Mrs. Draper; her sister married Paul Dana, Mrs. Draper's brother. Although not related, Ruth and the Phipps children, Margaret and Rachel, William and Paul Phipps, had a cousinly and devoted relationship. Paul was handsome, tall, charming, and, as a young man in London, an excellent ballroom dancer. He and Waldorf Astor were said to be the first gentlemen to "reverse" while waltzing, a maneuver hitherto considered "fast"! He married Nancy Astor's sister Norah Langhorne; their daughter Joyce is now the versatile actress Joyce Grenfell (see Bibliography). Margaret married a Phipps (not related). She and her daughter Anne, her brother Bill, and his wife Pamela were very much Ruth's London family. Rachel was en poste with her diplomat husband, Miles Lampson.

Mrs. Phipps, the subject of a striking portrait painted by her cousin John

Singer Sargent, was a remarkable and vivid personality. Lovely looking, somewhat formidable, with one green and one brown eye, she held a considerable social position in London and in later years served on the London County Council, being honored as a Dame of the British Empire. Ruth was a frequent visitor at Chorleywood and at family homes in London.

To Harriet Marple

> July 19 [1920]
> 120 Ebury Street
> [London] S.W.I

I'm weary and depressed so of course I follow my impulse and write to you! I wish you to know, however, that I've been much better for the past two weeks. I had been awfully slack and got quite scared facing the two weeks at the Coliseum, with no chance of rest or let up to get ready for it. I was fearfully busy right up to the last, then had 48 hours in the country, and the malted milk and the tonic I've been taking began to show effect so that I've felt steadily better as my job at the Coliseum progressed. Then the relief of finding I could "put it over" there was immense. The apprehension I had of failure, and feeling so down, worked on my nerves, I guess, more than I knew. But when I heard the extreme silence of those 3000 people, and heard the applause, a great burden fell from my shoulders and I knew I was saved.

You would have been as amused by it all as I have been. My name in the Tubes, on bill boards and in electric lights over the door; my charming room, and visitors after every performance. The queer orderly life it means, the lonely dinners at seven, the walks home at 9:40 with the sun just setting, the cooking of eggs in *our* little stove and digestive biscuits and milk before I went to bed and the contentment that comes from carrying out a definite job, the feel of the envelope of crisp notes on Saturday night—and the friends made of the theatre servants! I didn't meet one fellow performer! That's the funny part of music-hall life, you just do your turn and go home—see no one else.

To Harriet Marple

> August 6 [1920]
> La Douschka, Dinard
> [France]

Here I am back in our beloved France. The moment I saw the untidy, cross old blue bloused, brass labeled porters shouting for clients my heart leapt! And when I saw petits pains, warm, waiting for me on the breakfast table I seized one and kissed it!

I am here for a month with some American friends [Mrs. Storrs] who have a little villa, and, never having seen this sort of place before, am highly entertained. It keeps one's mind on a pretty low level, one does nothing but look and think about clothes, and wonder about the irregular relationships, and watch the gambling table. The people are pretty plain and very common—our countrywomen and English and French—none seem to be at all distinguished or refined. But the sea—my adored blue expanse of the sea expressing every changing mood of human nature—is the one exalting and satisfying thing about the place and one has but to look at it, when something inside one sickens at the shifting crowd on the Casino terrace, to feel refreshed and clean again.

I have to be back in England September 4th to begin work again. I had a strenuous life up to the time I came away. The week of July 25th–31st I was in Glasgow at the "Alhambra", the best music hall there, topping the bill, two performances nightly—7:30 and 9:30—and one matinee. Of all the gloomy towns, hideous, sordid, I think Glasgow is the worst I've ever seen. My things went very well—an audience of about 3000 and pretty rough. I did the Three Generations, the Dalmatian Peasant, the Scottish Immigrant, or the French one, and really was on my knees to the gallery, those weary factory workers, keeping still as mice, when they came to laugh and be cheered up.

This music hall work has been a great experience and I've learned a lot. I "turn on", as it were, about three times as much power, and the voice, the pauses, the gestures all seem to serve my will as well as in a small place. Of course I miss being able to do any of the lighter things; I can only hope to hold them by the dramatic ones but the managers seem to want me. I've been asked back to the Coliseum and to Liverpool and Manchester and may do a week each at the latter places in September. I don't want to do London again unless I had some startling new things, tho' they want the same program. I'd rather give my own recitals in new places even if it is more of a financial risk. My manager can't see this—wants to stick to the Halls and make more money—but it is a strain if I should keep it up continuously and, you can imagine, unsatisfactory just forever repeating the same three [sketches]. Still, it's fun and I shall intersperse my recitals and private jobs with an occasional Music Hall. I want to come home in November, I think it's better not to become too familiar here.

To Harriet Marple

August 20, 1920
Amstel Hotel
Amsterdam, Holland

It's cold as November and has been damp and rainy off and on for the last four days, so the week's jaunt to Holland with Aileen [Tone] has not been as perfect as it might have been from the point of comfort. But we've enjoyed it enormously—pictures too wonderful for words, the country full of quiet charm and the towns very picturesque. I look forward to a week in the country with Bill and Caroline Phillips and come back by Antwerp, Bruges, Ghent and Ostend to Dover. It'll be strange to be quite alone but I must confess I'm no longer a child and I can't bear to miss so much beauty as long as I'm so near.

The children call me terribly . . . the old friends and country, the old life tempt me, yet many fears deter me—fear that my work will not bring me the satisfaction it does here—the old shame of coming back without a wholly new repertoire—fear of the restlessness I know I shall feel, having no home—fear of being near Paul, etc., etc. O, I'm a coward all right. It's easier here and cheaper and I don't have to face problems that hurt and confuse me. Dorothea would like to have me share her apartment but to settle in New York I feel is the end of my making work my chief interest and God knows it has saved my life this year and I owe it devotion if I would keep it alive.

It's dreadful to burden you with my thoughts and worries, you dear patient old thing!

To Harriet Marple

September 1 [1920]
En route from The Hague
to Antwerp

I've just read The Times from cover to cover, studied the Baedeker on Antwerp, re-read all my recent letters, and we've just pulled into the station on the border where luggage is examined, so, while I wait to be questioned, I "take my pen in hand".

I still feel the strongest pull to return, tho' I can't tell what these coming two months may develop. Never in my life have I so wanted to go to a clair voyante, but I am resolutely keeping away! It is all right to go in a playful spirit but it would be a real weakening of my own decision to be guided by prophecy now. One can't really approve of seeking such guidance, and I feel I might be influenced, or at least disturbed by any advice or warning that anyone like that gave me. . .·. Emerson says: "Do the thing that is hardest" and I think going home is certainly less easy than staying here.

I felt quite badly after I'd written you that I didn't want to live with my sister. I adore her but prefer to wander forever or live alone. The truth is, I don't want to make *any* permanent arrangement and going in with her would rather mean starting a new home—which I can't bear to do.

Your letter of July 22nd in which you analyse my gift, goes almost too deep, and tho' you may not understand, hurts quite as much, and more, than any pain you caused me in Galway. It is because you touch the very "quick" of a truth that haunts me. It has long been in the background of my mind and has been growing and growing, as I see my talent growing in spite of my lack of effort to make it grow. You, alone, have touched on it—this truth that I've been blinking at—and I almost hate you for seeing it, tho' you pay me the most beautiful tribute. I wish I felt worthy of your estimate of my gift and my spiritual power. Harriet, my dear, dear friend, it's just because I feel too weak, too unworthy to accept this gift that I *should* so highly prize, and that I yearn only for what Browning calls "the obvious human bliss—that most men seldom miss".

As I stood on the great stage of the Coliseum and held that audience of 3000 with my "Vive la France" the revelation came to me that in thus giving all I had to give to those thousands, I must accept it as the alternative to giving myself to one. If I possess what you claim I do, I should be satisfied—I should be happy—it's a great and rare power. The point is, I should use it, I should work for it, live for it, rejoice in it—and all the while I'm looking over my shoulder for the other thing. It's this conflict, this choice, this acceptance and renunciation that makes life hard, and you turn on another light, as other friends have done in other ways, showing me what I know is true, and I *hate* the truth, with all its beauty and glamour and richness and possibilities, because it does not satisfy my lonely, human little soul. Gosh, I hate you for making me think and feel anew the force of this fear—that what I want can never come because God has given me something else to do.

Well, I'll go and worship now before Michelangelo's Madonna and get some strength from him!

To Harriet Marple

September 13 [1920]
The Palace [Theatre]
Manchester

I wish you were here—how we'd laugh—I'm in my dressing room waiting for the nine o'clock performance, just finished my first (7:30), brown shawl over my shoulders, red over my feet, electric fan going to keep the air fresh, strains of cheap music from the different turns "wafting" in thro' the cracks. I propose to read Don Quixote seriously between the acts, but tonight I'll use up a little time on you.

I have a huge tea at six, then come here, and eat again before I go to bed. I couldn't take off the paint and put it all on again in 1½ hours. So I shall wait at the theatre every night the way I did in Glasgow. There I had a delightful girl with me [Vera Gainsford], here I'm alone, and shall be next week at Brighton too.

Last night in London at a Sunday League Concert at the Palladium I had the most glorious audience, about 2500 and I could have hugged them—

you *never* heard such applause and such quick understanding! This afternoon, a matinee, it was fierce and I am beginning to experience the extremes of response. No understanding, save a few poor dears in the Stalls, laughter and noise thro' everything, even Vive la France. It was ghastly—do you remember that awful night on the Rhine, *your* night—it was that only ten times worse. My first really unpleasant but quite comprehensible experience, for these factory town audiences can be pretty rough—but when you do get them it's wonderful and I can never forget Glasgow. If only I had something [else] for the poor dears—how I'd love to hear them laugh! But I am only safe in giving them my dramatic and emotional things and even then, as today, it's a risk. I'm glad no one is here who cares for me—they'd die! As it is, it takes all the courage I've got.

I hope you've forgiven me that strange wild outburst in my last letter—the thought I expressed in it just took possession of me and nearly killed me and to have you feel it made it all the more forceful. If only we could entirely forget ourselves, in making something of our lives. I'm so sorry you've been downhearted and wish I could suggest a way out; why not nurse again—it's a terrible decision but might bring you the greatest satisfaction—wander a while and visit different cities, give yourself a chance to meet new people. There you're stuck in West Dennis thro' the whole summer, and apparently not a man has shown up. You arc *unquestionably* cut out for *one* thing (tho' you won't pay me the same compliment!) and you must not hide with little girls in a secluded watering place or stay where you know and dislike about every man in the place! Now don't think me cruel or calculating, I'm only honest and practical.

> . . . it is hard to remember an English artist who succeeded in making the art of the "diseuse" look at home in the music-hall atmosphere. At the Palace this week Miss Ruth Draper, whose performance revives and even betters the old tradition, should put new heart into those who have learnt since the war almost to despair of their music-hall's future. . . . But Miss Draper succeeds in a great deal more than characterization, and, while she acts, the stage is almost physically peopled with those others with whom her characters are engaged. The whole is a wonderfully effective and beautiful performance.
>
> *The Manchester Guardian*
> September 1920

To Harriet Marple

September 20 [1920]
Hippodrome
Brighton

I don't believe anyone in the world ever suffered as I do from laughing alone! My dear, I "follow" a tame seal! Now isn't that enough to set you off—I can hear you. If only you were here! I'm on the sofa in my dressing room—No. 1 as I *top* the bill—waiting between my turns. I'm on at 7:20 and again at 9:35 so I just wait in between and read and write and sew, and *think!*

First let me relieve your mind about last week in Manchester. It went beautifully after that ghastly Monday and the enclosed notice speaks for itself—or rather for the minority, but even the gallery were lambs and listened after Monday. I left Saturday midnight, had yesterday in town, saw several good friends and appeared at the Alhambra at a Sunday League Concert in the evening. Came here this morning and had a grand swim before lunch.

It went beautifully tonight—*wonderful* audience, lovely house and an excellent bill, and a very intelligent manager. He made a brilliant suggestion for improving Vive la France for these provincial audiences and I'm going to try it at the next show—just saying a few broken English words to the officer who speaks to me. They'll get the story better, and it can be done without hurting the thing at all. She might easily have picked up a few English words from the soldiers billeted in the villages.

[I shall] go and live a few days in the East End at a settlement. I want to try and get more of the Cockney accent—the hideous grimy element of the London slums. The Cornish Coast is more tempting but I feel I'd better do the other.

Things are fearfully exciting over here now and yet people go on serenely, with volcanoes about to erupt on every side—it's an amazing people. How horrible that New York bomb was [Wall Street bomb explosion, September 16, 1920]! Must we live in terror of that sort of thing now?

The seal is howling, that is the way he takes his applause, so I must stop and fly to the wings. O, Harriet, it's so strange, whatever led me to this life? I always thought it was difficult to know what "God's Will" was—I'd gladly obey if I knew—can it be for me to pursue the career of a music hall artiste? Gosh!

To Martha Draper

September 24 [1920]
Brighton

[This is] about the finest music hall in England. The trained seal is marvellous. A darling little girl of eight—one of the "turn's" children—sits with me every night, plays with my doll while I sew, and we talk, and dance together in front of my big mirror. Her father and I have become great friends—he's a clown.

I was alone the first two days and then, as everywhere, a bunch of friends turned up and I've been lunching and teaing out every day. Today I go to

Lady Sackville. She is a most charming and interesting woman, as you might suppose. No definite plan for sailing yet—as my success grows it seems more and more foolish to run away from it. I'm crushed by the sense of impending fame! In fact, it's already upon me and it would seem cowardly to run away.

To Harriet Marple

October 8 [1920]
120 Ebury Street
[London] S.W.1

Your sand dune post card has just come and I love it—so suggestive of our wonderful ride. I go over and over that and wonder often if you remember the bits of road I do and see again those woods in Kerry, the long slopes and the colors, and the other day I thought of those twin baby goats on the hill above Glengariff where we sat so long! Thank God we took that trip—could anything have so lifted up two wounded spirits—and will not the memory of it always comfort and inspire us anew.

I enclose a snapshot [of the Brighton Hippodrome poster] which will cause you to have one of your best laughs. Imagine my feelings when I met it on the street. Below my picture [the Sargent drawing] is a picture of the seal. I saw Mr. Sargent last week and told him his sketch was just above one of a seal and did he mind? He seemed much amused.

I've just come back from Norwich, where I gave three performances of my own in an adorable little old theatre that dates back to Norman times [Maddermarket]. It only holds 100, but it was packed each time and a most delightful intelligent audience, and I was full of pep. I came back to find a pack of letters—rather dull—and I made myself two lovely oeufs sur le plat on our old stove and had tea and milk and honey and one third of a loaf of bread and I feel full and comfortable. I've been sorting papers, answering business letters and putting in clippings—my book is so lovely—and now I must unpack and go to bed. I've a job tomorrow and Sunday—mixed concert programs—but grand audiences and, my dear, they applaud loudly when I come on now, showing I've really got the public—a fine new friend to have I assure you!

Two hours ago I was in the depths of gloom—all the old pain comes swooping down again at times. But I'm safe in my little pink room and fed and cozy and conscious of the love of friends, and grateful, and everything is all right now and I'll sleep and forget—and tomorrow I'll be busy again.

To Martha Draper

October 12 [1920]
Settlement House
London

You would be amused if you could see me. I'm in the Common Room of a Settlement in the East End where I came in the hope of hearing good Cockney and seeing the heart of London Slums. I arrived yesterday afternoon and leave in the morning, but it's been entertaining tho' not quite what I sought. Last night a Labor meeting on unemployment, at the Town Hall, very anti-capitalist, anti-Prince, violent, eloquent, pitiful and infuriating at once—for their arguments are so one-sided, so unthought out—and their cause so just. They're all marching to Downing St. next Monday, with other Borough groups under their Mayors, and of course it won't really do any good—poor dears—Gov. is so slow.

I visited with the Sanitary Inspector this morning and saw many typical homes and some sad cases—and adorable children by the score, seemingly bursting with health in spite of hardships. This afternoon I took a long ride on a bus top along the docks and thro' Limehouse, Mile End and Whitechapel Roads. Very interesting—tonight I wandered thro' the streets a long while—now after supper I'm going to watch a V. A. D. Class and then give a few monos to the Staff. I am crushed by the narrow, sanctimonious, dead atmosphere of the Settlement. I didn't know there were such people left in England—there is Terce before breakfast, Sext before lunch, Grace, and continuous talk of church and meetings and Saints' days, and a bunch of self-righteous old maids living in smug comfort, quite out of touch— human touch—with the people they purport to help. I am very wicked to say this—don't say the name of the place should you mention it. It's been very interesting to observe and ponder over and to find, as one slowly gets religion from living one's own life, one gets less tolerant of so called religion. I mean this kind.

I've met two characters, however, which have made the visit really worth while— I'll tell you about them some day—and tho' no immediate help to my monologues, I love the feeling of being immersed in all the vital force of this grim and appealing underworld: the beauty of the children, the resignation and courage of the women, the sinister smouldering power in the faces of many men, and the gaiety of the youth. Girls are much better dressed than they used to be, and some are so pretty. It's terribly depressing and desperate—the impotence one feels in the face of such problems. I can only hope something of what I feel will come out in my poor old monos.

To Harriet Marple

October 19, 1920
[with Mr. and Mrs. Evan
Fraser-Campbell]
Dunmore, Tarbert
Loch Fyne

Your letter came just as I was packing up to go to Edinburgh last Wednesday night. I gave a recital of my own there the 14th, and tho' not financially a success (and I didn't expect it to be), it went off finely and there was great enthusiasm. I find that contrary to my expectations a great London success does not necessarily mean fame in [the] provinces and one has to make one's way in each place. Of course I can't afford to take the risk often, for it's bound to be something of a loss, but I'd far rather go to new places, and make a start, than just stick in London, till they get tired of me.

I always seem to manage to combine pleasure with business, and I came on here Friday and shall stay until Wednesday afternoon. I am with very old friends—some I don't think I ever told you about (I can't believe there's anyone left to tell you about!). It's divinely beautiful and I've wished often for you.

Thanks for your last letter. I'm glad you weren't hurt by my outburst—but I'm bad as ever in not feeling ready or glad to have the responsibility of this gift; that's what I mean—I've *never* thought of myself as an artist—never considered that through me flowed a message, and that I must keep it a living power. You may be sure I won't deny myself marriage on the ground that it would interfere with my work! It's just the subtle consciousness that haunts me that I shall never have the thing I want, and must force myself to find everything in the development of the other. Gosh, why talk about it any more! There's no use, I see what I have to do—renounce the hope that haunts me—and I'll be free as a bird. And never a regret to warp enthusiasm!

To Harriet Marple

November 18 [1920]
120 Ebury Street
[London] SW1

I'm sitting up in bed with the sun streaming over me, my pink silk coverlet is shining and your knitted shawl keeping me very cosy. I'm in a desperate hurry to be up and out but I must scribble these lines to you. I'm in a great state of elation these days—the weather is lovely—and after days of hideous indecision whether to stay or return, a sort of fatalistic calm has descended on me and the silly self torture is over. Alice and the babies are here and it's lovely to have them. Arthur R[ubinstein] is here and I've heard and seen him a lot—wonderful as ever and such a true, fine friend. I've been busier and gayer than early in the month, and had very pleasant times with friends, and my new R.R. monologue is born at last, and perhaps that is the realest reason for my feeling happier. Not that I've been unhappy, save at moments and even in them I'm conscious of the wonder of it all.

Wilfred de Glehn is painting another portrait of me—and I should be on my way to pose for him now. I'm bringing the first one home, and I hope you'll like it.

By the way, I am determined to get work and make good at home—that is the real motive in my coming. Thank God, I believe I've shaken off the subtle drive of the desire to get nearer North Carolina. I don't want to boast, but after these 22 months I think the Albatross has fallen from my neck. Slowly but surely I feel possessed of a new spiritual strength. I don't know how it will stand the test of temptation, or disappointment if I don't get work, and the various complications of life that will meet me when I get home. I know I'm going back to meet all sorts of problems that I evade by staying here—but something makes me want to launch fearlessly into it all. If only I can hold what I feel I've gained! So I'm sailing on the Olympic Dec. 15th. Is there anything I can bring you? I *long* so to bring lovely presents to everyone, but the Customs takes the heart out of one!

My next public recital is the 25th and I'm doing the new monologue. It went well at Cambridge this week. It's fearfully hard, and elaborate, and capable of *such* effect if I *can* do it as it should be done. It's quite terrifying to face doing it at Æolian Hall—but I've felt new life since I see there is hope for its success.

To Harriet Marple

> The Hill School
> Pottstown [Pennsylvania]
> January 9, 1921

I landed the day before Xmas and have been in a rush ever since, very happy, amused and excited, but with a very active sense of the need of keeping my head, and not attaching any importance to anything but the planning of work. I had one job at a killing Woman's Club in Derby, Connecticut, and then spent New Year's and Sunday with Corinne Alsop, and had a wonderful visit, talking over the past eight months—she having been as active politically as I in my way, and being as thrilled by life and a sense of growth.

Yesterday I recited here, my third visit, and I love these boy audiences.

I'm letting J. B. Pond continue to manage me—he has gotten me jobs often in the past, and I think is entitled to it, and being rather free can put a good deal of personal work into it—and that's what I need. He has the best connections all over the country. M——wanted me, but I was warned against him—he hasn't half the connections of Pond, and, tho' he would boom me as a great artist, he would want money to start it, and could get no work *this* year. Work is what I want, and Pond can probably get me a fair amount, considering my late arrival, with no advance announcements. I've a press agent, who is working it up, and my New York recitals coming so soon should help bring in something for the balance of the season. I'd rather leave it to the public to decide if I'm any good—and as I never know where I may be next winter, I didn't want to enter into a contract with M——for 1922 which is what he wanted. The other big *concert* managers would look on me in the same way, so I think I'm doing right. What I want is a paying public—not primarily private jobs so I've gone up to $300. So much for my affairs.

I'm with Dorothea at 129 East 36 and later will go to George and Dorothy unless I take a room for a while. I'm taking some breathing, singing lessons, of a sort, from a wonderful person, Mrs. Carrington, and enjoying it enormously. Paul is teaching again, his play having failed. I've seen him once.

The reference to a press agent, in the preceding letter, probably is to Russel Crouse, who wrote, on September 16, 1957, to May Seymour, Curator of the Theatre Collection of the Museum of the City of New York: "My association with [Ruth Draper] *was many years ago as probably her first press agent. . . . It was a strange association for she did not want any publicity, refused to see me half the time, and every thing I did to help her sell out, which she did, I did in spite of her."*

Ruth Draper expected her managers and press agents to promote and to advertise—to fill the houses. She would do her part by performing, but personal interviews, details of her off-stage self, most definitely not! When, on occasion, she found herself obligated to being "met," as in so much of the academic circuit, she loathed every aspect and rarely found a redeeming moment. Over the years she came to accept, to some degree, the fact that interviews were part of the process, but always she protested and never enjoyed them. They were endured, however, with charm and considerable grace.

To Harriet Marple

June 17 [1921]
Brown Shipley's
Reading Room
[London]

I am back at my old lodgings in 120 Ebury Street. I'm very well, the weather has been simply perfect and the moon at night with a clear sky, and the romance and quiet of this adorable city, moves me as ever. My two recitals went off well, but were not packed as before. The season is *very* bad and all theatres half empty; that I do better than anyone else is all that can be said. I don't think it's yet permeated the minds of the seven million that I'm here!!! I've had *no* private parties yet.

I'll possibly try for a Music Hall in Paris. I long to be heard over there and don't know how else to start. My new sketch is working up well.

I sent for "The Golden Age" by Kenneth Grahame, who wrote "The Wind in the Willows". It is full of charm and deep tender beauty of feeling and observation.

To Harriet Marple

June 29 [1921]
[Wednesday]
Hotel Vouillemont
15, rue Boissy-d'Anglas
Paris

I'm in Paris, so of course thinking of you and wishing you were here to trot about with me! I've never been more thrilled by its beauty and charm, and the tempting shops, the food, and the general elation of the place, so crowded—so gay—is intoxicating. I only came over on Saturday and am going back to-night, for my fourth recital to-morrow afternoon. I meant to go this morning, and at the station suddenly realized I'd completely forgotten to get a British visa! Ass that I am—I'd been so busy and excited, it completely slipped my mind—so I'm missing a nice party in London to-night and having a hellish journey, and have a job to-morrow night, after my show, and two on Friday—so altogether don't look forward to the coming hours and the next few days. But I'm ready to pay for my stupidity, for the fun of these four days.

I came over to look into the possibilities, before I sail, of appearing here in the fall and, if by chance it should go, return next May for the Season. My dear, I met with the most wonderful luck and long to tell you about it. A regular concert manager, whom I first went to, sent me to a M. Lugné-Poe,

Director of the Théâtre de l'Œuvre which presents the most interesting and original things in Paris. He is one of those big, powerful Frenchmen—like Guitry, rather—and in ten minutes after I came into his office, had told me that he would present me in the autumn! I couldn't believe my ears—it's beyond my wildest dreams—at last to be "taken" and presented by one of the most important managers, and in Paris! And he's never heard me! I just told him as simply and directly as I could (in French) what I do—and he glanced at my notices and Sargent pictures—told me to write synopses in French of my programmes, send press copy, a story of myself and work, etc. which would come out in the Figaro. I am overwhelmed and won't believe it's true until it happens, but he is not in the least a man one would doubt—definite, direct, firm and a very strong personality, about 55, husband of Suzanne Déprés, the actress. Of course I shall have qualms—his taking such a sudden interest—but he does not strike me as a man who would do anything *for* that reason—he is supremely interested, obviously, in his productions, his work, and his position in Paris and from all I hear, it is the most serious and distinguished enterprise and the intellectual and artistic Paris goes to Everything that he puts on! I shall be terrified—but *think* what an opportunity!

I recited for Mildred Bliss [Mrs. Robert Woods Bliss], who had a tea for very smart Paris friends yesterday. It went surprisingly well; they all spoke English and seemed very amused and responsive, so I am a little encouraged about French understanding, tho' how it will be to a public that speaks no English, heaven only knows.

Lugné-Poe (1869–1940), French actor and producer, was born Aurélian-François Lugné, adding Poe to his name in homage to Edgar Allan Poe, whose writings he so greatly admired. Though he did not introduce Ibsen's plays to Paris, it was his productions that brought Parisian audiences to a knowledge and understanding of Ibsen's works as well as those of Maeterlinck, Gerhart Hauptmann, Bjoernson, Strindberg, and Oscar Wilde. He founded the Théâtre de l'Œuvre, which became known for its "Symboliste" productions and as a center of the young intellectuals, artists, and poets. Alfred Jarry's Ubi Roi *was one of his more sensational productions; and that of Maeterlinck's* Pelléas et Mélisande, *with costumes and sets designed by the young Vuillard, Bonnard, and Sérusier, so enchanted Debussy that he wrote from it the opera that helped to make him famous. The Théâtre de l' Œuvre became a Paris landmark at 55, rue de Clichy.*

This was the man who wrote in his memoir (Dernière Pirouette, 1946) describing "cette petite femme brunaude" who appeared early one morning to see the Director, asking about his theatre. He notes her business-like approach, her expert appraisal of the house and its facilities, "her eyes, very brown, blazing with a healthy light." Her troupe? "Non, oh non. Je suis seule. Je n'ai besoin de personne. Seule, moi. Un rideau, seul." He liked the "seule," which had something of pride, of ease, an air of defiance. The solitaries always fascinated him. Without doubt, before him was "un caractère." He offered her 60 percent. "But you do not know me . . ." "This interests me. I do not risk much. In your eyes I see the spark of fine theatre." He forgot to ask her name.

To Harriet Marple

July 10 [1921]
Colwyn Bay, Wales

I spent last night at Penrhos with the Sheffields, and have just come here for a show tonight at the "Grand Pier-Pavilion". It is a seaside resort about an hour from Holyhead. I wish you were here now. I'm sitting in a swing, under an enormous oak, overlooking lawn sloping down to the roofs of the little town and the sea beyond. The air is cool and the sun hot, and syringa and mown hay make a delicious fragrance. Dash it however, I must go in and dress for my show which is at eight—it doesn't get dark 'til 10:30 up here and I went to bed last night in broad light, with roses and hay scenting the air. My, the beauty of these English summer days—and these old houses and these children!

Incidentally, I look *very* nice and, of course as usual, there is *no one* to see how nice! I have on the most lovely white knitted silk and wool dress which I got in Paris . . . the loveliest softest thing to wear and I feel the way I *want* to look. Whether I look the way I feel, I can't tell! And, *always,* I dream of a pair of eyes who thought me lovely in my "Y" uniform—can you *bear* it, and do you blame me for still wishing that just once he could see me in something else! Don't think me vain—it's not me but this soft, sweet quietness and beauty, and loving it all, alone, that starts the longing again.

My first month here was very quiet—no jobs and I couldn't seem to get going like last year—and felt out of things, and at times depressed. It's been better lately—the same old story—I must keep busy. I sometimes wonder if I've gained at all—for I don't make much success of being "merry and bright" when life isn't humming with accomplishment and anticipation.

Ruth visited one of her war-time towns in France to see the well and pump which her gift of 500 francs had made possible. Then she continued on a week's motor trip to the Pyrenees with her sister Martha, and returned to England in time to look after Alice's children in a house near Hindhead.

Her nephew remembers: "Aunt Ruth was in a gay mood. When we pedalled thru villages and spied elderly couples walking along, she would break into some strange foreign language, intending, she said, to confuse them. 'Foreigners!' the village couples doubtless commented."

To Harriet Marple

September 21 [1921]
Shamley Green
Surrey [England]

I'm in a darling cottage bedroom, with branches of an apple tree fairly coming thro' the latticed window, birds are twittering and it's one of those misty autumn mornings and quite delicious. I'm here with friends and go up to town this afternoon.

Last week I spent with Alice's children in a house not far from here. I had a heavenly time playing with the children and going to bed nightly at nine. We bicycled, the twins and I . . . such lovely country—lanes, hills, breezy downs, and pine woods. We had our lunch on warm pine needles, and lay in hot hay, and we read aloud and laughed and I've never been happier.

My Paris dates are fixed for October 24th, 26th, and 28th, two evenings and one matinee, and if they go well, perhaps two more—31st and 4th. I sail on the Aquitania November 5th from Cherbourg. I think Alice [Carter] will come over to be with me—the little holiday will be good for her and it will be fine for me to have her. I'm not sure yet about what I shall wear, but I rather think my old Worth gold satin—it's been all done over and looks lovely, I love it so, and have had so much success in it! Worth has made me the most beautiful "robe Velasquez" out of an old brown velvet of Mother's—it's quite lovely, but much too exaggerated to wear for monologues, I fear. Then I've had an old flowered taffeta that came from a 2nd hand—or rather, an antique shop—made up, and it's quite the prettiest thing of its kind I've ever seen—apple green frillings and lace petticoat—but again, rather too "stylé" I fear for my work. I've had the gold satin copied in white crepe—it's very chaste and lovely—but perhaps not enough of a dress for Paris. So I suppose I shall be killing myself at the last minute and spending fortunes to get something quite perfect—if only I knew what it was to be. I looked at things in Paris, much is hideous, and one must in the end resort to one's own taste, inspired, of course, by them! I was only in Paris a few days, en route from the South, and gave them up to helping my sister find clothes—I couldn't seem to concentrate on my needs. I must get a winter day dress and an afternoon mono. dress anyway, and come prepared for the whole season because I begin work at once and shall have no time to bother about clothes at home.

I got my French synopses all done, and two excellent articles written by friends, and I'm awfully excited about it all. Lugné-Poe is a wonderful person; you'd be perfectly crazy about him, he's so full of force, so direct, and so full of charm, and the quickest understanding! He seems keen to make it a great success and his faith in me puts me on my mettle—he's not heard me yet! It makes a strange story—to tell on myself—as you can see, so it's better to say, I think, that he had heard all about me, and just happened to need something at that date, and rather wanted an American!

I'll write you again of any developments. I shall have a fair number of friends in Paris at that time, which will help a lot. Aileen [Tone] will be there for the first night anyway.

I still feel something may happen to spill the beans—it's such an opportunity, and the whole story seems such a stroke of luck and might be so wonderful, that it hardly seems likely my hopes can be realized.

To Harriet Marple

[October 25, 1921]
[Paris]

It's over! The agony of waiting for the first—nothing can be so scary again. I am warm and cheerful inside—this sounds *just* as if I'd had a baby (God, I wish I had!) and I didn't see how funnily it would read!! It really was a triumph and I wish you'd been here. Everything was with me— weather, acoustics, charm of the whole milieu and decor, and friends; dear old Alice to chaperone me to the nines, wonderful flowers, the most beautiful lighting; and Lugné-Poe announcing me in a way that made you fairly groan with pleasure—the distinction, taste, tact, beauty of form and content such as I never hope to hear equalled. It almost wrecked me to go on when he came off, but he had just tipped the audience off to a point of humor and friendliness and understanding that they greeted me in his spirit and I felt quite at ease. It was really a miracle.

I shan't make any money, I don't suppose, but never expected to, the honor and opportunity are enough. L'Œuvre stands for *so* much, I find, among the intellectual, literary, dramatic and artistic world. I'm in the greatest luck to have had recognition there. To have justified Lugné-Poe's confidence is what I most care about and as I evidently did, I'm smiling to the marrow of my bones.

I did The French Dressmaker, Three Generations, Quiet Morning in Bed, Vive la France, County Kerry, German Governess, R.R. Station, and two encores—Roumanian Lady and [Showing] the Garden. All went awfully well.

Jacques Porel came and was perfectly charming and is coming Wednesday; Mme. Lemaire—G[ermaine Wilson Rejane]'s friend—gave me a tea and lots of her friends spoke to me so cordially. I was much touched and very grateful for all the trouble she took to tell them about me.

The weather is like Paradise, Paris agleam, and one's feet can hardly keep on the pavement! I must try and take a nap now. I had a *lovely* party given me last night by Geoffrey Dodge and got home at 1:15, had rather a restless night and kept waking to see L-P's smile of approval! Another case of "our luck", Harriet, meeting a perfectly marvellous, perfectly unavailable personality—but I am grateful for so much, and what I miss must go with what I get into making me, and my work, of higher worth. O, if only I can hold to this philosophy for all my life!

Ruth Draper was to return many times, Lugné-Poe and his wife becoming her life-long friends. After Duse and Réjane he regarded her as his "trump card who came spontaneously and was spontaneously received." Just before his death in 1940 he wrote in Dernière Pirouette: *"Ruth Draper! Without doubt, one of the strongest personalities of the contemporary theatre; understanding the ills of the present dramatic art, she walks through it head high, and the contagion has never touched her. An artist of an entirely different* formation *than any I had known; fierce, admirable North-American, Ruth Draper observes herself, knows herself and suffers also like Duse, the Venetian, like Bady, like Réjane. In all her very great afflictions—and God knows this great friend has been stricken—I believe it difficult for her not to be objective, to censure and question herself; there is Hell in her depths. . . . I have never met an actress so sincerely humble when she steps out of her profession, whose success however she perfectly admits. . . . In my eyes she is always a great woman."*

The New York Times, *on November 12, 1921, noted Ruth Draper's return on the S.S. Aquitania from performances at the Théâtre de l' Œuvre in Paris, where she was "paid the rather unusual compliment, to a foreigner, to appear at one of the famous five o'clock receptions given by the Paris newspaper* Le Figaro *to people of both sexes who have acquired fame by their artistic or literary talents rather than as leaders of French Society." The reception was held on the 8th of November but Ruth Draper sailed on the 5th to keep engagements in New York, and regretted her inability to be present.*

She was on tour in the North-East and Mid-West right through April, in constant travel and having many one-night stands. Then, with Aileen Tone and Mrs. Frederick Keep she sailed in the S.S. France for Paris.

To Malvina Hoffman

April 19, 1922
Boston

My heart is very full, my dearest Mallie—of your pain, of the dumb acceptance of the great mystery, and of the almost joyful consciousness that you must feel, in the knowledge that her beautiful brave soul is free at last.

The fact that one is so sure that only supreme peace and beauty are her destiny, makes the long strange captivity of all these months, with the cruel suffering they brought you, of small importance now.

In my life I have not seen nor do I expect to see, more heroic or more lovely human qualities than your Mother possessed, and I am proud to count back the many years that I have known her, and to think of the loyal devoted affection between her and my mother.

The way you have borne the strain of these months, has left me silent with admiration and sympathy. So often have I wanted to let you feel how I understood, but it seemed too deep and too poignant to talk about. I know what your love was—the sustenance to all that was most sacred in you—the love and devotion that she gave you—but thank God we do not lose such possessions, and in their heritage we still find strength.

My dear friend, I know the agony, the baffling sense of loss, but I know that your head is high, and that the consciousness that all is well with her, outweighs the human sorrow.

But we are human, and my hand is in yours, and my heart aching for the pain that has been in your heart for so long, and that still must be, tho' of another kind.

Malvina Hoffman (1885–1966) had grown up as an intimate family friend of Ruth and Paul Draper and had her own distinguished career in the arts. She was the daughter of Richard Hoffman, who came to America from England in 1847 as a child virtuoso of the piano and who accompanied Jenny Lind on her American Tour in 1850 under the management of P. T. Barnum. He was internationally known as an outstanding concert pianist and teacher. Malvina became a sculptor, studying with Rodin, and achieving her most spectacular success for the Field Museum in Chicago: one hundred sculptures of The Races of Man—a commission that occupied five years of grueling work around the world. In World War I she directed the Bureau of Information and Research for the Red Cross in New York and, in 1919, was sent by Herbert Hoover to the Balkans for the American Relief Administration. She became a friend of Ivan Mestrović and was, for many years, active in Yugoslav Relief. Her sister, Helen Hoffman, married Ruth's elder half-brother, Dr. William Kinnicutt Draper, and became an indefatigable and greatly honored worker for the International Red Cross (see Bibliography).

To Harriet Marple

May 22, 1922
4, rue Henri Moissan
[Quai d'Orsay]

This is the most generous notepaper I ever saw, but I have plenty to say! I rejoiced over your letter this morning, and hope for one by every ship! How I wish you were here. So far I've kept my head on my shoulders but it surprises me to find it still there. In the paper on the 18th at Havre I read that I was appearing the 21–22–23–26–28 and I had a private party on the 24!!! Happily, Mrs. Keep (whom Aileen is with) and who has a beautiful apartment asked me to stay with her over Sunday, so I am most comfortably housed, and that has made a great difference, being with friends (my infernal luck) and with every care and comfort to hand.

I must describe my first day: the Bank, Vionnet—ordering two dresses, one afternoon and one evening (to be ready for Sunday!), shampoo and wave, the theatre—brief but delightful talk with L-P. Lunch, rest for half an hour, corset place, theatre to see about properties and programmes, etc., tea with my friend Raymonde Glaenzer whose apartment I found was for rent, and which I took [until July 6th]! Home, several telephones, dinner and early to bed. All this with the beauty of a perfect day eating at one's vitals—horse-chestnuts, fountains, noises, smells, colors, familiar views and mellow lights and everything else to make one completely intoxicated—and muguets and lilacs at every corner! And Vionnet's dresses as lovely in their way.

I move tomorrow to my apartment and I'm in great luck to have got it. The hotels are very crowded and terribly expensive. This is an old house, 20, rue Jacob, it runs off the rue de l'Université and is near the rue des Sts Pères and rue Bonaparte. I have a salon looking on a little garden, two bed-rooms, a little salle à manger, and a darling maid [Léa Dessay] whom I've known for several years, being the devoted slave of Raymonde, to cook and wait on me hand and foot. I pay her 150 frcs. a month and 600 for the flat—think of it! Aileen is dining with me to-morrow—my first night—and over the telephone I ordered our dinner—potage, poulet rôti, salade, légume vert, coeur à la crème! Can you bear it— I am cruel—yet you'd rather get a letter than none, I guess, and what can I say but what is going on! It's hot—too hot—and I've been so preoccupied with my work, I've not been to dressmakers until to-day and I ordered a blue, sort of poplin serge stuff, dress and cape lined with a queer green, and a crêpe toquet, a new stuff, the brown of autumn leaves. My Vionnet is a screaming pink flame, a perfect dream, wore it last night, and a golden yellow—rather the color of my Worth—in crêpe romain for the afternoon. I expect to fall for a white diamanté crêpe—quite the loveliest thing I ever saw, an absolutely simple Greek design. I've got a party at the Embassy June 9, very smart, for the Princesse Murat.

Well, about last night—I feel just as if I'd had a baby, the lifting of the strain is such a blessed relief. The rehearsal of my Philip IV went too awfully—Lugné was very severe, very skeptical, and wanted me to put off doing it! I was terrified, distressed and worked hard over it. I knew I must not lose confidence in my power and postponing it meant a sort of failure. Well, I did it and it went all right. The costume was really beautiful and I've never seen such lighting as they gave me—the most wonderful effects of blues and reds that gave reflets of the silver that were too lovely. They put paper in the piano, most ingeniously, to make the sound of a clavecin, and only a flute besides, so the music was very simple and very perfect. What is so interesting here, so good for me, is their accurate knowledge and finished taste. Nothing sloppy, imperfect, or not perfectly "aux pointes", as they say, goes. I tell you it jacked me up to see I could not think of putting over the sketch as I did in New York, and it's 50% better already. They are all too adorable at the theatre—all so glad to see me, so solicitous and sympathetic when they saw L-P. finding fault. He was adorable, but perfectly honest in his criticism.

The audience was very small but keen and appreciative as could be and all French but about ten Americans. They applauded the bandaged finger which is always a good sign, and the silence in the Spanish sketch was breathless. Lugné was thrilled and in his wonderful simple "c'est très bien, c'est très très bien" I got all the recompense I needed for the agony I'd gone thro', and the deep tribute and tenderness I know he feels. Aileen was with me, and thrilled, and felt the atmosphere of the place and of his quality as I've tried to make you feel it, and I'm so glad she did.

Good-bye dear friend—I won't say what I wish, this letter will have made you sufficiently envious. I'm resting all afternoon, from lunch till dinner, for my show tonight, so don't worry about me—I'll be careful. No word from "Spain". Lugné wants me to go there in October so I guess I will.

At the Court of Philip IV is the only one of Ruth Draper's dramatic sketches that was based on a historical incident, and the only one in which she wore an elaborate costume. This was designed in the costume workshop of the Neighborhood Playhouse; with its panniered skirt, of the type known as "guarda infanta," it seemed straight out of a Velasquez portrait. She wore it, and moved in the Minuet, with great grace, and her Spanish accent in speaking French was considered by Spaniards to be remarkably accurate.

To Martha Draper
at Dark Harbor

June 23 [1922]
20 rue Jacob [Paris]

Thank you for your letter, I smell the air off the water and the damp sweet smell of the earth and trees, just as keenly as ever and wish I were there, to teach the boys to sail, and to re-live those happy days. I can honestly say, thank God, that I have not ceased yet to enjoy with equal zest any one thing that I have loved in my youth, and I would revert to myself at fourteen were I there again.

Well, with me the days fly by on wings of beauty and interest. My little home is a constant delight, and the beauty and charm of Paris sinks and burns into me as never before. I meet delightful people—distinguished, charming—all full of extravagant praise for my work, and the finest perception and analysis of its originality and virtue. All of which is pleasing, of course, but continues to leave me quite unsatisfied with any but my own estimate, which seldom reaches par. The Spanish piece has improved vastly, and the dress is really beautiful. (Wore it to the great Venetian Ball at the Opéra.)

I had a very great, an unforgettable moment a few days ago. I was at tea with a charming Countess Boisrouvray, who was singing—only ten or so people, among them General Mangin. She asked me to do a piece in French—no one spoke English—and there was a blind man present, so the Retour [de l'Aveugle] was impossible—so I seized a little pillow, threw off my hat, and did "Vive la France". When I got thro' there was a suffocating silence, and the General rose from his chair, tears pouring down his cheeks, and without a word seized and kissed my hands. No one spoke. It was a solemn moment—and a long moment—and I felt strangely moved, for there was the great man who had driven thousands to the slaughter, not just slightly moved, but controlling himself, obviously shaken, as if he were suddenly overwhelmed by the consciousness of the agony of all those wives for whom I had the privilege of speaking. I shall never forget it as long as I live for I had the actual sensation of transmitting, in that moment, the pain and the heroism of all the sorrowing women. So it goes—the strange round— beauty born of pain, in one way or another the two are inexorably linked and, after all, the best thing that a man or woman has to offer in their sacrifice.

I'm looking at a branch of blue hydrangea, a vase of lilies, and a bowl of red roses, the smell of a soft rain is floating thro' the window and birds are twittering.

I must now get up and put on my blue, peacock blue dress, and a nifty little toque with a veil over the eyes and dribbling over one ear, and go to a musicale at Aileen's. To-night, I recite at an American-Franco Fête, tomorrow an Anglo-Franco Fête, Sunday my own last recital. Next week I'm going to see pictures and sights madly, and probably go to look for a place on the coast.

I've got a *lovely* new hair ornament from Worth, Egyptian diamanté effect, and très séante, and my yellow Vionnet afternoon dress is a *dream!* I know all these details divert you! Dearest love to the boys—I hope all goes well.

In Paris Ruth enjoyed to the full the apartment on rue Jacob and Léa Dessay became her great and life-long friend. "We had the happiest combination."

She was taken by Raymonde Glaenzer to call on Sarah Bernhardt where, in all the dusty confusion of possessions and pets, she recited for the mettlesome old actress, so strong and full of vibrant energy. Bernhardt was charmingly appreciative, telling Ruth she must *become an actress. But Ruth was unimpressed by this advice and remained interested only in Bernhardt's dynamic, intense personality, thinking it vastly amusing to find herself reciting in that setting. More moving was the Sunday she went to St. Sulpice and sat next the great Widor at his organ while he played.*

With rare exceptions, Ruth Draper's blue leather Smythson Diaries contained no more than notations of her social engagements—occasionally with a comment such as "marvellous food," "great fun," "delightful people," "wonderful audience," "sold out"—very useful, however, as reference in dating the many letters headed merely "Sunday," or "Tuesday"! Even so, these "diaries" are available for only twenty-four out of the thirty-seven years, and often contain long series of blank pages. For 1922 she had a thick red Day-by-Day Diary, though she found life too diverting for daily entries after the first few weeks. On board the Majestic, en route home after Christmas, she attempted to write up the year while struggling to keep herself awake for a New Year's Eve party with friends. This is the only running account in any year and proves an invaluable supplement to the available letters, which do not describe all the year's events. Therefore, gaps between letters, for this one year alone, have been filled in by a reordering of this rambling letter to herself. Excerpts are noted as "Diary."

Diary:

[In Paris] one morning at 4:30 I went to market with Léa—great fun—going with our baskets, no hats, and coming home laden with flowers and supplies of fruits and vegetables. At last to get away from hotels and feel "at home" in Paris. I loved every single day and night in my enchanting room. I loved climbing the dark stairs with my little electric light at night. The sunsets, the roofs, the rain in the court, the rue Jacob, the shops and people, the lovely St. Germain-des-Pres—the whole Quarter. What a lovely time I had, chiefly in having such an enchanting place to live in.

I had a great opportunity in Paris and met dozens of very interesting and distinguished people—but I can hardly remember a name, alas, as I never wrote anyone's name down. At first I fought the usual Paris nervous fatigue that always gets me and it was *awfully* hot and my shows were not thrilling, the audiences were so small, but very serious, enthusiastic, and the critics were very generous in their praise. All the time I realized how much more success I should have had—for people were talking tremendously in the "monde", I heard. If only Lugné had followed it up with more skill. I felt it was all badly advertised and carelessly handled and realize the shortcomings of the "Œuvre" in spite of the honor and prestige of appearing there. But I'm bound to Lugné and see no way of expanding unless I spend a lot of money and take a theatre which doesn't seem worth while.

Travelled over to London [early in July] and went at once to my little home, 20 Halsey Street. Mrs. [Yates] Thompson had got the house for me, and it was full of flowers to greet me—a sweet little maid, Nellie, and a most respectable cook, Mrs. Tobin. Mrs. Thompson had sent vegetables, fruit, butter and eggs, and continued to do so for the three weeks I was in London. My three recitals went beautifully, the last two sold out, and besides I had parties at Mrs. Thompson's and the American Embassy for the Duke of York. Will [Draper] came for the last ten days of my visit which was very nice. I enjoyed being able to put him up and play about with him. The days fled. Of course I took enormous pleasure in my little house—having friends to lunch, tea, and dine. Wrote a lot of letters in my darling drawing room and really resented going out. I felt I had come late in the Season to get really into things, but then I would not have shortened Paris! I missed several nice parties by not letting friends know before—my usual failing! Went to see various friends in shops along Ebury Street—in some ways missed my old life in lodgings. The house was *so* charming, it made a new interest and made me less dependent on outside and friends for amusement and occupation. Also very expensive but well worth it as an experience.

Also had an evening recital at Lady Bathurst's—very smart, delightful evening—Princess Christian was there and Sir Edward Carson, [Philip de] Laszlo, Kipling, and the Duc de Guise whom I'd met in Paris—very attractive.

To Harriet Marple

July 21 [1922]
20 Halsey Street
[London]

Tonight the de Glehns are coming to dine, and another man, and we're going to "Loyalties", the new Galsworthy play which is having a succès fou. I had my second show last night and the people were turned away! Every seat sold! I am far from happy about my work however, tho' the public seems more than satisfied.

I had a lovely dinner at Hugh Walpole's the other night—14 men and women, every one of whom did something—there was such an atmosphere of self and mutual respect, and no jealousy or smallness—it was intensely interesting: Karsavina, Walpole, Melchior a great young Danish tenor, Rose Macaulay the novelist (Dangerous Ages), Beizel (the singing teacher), a splendid woman pianist, another woman writer and critic, Kelly a well known painter, me, Dennis Eady a 1st class actor, Edward Knobloch the playwright (Milestones) etc. It was so delightful—lovely house—good food. So dignified and clean—the host too nice, so wholesome and enthusiastic, and we all enjoyed ourselves and had music and monos. after.

I'm going to the Royal Garden Party at Buckingham Palace this afternoon. My ticket No. is 10,461 so there will be a slight crush but I expect to be enormously amused.

Thanks for your letter. Please remember that I'm only all stirred up like that when I receive your letters—and his—and quiet down and am quite happy in between, so you needn't worry about me at all.

On July 29th Ruth joined the Carters in Southampton, crossing on the boat to Le Havre en route to Houlgate where she had taken a villa for six weeks. Léa Dessay came to help with the four children and to speak French with them. "The twins [aged 13] were wonderful companions; we played games after supper and went to bed at 9:30." After a time she became fretful, not working, even though enjoying the relaxation, the seashore life, and the good food. She was concerned about material for new monologues, but after the Carters left, ideas suddenly began to form.

To Harriet Marple

Sunday 10th [September 1922]
Houlgate [France]

Alice and the children left Thursday evening. Friday was general cleaning house, changing one's mood to the peace and emptiness of the house without them. Saturday, wonderful rainwater shampoo, terrific cleaning, mending, brushing and repairs of my wardrobe with my lovely Léa. It's rather a dreary day however and I'm cosily sitting in the wee salon, with a fire, reading and writing, and soon I shall go for a wild walk before tea. I miss the children but in many ways I'm glad to be alone, to descend within myself with no distractions.

I simply must conceive a work out of something new. Do you remember the crazy drive from Springfield when I sang all those songs? Well, it's a vague idea I've long had to use a group of songs if ever I could catch and hold the melodies I create. Gladys Lea comes on Wednesday to stay with me and I'm going to try to get her to take down the notes if I can conveniently have a "seizure" while she is here. Then, you see, I can learn them for safety and compose my words in appropriate rhythm (fake language). My plan would be to call it

Group of Folk Songs in Costume
Balkan Lullaby
Swedish Polka
Corsican Love Song
Hindoo Chant

and just wear different shawls to give vivid contrast to each song. I'm getting quite excited by the idea and hope I can put it through. Don't say anything about it, will you. I'll let you know if anything develops. I'm staying on here at least a fortnight more. Nothing is so important as to work out something new and my best chance is here, so here I stay.

To Harriet Marple

September 22 [1922]
Houlgate

I'm not in a mood for writing, but want to get this word off to you. I'm feverishly sending off notes to bankers—changing address, friends in Paris, planning my little trip to Tonnerre, Châtillon, and Nancy and writing ahead for rooms, etc. The fit of moving is on me and I can't be happy idling any more. I've written five songs, words and music, and am eager to get the music written down, and possibly orchestrated. It's frightfully difficult to memorize these crazy words that mean nothing, but being composed with care I must of course learn them perfectly. You'll die over the Swedish polka—*never* heard Swedish, but I am convinced the effect is perfect. I almost have hysterics over it myself (this is a bad sign!). The others are promising. I feel a lot depends on my freedom after I know them perfectly, and on the costume.

I've worked up the Children's Party and it promises well, and I'm determined now to work on the Telephone Switch Board. I'm not by any means happy over what the summer has brought forth, but I am much happier having pulled myself together, and feeling my brain kindled again, and if these songs by chance take, they might be a great addition. Don't say anything yet. I'm terrified someone may take the idea and do it before I get back!

Gladys Lea is with me now. She has a sore throat and is in bed—brings back old days. I must have a bad influence on throats of my companions.

I've another letter from Lugné with [a] most splendid offer from the Spanish director. Gosh—*why* aren't you here to go with me! I *must* go—no matter if my feet drop off with cold! I'm just trusting to fate to drop a companion beside me.

Thanks for the book—I'll read it someday, not now. I must try and not read—when my mind is working on new things—it's an easy way to escape work, and you know my inclination.

Come to think of it—I *did* answer your last letter. Am furious to have used all this time on you!!

A long fragmented letter to Harriet Marple written over four days early in October records a nostalgic visit to the towns where they had entertained American troops in 1919–20.

"I walked over the roads that are stamped in my memory forever. It's raining and the smells of the wet stucco and the feel of the pale mud on the cobbled streets at Is-sur-Tille brought such poignant memories of our days to-gether in all the villages we lived in."

In Châtillon she stayed two nights with Mme. Beauvoir, renewing their friendship. "Bitter cold in that old stone house. We talked late huddled about the stove. Sunday afternoon a large tea party for me—a wonderful scene, such types—out of a Balzac novel."

She continued from Paris:

To Harriet Marple

[October 10, 1922]
[Paris]

I find piles of mail and much to attend to here. Madrid dates don't fit until November 25th so I shall stay in England and get more work there, I hope. I doubt if I attempt Italy and may come home by Xmas, but you never can tell! Gladys Lea is staying over to do some work with Mühlen and goes to London with me to-morrow.

Of course, you really want to know about [Emile] Coué. Well, I was deeply impressed and moved. The first thing that strikes you is his intense simplicity and sincerity—just a dear funny little old man, shabbily dressed in a neat but shiny black suit—about my height—white hair and pointed beard, piercing deep-set sparkling brown eyes full of *humor* and kindness. The house is a scream—a little ugly modern villa, with dreadful "objets d'art" and pictures in embossed metal frames which he evidently makes himself—all signed E. Coué. There was one plaque of a nude lady riding on a dolphin's tail—guided by a cupid. About 100 chairs all around the edge of the room, and the most motley crowd. Rich Americans, French peasants, English middle-class, and professorial types—Aquascutums and projecting teeth. The spirit in the whole thing is amazingly cheerful and friendly and easy, and there is absolutely *nothing* that offends one's taste or sensibilities—like the jarring language of [some] other "New Thought" cults. That's what struck me most. It is entirely compatible with any religion, with any religious feeling one may have, lucid, logical, human and directly appealing to one's intelligence and one's finest feelings—anybody's. It is easily understood and can begin its effect at once! Of course one's analytical sense is a barrier, one *thinks* too much, and one's mind puts up objections and denials, even while one's desire is working and believing, but I'm sure this lessens in time if one mechanically continues to do what he says. I'm enclosing a little cord which his sweet peasant maid *gives* you at the door. I'm awfully glad I went, for to see him working one cannot but be moved and think of St. Francis, and Christ himself, who in such simplicity desired nothing but to help suffering and erring souls. Do tell Doro about it all, I'm sure she'll be interested.

Émile Coué (1857–1926) was a French doctor whose form of healing by auto-suggestion (psycho-therapy) had a considerable vogue in England and the United States in the early 1920s, his followers repeating to themselves: "Day by day in every way, I am getting better and better."

Diary:
Gladys Lea and I went to 9 Pembridge Gardens, Notting Hill Gate, London, Miss de Casagrande's new house—clean and comfortable but a dreary household. Very cheap, however, and conveniently near Mühlen where we went every day for a lesson. Enjoyed this enormously—he is a strange lovable personality and I'm sure knows more of the art of song singing than anyone in the world. I loved him and the rare privilege of working with him on voice production and breathing. Fortunately ran into Pedro Morales who gave me splendid letters for Spain. Paid huge Income Tax.

That curiously humorous, half-imitative, half-creative art which is Ruth Draper's held a Wigmore Hall audience captive yesterday afternoon. For truly her character sketches are unique, from whatever angle they are regarded, and their variety, within the compass of one recital, quite astonishing. . . . Her technique (unlike that of so many famous artists we could name) is, as it were, an invisible thing. . . . Miss Draper, like the fine artist she is, is not content with one sort of technique for all; she has many techniques. . . . Miss Draper went on to give a series of imitation folk-songs in the spirit of parody, an authentic costume for each. . . . To sum up, the whole recital was a tour-de-force that defies analysis. The alternation of comedy and pathos, hard-bitten naturalism, and simple fun, leave one just a little bewildered at the cleverness and truth of it all. We have praised this lady's technique because we must. But it is only the beginning of her art, the pot-hooks. "At a Telephone Switchboard" is as good a slice of life as we have seen on any stage for many a long day.

The Daily Telegraph, London

To Harriet Marple

October 20 [1922]
9 Pembridge Gardens
[London] W.2

I'm enjoying enormously working with Mühlen and he is a goldmine of knowledge and wisdom and inspiration. I believe he could make me sing!

This [notice] will amuse you. *The Daily Telegraph* is a faithful friend and admirer so one must not take it too seriously, but on the whole the new things went well. I was very excited and nervous but feel so happy they're launched. Now they'll improve, I hope. The changing of costume in front of the audience [in the Folk Song Group] is very original to say the least, and amusing it appears. How New York will take such an innovation remains to be seen. The London public is adorable and cosy and friendly and one can trust them and confide in them. The Swedish Polka and Arabian Chant are much the best—I'm not happy about the others. The Switchboard, if I can perfect the appallingly difficult technique, will, I believe, be one of the best I've ever done; and the Charwoman has suddenly such a very deep note. But, oh, they're far from right yet. Cambridge was adorable as ever, Winchester School, thrilling.

I've decided to go to Rome. Duse will be acting and I shall meet her and that alone is worth the journey.

To Harriet Marple

November 2 [1922]
9 Pembridge Gardens
[London] W.2

Your description of being all settled, and of Paul's little place, and the news of my dear old Christine's death, makes me really homesick, and I feel far away. I am so sad about C. and full of the usual regrets after someone dies, that I wasn't loving enough. (I only sent her two post-cards all summer.) I only got news of her illness in a letter from Dorothea last night, and was going to cable my love to-day, but I'm too late. She loved me so and I loved her dearly, with all the affection of my childhood's memories—it was from her I got my Scotch—and all my life I shall not forget her standard of perfection in her work, she out-Lizzied Lizzie—and if ever I have a home her example will keep me to the mark. O, the tragedy of a lonely old servant—and we didn't do enough for her. I wish I'd been home—tho' I know everything possible was done at the last. Martha and Dorothea and Will I know did everything.

To Harriet Marple

November 21 [1922]
Hotel Ritz
Madrid

I'm madder than ever that you are not along! It's desperate having this beauty so personally and so alone and not even being able to communicate my feelings to a policeman or guard. I crave knowledge of the language, and find it very hard and myself very stupid. They're very friendly, these people, and the streets are gay and amusing—glorious sunshine, clear air, enchanting babies and nurses, and girls in black with veils on their heads—I've never so appreciated the value of black. It's a modern bustling city—but the Prado is supreme as a picture gallery, the Velasquez are perfectly marvelous—not to speak of others.

I've delivered a lot of letters, and am awaiting results—two callow youths from the Embassy called. I can't tell at all how my shows will go—it's a great gamble, and perhaps a crazy thing to have done, but how could I not follow when Lugné opened the way? He came to see me off—it was a tremendous, if brief, moment—our relation is very fine—so little said—so much felt, I know, by both. He is so noble, so full of tenderness and respect for me but I can see how he restrains himself, and it only makes me care more. He is a strange interesting creature, who has suffered terribly I guess and is in a way bitter and hard, with a nature that was not made that way and which is generous and noble still. Aileen was with me, and saw it all, and was a great comfort to me in some bad moments before the train pulled out. Oh, well I am thankful to have such a friendship—but it's the kind of happiness that is akin to pain at times.

I have a maid with me—a luxury but a bore, I'm not used to service, and it makes me feel unnatural—but it's an experiment—and I know I don't like it—it might be O.K. if I had a friend too. I almost got a charming friend in London to come with me and at the last she failed. The maid is an awfully nice creature, but she thinks laundry hanging out of windows in the little towns "assommant" and is a great snob, and sees no beauty where I see it, and it's amusing to watch her make a day's work out of "maiding" me!

I can't make up my mind whether to go alone to Seville and Granada—it seems a shame to miss the chance, but I'm almost afraid of seeing it all alone, and so briefly—for if I go to Rome I've not time to linger here. The journey to Italy is bad, but seeing Duse will make it worth while.

And to think I am going to do Philip IV on the premises!

To Mrs. Yates Thompson

[November 26, 1922]
Hotel Ritz
Madrid

The first ghastly day is over! The critics have been abundantly generous and enthusiastic in their praise, the audience was absorbed (if chiefly by perplexity I think) and very kind in its reception. I think all the American and English people in Madrid were there but the bulk was Spanish, and I fear few of these understood English. All my French things went beautifully and the Balkan scene—and I only wish I had enough French to fill the programme. The "Court of Philip IV" went well but I've been advised by Embassy people not to do it to-morrow when the King and Queen are coming! I'm sorry there should be this feeling, as it is a useful number, but I quite understand it! I shall do the Songs instead.

The weather is superb, sunny and warm, and the Prado my consolation and delight in many lonely hours. I'm going to Toledo on Wednesday with the First Secretary [Sillems] and his wife, of the Dutch Legation, a charming couple whom I met last June in Paris, so that will be a great pleasure to look forward to. I had a wonderful afternoon on Friday, going over the marvellous collection of Sr. Lazaro to whom I had a letter. He was delighted to know I knew you, and apparently knew all about Mr. Thompson's books. A dear old gentleman and his wife, so alone in a great palace full of wonderful pictures and precious things. They gave me tea, a huge bouquet, and sent me home in their motor. I hope to see them again.

To Harriet Marple

> Monday 27th
> [November 27, 1922]
> Hotel Ritz
> Madrid

Your last letter came very opportunely with a delicious one from Dorothea and several others, at a moment when I was very low fighting a cold, and in those terrible hours before my first show with no one to understand my peculiar state of mind. The letters set me up considerably, particularly one from Lugné—just a few words—but *so* beautiful, so just exactly what I intuitively feel he feels about me and our friendship, that I seemed suddenly to be lifted up to a very high and lovely peace. Some day I shall show it to you. Of course it made me cry, but such solemn, happy tears, and it has sustained me thro' strange and difficult hours here. I ought to be contented but you know me—the criticisms are wonderful, the audience very quiet and absorbed, but I feel truly they are terribly polite and flattering and more perplexed and interested than anything else. The King and Queen are coming today; so that is another excitement.

The weather is glorious. I've met several nice people who are terribly kind, a few whom I knew before, among them a darling Dutch couple who are motoring me to Toledo on Wednesday. I've got letters to present in Granada and Seville so, tho' the travelling is lonely, I'll find someone to speak to in each place I stop so I shouldn't complain, but oh, if you were along how this whole journey would be suddenly perfect! At least I know now how great a chance I took in undertaking such an adventure alone—I rather outmeasured my courage and enthusiasm but I believe good must come somehow out of such an effort and I shall be glad I came. I am terribly comfortable here at the Ritz but I shall really be happier when I get into a more Spanish atmosphere.

I have seen one fine dancer and some splendid acting.

I hate my new clothes, Vionnet's at that! You'll be pleased to hear I have a lovely new neck piece—beautiful soft skunk—tell Aunt Nin! Fido II looked very mangy but I haven't the heart to throw him away!

Ruth spent many hours in the Prado, overwhelmed by Velasquez and El Greco and her new understanding of these paintings so long known from her childhood education with her German governess. Her visit to Toledo, with the Sillems, remained always in her memory: the scenery, the light of sun and of moon, the Cathedral Choir, the Count Orgaz painting by El Greco. The continuous sunshine and high air exhilarated her.

To Mrs. Yates Thompson

December 20 [1922]
Hotel Cavour
Milan

I've thought of you both so often on my great journey. Tell Mr.
Thompson that I took luncheon with the Duke of Alba, and saw the beautiful velvet and gold box of the Bible—[which] was still away at the publishers. I saw such wonderful things there, and we lunched in a room with
tapestries woven with gold thread under the colors, made to celebrate his
ancestor's victories, (and for which he possesses the original bill) and so
beautiful they were, that I was distracted from eating and almost from talking! I went to the Palace, as I believe I wrote you, and the Queen sent me a
lovely platinum and diamond bracelet. I spent a marvelous day in Toledo, a
morning in Cordova, two and a half days in Seville, two in Granada, and
also stopped a night at Ronda en route to Algeciras. At Gibraltar I took the
ship to Marseilles and I had a delicious day and a half of rest in a ridiculously calm, blue, sunny sea. Then the beautiful journey along the Riviera,
and a night on here. Everything has been quite perfect.

To Harriet Marple

December 17 [1922]
Hotel Cavour
Milan

I arrived at 6:30 a.m.—it's now 8:00—and I've had a delicious hot bath
and a good breakfast, am all clean and fed and cosy in my "costly bed,"
littered already with letters and telegrams. I've had a marvellous journey,
and my goal is reached. Duse is under this roof—and I shall see her act to-
night! Toscanini is also conducting at the Scala this afternoon [*Falstaff*], so I
shall go to hear him. . . . I envy you hearing R[ubinstein] and K[ochanski],
it takes me back to Edith Grove—I've heard them there and never can
forget. I wish I were back to enjoy them now.

About my self and my journey—I don't know where to begin—I think I
wrote you last from Madrid. Things wound up beautifully there, and I made
2000 pesetas out of the four shows at the Theatre and 900 out of the evening affair at the Ritz! A small public of course, but a very interested and
enthusiastic one, and I suppose I should be thankful to have got thro' as
well as I did! I left the 5th and then spent the most wonderful week. . . . I
am crammed with such wonderful pictures, such beauty as I've seen this
past month! I've had great luck, and met delightful people to console me for
my lonely journey. Granada was beautiful beyond words. I spent an evening

with Falla and he played to me—his own magical music—as the lights came out in the valley below the Alhambra! Seville was marvellous, and I saw the boys dance before the High Altar—a thing that only happens twice a year. I wept at the beauty of it all—the colors and lights, and the great pillars of the Cathedral hung with 16th Century red velvet that made your mouth water (how horribly that looks written!). I've had the pleasantest experiences with Spaniards and nothing unpleasant.

[From] Gibraltar, a day and a half at sea, calm and blue (with delightful friends whom I'd met in Pasadena in 1915! [Dr. Hale, the astronomer, and his wife]) and yesterday from Marseilles to Ventimiglia—past St. Raphael and that whole wonderful coast, where memories that burn are all mixed up with mimosa and the sunny air and blue sea! Last night on the train, and here I am for three or four days.

As I look over my schedule—my time at home is painfully short—only until January 29th! Back for the 4th of Feb., and away, and then back for the 17th and 18th of Feb., then away for the rest of the Winter and Spring; and if I go on to Japan and China, from California, until August! That is of course only vaguely thought of. I really long to spend next summer at home—to sail at Islesboro, and to have the children—and after *five years* to taste green corn, melon, and Delaware grapes and baby lima beans! It remains to be seen where my strange destiny drives me next.

To Martha Draper

December 18 (1922)
Milan

I'll be sitting by your fire before very long (D. V., as the Kents would say) and talking you to death about all my adventures. This last month has been wonderful—all seven have been for that matter, but this last has been the most dazzling and swiftly moving and exciting of them all. And the climax has been here—fifteen minutes [to-day] in a little hotel sitting room sitting beside Duse on a sofa by a little stove. And I somehow don't feel the same person, so deeply have I been moved by her tragic personality and her acting—last night in "Ghosts." She is beautiful beyond expression—frail—whitehaired, but her grace and movement and the line of her throat—her gesture and voice—and a haunting sadness that simply wring your heart, seem to belong to the immortal beauty in the world.

I am going to recite for her to-morrow—I suppose my French things as she can't understand much English—and you can fancy how honored and thrilled I feel. I shall see her once more (alas, she can't play every night) and am staying until Thursday and then leave for Paris. . . .

I must go to sleep now—the Brera to-morrow and lots of lovely things to see here. Please book an early date for a cosy dinner and a long talk!

Bernhardt had said to Ruth, briskly:
"Pourquoi ne faites-vous pas la comédie?"
But Duse, gently:
"Mon enfant, ne faites jamais la comédie."

To Harriet Marple

December 21 [1922]
6:00 p.m.
En route Milan to Paris

Darkness has fallen, so I can't see the wonderful mountains any more, and it's too early to dine, and I don't feel like reading, so, having made a list of all I have to do in Paris in two days, here goes for a drool to you!

My four days in Milan have made a wonderful ending to my journey and nothing could have been more perfect than the sympathy and "accord" I felt with [Duse]. I went four times to see her in her room—and recited twice—and she said such beautiful things to me—and just to see her and feel her personality does something very strange to one's heart. You've never seen such suffering in a face, nor felt more forcefully the presence of an immortal soul. I saw her in Ibsen's "Ghosts" and in a modern play—but in which she was very beautiful. I'm deeply thankful that I came.

I'm going to my dear friends the Starrs in Dinard for Xmas and Aileen will be there with her sister, so I'm looking forward to a happy visit. I go direct to my ship from there [on the 27th]. I have much to do at home—Income Tax, dentist, general overhauling and repacking of everything, with my American tour beginning so soon—to say nothing of all my family and friends—and all the talking I have to do!

Paul wrote me a letter about my old brown coat, which is the most screamingly funny thing I've ever read! I'm quite sure, if you've seen him, he will have told you about it—it's brilliant—so like him . . . there is *no* one like him. The coat remains exactly what I want—it's been all cleaned, the fur lining done over so it's like new, and I've got very handsome skunk collar and cuffs on it now. It's not as if I lived in New York—for the travelling and motoring, storm and cold, I must have a rough coat like that and it is a joy and comfort for warmth! *Worth* did it over and put his sign inside and said it was quite à la mode! So there!! It has been perfect during the journey of the past month. Lord—I hope you'll all like my clothes—I don't altogether, but then, such is life.

In Dinard on Christmas Day Ruth wrote, with some effort, to Duse and to Lugnè, and read De Profundis.

To Eleonora Duse

Dinard
Noêl

Madame—

J'ai beaucoup regretté que je n'ai pas eu la chance, tellement le temps à fuit pendant mes petites visites avec vous,—de parler de notre ami Lugné-Poe. Plusieurs fois en parlant de vous avec lui, j'ai senti qu'il était étonné que vous ne lui aviez pas faites signe en venant à Paris, et j'ai deviné qu'il était blessé, et qu'il souffrait d'un mélange de perplexité et d'amertume.

Quand je suis rentré de Milan, je lui ai parlé naturellement, de vous, de mon bonheur á vous connaître, et quoique je n'ai pas répété tout-ce-que vous m'avez dit sur les difficultés qui vous entoures, j'ai parlé avec lui de vos projets de venir à Paris. Içi, il faut que je vous dise combien Lugné Poe était pour moi, l'ami genereux et noble—que sans lui, je ·n'aurais jamais pu commencer à Paris, ni à Madrid—qu'il à travaillé pour moi avec un enthousiasme sincère, et que je le suis reconnaissante à jamais. Souvent je lui ai dit, que si un jour le moment arriverait que je puisse lui rendre un service, que je le ferai de tout coeur. Il parait que le moment est venu,—car après mon reçit de ma visite à Milan il m'a prié de vous ècrire, et de vous dire, qu'il avait souffert d'une folie amère,—qu'il à beaucoup reflechi à votre égard, et qu'il vous fait l'offre de son théâtre, et de tous les arrangements, gratuitement, sauf les impôts. Qu'il fera un abonnement, une réclame speciale, qu'il vous guarantira un profit de pas moins de 6000 frcs. par représentation, et qu'il se mettra entièrement à votre disposition. Je pars maintenant pour New York, donc je n'attends pas un mot de vous, mais j'ose espérer que votre réponse sera dans l'affirmative à celui qui ma lettre concerne, car je vous assure que son désir à vous aider et à vous présenter pour le mieux à Paris, est d'une sincérité profonde.

Je ne peux pas fermé cette lettre, que j'ai écrit avec un désir brûlant de faire, en ceçi, une bonne action, sans que je vous exprime encore le bonheur poignant que j'ai eu en vous voyant jouer, et en faisant votre connaissance. Vous m'avez inspiré dans deux façons inoubliables, comme artiste, et comme âme humaine, et je suis reconnaissante pour toujours. Les moments que j'ai passé, seule avec vous, seront parmi les plus sacrés de ma vie.

Avec mes souhaits les plus sincères pour la nouvelle année, acceptez, je vous prie Madame, mes hommages et mon affection.

Then to Cherbourg to board the S.S. Majestic. *"Marvellous ship, very rough crossing. Recited for Coué and at the Concert. Nice talk with Stanislavsky—wonderful man!"*
The "damn diary" was finished!

To Harriet Marple

Tuesday 9:20
[February 20, 1923]
Pittsburgh Station
Women's Room

My train from Wilkes Barre being an hour late, I'm waiting to get on the night sleeper to Cleveland.

It's just as well there was no chance to do more than look into each other's eyes yesterday; words, or being alone, could not have signified more than what I read in your face and in Dorothea's and Zoscha's and what I hope you read in mine. How terribly worth while is life—if only to feel the flood and warmth and inspiration of such affection and such trust. Gladys Waterbury was at the train, with another God speed, and it helped the start of a difficult journey—for I hated to go. But the quiet hours, and the lovely country and working hard over my portfolio, sending back dozens of letters and papers I'd had no time to sort at home—helped to pass the time. I was desperately tired after the 48 New York hours! Could eat no dinner and felt chilly and wretched, but as I worked my strength came back.

I'm gathering courage for what's before me, and a beautiful little word from Lugné came to bless my departure. He ends, "votre joie de travail en enchante et je vous fais un bien beau et bien bon signe à travers les mers et les continents. Amie—au revoir!" No signature, no beginning—but a tender little line of how moved he was to receive my letter—it was midnight and he was answering at once so that I should wait less than he had waited—but that I should know he was ready to wait—how beautifully they put things!

To Mrs. Yates Thompson

April 2, 1923
Santa Barbara
California

I have wanted to write you for many weeks and have thought of you so often in my wanderings. Thank you for your letter. I am glad that mine from Spain gave you pleasure. That was a wonderful journey, but I've been moving over vast territory since my return! I enclose a list which may amuse you and will show you the extent of my tour! I am nearing the end and am loath to leave this wonderful coast and turn back to the East which is still cold and dreary, I believe. I have been basking in sunshine while they've been having terrific blizzards and cold winds. It was very exciting getting home again, tho' I was only there three weeks before I started off touring. I was with Dorothea, and fearfully busy and gay, seeing all my friends and going out a great deal. When I return I shall be with Will and Helen.

This country is beautiful and hideous at the same time and very confusing to one's emotions and one's thoughts. I've never breathed such air and the flowers and blossoms are enchanting, mountains and sea and, in this place, beautiful woods and trees. Here there are charming people, very lovely places, but the South is over-run with such dreadful people, and the vulgarity and ugliness of everything man has done is appalling. The "movie" world is quite fantastic, and Los Angeles really a revelation of all that is ugly. One's spirit fairly winces. This place is really a dream however and I'm so enjoying my few days here. I go to San Francisco to-night, and that is beautiful too, and interesting in many ways.

I am vaguely planning . . . to be in London for a short time only and then go to Norway and Sweden for my holiday—possibly working a little here and there, just for the fun of performing to new audiences and making a reason for wandering, apart from the pleasure of it. I will let you know when my plans are settled.

To Lugné-Poe

[August 1923]
Stalheim
Norway

Me voilà bien fondue dans un fauteuil né de l'herbe et d'un rocher, je regarde devant moi cette vallée superbe, ce ciel bleu, ces ombres que font les nuages flottant sur les montagnes qui à chaque instant modifient la lumière sur les choses. C'est à la fois très beau et très sombre. Mes misérables pensées voudraient pouvoir se plonger dans l'idée de Dieu, de l'univers, de la puissance et des lois de la nature. . . . Oui, je voudrais tant savoir, connaître tant de choses . . . les sciences occultes, la métaphysique, et même toutes les pensées de tous les surhommes. . . .

Les grands spectacles de la nature me trouvent toujours ainsi, interrogatrice, cherchant la réponse à la voix intérieure. Ah! Après avoir senti ce tremblement de l'âme, et des efforts exaspérés de lier nos pensées à l'Eternel pour comprendre, combien l'on serait heureux de saisir la main d'un ami et de se reposer dans un jardin, de regarder les fleurs ou les enfants, de se sentir plus à l'échelle de ce qui nous entoure. . . . Qui sait si ce n'est pas seulement cela qu'il nous faut?

Arriving in England after their Scandinavian holiday, Harriet Marple and Ruth Draper spent several weeks in August and September at Steyning studying voice with von Zur Mühlen. Ruth sailed home September 22nd, moving into a small furnished apartment at 144 East 40th Street, near the Cosmopolitan Club.

January
10	New York	
14	"	
16	"	
17	Garden City	
18	Philadelphia	
19	New York	
20	"	
21		
22	Brooklyn	
23	New York	
24	Providence (?)	
25	Hartford Conn.	
26	New York	
27	Baltimore Md.	
28	New York	
30	Boston	
31	Cambridge	

February.
1	Boston	
2	Northampton Mass.	
3	Springfield "	
5	Pittsburgh Pa.	
6	Pottsville N.Y.	
8	Buffalo "	
12	Toronto	
13	Quebec	
14	Ottawa	
15	Montreal	
16	Albany	
19	Wilkesbarre	
21	Delaware Ohio	
23	Ann Arbor Mich.	
24	Detroit "	
26	Grand Rapids "	
27	Chicago	

March
1	Chicago	
4	"	
5	"	
6	"	
7	Webster City Iowa	
9	Omaha Nebraska	
10	Kansas City Missouri	
13	Denver Colorado	
16	Salt Lake City Utah	
19	San Francisco	
21	Los Angeles	
26	"	
27	San Diego	
29	Pasadena	

April
2	Santa Barbara & San Remo	
3	San Francisco	
6	Santa Barbara Home!	

**To Harriet Marple
in London**

[c. October 7, 1923]
[New York]

I am in my new apartment and it is so nice and cozy. My maid seems quite nice, I hope she'll prove a decent cook. Having hoped for a French maid, I have one named Mary McGorty! Artur [Rubinstein]'s concert was this afternoon—marvelous—and he and Paul and Zoscha [Kochanski] and Countess Drew came back to tea—it was lovely—my first party, very sudden and unexpected but I tore home ahead and got everything ready.

My mind and heart are obsessed with my new sketch—living into it—in preparation for next week. I've never approached anything with such reverence and longing and fear. The fact that the idea is my mother's gift to me—and that probably its flowering and growth are all from my own suffering make it precious beyond words to me. I feel unworthy of it, so beautiful is the idea, and the possibilities of its expression. Lee Simonson is doing the setting and will be in charge of lighting so I depend much on him. I've got very beautiful chimes and shall have several rehearsals this week. My clothes promise to be nice—the white velvet is lovely, I think. I wish you were to be here. I am hoping Gladys may come down for it, and of course Ba, Anx and Alice will all be with me.

On October 29, 1923, in New York, Ruth Draper performed The Wedding Bells, a three-part sketch with scenery, lighting, costume, and music. Both Alexander Woollcott and Percy Hammond were severely critical of it and John Anderson wrote in the Evening Post of December 4th that Ruth Draper, fully understanding the importance of the imagination of her audience and of bringing them up onto the stage with her, is reported to have said: "It was just as if I had asked the audience to leave off its end of the performance, saying 'you needn't help me in this, I have scenery and costumes and I can do it all by myself.' They don't want to be treated that way. Anyway, I got a chaise longue out of it and a beautiful white tea gown which I had wanted all my life. So, you see, I snatched some rewards from The Wedding Bells, after all!"

Paul Draper, who had been divorced for several years, was now in precarious health and, at 38, remained unable to grasp a career in music in spite of his knowledge, in unusual depth, of a wide range of musical literature— particularly in his own field of German Lieder and the songs of Elizabethan England. In the hope that she might be a steadying influence, however tenuous, Ruth decided to remain closer to home in 1924, and toured only in the

United States. During all the winter of 1923/4 she was solidly booked in the
East—mostly in the New York area—and planned a series of joint recitals
with Paul for the summer months in the Adirondacks and Long Island re-
sorts.

In June Ruth Draper went to Utica, New York, to receive from Hamilton
College the Degree of Master of Arts; this was the first time Hamilton
awarded a degree of any sort to a woman. The citation read, in part: "Edu-
cated not by any college, but by your inheritance of all the best that the cul-
ture of our greatest city affords."

At the luncheon afterwards, Elihu Root, with whom she was staying,
made the principal address, but Ruth Draper was asked to perform; handed
up onto the heavy oak speaker's table, she gave three monologues, the press
reporting "most spontaneous and violent applause."

To Harriet Marple
in Bexley, Ohio

[June 18, 1924]
[Utica, N.Y.]

It all went off beautifully. I didn't have to make a speech!! They insisted
on monologues instead and, as the occasion was informal, I guess it was as
well. The speeches were all good, Mr. Root's wonderful. He is the most
lovely person and it is a privilege to be here with him. The baby in the house
is too adorable and giving me the kind of pleasure that is a mixture of pain
and exuberant delight. We are having delightful talks—it is a joy to be
among such high-minded, high-souled, intelligent people, who are deliciously simple, profoundly real, full of sensitive humour, appreciative of the
finest, and as completely happy as it is possible for mortals to be—though
he is nearly stone deaf [at 80].

The country is too beautiful—woods of huge glorious trees, old lawns
and elms and brooks. Yesterday I went in bathing (au naturel) in a darling
pond, with a 16 year old girl who was so beautiful in the sunlight and green,
with blue sky and blossoms about, that I saw with the eyes of an artist and
longed hopelessly for the gift that could catch such beauty and put it down
in lovely form!

Edward Sheldon, only fourteen months younger than Ruth, had been a
friend of many years and his increasingly brilliant success as a playwright
must have added an important dimension to their friendship. Since 1921,
Sheldon had been rigidly immobilized with a progressive arthritis, and
within a few years had become totally blind. He had been idealistically in

love with Doris Keane, who starred in Romance, *the play he wrote for her, and he remained so throughout his life. After her death, of cancer, in December 1945, he lived only three months.*

To his bedside in his New York penthouse at 35 East 84th Street came not only his family and old friends, but an ever-widening circle of new friends, particularly from the worlds of the theatre, music, and writing. Of great strength of personality, tremendous charm, and extraordinary memory, he was kept widely informed by his friends who brought the world to him. John Gielgud, taken to call by Mrs. Patrick Campbell in the winter of 1936/7, describes the experience as one of the most impressive of his life. Sheldon, lying on a blue-draped bed like a catafalque, with his head bent right back and a black bandage across his eyes, received endless visits in a cheerful penthouse room full of flowers, books, and photographs. Neatly shaved and wearing a jacket, collar, and tie, but with his hands hidden under a coverlet, he could talk to strangers as if he had known them all his life. "He seems quite removed in some marvellous way from everything but the mind; like some extraordinary human oracle."

Compassionate, wise, generous, and great-hearted, he inspired devotion and trust, his friends coming freely with their hopes and fears. Anne Lindbergh writes of his "uncanny powers of perception," adding, "many would have said 'he understood me—nobody understood me so well.' Everything became more beautiful in the light of his appreciation. . . . One always talked too much and stayed too long. One went away refreshed and stimulated, with a hundred new paths shooting off in the mind." Thus he gave of himself, uniquely, to each person, so that his gift of intimacy led to personal confidences that never, under any circumstances, were betrayed; all letters to him appear to have been destroyed after his death.

Often Sheldon would say to a friend overwhelmed by personal problems: "Come, let us do a play together," and quickly anxieties would disappear in the absorption he inspired of creating character and dialogue. During this summer of 1924 he had led Ruth Draper into writing a fantasy (and fantasy was not the forte of either of them) on the return to Earth and contemporary life of the Three Fates. He suggested and developed the scenario; the episodes and dialogue were her work. This collaboration was, of course, his device to occupy and distract Ruth from her intense and mounting anxiety over her brother Paul.

To Harriet Marple
in Bexley, Ohio

[August 19, 1924]
[New York, N.Y.]

I've just finished the 1st scene of Act III and it sounds good to me. I'm going to Ned's tonight to read it. I hate the last scene of Act II and have been miserable about it—he says just to leave it and go ahead—he doesn't think it's as bad as I do—but I don't see what to do with it—it's an ugly scene and I can't get into it at all. This next act is thrilling—the Russian woman—and I do so long to reach the heights and make it really beautiful.

I had a terrific evening with Ned on Sunday—laid bare my very soul and sat there sobbing—and God knows what he felt—I haven't the *remotest* idea—in the semi-darkness with that damned patch over his eyes, saying beautiful, calm, wise things—without a trace of emotion—I thought I should scream, to know the truth, and knew I couldn't ask. It would seem as if it were some consolation to him to see another's agony; nothing could have been gentler or more helpful and sincere—but it is as if he had shut tight the door to his own inner life and thrown away the key. I suppose one must just accept his terms.

Paul went back to the Adirondacks to arrange for a joint recital at Lake Placid, Keene Valley, and Schroon, so with my engagements it should be quite a help to him. On the 29th we have East Hampton and 31st Southampton.

To Harriet Marple

[August 26, 1924]
[New York, N.Y.]

I don't want you to think I suffer about Ned (in the way of longing for what isn't possible), for it is only those moments—and they've been very few—when I show him something of my own suffering, that it seems so terrible I can't share his. I am not at all in love with him, and doubt completely if I would be were he well, but of course to have a man so sympathetic and so believing in you, and so steady, and so searching in his interest, breaks one up terribly—for the time being, and it was then I wrote you, when the memory of my hour with him was very green. I love him, and admire him enormously, and am conscious of the privilege it is to mean something happy and vital in his life—and of the good it is for me to have him believe in me—but at moments I almost rebel against the hold he has on me thro' this work (which I still cannot believe in) and thro' his tragic situation. This sounds little short of wicked in its selfishness and ingratitude but of course is only a mood that comes and passes.

I've been to see Ned twice since I got back—I had so much to talk over in regard to the last act. The first scene doesn't seem to be right according to his idea—tho' he finds no fault with the writing—more with my interpretation. How in heaven I'm ever going to get this mystic lady I don't know—it's 8:30 and I mean to work tonight. It's cool and quiet and I was at the tennis all afternoon—very exciting games.

I just put Paul to bed with a bad sore throat. He got home this morning and plans to go to East Hampton tomorrow in order to practice for our show on Friday—I hope he'll be ok. Our "joints" went off well tho' we didn't make a great deal of cash.

Heaven be praised MARY McGORTY RETURNS ON MONDAY to be with me till Oct. 1st. GOD IS GOOD!

The typescript of The Three Fates *exists, but it was never performed. Three years later, in London, Ruth Draper showed the play to Sir James Barrie and wrote Sheldon: "I am sure that Barrie's estimate of the sustained, tremendous dramatic quality will please you. That is all yours and I am proud to think I kept it alive with you. What fun we had, anyway, working on it that summer!"*

The following letter is inserted out of sequence in order to complete this episode.

To Theodore Sheldon, Jr.

March 5, 1953
39 Hyde Park Gate
London

My Secretary in New York has just announced the receipt of the typed copy of "THREE FATES". It was in the summer of 1924 that Ned and I wrote that Play together. It was a terribly interesting work to get his ideas, write the text, and read to him what I had written. I am so sorry nothing ever came of it. The Producers who saw it (though I don't remember who they were) felt it involved far too elaborate production. It was originally intended as a full-length Play, not as a possible monologue for me, though Mrs. Woods suggested this, but it was not Ned's or my idea when we did the work. He always wanted me to do a play, apart from my own particular work, and I know it was a great disappointment to him that a possibility of appearing in a production of "THREE FATES" never came, or that I never even considered playing a role in an Ibsen or Shakespeare Play, which he would have liked me to do. The idea of "THREE FATES" is certainly a very interesting one, and I am sorry but I am afraid it will never be used.

I am sorry that I could not be present at the Dedication of the Library [Edward B. Sheldon Memorial Theatre Collection at Harvard]. I read the report of it in the charming little brochure with the greatest interest, and shall hope to see it when next I go to Harvard.

At this period Ruth Draper's romance with N.C. appears not to have developed. Haunted by a sense of loneliness, longing for love and marriage, yet

driven by her talent and the need to give it expression, she often was over-
whelmed by depression, particularly when away from the stimulation of her
work or when a letter or word or scene triggered this emotional response. It
was in October of this year that she spoke of her heartbreaking fears to a
friend, saying: "I'll be lonely—I am lonely—but I could never live with a
woman! Perhaps I shall never marry, but—when a man and woman go
away together—where do they go—how do they do it? Three of my best
friends have made messes of their love life and I don't want to make a mess
of mine."

She wrote Harriet Marple: "What fools we are—for the 100th time I say
it. . . . The joke is I feel I know so much about the game but I can no more
play it than I can fly to the moon!"

To Mrs. Louis Graves
Chapel Hill, N.C.

November 6 [1924]
The Drake Hotel
Chicago

I've been waiting for a moment when the right mood was uppermost—in
which to write you. I refuse to drag you down into an abyss every time you
open a letter from me! With the activity and distractions of my strange life I
am often cheerful, but then writing is impractical, and when I am alone and
quiet, the clouds descend again. Your sympathy, and Louis', is very dear to
me but I must not always be bringing you my pain. I crave and need your
sympathy but it shatters me. I must listen to Nietzsche: "Be hard, my breth-
ren be hard!"—and "Wass ist gut? fragt ihr? *Tapfer sein*, ist gut!" isn't that
wonderful? And Goethe: "Entbehren sollst du—sollst entbehren!" That's
the answer! I have a little book in which I've written many things that help
me, to read and think about.

I have another sorrow [brother Paul]—haunting and constant in my
life—which at moments wipes away this sorrow; I have a host of friends—a
few of great intimacy—and my work, this driving urgent active thing, and a
love of beauty that sometimes seems sufficient compensation—(though for
such fleeting moments is this true!). So do not pity me, I am rich, Mildred,
rich—and ashamed of my ingratitude that I should murmur—and one day,
when this spell that nature casts over us is removed, I will see it all, and
laugh at my tears. So don't be too sympathetic—it softens me. All that you
say is so wise, so discerning, I could talk to you for hours—of life—getting
quite away from myself. I know I could and someday we shall do it!

This is the strangest life, Mildred, and many envy me. I would delight in it
if another picture were not continually coming before my eyes; and so do
others long for freedom such as mine—it is funny and foolish and so human, this looking at the other side of the road for a better strip to walk on!

To Mrs. Louis Graves
Chapel Hill, N.C.

December 10 [1924]
Mt. Carmel, Connecticut

I have been feeling so ashamed of the last letter I wrote you. I should not write at those moments when inside and out the gloom descends. Altoona was the last thing in grim ugliness, smoke and fog and black snow, and I was physically tired and spent—what victims we are of physical conditions!

I took the train that night after a happy evening at a girls' school where to my surprise and pleasure I ran into Miss Jones of Chapel Hill! We had a good talk and I was so glad to meet her and talk of you and Louis and that sweet place. The next day I was furiously busy in New York and left at three for Albany where I recited before a huge audience in the evening, returning to town on Sunday, and a long evening with my dear Ned [Sheldon]. Monday—a hectic morning looking for a flat and in the afternoon to Trenton, coming by train to Boston after the show; Tuesday with delightful friends and in the evening to Wellesley College; Wednesday here, again to friends and in beautiful country, and in the evening at Yale before the Dramatic Association. Such an audience and such response—I was at my best and knew it—a rare happiness—how I wish it could always be so and that all the people I love could see me then!

I am writing in bed in a lovely room looking thro' trees down to a river and hills beyond, and the crackling fire is warming the sweet frosty air of the night. At eleven an old friend is coming to motor me to Farmington where we will lunch, and then go on to Holyoke where I perform to-night. He will then put me on the train at Springfield and to-morrow I shall be in Rochester, reciting in the evening before a huge audience and returning to New York afterwards.

Saturday afternoon a great friend of mine gives a concert in Carnegie Hall, Paul Kochanski, a Polish violinist, and I am taking some people to hear him. His wife is one of the rarest loveliest creatures in the world, and after long years of struggle and suffering and patience, he is rising to a high place, and I am so happy about it for he is a great artist and so worthy of success. In the evening I recite at Mrs. Pulitzer's—a soirée for the Grand Duchess—and it is sure to be amusing. These foreign Grandees completely destroy the equilibrium of the public (a very small public to be sure) but it is a ridiculous sight, the excitement they cause.

Then my work is over, for the present anyway, and I don't at all know what the winter may bring forth. I've decided to try and find a flat again and have my brother Paul with me. It is some security to him to be with me, and have a home, and I am happier to make one for him tho' it is a great strain at times—but when one loves a person one faces anything. I may go off on a

Western tour later on, but perhaps it will be good for me to stop reciting for a while and try [to] compose new things. I want new sketches dreadfully and will try and force myself to work some up. I can hardly wait to get back to New York to see the [J. P.] Morgan books and mss. at the Library. How I wish you and Louis could come on! Did you read the list of what is there? It gave me such a thrill. Let me know if ever there is a chance that you will come—it would do you a world of good, Mildred—and give me such happiness.

During the last few months of 1924 Ruth Draper filled more than thirty engagements, mainly in the South and Mid-West, but she was in the East when Paul Draper died of heart disease early in the morning of February 15th at the apartment she had taken at 147 East 61st Street, New York. His death was a great and continuing grief to her but, trouper that she felt herself to be, she maintained her schedule, leaving early in March on a six weeks' tour to the West Coast. Late in April she sailed for Europe. At the American Embassy in Brussels, where she stayed with her long-time friend the Ambassador, William Phillips, and his wife, she performed at a party on May 7th.

Following so soon upon the long strain of her brother's illness and death, with the additional strain of being "artist in residence" at the Embassy, this is one of the few recorded times when Ruth assumed her personal, and defensive, role as the diva. Caroline Phillips noted in her Journal: "Ruth Draper always gives me a feeling of strangeness; I could not ever feel intimate with her. There is an element of something very ancient or primitive in her nature, or as of a gypsy or alien race, beyond my understanding. I always feel her (unconsciously perhaps) acting a part. We all probably do this more or less, only I am particularly conscious of it with her."

To Martha Draper

May 12 [1925]
[American Embassy]
Brussels

It all went off beautifully and was a superb affair. The house is the finest in Brussels and grand for entertaining, with a great sweeping stairway and beautiful rooms. Caroline [Phillips] looked *so* distinguished and Bill too, I was very proud of them. We were 23 assembled promptly, well before eight, and then the Cardinal [Mercier] arrived with his "chanoine", and a little later the Queen and King and their suite. We were 30 in all. The King was dressed in an ordinary dress suit, not a ribbon or medal, (which was a great disappointment to me), the Queen in white velvet and diamonds, very simple and attractive, and the Cardinal too superb in his red robes—I never saw such a glorious color—there is nothing like it—moiré, very rich and thick—and too dazzling and beautiful. His face is very beautiful, so gentle but so intelligent and strong. Monsieur Max the famous Bourgomaster and various important government officials and statesmen and [U.S. Ambassadors] Mr. [Myron T.] Herrick came from Paris, the [Robert Woods] Blisses from Stockholm and Mr. [Richard] Tobin from the Hague. Eleanor Tweed looked lovely, Edith Coolidge from Boston, the Sterlings our 1st Secretary (or counsellor) from London, Waldorf Astor, Mr. Parker Gilbert the brilliant young Dawes agent in Berlin—a mere boy, and they say one of the great financial experts in the world; the Nelson Perkins and various other Americans, and Secretaries and Belgians made up the 30—and about 15 more came in later, including Mrs. and Miss Burgess—who sang a group of songs before my monologues. She was very good and the whole show went off well.

My dress was really lovely—very white and fresh and graceful—long lines, Grecian sort of thing, with a sparkling girdle. (I'd had a very successful shampoo with "eau distillé" in the morning and my hair looked lovely.) I had a nice little chat with Their Majesties, and I may say "a pleasant time was had by all". Sunday we went to a superb Pontifical High Mass with the Cardinal officiating and a wonderful choir singing a Palestrina Mass—at Malines. It was very beautiful. In the afternoon Mr. Herrick, and Waldorf and I went to Waterloo—which is a very moving thing to see still, in spite of the more extensive battlegrounds that cover this country now. Yesterday I went to the museum in the morning and Caroline, Eleanor and I went to Louvain in the afternoon—it is entirely rebuilt, a most remarkable achievement—fresh, clean and orderly and perfect reproductions of all the good old houses. The library is not finished yet—it was promised by the U.S. and the money has given out—rather an awkward situation.

It is lovely and restful staying here, and the weather is fine—the country a dream of blossoms and dazzling green. Donkeys and old women and dogs pulling carts, and children babbling French in the parks, and the hundred and one things that one observes with pleasure keep me busy and enchanted. We start South at 6 to-night and reach Vienna at 10 to-morrow night and stay for 36 hours, then Buda Pest for a night, and via Belgrade and Sofia to Constantinople. We are due to arrive there the morning of the 18th [of May] and stay till the evening of the 28th. Then Athens, Hotel de la Grande Bretagne. I shall join up with someone after Eleanor leaves on the 6th, probably Joan and Gladys Waterbury, for I don't want to feel hurried, and if it's not too hot, I'll stay till about the 20th I think.

I bought a lovely green Chinese bowl in Paris for Elizabeth [Lindsay?], and want it myself, so you can know it's very nice—one of those shapes you just want to sit and look at, a heavenly color, living and rich, and a lovely soft dull texture, on a beautiful old stand. I hope she'll like it—it's small enough to carry about when she moves. I'm going out now to see a few sights and buy a little lace, so will close. I shan't get any word from home till I reach Constantinople.

The schedule in Greece was grueling: twelve- to eighteen-hour days of sightseeing: from Athens to Olympia 4 A.M. to 10 P.M. by train, to Marathon, by motor to Delphi, three twelve- to fourteen-hour days motoring around the Peloponnesus. Then, on June 11th from Patras "sailed at 5 pm in a nasty little ship" and the next day "touched at Corfu—terrific sea—awfully sick." Then, on the 13th, "got off in the evening at Cattaro and spent the night. Took glorious motor trip to Cetinje in the mountains of Montenegro, sailed at four, arrived 9 pm at Ragusa—dark and raining. Two beautiful days in Ragusa, enchanting town, and sailed 8:45—marvelous coast."

To Harriet Marple

June 17 [1925]
Fiume Station
[Yugoslavia]

Arrived Fiume [this morning] where I now am awaiting the train to Venice where I shall arrive about three [P.M.]. Pretty strenuous trip and what with the queer food, queerer hours, and queer water I am a bit weary and my insides are somewhat upset. I was in grand form for the two weeks in Greece and enjoyed every moment of it. Ragusa is the most enchanting little town I ever saw and I longed to stay, but I thought I'd best come along nearer somebody in case I needed a Doctor. The food was very bad there.

I am hoping to find letters in Venice. I've not heard a word in a month now and must have missed something somewheres. I hope you've written me of all your visits and your plans. I have none. I daren't go to London and give recitals anymore than at home tho' I know the public would like to see me again. It is the same awful impasse and just the same "misery" is waiting to engulf me the moment I openly face the future. This trip has been a lovely interval, deeply interesting, very distracting from unhappy thoughts, and full of beauty that will enrich my life forever—but as for changing the situation, or my point of view, or giving me a fresh outlook or new courage—I can't say I notice any difference! It was too much to expect I suppose. Everything has gone beautifully and I've got a LOT of pleasure out of it, but one cannot lose the facts of life—the facts that burn one's memory and break one's heart and make one fear the future. As one has been, so one is, and will be. I see no escape really—according to one's health, one's sense of humour about it all sinks or soars, that's all.

You can't think how beautiful Greece was—the high plane on which one's imagination swims—it is beyond anything I dreamed possible and I thought often of you in the mountains and my "sea"—"Thalassa"! It was sublime.

To Harriet Marple

July 24 [1925]
Pension Amisbühl
Beatenberg [Switzerland]

Gosh I wish you were here—it's pouring rain, and I'm in a great mood for a talk. I think my last letter to you was a bit on the discouraged line—it is always a mistake to write so, for it's hard for the reader to believe that by the time the letter arrives things have changed for the better—which was of course the case with me. The cold didn't amount to anything, nothing but a signal for soda and light eating. I was all right—but I was rather depressed, and decided I'd better get away from Venice. Much as I love it, it is rather enervating and I'd been there nearly a month. I ran into that quaint character Gretchen Green at St. Mark's, the day I was leaving for Ravenna and I asked her to come along to keep me company, which she did. She looked frightfully thin; and was very lonely, and glad to see me, and we had a fine day in that fascinating city. The knight for whom I've always had a secret passion—Guidorello Guidarelli—lies there in marble, more beautiful even than I'd dreamed he was, and I had a wonderful moment standing beside him. How marvellous those mosaics are—I forget if you were there or not. Gretchen returned to Venice and I came on to Bologna for a day, then Milan, and then Berne. The moment I struck the mountain air I felt better, and curiously enough in the train I got a fine idea for a mono. and suddenly I got excited, and the mood has lasted, and I've done quite a lot of work for me! I've been trying to make up my mind whether to go to see this Doctor in Berne—I had several friends there who are terribly enthusiastic. I don't think there is anything the matter with me, and I loathe the idea of going, but perhaps it's a chance not to miss, and as I'm here and have the time it might be a good idea—just to have my blood examined, and have a consultation anyway. I needn't stay and take the piqures if he doesn't feel it's imperative—it might take three weeks or so.

I had a terrific longing for the country. I stopped at Berne as I wanted a taste of Switzerland before going to Paris to enter the clothes arena, and from there I came here, only one hour away and 4,000 ft. high. I've had nearly a week of this glorious air, and feel so well. I go to bed at 9, drink quarts of milk, walk a lot and rest after lunch, and make hay with the sweetest peasants, with whom I made friends the first day. The haying season is at its height, and the air is so sweet, and I love the exercise of raking and pitching with a light wooden fork, and I lie down in the soft piles and watch the others work. It's quite idyllic, and I've longed to do it whenever I've seen peasants making hay—it's wonderful exercise. Travelling, one only seems to live in cities, and one sickens of hotels. This little 3rd rate pension, full of the simplest people, I really love—it's clean, and there is a bath which I alone use (no one else has washed in it since I came I believe), the food is *very* bad—that's the only out—but I have milk with, and between meals and I've been twice to the good hotel 20 minutes away for a full meal.

Now about my mono. I just got a streak of work—I don't dare breathe, for fear the old discouragement will return, but a sudden determination and courage seems to have been born. I lit a candle to St. Anthony, and asked him to help me, so perhaps he did it. I've worked up, and enlarged, and finished and *learned* that "Busy Mother"—it's really funny, I think—much better than it was. Then I've worked out one I had long in mind to do and which Paul wanted me to do—that dreadful woman who laughs gently and says "yes indeed—ah—ha—um—um" in a restaurant with 3 friends, all are dieting and discuss doctors and maladies. I'm not sure if it's funny or not and am anxious to try it on my friends in Berne. The really new one is an original idea—I'm not sure if it will work—it requires some rapid tho' very simple changes of costume. Scene is "In a church in Italy". Curtain goes up on me as an English girl sketching, and talking to a friend at the end of their morning's work, so she needn't be on for more than 2 minutes—I'll just have a brush for property and a loose smock and flat hat to make me look the part—and you know the funny faces people make when they sketch; I go off left, talking, and come on at once as an old, old ragged Italian beggar woman, with a torn old shawl, asking for "soldi" in a cracked voice; go off right and come on as an American tourist with a party of girls. She reads from a Baedeker, endless measurements and dates, real Baedeker lines, and looks casually at the chapel where they are supposed to be, and everything in it; go off left and come on as an Italian mother with baby and little child, staring the way they do, rapidly praying in front of the altar, yawning and talking to child; off right and on as charming young girl with lace head scarf, meeting her lover, and making rendezvous for that night, young and sentimental; off left and on as one of those garrulous gesticulating Italians with a colored handkerchief on head, talking to a friend in a heated way, she puts away chairs used by the artist and is full of trouble and chatter—raucous whisper—"Dio Mio's" and "per Bacco's"—you know, quite different from the lazy mother and the old beggar; off right and on as a German tourist, with eyeglasses, cane and Tyrolean coat, full of loud adjectives, with a party of friends and 2 children, on their way to a restaurant; off left and on as a woman alone in a black shawl, who walks quietly to the altar and looks up, kneels, crosses herself, and prays with eyes closed and hands clasped as the curtain falls. This last would be very brief but very intense, and must be done so that there is no feeling of embarrassment. I don't know at all how it will go—but it seems to me to have great possibilities. I feel as if Paul were helping me get hold of myself— I've been grieving so terribly for him, and it seems as if I must use myself to better purpose—for his dear sake. If only I can hold on, if only these things prove to any good!

To Harriet Marple

August 7 [1925]
Bellevue Palace
Berne [Switzerland]

I wished for you so to-day because, having decided to stay and take the "cure", I've got myself a lovely bicycle and went off alone into the most beautiful woods you ever saw, and missed my little "compagne de bicyclette"! Dr. K. says he can, he thinks, help me very much in 3 weeks (if he'd said more I wouldn't have stayed!) but that doesn't seem too long, for it's really a nice little place. I've arranged to play tennis, I've got a bike and there is lovely country as well as the forests, right near town. I'm going to give a show I think to help cover my expenses! [Dr. K.] says my blood is too thick—just what Dr. Finlay said when I had it taken 2 years ago but I never did anything about it—(I don't know if they knew what to do *for* it then) and there is something wrong with the white blood corpuscles, and too much phosphate or something. It appears to be a condition with which he has had his greatest successes, so I am hopeful of a good reaction so I can surely get away by Sept. 1. I'm feeling less harassed since I made up my mind and really think that probably my blood will be better, if the glands that stop secretion when you "worry" get going again. I hated to decide to bother and go to a Doctor with no real ache or pain, yet something seemed to bid me go.

Friends and acquaintances pass thro' and the time passes rapidly enough. I've been reading *Mrs. Dalloway* by V. Woolf, and *Leonardo da Vinci,* in French, by Merejkowski, a delightful book, and working on my 2 new monos. which promise really very well, so I'm in a happier state of mind. My clothes are holding out nobly—they've really been perfect and just what I needed. Here I need very little— I bought a cheap little cotton dress for hay making, and I use it now for tennis. This hotel is very costly and very comfortable and de luxe, but these grand hotels have a strange effect on me. I'm really happier in a simpler place, so I'm moving next week to a very nice pension. I can see Paul smiling in despair "wouldn't you know Jane would go to a 'little' pension?—of course the hotel manager should be giving her his best suite, etc."! I think of him and miss him more and more it seems to me, and look ahead to returning and giving shows in New York, and Christmas, with perfect horror—or rather a sort of shuddering—and its still a sort of amazement to me to think of him as gone. The other day I came in and sort of wondered what I'd do, and I actually started to think I'll write a long letter to Paul—and then——————. I want to come to see the boys [Paul's sons] not be too long quite out of their lives; I want to see Ned, for I think I give him something real and maybe helpful, otherwise I would not come, but linger in England and France and then Italy. I don't know—I want to be hard at work, which I can't well be over here—it is bound to be sporadic and desultory, and at home Pond can keep me right at it. I want the money too. So I guess I'll come in early November or late October.

To Harriet Marple
Columbus, Ohio

August 16 [1925]
[Berne]

I have my second blood exam tomorrow and I shall be awfully interested to know what change, if any, has taken place. I shall be terribly disturbed if he asks me to stay on longer than the 3 weeks he originally spoke of, as I am getting bored and impatient to be on my way. . . . I feel no effects, but then I really didn't feel ill at all and as a matter of fact, a sort of moral change had taken place before I ever began. It came with the new monologue and with the breaking away from Venice and coming into high air.

The little show here was a small affair [on 12 August at the Bellevue Palace Hotel] but gave me a chance to try out the new sketch of the Busy Mother and I think it went very well. I'm now planning to give a show in Geneva and have great hopes of that being a success. There are quantities of English and Americans there and I'd be glad to "try out" the new church sketch, and make some money for use in Paris!

To Harriet Marple

Sept. 18th [1925]
4 rue Henri Moisson
[Paris]

It seems a long time since I've written you. I've been in a nightmare of looking for and ordering clothes for the past two weeks. I shall probably hate everything and I seem to have much too much, but I've tried to get everything for a year and not be bothered again. I hope my plan works. The idea of going out of black nearly kills me and I dread putting on colors more than I can say. There is some psychological satisfaction in wearing black, and yet how silly to think that clothes should affect one's own recognition of one's sorrow—as if in changing my clothes I could be disloyal to my thought of [Paul]—too silly—yet it is a very distinct feeling.

I've had one lovely evening with Lugné here—just we three—and later alone when Aileen left us. He was so sweet, so amusing, so interesting, and Aileen loved him. We are installed "en luxe" in Mildred [Mrs. Robert Woods] Bliss' flat. She wired to ask us when she learned Aileen was coming to Paris to be with me. Mr. Tone seems quite happy in Dinard, and Aileen plans to stay here thro' next week, so I'll stay on, as my clothes won't be ready before, and we're having a lovely time. Such peace and luxury and comfort; cosy old servants and my sweet Léa [Dessay], running in and putting all my things in order. The days fly by full of tiresome, silly activities but I'm trying to be philosophical about this horrid business. I hate spending the money but keep thinking how pleased Paul would be, urging me on! Pond is planning a big tour—a full winter I guess—so I shall need a good many things. It's hard to know what to do—if I decide to come abroad again in March for the spring in Italy and here in May—Lugné thinks I'd better come back—and a real season in London again   yet I know once at home I'll probably hate to start wandering again. But so it goes.

Your letter made me sad of course but I assume your black mood has passed, and that you are on top of yourself and the world again. Of course we can't help each other really; because few of us have the tact and gentleness and insight to give sage advice, and few of us are humble and generous and open minded enough to accept it. Fond as you are of me you would not want to listen, and fond as I am of you, I would be afraid to speak—even if I saw you wandering into a trackless waste. It's a curious thing how unhelpful we really are to people whom we most care for and would most willingly serve. Isabella has as usual been an inspiring and wonderful figure to me—just seen her twice—but she is so rare, so amusing. We were talking—pretty deeply—about the sensation of missing something, and she said "franchement—je ne sens pas de vide"! Imagine the mastering of her problems and finding peace—it made me feel like a worm.

The weather is lovely. Paris jammed with Americans—but strangely I've run into very few friends—and it's such a bother to look them up. We spent a delicious Sunday at the Walter Gay's—such peace and beauty and they are such dears. I've got your gloves, and a purse which I don't like much. I am *no* good on commissions—somehow just can't choose for other people— and go thro' agonies worse than for myself. Hope you're full of bea*n*s again—wish the n were a u!

To Harriet Marple

[c. October 15, 1925]
13 Norham Gardens
Oxford
[with Lady Osler]

I love this place—all my friends have been so lovely and the public so loyal and so warm. I don't think I've ever had such a reception—they cheered me at the last recital—almost reduced me to tears! The house could have been sold out twice over and they were standing three deep. The new sketches go well, tho' I see lots to be done on them yet.

Arthur [Rubinstein] has just turned up in London and I'm lunching with him tomorrow—he is so afraid to see me—I'm afraid too. He is terrified of emotion and of seeing pain, yo know—it's a strange cowardice on his part. And of course it will be for me perhaps the biggest emotion I've felt in seeing one of Paul's friends and I must try to be very cool. You will understand what it will mean. He really adored Paul and knew him so well and you know what Paul felt for him.

Reluctantly Ruth Draper sailed in the French Line's de Grasse *on October 21st with the Kochanskis and Aileen Tone also on board. She stopped briefly with her sister Dorothea at 129 East 36th Street and then toured until late December.*

At Christmas she wrote Mildred Graves, "Life is just tearing along for me and I am off on tour January 3rd. My success is at times almost a burden— such a perpetual challenge to further effort."

A fairly rigorous tour was scheduled through the Southeastern states for the first three months of 1926. Early in February Ruth Draper came down with influenza and for the only time in her career was unable to go on. Mrs. Kenneth Terry Martin of Stillwater, Oklahoma, wrote of this to Alice Carter in 1957:

"We were a tiny town then and because the hotels were horrible we asked her to be our guest. She had been awake all night with this virus, flu . . . and could only whisper. This was the only time I ever saw her look old. She was in the depths of despair but we got her home, with a comfortable bed, got the doctor, who said she must under no condition appear that night; my husband got Mr. Pond (her manager) on the telephone—he rearranged her schedule and Ruth stayed with us for a week, to our delight, but she never forgot us and all her life was thanking us for this little thing."

Over the years, Grace and Terry Martin became great friends (he was

Chairman of the Department of Speech and Drama at Oklahoma State University in Stillwater, and Mrs. Martin was a Professor of speech and drama). Always, when her touring took her near enough, Ruth Draper stopped over to visit them, or Mrs. Martin met her for a day or two along the way.

From Houston, on February 22nd, Ruth wrote her sister Martha: "My voice is restored, and I feel stronger each day—it's amazing how such a mild attack can take it out of one. I must have had the real flu, as far as I know for the first time, for other colds I've had have never affected me this way. I've been lucky in finding exceedingly nice doctors, particularly here in Texas, one had worked under George and one remembered father. I am bravely swallowing Scott's Emulsion and it takes me back to the pantry in 47th Street and Bridget dosing me. I've not taken it since—it's grand old stuff." A few days later she wrote Mildred Graves: "I'm resting three days here in Galveston but my strength returns slowly and it's an awful fight to struggle on—but I'm thankful to be turning toward home—I feel so far away off here." En route she returned to Stillwater and Tulsa to make up her postponed performances.

To Mrs. Louis Graves
Chapel Hill, N.C.

March 5 [1926]
Stillwater, Oklahoma

I have to think out what I am going to do in the spring and summer, and whether to take a place in New York for next winter. In many ways I'd like to have a little place with my own things about me, but I dread New York for any length of time and in my heart don't want to *settle* anywhere! It's a great problem, and I fear my life will be over before I ever solve it! It's strange because I doubt if anyone cares more intensely for domesticity and all that a home implies; as a tiny child cleaning and cooking and caring for things—dolls and babies and animals—sewing and generally fussing were my chief delights and are still; yet this warning to deny oneself all that, lest it usurp my time and strength to the sacrifice of this other form of self expression—what I call my work—is ever at my shoulder, and urges me to keep free from "entangling alliances" with all lesser loves! That's really what it amounts to, and I am convinced that I have not been given this great freedom for nothing; few people are so utterly free as I, so completely unfettered and equipped for freedom—by nature as well as circumstance. I see my destiny, and I must ever onward and not be lured by moments of weariness and longing for peace, and the anchors of little tender human things.

I write thus—but I am seriously considering getting a flat; if I have a long season in New York next winter it is worth while from a practical point of view—and once I have it—God knows where my theories may fly to!

I can't waste any more time gabbing to you—I must write many letters, and doubtless you have things to do.

"I go quite drunk in a bookshop!" Ruth noted in sending some books to Mildred Graves in 1925. She was an avid and selective reader, the long tour-journeys providing a bonus of time, her wide-ranging curiosity the stimulus. Her comments have interest, but mere listings of books read tend to be tedious and have been omitted; it is sufficient to say she read everything worthwhile, in whatever category, as it was published.

To Harriet Marple
New York

[May 21, 1926]
Thursday Night
At Sea

The sea has been calm as a lake, the weather mild and grey. The food is poor, the passengers unusually quiet and attractive, not a soul we know, save a nice young English actor. The children have been very good and Alice and I have had a nice cosy time. I've written lots of letters so as not to feel the burden of them when the rush of life begins in Paris—dull but necessary communications. I've read *Lady into Fox* and hated it; *Lolly Willowes*, beautifully done but too clever for pure enjoyment—I sometimes think I have no imagination—strange stories bother me so—I like real tales! *My Life in Art* by Stanislavsky—not interestingly written, but many interesting ideas that line up with some I've had, and a great story of well spent effort that makes me feel ashamed of my effortless success! Now I'm deep in Dreiser's *American Tragedy*. I've helped Alice with some sewing, done a bit myself, rested a lot and now have a slight cold, so am staying in bed. The fog horn is beginning to blow, and I'm fighting against the blues by chatting in this inconsequential manner to you.

I got a wireless [that there is] a room for me at the Port Royal [Hotel] and I'm trying to get rooms for A. and the children there too. She says she'll stay over for my first matinee on Tues. 20th. Had a wireless from Ned [Sheldon] saying "Ruth dear I send my loving thoughts." I answered "Thanks I need and cherish them". Do I need them?—Gosh! Had a wireless from Lugné saying he advised evening show on the 31st, so I wired to confirm. So that's that. Things appear to be going well. I've been in a state that is indescribable save to you—so foolish, so weak, so desperate, but I've skillfully managed to hide it from Alice.

I've thought of staying abroad—telling Pond to stop everything—going round the world—selling the flat—anything to get far away from this entangling affair—yet do I want to end it, even if that would? Such little sips of joy for dregs of pain. Need life be that way? I'm beginning to think I can only hope for a better time in the next—yet I love life—wass ist gut fragt ihr? Tapfer sein ist gut!!

To Harriet Marple
New York

> May 26[1926]
> [Wednesday]
> [Port Royal Hotel]
> [37, rue du Bac]
> [Paris]

Just a line to say I'm o.k., the show went well, tho' as I anticipated (and regret) the audience was mostly U.S.A. It would be a long, patient and costly road to 'get' a French following—tho' I'm sure I would ultimately if I gave the time and money to it—which I won't. Lugné is wonderful—darling, generous, fine soul. His delicacy and "savoir faire" just makes me feel about one and a half years old—his sensing of a situation and his consideration and feeling for the essential and the appropriate. It's been a ghastly nervous rush—arriving twenty-four hours before the show—but all is safely over and I breathe! We had a drive in the Bois Monday afternoon but I was weak with fatigue from the journey and 5 a.m. rising. He just gave me a feeling of confidence and peace and I made no effort, nor did we touch on dangerous ground. How can I grumble—with such friends—gosh!

Paris was followed by a four-week London season at the Garrick Theatre and a Command Performance at Windsor Castle before Their Majesties King George V and Queen Mary and about fifty guests of the Ascot Week house party.

Queen Mary's Diary for Friday, June 18, 1926, records: "We dined in the Waterloo Gallery being Waterloo day and afterwards Miss Ruth Draper gave us amusing recitations in the Crimson Drawing Room. She is very clever and original."

Ruth wrote, "I did ten sketches—the King roared."

To Martha Draper

> [June 20, 1926]
> [London]

I'm tired of writing but must just send a line to say all is well. The week has been phenomenal and I'm doing another! Windsor was *thrilling*—too marvellous and I got a diamond and ruby pendant!

I've taken a house—20 St. Leonard's Terrace—near by and quite sweet. Alice comes the 25th and I hope George the 30th. Am sending you a delightful article in The New Statesman on me. I hope you're having a nice time. I'm overwhelmed with work and having a lovely time too. I flew back from Birmingham yesterday and it was nothing less than sublime! My own little machine—a great war hero as a pilot—perfect flying conditions—sunset-grey clouds too wonderful—only cost 25 guineas and my manager paid half!

I'm nearly crazy with the newspapers and resolutely refuse to talk of the Royal Experience. I just can't and won't—and if the houses are packed, what need of publicity? They make the best they can of the crumbs they catch.

Feeling that she might have reached the high point of her career, it was with reluctance that Ruth Draper closed her season at the Garrick Theatre on June 25th. As always, family associations were deeply a part of her consciousness in the present—so, responding as she did to her success, uppermost in her mind was the awareness that her grandmother (Eunice Dana) had longed for a career in the theatre—and longed in vain. Now her granddaughter, without work or effort—without really desiring it—had all that her grandmother could have wished for.

To Harriet Marple

July 5 [1926]
[en route from Steyning]
[Sussex]

I meant to have written you from the terrace at Master's looking out on that lovely lawn and view, with the pigeons and dogs; it was enchanting as ever and the old darling heart-breaking and adorable as ever—shouting epithets and contempt in his inimitable way, speaking a world of tenderness to the animals, and smiling occasionally with that melting beauty—roaring with laughter, delighting in his flowers and the place which he has made—nursing a sick puppy—cursing the foolish servants—raging against Wagner—describing his old house and his mother and the linen press and preserve closets—all with his vivid, magical charm. Paul seemed there, delighting in it all—laughing with us—adoring his scorn and fierceness, his tenderness, and pride and joy in my success—and his thinking of him (Paul) in it all, his picture in the center, and only one on the mantel, and he says he talks to him so often, when the news of my triumphs come—always he says "Paul, Paul," - - - - it was all very wonderful—and I am so thankful to know him as I do. Somehow I feel that Paul and I are locked to-gether in his sad old heart—so wise, so all knowing—so broken, yet so vibrant still—so fighting for truth and beauty. He has plenty of pupils—no striking ones—the same tragic situation, wretched servants, endless tiresome worries. Mrs. Carrington motor'd down for tea, with two young men—tired and bored Master dreadfully—he was too funny and furious. Crowds fuss him dreadfully.

Thanks for your last letter. I've been very bad about writing, but I can't tell you how hard it is to find time, even for the family. I've a sweet little house now, Alice was with me for a week—and George is coming this week for ten days, and I look forward greatly to have him by myself. He is busy seeing doctors and clinics, but I hope to take him about a little, and I love to think of the little intimate moments we'll have to-gether. He seems to be in good form—like all married people, freer and happier away from their mates!

I don't feel that I shall ever catch up in letters the wonderful events of the last weeks, but someday you'll get it all in detail! More and more I regret having to come home, but I'll take the winter as my farewell tour, cram it with work, and then come abroad with no ties to compel me to return. Planning this now probably means I shall marry and settle in Greenwich, or some like spot, but I realize now how far freer and happier and more related to my work *spiritually* I am over here, consequently I'm safer and more concentrated and calmer in my determination, and my capacity of growth. I long for a good rest and change, and hope then for new ideas to take hold; here and now life is too swift and colourful, but it's marvellous, and I know I shall never touch such peaks again. I'm lunching at the House of Commons to-day with a charming and brilliant young member; Alice and Billy James are coming to tea; I'm dining with my beloved Lady Antrim, quite alone, and reciting at a swell party with a party at Hoyty's [Mary Hoyt Wiborg's] late and Kochanski playing; and a fancy dress ball, if I want to, later! But don't worry—I shan't attempt that too! My shows continue packed every time—I've six more matinees—did you see the last Punch—another delightful poem.

To Harriet Marple

Sunday, July 25 [1926]
Longparish House
Whitchurch, Hants

I was glad to get your last nice chatty letter—how I agree with you re the July 4th celebrations!—but this "dear old world of ours" is made up of *such* dreadful people—who will do such fool things, and enjoy them—which is worse!

My happy sojourn in London is nearly over—if you could have seen my darling house I believe you would have been captivated in spite of your prejudice and indifference. I've grown so fond of it, I can hardly bear to leave on Friday next. George has been with me a good deal and I have enjoyed having him so much. Alice was with me nearly a week—I've had three or four little dinners before plays—several tea parties—but I've been out almost every night and lunch. Such a two months—there has never been anything to equal it in my young life! And I've been in fine form until two days ago when I contracted a slight cold, which I've been nursing to-day—instead of enjoying myself out of doors. Fortunately there is no party, so I haven't minded keeping to my bed—tho' it's been tantalizing to see the sunshine and lawns, flowers and children, and the river flowing by and not be out. But I've been gargling, steaming, "sodaring", writing and sleeping, reading, and saving my voice, and I think I'll be all right! I have one more show on Wednesday and it's for that I'm anxious to be O.K.

George leaves me Wednesday for Paris. I leave Friday for Cowes, where I have a charity performance at Carisbrooke Castle, & stay over the Monday Bank Holiday [with Princess Beatrice, youngest daughter of Queen Victoria, who married Prince Henry of Battenberg]. Then, I hope to motor to Cornwall, where I've taken a room on a farm near the [Wilfred] de Glehns'. If I like it I'll stay, if not I'll move on to Scotland. I have lots of invitations but I feel it would be better for me to be alone and very quiet for a while. It's been too amazing—my success this time—all past experiences pale before it. Of course I long to stay over here—more and more—and curse my stupidity in linking up with Pond. I still think of breaking tho' it would cost me some $5000. now in forfeited commissions which I would feel impelled to pay him. But it would buy my freedom. I am torn! If I'd had the courage to do it in June it would not have been so bad, now it is pretty serious. Of course one can say—do it another year, but who knows about next year—here is the great opportunity—here and now—still [the] U.S. is my native land, they want me too, and I think of my family and friends and Ned, and I suppose I'll enjoy it when I get going there again. It's the tour that terrifies me, fills me with horror, those dreary towns and hotels and trains. I've done it enough, enjoyed it too, but life is too short now, not to do just what I want to do, and my enthusiasm for that particular phase of my work is past. O dear O dear!!!! I had such a good chance to cancel in June—but Pond's pathetic cable weakened my resolve—I was also then not free of the N.C. influence—and felt I'd better face that again—give it a *real* chance—not just an hour or so—and know its depth. Now—I'm strangely free of that—the preoccupation of this tremendous season has put it far away.

From Scotland, on September 7th, she reported to Harriet Marple that she had had "a charming letter from N.C. which has disturbed my peace of mind. . . . Gosh, how I wish I were a light hearted jade!"

Sailing on September 15th she returned to a three months' tour along the East Coast from Virginia to Boston, then, after Christmas at home and two weeks at the Selwyn Theatre in New York, she set forth again until mid-April: Pittsburgh, Chicago (January 28th, "frozen legs"; January 30th at Harris Theatre, Lake Forest, "legs in agony!"), Wisconsin, Indianapolis, Chicago again, Boise, and on to the West Coast.

To Harriet Marple

[February 5, 1927]
Willow Road
Winnetka, Illinois

I'm having a lovely rest out here—from yesterday afternoon to to-morrow morning—with Sue Hibbard—a friend I guess you never heard of! I always love to surprise you with perfectly new ones—known her for years too!—I'm looking out on lovely lacy black trees against a foggy sky. It's warm and cosy and utterly silent. I've just written a long letter to Lugné after months of silence, I guess spring must be on its way! I got a cable—crazy—I mean a letter—rather pathetic—before Xmas—and have never answered it, and now have that puffed up virtuous feeling with a warm little pang in my heart as well. If only he were not old and worn and fat and sad. Everything going fine—my frozen legs slowly improving, but I haven't walked for ten days now and probably can't for another week or so. It's maddening because I depend on walks so when I'm on tour, and the weather has been lovely for walking. I heard the lovely Schumann concerto yesterday—with Gieseking—a fine performance—and I love the thing so. I've done fourteen jobs since I left and have thirty to go. Indianapolis to-morrow and tea with Booth Tarkington. These weeks in Chicago have been fairly easy—thanks to my having cut out Memphis. From the 10th I have nine one night stands in different cities so I'm bracing myself for that. The idea of Honolulu grows and grows on me, so you'd best abandon Italy, I don't think I can do both—I'm sorry to disappoint you. I may just go to Rome with the twins, for I definitely asked them, and not attempt any other travelling there.

I've read Tin Wedding, Revelry, The Plutocrat, The Sun Also Rises, To-morrow Morning, The Royal Road to Romance, and Vie de Balzac—since I left! The Sun Also Rises is an extraordinary book—unpleasant—and touch-ing on an unmentionable subject—but most poignant and very well done. A supremely wonderful description of a bull fight and descriptions of Spanish, or rather, Basque Country; enlightening and sad—dealing with decadent drunken young men and a woman—a lost generation indeed! "Have another drink" beats like a rhythm thro' it all—written in short sentence dialogue; a marvellous picture of Paris night life and these sunken American youths—horrible—with absolutely no standards or ideals or object in life—really an amazing picture—done with a purpose and painted in a uniform key—so that it rings true. Some bad English in it irritated me dreadfully, but one is left with a sense of having read a vital and searching book, unpleasant, but real, and a touching and lovely note of a love that cannot be consummated—but gives one a sense of deep and quiet permanence. Not a book for everyone by any means. Glad you had Gladys and A. [Aileen?] to tea. G. wrote me she finds such peace and beauty in your little home. Hope A. wears those woolies—she looks so cold and thin. Gladys worries dreadfully about her—never did anyone so need a child—it certainly should be arranged. This code of "sin and shame" is sacrilege, and ethics and convention are gangrenous with hypocrisy. What are we going to do about it?

Well, I must now glance at the news, dress, and go down to lunch. I wrote Lugné: Je suis suspendue—je pense peu—rêve peu—souffre peu—le travail réponds à tout—un succès fou—je suis reconnaissante. A true description of my moral state.—But spring is on its way! God help us all—!

To Harriet Marple

> Feb. 28 [1927]
> 212 West Idaho Street
> Boise, Idaho

It seems a long time since I've written, but longer since I've heard! How are you? Everything humming along with me; it all comes down to health in the end! I've been in wonderful spirits for so long; even the slightly negative mood expressed in my letter to Lugné was not really true, only induced by the thought of him and the temptation to express it in French! I've gotten enormous pleasure and satisfaction out of the tour, and find life very amusing. Mary [maid] has added to my physical comfort and I fear that in future all the things I've never questioned as being easy to do for myself will seem very boring. She is a good creature, but a snob, and I feel concerned about her, for I have to send her to hotels when I visit my friends; and I think she thinks I've very queer friends, who can't put up a maid! My legs have been cured for weeks.

To Harriet Marple

[March 27, 1927]
Sunday, 6 p.m.
Fairmont Hotel
[San Francisco]

You must think me 'very much all right' not having heard from me in so long! And you are about right. I'm simply blooming—I don't think I ever in my life looked so well—I look in the glass and am almost startled with the glow of health and vigor, and it seems a pity to waste it on so many strangers; I've been in such wonderful spirits—the whole tour has been grand, but these last weeks particularly happy. I feel as if it couldn't last, such inward peace and cheerfulness. I'm out of a letter writing mood, and resting after a successful matinee. To-morrow I'm motoring down to San Mateo and performing in the evening at Palo Alto (Leland Stanford) and we're spending the night at Philip Lansdale's—do you recall him?—He is still keen on the Yosemite trip, and I hope to go when I return from the South. It was such a success there this year, that I'm going again, once more in Santa Barbara, once more in Los Angeles, and in Hollywood. I've given up Honolulu. I gathered from reports it would be a terrific crowd of tourists, and a frightfully expensive affair, and being alone, I couldn't get off to remote romantic places, but would just have to stay in the big centers, and it wouldn't be much rest. I'm ready to stop in one way, but now I'm here, I might as well respond to the demand and feel I've really 'done' California, and got it clinched! I lunched with Mary [Pickford] and Douglas [Fairbanks] and dined with Jack Barrymore last night; *such* an attractive creature, and he makes me think a little of Paul, of whom he was fond; he was crazy about my things. Douglas F. [Fairbanks] and Norma T. [Talmadge], Gloria S. [Swanson] and a lot of others were too, and I think I could easily get a job if I wanted it! Such an awful place,—but aflame with youth and zest and enthusiasm. I was awfully amused at the whole scene, and they were terribly nice to me. Douglas F. is very interesting to talk to, full of ideas and theories and ideals about his work, and the possibilities and their ignorance of the whole vast field.—

Mary [maid] was completely renovated by her Santa Barbara visit, the poor thing hadn't had a soul to speak to really in all these weeks, and she knew several rich maids there, and felt at home. We went on a glorious picnic in Santa Barbara arranged by Anne—you would have loved it—long walk in [a] marvellous ranch where we all lunched by a brook in a beautiful sycamore grove. And a 2 hour drive there and back!

Do write soon—I forget what your last letter said, it's so long ago—hope you are well—Still no news of Aileen? Have you seen anyone *new?* anyone amusing? Aunt Nin? new clothes? books? plays? thrills?

On May 10th Ruth sailed with her sister Dorothea in the Conte Rosso *for Naples where, ten days later, they were met by the twins, Ned and Bill Carter, now 18 and fresh from a year in Geneva and Germany (Tübigen and Heidelberg), who were to be given an Italian "grand tour" before going to Harvard in the fall.*

When sightseeing Ruth was possessed of such inexhaustible energy, such overflowing enthusiasm that it had become a family joke. Historical sights, museums, buildings, views, and picture galleries—all had to be visited, and she was ecstatic over whatever aroused in her a response to its beauty, history, humanity, or association. Throughout her life constantly she revisited scenes or galleries, noting "saw again many beloved pictures." All this she quite simply needed *to share—most eagerly with nieces and nephews, whose independent looking received little, if any encouragement.*

After "a horrible day among 4,000 tourists" seeing Pompeii and Capri, they journeyed through Rome and Florence to Venice, missing little along the way and lunching with Iris Origo at La Foce, supping with Berenson at I Tatti. At Venice on June 10th they separated, the boys to Germany and Ruth to Paris, where she promptly went to bed with a cold, gave three recitals at the Théâtre de l'Œuvre, and a week later left on the Golden Arrow *for London and a house at 18A Charles Street, Mayfair: "Paradise!"*

The next six weeks were filled with recitals and friends: a "season" of two full weeks at the Garrick Theatre and a month of matinees at the St. Martin's; a Garden Party at Buckingham Palace; "a good talk with Sir James Barrie, who came to supper!"; a weekend at Cliveden, where she arrived by motor at 3 A.M. after the theatre; a big party at 18A; "Paul Kochanski came to stay [and we] talked 'til 2:30 A.M."; then, on August 1st, to Wales for a week—"the Eisteddfodd—marvellous!"

On August 10th she traveled from Basel to Salzburg, "the most beautiful journey I've ever taken," and a few days later attended a party at Leopoldskron and "did monologues." Again on the 15th, "dined with Max Reinhardt, a distinguished group, and did monos." She wrote: "Reinhardt was more excited and impressed than anyone who has ever heard me, I think, and, quite unsolicited, he wants to present me in Berlin. A finer guarantee for a start I could not have."

Returning to Paris and on to London ("hideous crossing"), she spent a day in Steyning "to see my beloved Master [von Zur Mühlen]—lovely evening and long talk"; spent a long weekend with Miss Eliza Wedgwood at Stanton with Barrie and Cynthia Asquith dropping in; dined with Luis Bolin to hear Spanish music; then went to Scotland at Drynachen Lodge, Nairn, for "10 wonderful days, delightful company—a perfect holiday. One evening I did monos. and all the household came in. Such fun!"

Sailing home in the France *with the Kochanskis and Anne Phipps, she reached New York the middle of September for two months; a short stay in Islesboro, and visited family and friends during October. After returning in the* Majestic, *she opened November 11th at the Criterion in London for a full five-week engagement—matinees and then nine performances a week for four weeks.*

To Martha Draper

December 15 [1927]
In train to Birmingham
where I have a big char-
ity mat. this afternoon.

I close Saturday—but the demand is *so* enormous that I'm strongly tempted to give matinees the week after Xmas and leave for Switzerland, for a holiday, getting to Berlin the 12th [January]. I feel I must take a little rest in between—I shall go next to join Phyllis Brand and her children [at St. Moritz]. Lots of nice English friends will be there, and it should be great fun, tho' I already see myself lying in splints with front teeth knocked out, arms, legs and fingers broken, and a large black eye! However, I also see blue skies and sun, and long walks in the snow, and long quiet sleeps in that bracing air. It will be hard to leave dear old London, my darling house, and all my friends and I shall weep to leave the theatre! It has been more wonderful, if possible, than ever, and I love them all so—the public—the stage hands— the dingy underground passages—it's a strange intense and wonderful world of its own, the theatre, and once you've known it, it becomes a part of your very self. Arnold Bennett watched me from the wings on Tuesday; Bar- rie was with me last night [in the wings]; A. A. Milne comes to-morrow; and Hugh Walpole on Saturday; no seats ever left over and hundreds turned away. How Paul would rejoice—he must know—he is there with me every night. I'm doing fine work—most of the time.

On this same date she wrote also of these backstage visits to Ned Sheldon, adding: "How I long to come into your quiet room and tell you everything. I feel your friendship with me constantly, warm, safe, and tender and I hope you feel mine."

To Martha Draper

[December 26, 1927]
[visiting Lord and Lady
Astor over Christmas]
Cliveden, Taplow

Wasn't it too thrilling! Of course I was so excited I couldn't think of a thing to say and was so afraid of the three minutes ending before I'd spoken to you all. I rather hoped there would be relays of you all on each of the three telephones so I'd get a chance to hear each voice. . . . I was just one hour later (11:30 P.M.) than the time I'd bargained for, which was most annoying as I'd longed to catch all the children and hear each of them in turn. . . . . Who was still there? I long to hear all about it! Were you all excited? I couldn't get to sleep for about an hour, I was so stirred by the mystery and magic of the sensation! Eight people were in the room while I spoke and I felt so hurried and conscious and excited I don't remember even asking how you all were, if the party had been fun, and to thank you for my lovely gold necklace. I'm afraid I yelled too loud over the wire, I had the foolish impulse to get over that ocean. . . . . . I wanted to give a whole list of friends to call up and give my love to—and forgot. I was trembling with excitement and felt quite as if I'd been thru' a great experience. Isn't it too uncanny and amazing for words? . . . . . . I was terribly disappointed not to speak to the other children—it would have given them such a thrill, as it did me and made the cost of the thing worth while—but I suppose they couldn't wait any longer. It made me quite homesick to hear all your voices.

We are having a very happy time here—Mr. G. B. Shaw is too delightful. I did monos. for the whole party (28 of us) and the garden, garage, stable and house staff—about 100 in all—yesterday afternoon and it was great fun. It is lovely and snowy here today and it's too beautiful in the woods and we've been sliding on trays and skiing and hitching behind a motor—a very merry party.

To Harriet Marple

Dec. 29th [1927]
18A Charles Street
Berkeley Square

I'm having a permanent wave—come to it at last! What do you think of it? I thought, with winter sports at St. Moritz and then travelling about for 4 months, it would be an enormous comfort—do hope I shan't be sorry! I'm feeling my usual blues at moving on—but once off I'll get the thrill of change and fresh adventures. I long to see the mountains and sunny blue skies—I need them in more ways than one. I'm in a queer mood and a change is indicated as the best cure. So easily do I react to it that I sometimes wonder how real my feelings are. The challenge to make the best of an opportunity is always strong and if life has handed me a few difficult things to endure—it has certainly handed me marvellous ways of escape from a too heavy burden. I've had some bad moments—some marvellous ones—much food for thought—the weighing of values—it's all very well to say I think too much—but there has been good cause to think, and such a delicate situation to be met with courage and control. Of course my searching faculty of seeing the truth always makes me suspicious of motives; as again and again in life I've seen the currents of conscience and cowardice mingle in an almost inextinguishable stream—but the facts are plain—the man is not free—and whether we are both really fine or really afraid will always intrigue me, and dampen my confidence in the reality of right. Fate, as usual in my case, seems to arrange things. It is exceedingly difficult for us to meet and so I go my way making myself believe that all experience and all pain is but grist to my mill, to be used in laughter or beauty or whatever it may be for the delight of others and the deepening of my own nature and accomplishment. I write calmly—at the moment secure in my philosophy—but alas, it is not always in control of thoughts and tear ducts and the ability to enjoy the passing scene. [You and I] have warm assurance of our mutual understanding—God bless you and a Happy New Year. We must believe and go on wishing and hoping and loving. That's the only rule I know.

New Year's was spent at Bixley Manor in Norwich with the Geoffrey Colemans "skating and coasting—perfect day. End of a wonderful year."

[*1927 had, indeed, been a wonderful year. At the end of her diary she noted:*]

Made U.S.	....	$41,971.82		Less managers
" England	....	42,718.40		commissions
" France	....	425.00		(more fool me)
		$85,115.22	(Gross c. $110,000.00)	

Estimated professional expenses	$9,922.18	

Living expenses U.S.	....	$3350.54	
" England	....	3671.98	
" France	....	184.00	
		$7206.52	

Gifts, personal—U.S./England	$7238.43
To organized charities	7451.00
	$14,689.43
To P.K. [Paul Kochanski] for violin	5000.00
	$19,689.43

[*This record of personal gifts is an indication, and only that, of Ruth Draper's constant generosity and practical concern for her friends.*]

1928–1931

To hold in my heart as my 'panache'—
my reason of life—
your love.

Ruth Draper to Lauro de Bosis
(probably 1931)

To Aileen Tone
in New York

Jan. 5, 1928
Suvretta House
St. Moritz

Your lovely letter came to-day and I'm so glad to hear from you and feel so close in consequence, that I must write you at once! I meant you to give that money to Rose for all her expenses—because I thought you might just feel a little uncomfortable at taking it, and wanted to avoid that, but it all comes to the same thing in the end—I'm glad you were able to give her some for a present. I meant there to be some left! Darling, don't ever mind taking from me—what can I do but use it—what is it for but that? I hope you got a very lovely pocket-book or rather evening "pochette" I sent you—it was a little dream, I thought and so like you! A charming Spanish beau brought it I hope safely to Dorothea.

I telephoned the family on Xmas, and hoped to catch you there, but the call got thro' later than I planned. I wanted to catch all the children—give them the thrill of a word across the ocean. I got an enormous 'kick' out of it, and couldn't go to sleep, and thought of it for days! The sound of D's—A's—Ba's—the children's voices was too mysterious and magical. I was disappointed not to speak to Paul's boys—and George and his children and I hoped you and Harriet might be at the tea party too. My work—5 weeks—40 performances, stopped the Saturday before Xmas. I had a week free for friends and theatre and shopping and went for 4 days to Cliveden for Xmas. The Bernard Shaws were there, he *most* interesting and *very* delightful—and a pleasant enough party besides. Then I came back to town for 3 matinees, and spent Sunday with some friends, and left Monday afternoon for Paris and spent the night with Esther [Logan, sister of A. T.]. She had a huge dinner for me, not knowing when I was arriving, and I got there more dead than alive at 10 after a hideous journey—the channel has been bad lately and it was wet and cold besides! So I was a poor guest and had to go to bed, and was not very entertaining! She did not warn me, and didn't know when exactly I was coming till after she'd made the party! The next day I saw—Léa, Lugné, Loudons, Rudyard Kipling, bought a few things, went to the bank and had tea with Isabelle Malet and left at 8:30 in the evening; a full day, and I was glad to get to the lovely silence and whiteness of this high world! The air is divine. I've been skating already—it's so beautiful, and I shall enjoy my week's rest here, and get full of health and new energy for my German adventure. A huge party to introduce me is planned for the 14th. I hate this sort of thing, but I am advised that is the only way to get started in Berlin—coming as I do quite unknown. My London triumph, there, counts not at all—so I'm doing this, and expect to be amused—if as I hope Elizabeth [Lindsay] can go with me, to laugh about it. The 17th she is giving an important party at the Embassy at which I shall be featured and perform and the 21–22–23 come my 3 public shows at the Komödie—the very chic and attractive (I hear) theatre that Reinhardt is putting at my disposal. I shall have plenty of free evenings to do the theatres and hear music and shall enjoy the museums and the wonderful Egyptian things.

If my work goes well I may plan more shows—or else go on to visit other towns—work wherever it seems advisable. I hope [to] go also to Vienna and Prague; possibly North—possibly Russia, or to Holland and Belgium—God knows where—then Rome and Florence—then for a holiday to Sicily—to Tunis—Algeria—possibly Morocco too. Then Paris, to you, possibly work too—then perhaps London for a short season and sail early in June to get servants, and make preparations for my Islesboro summer! You must come to me there for a real visit. I wonder if it will really come off—it is hard to plant one's heart and mind in America when for the moment they are wholly here. But I must keep the family close; the children must know me now, before they go their separate ways and I begin to break up! I must begin to weave them more closely into the pattern of my life—because I suppose in the end, one turns to one's own for the warmth one needs, more than to those one chooses for friends and companions in the bright years of one's life.

I have often longed for you and needed you as never before—hold me close in your heart, and pray for me—that I may have more courage, more light and more strength to endure pain—such as I've not felt before. I can't write more—say nothing to a soul—because there is nothing to say. I am well—I swear I am quite all right—I am always with friends—I have a nice maid. I see my way plainly—work, distractions of travel and new experience, and faith in the purpose and end of renunciation. It must be to serve some vague plan. Again must I try and use suffering to make beauty and laughter! Again! And the mockery of knowing poor old ——— is there at home, his one desire to serve and comfort me—and I could not possibly let him. Less than ever before!

Lugné was darling, faithful and full of the knowledge of life and its fantastic toying with our hearts and our purposes. His "Eh bien—vous savez que je suis toujours là!" was a kind, very real kind, of comfort—and my darling Léa's passionate devotion—her embrace is like a warm and sunny day in a field of hay or a mass of glowing flowers—and a strong wind and a blue sea and all vigorous beautiful young elemental things springing from the heart, and nature itself. She is full of work and a quiet philosophy—illusion gone—but character and goodness and a gay courage to fill her life.

Well, my beloved—I must jump into a hot bath and dine with the delightful Cavendish family and dear Bob Brand—Phyllis is a wreck after a too strenuous skiing trip. I skated to-day, watched the coasting, and it's glorious here—so bracing and so white, quiet and clear and cold.

Don't be unhappy about me—these things will happen—and I was about due for another turn—I thought and dreamed the next one might be marked with happiness—but again it's not turned out that way. Lovely it's been—worth a great price—but not to be in its entirety.

Although there was no question as to the success of Ruth Draper's dramatic sketches, she continued to seek and explore further development of her talent, as shown by these entries in The Journal of Arnold Bennett:

Tuesday, July 26th 1927. Lunched at Sybil Colefax's. Rather learned. Balfour, Lewis Malet, Garvin, Julian Huxley. Women: Ruth Draper, Mrs. Garvin, Lady Edward Grosvenor. More men than women. I sat between Ruth and Mrs. Garvin. I talked to Ruth about the critical work she might do on men. She wanted ideas for this.

Friday, December 30th, 1927. We went to lunch with Ruth Draper, who has a little house in Charles Street, belonging to an American named Chubb. Present: the Alan Herberts, and Mrs. Phipps, sister of Lady Astor. She was full of Bernard Shaw's conversational liveliness. She is very lively herself and I liked her. Ruth Draper again talked to me about writing a play for her, and I promised to write to her about such a play.

Thursday, January 5th, 1928. . . . walked up to Piccadilly Circus and back, thinking further over my scheme for a play for Ruth Draper. I got this scheme into order, and wrote to Ruth about it immediately after lunch.

To Arnold Bennett

January 18 [1928]
British Embassy
Berlin

Dear Arnold Bennett,

Thank you for your letter. I have been thinking about your plot. It seems to me that if I do anything with another person, it should be for the whole evening—not to mix my monologues, where I deal with invented characters, with a piece where I do straight acting with a living companion! What do you think? That was the reason for my suggestion that there be three acts—like three short plays, that had a common idea, motive, or "message"—what you will,—running thro' them. A man and a woman—in three vividly contrasting walks of life, or periods of history, or age, where clothes, and make-up would make effective and pleasing variety for the eye, and give us each a chance for character acting. See what I mean? It just occurs to me—take the problem of infidelity—poverty—thwarted ambition of the man (or woman!), conscience, or some 'complex'—problems which defeat or exalt human beings, and that mates have had to work out since the beginning and will to the end. Anyway—I feel it must be something to sustain for an entire performance, and that if I tackle this new form of work my old specialty must be laid aside for the time being. Let me know what you think.

I see that the synopsis you sent me could be worked into a very interesting dialogue and action but it would leave me to fill my performance with the old bag of tricks, and if I do the new thing at all I must come out bravely and not lean on them for security. Don't you agree? As far as possible, of course, make use of my particular gifts in conceiving the characters and situations. I hope you see a rather new idea in the above suggestions—each act might work out a given problem—taken up where it's left off—or each might find a different solution and finish it in each act.

This address will find me for two or three weeks. My best regards to you both.

Yours sincerely,
Ruth Draper

P.S. I should think if there is costume there should be scenery; don't try and stick to my particular medium, I want to try yours! and I always want beauty—even if it's beauty in ugliness, and whatever is needed to enhance it. In my line visible aids to the bare idea block the imagination—but with costume and another character it's different, don't you think?

R.D.

To Arnold Bennett

January 23 [1928]
British Embassy
Berlin

Dear Arnold Bennett—

If there was a misunderstanding it was certainly my fault—as I fear I am often not quite clear!—but I hope you agree that it would be a poor plan to mix my monologues and a play. I don't feel it would be impossible to hold the interest for three acts, but I must submit to your wide experience in this matter. I do not feel that [———] is the person to discuss it with, and I do not feel any particular confidence in his judgment about such a thing. I expect you are right about the advisability of discussing it, and that, alas, is impossible. It just will, or it won't happen—if the idea hit us strongly enough, and was worth while—it would happen—that's all—because that's the kind of people we are—and if it doesn't, it only means it wasn't worth while!

I find this a very convenient philosophy. Things are going wonderfully with me here but I feel about my work rather as I think the English ought to feel about boiled potatoes.

My best regards
Yours,
Ruth Draper

To Martha Draper

January 24 [1928]
[at British Embassy
with Ambassador and
Mrs. Ronald Lindsay]
Berlin

I can't say I'm drawn to Berlin or that I've fallen in love with the Germans! I've had my two shows—the theatre is *exquisite* and nothing could have exceeded the response and appreciation I received. Critics all excellent but two very adverse ones which is probably good for me—anyway it is a new experience!

I'm amazed at my German—it's coming back with furious fluency and is constantly termed "fabelhaftig."

After her two performances at Max Reinhardt's Komödie on January 21st and 22nd, Ruth Draper gave two more to packed houses at the Kurfurstendam Theatre, a benefit for the Actors' Association, and a farewell performance on February 5th, leaving that night for Vienna.

In the intervening days she went "to Dresden to see pictures" for nearly four days, where she drove and dined with the von Klemperers and attended a performance of Salome *at the opera.*

To Harriet Marple

February 15 [1928]

Here I am again—writing on the train—having left Vienna for Frankfort-on-the-Main! A Poem! Grussen mein schatzel! I've become so German you wouldn't know me. It simply pours out, full of faults, but fluent and facile and lots of fun! Well—I've had perhaps the triumph of my life in Vienna! I *adore* the place and the people are so nice, and the public *too* wonderful—*packed* houses and such quick, keen appreciation. I hate to go and believe I am a fool, but what can I do? I have Frankfort and Munich, Florence and Rome all planned! They urge me to return—it really was "*colossal*", the whole town talking, and never have I seen such critics; I played in [Max Reinhardt's Theater an der Josefstadt] the most beautiful theatre I've ever seen—a perfect gem (about 800 seats) and had *such* a *thrill* when I learned that it was opened by Beethoven's music, (and he there) the first time it was publicly performed in Vienna! I keep saying to myself 'Be thankful' for all these wonderful impressions and thrilling moments! I certainly have had a far greater success than I dreamed of. Munich and Frankfort will be more doubtful perhaps; smaller groups, possibly, of people who enjoy English and understand. The Italian Lesson and Church are the favorites; Three Generations and Dalmatian Peasant perhaps most seriously appreciated; but all go well; not the Garden because it's too English and they don't get the humor, just like the American audiences, because they don't know flowers and gardens or that type of woman very well. I believe I'm in a charming theatre in Florence and it's already sold out. Rome is not yet fixed up, but will be soon. I expect to go there March 1.

I had my fur coat recovered in Vienna [in] a *very* smart and rather 'loud' tweed—a real travelling coat now and very good looking I think! My clothes hold out wonderfully and naturally are new to everyone! My ruby velvet looks *lovely* now with [the] old garnet necklace and earrings I got in London.

I've met many delightful, friendly people—some interesting—and seen several eyes glow and hearts flutter but none have had a like effect on me. I found a real old beau in Vienna—told me he'd always loved me—a Doctor whom I met 25 years ago! He's now about 70! Fine old boy. The weather is cold and damp. I had a slight cold in Vienna but no harm, fortunately I could stay in bed, and was O.K. for my show. The maid is grand—bores me but is a tremendous help. My trunks are so full I *can't* buy any presents for anyone! I've at last done my income tax, a stupendous job, and sent the information to the bank. Hope to heaven the papers don't all publish it this year! It's been a rich year and makes me laugh. I've certainly done a lot with my money this year, and put away a lot too.

I'm just drooling along now. It's a long tiresome journey—seems foolish to come all this way back—but no other dates were available and I thought I'd better do all I could in Germany but I'd far rather have stayed in Vienna, appeared there 2 or 3 times more and gone straight to Florence. They thought me quite mad to leave such a success. They say no one has ever had anything to equal it—not even Duse and Guilbert, and the manager said in 26 years experience he'd not seen anything like it before!

After arriving in Florence February 21st, Ruth Draper gave three sold-out performances and an additional one for charity. "Out for every meal. There is immense excitement about my coming. Seeing Iris Origo, Carlo Placci, Reginald Temple and gave a private show at Mrs. Lathrop's. Will stay ten days and then go to Rome."

In Rome on the 1st of March she went to the Hotel de la Ville in the Via Sistina; gave evening performances at the Teatro Quirinetta on March 10th, 11th, 12th, and 13th, at the Odescalchi on March 20th, 21st, and 22nd, and recited at private parties. Every day she was entertained by Roman friends and those anxious to meet her, and on the 29th Pope Pius XI received her in audience. On the 14th, at five o'clock, she recited for Mussolini in his vast office in the Palazzo Chigi, giving him a moment of apprehension as she entered with her shawls rolled in a bundle—concealing what? The next day she noted: "flowers from Mussolini."

Earlier on the 14th she had attended a luncheon at the Palazzo Borghese given by the Marchesa Presbitero. There she met Lauro de Bosis, Italian poet, scientist, brilliant classical scholar and translator, handsome, charming, and twenty-six.

For so many years Ruth had yearned for romance—for love on a high plane of peace and beauty and poetry—but always it had eluded her. Now, suddenly, without warning, when she was exhausted, disheartened, and aged forty-three, the lightning struck.

She met de Bosis again casually at an evening party of the Contessa Pasolini on the 17th. Two days later he drove her to Frascati for the afternoon; they dined at Alfredo's and went to a Pirandello play. Then, until she left Rome on April 7th, they met every day. He took her to concerts and sightseeing in all of ancient Rome; to churches, the beach and woods at Fregene, the Villa d'Este. And they walked, they "walked miles thru the streets and along the river," on the Pincio and the Palatine, in the Gardens of the Villa Borghese and the Villa Medici, again and again they walked and talked under the trees. On the 27th he took her to meet his mother, for whom she recited. The next evening they dined in her rooms at the Hotel and read aloud together, and on the following evening they dined with Signora de Bosis. On April 7th they walked both morning and afternoon in the Gardens of the Villa Medici, before he took her to the six o'clock train for Florence. All this is set forth in her own hand in a memo dated April 20th, and headed "Lauro—Here is the record of our happy days!"

To a mutual friend in Rome, well aware of the situation, de Bosis had spoken of his misery, his fear that his impetuous, ardent pursuit had been a hurt to Ruth; and Ruth in her great distress had spoken of her reluctance to leave, of the doubts torturing her, and of her very real pain and dismay at the turn of events. The counsel she received was to rest during the summer at Islesboro, and then to make the decision—that she alone could make—and *to make it, not in pain and dismay, but in joy and wonder at the love that had come to her.*

In Florence, where she visited her old friend Mrs. Parrish at Il Poderino, Ruth went on the 11th to dine with Lauro's brother, Vittorio de Bosis, a surgeon, and to drive with him a few days later. Then Lauro came and for three days they were together, motoring to San Gimigiano, Prato, Pistoia, exploring Florence, having tea with Berenson at I Tatti. He returned to Rome and two days later she left for Switzerland.

After a stop-over in Vevey with Aileen Tone, Ruth arrived in Paris to fill six engagements at the Théâtre Athénée; then on to London where she appeared for a week at the Haymarket, and, rare for a working actress, was presented at Court on May 23rd by the wife of the American Ambassador, Mrs. Houghton, saw her English friends—Eliza Wedgwood, von Zur Mühlen—lunched at Knole with the Harold Nicolsons and at Wadham College, Oxford, with Lord David Cecil. Her brother Charles came to stay with her at 18A Charles Street, Berkeley Square, and, finally, on June 20th she sailed for home in the Ile de France; with her sailed "Jock", a cairn puppy, brought to her at Plymouth as a gift from Lauro.

To Harriet Marple

[c. June 22, 1928]
S.S. Ile de France
At Sea

At the moment I'm terribly bored—trying to sleep—can't—tried reading and can't—too rough—grey and dismal on deck. My only friend—delightful Mrs. Ryerson of Chicago—(now Mrs. Sherpesee) for the sake of travelling with whom I took this ship,—is very ill with influenza and can't even see me. I'm so sorry for her. Mr. S and I eat to-gether. No one else on board I know—rather nice, that. I have a lovely cabin and shall rest extravagantly all the way over. I've got a darling little dog and he's so good—never leaves me. A little Cairn, like Edith Lindley's. I thought it would be nice to have a dog with the children this summer, and a friend gave me a perfect darling—Jock, 8 months old, brindle, a lovely head and the most affectionate cheerful nature. I love him, and he loves me already and is a darling companion. I've got lots of interesting books.

It is disgusting to miss you—if *only* you'd just thrown everything to the winds and come when I called. But I understand your difficulties and only hope staying was worth while, and that you landed a job. Hope you'll still find Aileen in Paris—her plans are vague. It was lovely having her in London and I think she enjoyed her stay. It was also nice having Charles. I had a marvellous party while he was with me—Paul Robeson sang too beautifully and 116 people came—delicious food—a pleasant time was had by all. I stayed on longer, when I heard Charles was coming. It seemed such an opportunity to do something pleasant for him; my work was going so marvellously, I just couldn't leave, making so much money as I was, and with the enthusiasm greater than ever! The Haymarket is a beautiful theatre, seats 1000, and was full every time! I gave 10 shows of my own and 5 for charities—counting 1 in Oxford, 1 in Stratford and 3 in London. No private parties, thank heaven.

I shall miss you terribly at Dark Harbor for I longed to have you, and your influence with the children would have been so good! I'm getting very cold feet about handling them all and hope the twins will come, at a tutor's salary, to help me. I hope I can keep clear of the social life—not playing bridge or golf will be a help. I hope to go to bed with the children about 9 and have a really good rest.

This radical change of life and surroundings I hope will do me good—yet can I venture to hope for a change in my strange nature? God—I am baffled by myself, and the way I take life. Here I am loved by several men—adored by the public—with the most wonderful friends anyone ever had—and a triumphant success wherever I work—and I'm just fighting tears most of the time. Love certainly plays havoc with me—would to God I could take it lightly or that such strong doses hadn't come to me so late. I am determined to be happy—no one ever had a better reason to be—to beat this melancholy, and fears and take each day as it comes—so don't write to me in sympathy—I deserve none—I deserve lashes for my ingratitude and mockery of my egotism and my selfishness—that's the fundamental cause. Never have I dreamed that such love and such beauty could come to me—it is partly amazement and unpreparedness I think that makes it so difficult for me to accept it—it somehow terrifies me and I feel hopelessly unworthy. Because I'm not convinced of my own feelings and cannot love as he does, I am wretched and almost spoil its beauty with my suffering. I demand too much of myself—too much of life—failure to rise to my ideal is hurting badly.

I think I was right to come away—I must wait and see what time does to the situation—to me—for of him I am certain. The distractions of the summer, and the rest and change, and trying to acquire a new philosophy and determination to be happy, and beat this tendency to take life 'au tragique', I hope will work wonders. Whatever made me such a fool about life—so cowardly about accepting pain—for it is a part of love and a large part of life. This last winter has been so crammed with feelings—I'm tired—my very soul is tired—I must just try and be a potato for a while. I was worn out when this last whirlwind hit me in Italy—that's why perhaps it took me so hard, and my distress at not having the nervous or physical vigor to cope with it—was one reason for my misery. I am better, the sea and the silence has helped me already. I have talked too much of it all—and hate myself for that—but my need of wisdom and sympathy was too much for me, and I simply couldn't help it. How often I wanted you—you could have helped me I know. I *loathe* the idea of a psycho-analyst as you know—but often wish I'd had the courage to go to one. But I guess I'm impatient, and that all I've gone thro' is amply justified by circumstances and my complicated, over thoughtful nature; I wonder tho' if I shall ever *know* what I want—ever be sure that I love *enough* to live with a man— either married or not—it's all in the lap of the Gods. My great object is to stop *thinking*—stop *worrying*—rejoice in the fact that I am loved—in the wonder of my life and its richness and beauty. I seemingly have everything—yet I can't *grasp* it—that's my trouble. I shall go home and do this job with, I hope, a grace and joyousness that will give all these children a glorious summer to remember. It is sure to be full of fun and interest and I am looking forward to it. I hope Ba will enjoy it too— I've done nothing for her for so long and given her so little affection.

Diary, June 29th: "Arrived Dark Harbor with Ned, Ruth and John [three Carters] to find Ba, Diana, George, Smudge, Penelope all here [sister and Draper nieces and nephews]. Tennis, bathing, sailing, sleeping, eating, reading—life too uneventful to relate from now on." Bill Carter, Aunt Nin, her sisters, with their husbands, her brother George, the Kochanskis, Corinne Alsop and her daughter, Edith Lindley, and various other friends, all came and went. "Anxie" was there to help and Harriet Marple turned up later in the summer and stayed until the house was closed on September 27th, when they left, via the Bangor Boat, for Boston. Ruth visited friends there and on October 8th arrived, by bus, in Avon, Connecticut, for a week's stay with Corinne Alsop.

All during the months since leaving Italy Ruth had, in her torment, won-dered if it might not be better to keep only the image of those days in Rome and Florence, unable as she felt to cope with this passion. Sensing this, Lauro remained silent for weeks, giving her undisturbed time for adjustment in her own climate of home and family and friends. He had said from the beginning: "If I had to choose between the power of making you love me or of making you love your great art—I think I would choose the second." He was uncertain, now, about going to New York—where he had a job waiting for him—and wrote of postponement, leaving the decision up to her. Few of Ruth's letters to de Bosis exist, but his letters clearly indicate the doubts, misgivings, and inner turmoil that possessed them both at this time. It was early October when he arrived in New York to take up his work as Execu-tive Secretary of the Italy-America Society at the Casa Italiana at Columbia University.

To Harriet Marple

[October 11, 1928]
Wood Ford Farm
Avon, Connecticut

I've gotten to the point now of 'near' terror at the thought of the meeting—and woke at four this morning, sure that I hated the idea of seeing him, and had no love for him at all. I certainly was not made for love affairs and it's well I've had so few of *this* variety! I need several friends, doctors, priests, philosophers, and psychologists to hold my hands, and guide my every step! You see I'd like to be the type of Francesca da Rimini and a *great* artist all rolled in one—putting myself far far out of the picture—and I have to admit I'm none of these, and accept myself *as I am*—and that's not so good! I can hear you roaring, but this particular joke can go no further just now!

Everything of course is perfectly indefinite until I see Lauro. I hated the idea of coming to New York and if I had come I would have had to go to Dorothea's as promised and taken him if Lauro could have gone and it would have been difficult. Corinne proposes he come here—we shall be alone and it's so lovely and quiet and she is going to be away until Sunday night. I've written him to propose this—hope he will phone on his arrival.

By December Ruth came to accept the great love that Lauro de Bosis laid at her feet, although she could not overcome her fear of herself and of her own unworthiness.

To Grace Martin
(Mrs. David Terry Martin)

[November 24, 1928]
Hotel Westbury
New York

Indeed I'd love some berries to decorate my new, and first own home! I'm just about to move in [to 66 East 79th Street on November 30] and it will be lovely to have berries picked by you to decorate a table or window ledge. I'm opening in Boston December 3rd at the Plymouth Theatre for a week—and at the Comedy here December 25th for a real run—eight shows a week—a daring venture, but I feel a step forward, getting beyond Sunday nights and trying to go alone! Wish me well—I can't tell how long it will last, and I may be a flop, or it may kill me, but I'm going to try! It's very exciting having my own home—I'm very busy moving now and buying things for it. I hope "things" and domestic cares aren't going to wean me from my work! I fear I shan't get West this year!

Macbeth is *awful!* The old traditional costumes in the Craig set look all wrong and the lighting is fantastic and multicolored for *no* reason and surely was not what he meant. I hated it all!

Backstage Ruth Draper was all business and, apparently, entirely without temperament—brisk, contained, assured, completely knowing her job. She could spend two hours after breakfast telephoning, writing or dictating letters, visit a museum or exhibition to look at paintings, lunch with a friend—chatting, carefree—and arrive at the theatre twenty to thirty minutes before curtain-time. She would glance at her mail, ask her stage manager which "sketches" were on her program for that performance, and then, with the help of her dresser, slip out of her dress or suit, and don her pinkish kimono while she supplemented—really only strengthened—her makeup: a little blue eye-shadow, the minimum of mascara and brown eye pencil and rouge—very little—dark lipstick shaped on with her little fingertip, powder with a rabbit's foot or soft brush. She simply wore her own face—her primary tool of expression. Dark brown wavy hair, large brown eyes compelling, expressive, and all-seeing, skin clear with a tone slightly—very slightly—tawny.

Then into her stage dress: brown or beige lace, a dark brown velvet, always sleeveless, basic, unobtrusive, to which could be added shawls or bits of costume for her characterizations. A final glance in the mirror and she walked quickly out to the wing where her dresser had laid out on a table the "costumes" and props for that performance, put on the necessary items; the curtain rose, and with a final word to whomever she was chatting with, she walked into the stage lights—a different character and personality. No more ado than that, no rehearsal, no moment of reflection or of gathering herself together—she was always collected, aware, "in character." She could come off-stage into the wing, speak in stage-character to whomever was standing there, switch shawls, finish her remarks in the manner and voice of the new character, and whip back into the lights; too quick for the eye to see or the ear to mark that precise instant of transition; it was unbelievable—but it happened.

Ruth Draper's season at the Comedy Theatre in New York was a spectacular success; she played eight performances a week for eighteen weeks—to April 28th. On May 18th she sailed for France in the S.S. St. Louis of the Hamburg-America Line. Lauro de Bosis was on board.

To Harriet Marple

[May 25, 1929]
At Sea

There is a fancy dress ball assembling—for the moment I've lost L. (you can imagine we are not attending) so I'll seize the chance to write you as all the desks are empty now. It's been a wonderful trip and I simply can't believe 8 days have passed—they seem like one. Heaven knows how they've gone! I've done very little reading—the heavy books on Russia didn't tempt me. I've written the Private Secretary Monologue—it's not bad—nothing striking however—just pace and rich content, type of the Italian lesson, and depends of course how I do it—whether it is any good. I've also started the "Opening a Bazaar" and tho' not far along, it might be funny. I wish we'd brought more lovely things to read aloud to-gether. I concentrated so on improving books for my trip I never thought of poetry and lovely essays etc. and we've started several things we didn't much like. We had a lovely read in my cabin this afternoon, "Civilization" by Clive Bell. It was cold and wet on deck, and lovely and cosy there. The big cabin and bath have been a great luxury; we found a lovely remote sunny corner for our chairs and have lain hours in the sun. The ship is delightful—small, well planned and *such* restrained, *un*German taste—you'd be surprised; the people are awful but inoffensive and we've said a dozen times how glad we are to be on such a ship, unknown to anyone. It was plain last night at the concert that very few knew me; two ladies sang, a gentleman played, and I did 3 pieces. Mr. and Mrs. Hapgood and Prof. and Mrs. Counts and their children have been our only companions. L. is too adorable with children—they collect around him like flies, and he radiates a kind of magic and understanding that is rare to see. We've discovered 2 interesting Professors since last night— I guess he's talking to them now. The food is good, and I had lots of cake and candy, fruit, coffee, flowers and nuts, and we nibble something most of the time. He comes to breakfast in my room and we're together every moment, and it's been *so* lovely! The nights have been too cold to enjoy the moon—and damp and cloudy most of the time but not rough. I'm going to try and go to Mont St. Michel if I find it's possible as we are due to land at 4 a.m. on Monday.

L. has now returned having been talking with the Ex Austrian Minister of Finance, now at Harvard as Prof. of Comparative Law. He's drawing winged horses at the opposite desk—he draws them in chalk all over the deck to the delight of the children. He went to Deauville once and spent all his time drawing seven gigantic winged horses on the sand, and then went away—all he saw of the place—all he did there! I plan to leave for Warsaw on Wednesday.

Thursday [May 30th]—*6 p.m. enroute to Warsaw.* To continue this dull letter which I've just found in my bag: We motor'd to Mont St. Michel and had a marvellous day there; the country was divine—blossoms, lilacs, young green and young animals and of course Mont St. Michel a marvel. L. had never seen it and it is thrilling to see beautiful things with him—he reacts so instantly, so genuinely. We had rather a tiresome journey back to Paris and felt sort of done up the next day but we enjoyed the play that night and had a lovely 2 hrs. at the Louvre and a drive in the Bois yesterday before he left for Rome. I saw Léa and Lugné and Isabelle to-day and did some errands and packed and got off at 4:30. I sent you a very uninteresting but nice little white dress from Le Breton's, and a lovely one to Aileen. They are at the Colony Club, or will be, addressed to *her,* so please tell her—Hester Pickman is bringing them on The Homeric sailing next Wed. and will leave them at the Club. I'm sorry yours isn't nicer—they just happened to have it—it's a new model—but slightly soiled—they assured me it would clean beautifully and ultimately dye well. I thought it quite smart and useful—it's wool—silk Rodier material. I hope to heaven it fits!

I wish you were here right now— I need you so often to straighten out my crazy moods. I despair of understanding myself and Lauro grows to me in beauty all the time and I remain hateful to myself.

P.S. Did Doro find out L. was on board? Don't say I went to Mont St. Michel.

Lauro returned to Rome—uplifted by his love and all that Ruth had come to mean to him.

Ruth Draper remained for ten days in Warsaw, where she performed at the Conservatoire on the 6th of June. While impatiently awaiting her Russian visa she saw the sights of Warsaw under the guidance of her great friends Zosia and Paul Kochanski, Arthur Rubinstein, and Karol Szymanowski, all of whom had been friends of her brother Paul in the "Edith Grove days" in London just before World War I. Her diary records, "June 6 – Party at Richard Ordynski's—Brahms Sonata, César Frank, Barcarolle, etc. etc. - - - dawn!"

To Harriet Marple

June 5 [1929]
Cracow

Here I am just for the day to see this interesting old town. Richard Ordynski had to come to see his mother who lives here, so I joined him and we left last night after the ballet at eleven and arrived at six! I'm resting . . . till dinner and we take the train back to Warsaw. My show there is tomorrow night—the town is covered with Polish posters in pea green!

Warsaw has charm and the food is something to dream of! But I've been awfully lonely for Lauro and the week has seemed like a month. I don't think I can face Russia and two weeks more separation. I wonder why I ever thought I could! In my heart I never really felt keen, but thought I ought to see more strange places, that the separation would be good. Everyone in Warsaw tries to dissuade me and it does take a heap of courage to face two days on the train alone—and no one I know at the other end, and for no particular reason for frankly I'm not much interested in Bolshevism—it is anti-pathetic and will be dreary and awful beyond words they say!... It's been awfully cold, wet and gray—I've lived in my two suits and longed for a fur coat at night. All my thin dresses are useless and how I've wanted a fur piece—and I forgot any rubbers!

If I force myself to go to Russia it will be with a heavy heart impatient to get thro' with it, yet if I don't go I'll be a little ashamed and embarrassed to explain my change of plan. So long old thing—I can hear you laughing at me. Shall I ever grow up? I think I've grown more helpless and weak minded instead of less in the past eight months.

The Diary entries for the Russian trip.

June 12—Arrived Grand Hotel, Moscow
(Wednesday) Drive about city—Monastery—
*   Bob Littell, Walter Duranty,*
*   Alexandra Goncharova, Ballet*

June 13—Children's Playground—Art Gallery,
*   Museum of 1840—Museum of Modern French Art.*
*   Cherry Orchard.*

June 14—Kremlin—Tolstoi Museum,
*   Tea with Tchzekova*
*   Workers' Restrooms*
*   Theatre—Armored Train*

June 15—Leningrad: Hermitage—Tsarskoe Selo—
*   Drive about city—Revolutionary Museum,*
*   Market—Tea with Tolstois*
*   Leave for Warsaw*

June 17—At Warsaw Station
*   Karol & Mylnarskis.*

June 18—Arrive Vienna.

To Harriet Marple

June 18 [1929]
Hotel Bristol
Vienna

I'm well, *quite a lot* thinner and so glad to be out of Russia! I've nearly died longing to be with Lauro again and three weeks has seemed like three months! Russia was *awful*—so depressing, so uncomfortable, but terribly interesting and I'm glad I've seen it. My passport was six days late and I was so impatient, after waiting on in Warsaw that I couldn't bear to stay away any longer—please keep it a dark secret that I only stayed five days in Russia! I'm ashamed to admit it, but I saw an awful lot, distinctly all I wanted to, for I wanted to leave the minute I arrived! The flesh is weak (my flesh, not theirs) and I rejoice to be back to cleanliness, good food, security and order. Vienna is divine—I love the place and if only Lauro were here would love to stay—but I'm hurrying on, having spent the day *scouring* and airing and repacking.

I was four days in Moscow, one in Leningrad, and five nights on the train going and coming away!

I'm dropping with fatigue. If this *is* my last night on earth, tell everyone I was terribly happy, flying to join my lover, and what a lover! I can find no flaw in him—this separation has taught me so much—so, tho' it's been awfully hard, I'm glad of it.

To Dorothea Draper
(Mrs. Linzee Blagden)

June 26 [1929]
Ancona

I wrote Helen a long (and intelligent sounding!) description of my Russian visit and perhaps she'll tell you about it. It's so hard to say what one feels—for one is so hopelessly confused and troubled and depressed and frightened by the whole thing. I loathed it and feel sure that even with a fairer, longer time to absorb the atmosphere it would still leave one completely torn in one's judgment and sympathies. Walter Duranty, the Times correspondent who's been there seven years, is quite non-committal tho' very informing and interesting and was very kind. Bob Littell (husband of Anita Damrosch) was so nice, and it was a great comfort having him 'around'. He is staying a month more, and I think is longing to get out—I never was so glad to leave a place! But I'm *very* glad I went. The world they are making seems utterly unbeautiful, that is perhaps what one notices most. The Hermitage restored one's soul, that alone was enough to take the journey for—and that is the lasting symbol of what the old world accomplished after all! One's brain is *so* stimulated, and one's heart so troubled, by being in Russia, that possibly that is one of the chief virtues of the whole thing— and the chief privilege and advantage of going there! And one can't fail to be awed and humbled by the brave acceptance of those that hate it all and have suffered so terribly—their patience and renunciation; and thrilled by the vitality and hopefulness of the young. And the memory that haunts me (as a sentimental woman I suppose) is the picture of the [Czar's family] rooms at Tsarskoe Selo—the intimate things left just as they left them that night, the boy's toys and little uniforms and books, and the girls' old dolls and all the little beds and such lovely dresses—pretty silly things, and photographs— and supper table laid—all the feeling of a nursery and a school room just left—it was terribly touching. I had a nice little interpreter, and asked 1,000,000 questions, and ran into a nice American and travelled out with her.

I flew from Vienna to Venice too beautiful for words—I love Vienna— the joy of getting back to an old familiar civilization and such beauty and freshness of style after sordid ugliness was very great. Venice was lovely as ever. Now I am visiting the de Bosis family in an old town on the shores of the Adriatic, a wild and most beautiful spot—the grandest place for rest and work—I hope to make myself write, when I can clear up all the letters I owe—it's always a temptation to do them first! I'm going to swim now— it's very beautiful and remote here. I'm scribbling this on my knee, looking at surf on rocks and a long line of cliffs and blue sea.

To Harriet Marple

June 27 [1929]
Pietra la croce

I only spent one night in Vienna, repacked and got thoroughly washed and cleaned and flew on a glorious morning at nine across the mountains to Venice, landing at the Lido at 11:30. As I descended from the machine, I heard a whirr above me, and said—where does that machine come from— "from Rome, signorina"—and in three minutes Lauro and I were rushing toward each other, having started and landed at the same hour, moment literally. It seemed miraculous! (it's fifteen hours by train from Vienna). By twelve we were swimming in the sea and then after a good lunch, we rested in a nice room in a hotel at the Lido and at sunset crossed over to Venice. Lauro had never been and had been waiting to go with his love so you can imagine his excitement and mine. We had six enchanting days there, full moon, warm bright days—went to Padua. We had a lovely room in a quiet little hotel, and can you believe it did not run into or see one person I knew. It was all so lovely—and we flew on a perfect morning in two hours along this coast to Loreto then motored here.

His mother, sister, three little nephews, and brother from Florence are here—it is all very sweet—easy and natural and tho' we wish we were alone it is quite easy to get off and the beach is limitless and not another soul within miles.

Ruth Draper stayed six weeks at "The Tower" with Signora de Bosis and her family. Lauro's mother, born Lillian Vernon of St. Louis, Missouri, had, since childhood, lived in Italy, where her father, of New England Methodist stock, served as a clergyman for many years. Brilliant and cultivated herself, she had married Adolfo de Bosis, a successful Roman lawyer who was even better known as a writer, poet, critic, and, particularly, as a translator of Shelley. This intellectual, literary, bi-cultural background, and their devotion to her revered Shelley, drew Ruth to them all. Adolfo de Bosis had died in 1924, and the youngest son had died in a fall from an airplane. Between Ruth and Lauro's mother there was an immediate rapport that grew in time to an extraordinary closeness. She came to look upon Signora de Bosis almost as her own mother and, with Lauro's two sisters, Elena Vivante and Charis Cortesi, regarded them as her Italian family.

After ten days in Switzerland with Harriet Marple, and a "delightful" weekend house party at Donsbühl Schloss, near Nuremberg, she sailed, with Lauro, from Genoa in the S.S. Augustus; arriving in New York in time to see her sister Alice, who was to sail on a trip around the world.

She brought her cairn back from the kennels in Chappaqua, writing: "I brought Jock in, and I love having him but he misses the country and other dogs and makes me sad. It seems cruel to keep him—but it's a great expense there and he seemed happy last winter. Perhaps he'll forget but the poor darling really seems sad and bored. He's happy when he's out but gets tired as the flat is very dull after the kennels, I suppose! It's really a problem and I almost wish I didn't have him—I knew I would care too much!—for his happiness I should let him go to some nice family in the country yet I can't bear to send him away."

With Harriet Marple Ruth spent three weeks in Islesboro, where Aileen Tone joined them, and Lauro came for the last three days–his only visit there. She returned to New York to repack and went to the MacDowell Colony at Peterborough, New Hampshire, for four days of concentrated work—"enchanting place, glorious weather"–then spent an early October weekend at Avon, Connecticut, with Corinne Alsop. Lauro joined her there.

November and December were well booked in Kentucky, Ohio, and the Selwyn Theatre in Chicago; she returned home only two days before Christmas and on December 26th opened again at the Comedy Theatre in New York.

To Harriet Marple

[December 14, 1929]
The Lake Shore Drive Hotel
Chicago

Sitting up in bed—old scene—letters, papers, monologues covering me. I enclose my notices—too good—I am greatly disappointed in all my new things and only see slight improvement. I think the Bazaar is the best—in its way, one of the best things I've ever done. The [miner's wife] fails as all the things I care most for fail, the way the Embankment did, I mean; it's a superb idea—most imperfectly carried out—it's loose, rough and inadequate in construction, and gets no better. I'm very hopeless about it; a certain "kick" gets over by the horror and drama at the end—which leaves an impression of a big thing—but that covers the rest, which is *very poor.* [In Three Women and Mr. Clifford] The secretary is good and the wife—pretty good—but Mrs. Mallory is miles from my idea—and it breaks my heart and I see nothing more to do. I just can't do what I want. The whole is evidently impressive—for it's immensely popular—much talk, and they insist on it at every performance!

I've had good audiences growing in numbers, it's been *very* badly handled—great enthusiasm but not full houses yet. No local person was employed to superintend the advance. I can't complain really because I took no responsibility myself. I've had the chance to practice, and make a good deal of money—but it's a pity it was not better handled! I assure you I look well dressed. I wear my green *every* day. I have my black fur coat and wear that too—red is cleaned and all admire me in it, so there!

I'm seeing people at lunch every day, but have lonely little dinners and have had very low moments— I've telephoned Lauro about four times and that is wonderful! I'm embarrassed to do it more often because hotel walls are thin, and telephone operators not above suspicion!

During this year the question of marriage appears to have been very much in their minds. While there are no letters of Ruth Draper's that mention marriage at this time, a few of the existing letters of de Bosis refer to his desire for it. The most significant of these was written early in December to Ruth Draper on tour in Chicago: "I had yesterday evening a most marvelous time with Ned [Sheldon]. He is really a God and I felt as if I was talking with the oracle. He feels as I do, as we do, that whatever we will choose will be perfect so we must feel confident and happy . . . that our present freedom is a great value for love. . . . Marriage would hardly add anything except *we felt we wanted for the sake of a child. I will be overjoyed to think of marriage though I doubt whether you really wish to have a child or not. The ultimate decision must lie only in your having or not having a craving for a child."*

Ruth Draper's season at the Comedy Theatre, with eight performances a week, lasted over twenty weeks until May 4th. At the end of the month she sailed for England and opened June 9th at the Vaudeville Theatre in London for four weeks. For this stay she leased a small house at 28 Chapel Street, near Belgrave Square. Lauro, who had crossed with her, went directly on to Italy. In the middle of July Ruth Draper flew to Switzerland, visiting Lucie and Ernest Schelling at Céligny on Lake Geneva, then motored to Venice and flew on to stay with the de Bosis family at Portonovo for six weeks. Returning to Switzerland on August 30th, she joined Harriet Marple at Gryon for a fortnight. Then, after a quick trip to Paris and London (where she spent two days with von Zur Mühlen at Steyning), she returned to Italy and sailed with Lauro in the Roma on October 4th from Naples. November and December saw her giving recitals in the East and on December 26th she again opened in New York at the Comedy Theatre—but this time for only a four-week season.

On the face of it this appears to have been a routine year. In actuality it was a turning point for Lauro de Bosis and, consequently, for Ruth Draper also. Now, until the end of 1931, his story becomes essentially her story.

At first sympathetic to the Fascism which had come to Italy in 1922, embellished as it was by Mussolini's rhetoric, Lauro had begun to understand the reality, which to many Italian intellectuals was nakedly revealed by the ruthless murder of Giacomo Matteotti, the Socialist Deputy, in the spring of 1924. Increasingly alarmed by the terror and totalitarian tactics of the Fascist regime, and the slowness with which Italians seemed to recognize the seriousness and potential of Fascism, he determined to work for its overthrow. It was with this in mind that in 1928 he had applied for the semi-official appointment as Executive Secretary of the Italy-America Society in New York, in the hope of emphasizing Italian culture and civilization rather than Fascist propaganda. In fact, this position would give him access in the United States and in England to those opposing Fascism and actively working for Italian liberty. Now, in June 1930, without any previous political experience, he resigned his position at the Society and organized in Italy the Alleanza Nazionale, a resistance group, to bring together the doctrines of liberalism, monarchism, and Catholic Action, and to form a union of all parties working against Fascism and for a liberal monarchy. Beginning July 1st he was, alone, writing and circulating 600 bi-monthly letters, not aiming at rebellion but "of a strictly constitutional character," calling on "all men of law and order" to join in accord and organize in preparation for the fall of Fascism. He hoped these would circulate by the thousands in a chain-letter action and have a considerable effect.

Also in 1930, his verse-drama Icaro *was published in Milan. Written in 1927, it had been chosen as the only verse-drama to be entered by Italy and had won the Olympic Prize for Poetry at Amsterdam in 1928. Modeled on the ancient Greek dramas, this play was based on the legend of Daedalus, who fashioned wings to fly from the tyrant Minos; his poet son Icarus flew so near to the sun that the wax of his wings melted, plunging him to his death in the sea. De Bosis wove into this play his own faith in scientific truth and in the ideal of freedom of thought and action—all of his vision so influenced by the tradition of Shelley in his family.*

Having sailed from Italy on October 4th with Ruth Draper, Lauro spent six weeks in New York to transfer to a new Executive his work at the Italy-America Society and to seek nomination by the League for International Education as its representative in Italy. In this work he would have broader contacts in Italian intellectual circles, where he hoped to exert some political influence. He secured the nomination. But then he made a serious mistake that was to return to haunt him: he wrote a letter to the Italian Ambassador in Washington, in which he expressed admiration and support for the Fascist regime—hoping in this way to avoid suspicion in Italy. He then started for Rome on November 26th in the S.S. Mauretania *via England. Before leaving Italy he had arranged with two friends, in whom he had recently confided, to get out the bi-monthly letter while he was absent. Those were Mario Vinciguerra, well-known writer, liberal, and associate of Benedetto Croce; and Renzo Rendi, head of a literary agency in Rome and literary correspondent of the* New York Times, New York Evening Post, *and the* Chicago Daily News. *A third associate had promised to substitute for Signora de Bosis, who was too ill to carry out the printing of the letters, but he failed to keep his commitment and before someone else could be enlisted they were betrayed. On December 1st Vinciguerra and Rendi were arrested—one of them while posting the A.N. letters. Two days later the police searched the de Bosis house, found the mimeograph machine under the bed of Signora de Bosis, and arrested her also. All were charged with writing and circulating anti-Fascist propaganda. Five others, including one woman, also were arrested in Verona and held for complicity.*

As the ship neared England on the evening of the first, Lauro received a telegram from a friend telling him that his mother, three members of his family, Vinciguerra, and Rendi had been arrested. Lauro's first instinct had been to continue on to Rome to face trial with his family and friends, but word was brought to him from his family not to cross the frontier, and to this was added the protestations of his associates in London, Paris, and Switzerland. After conferring in Switzerland with other activists it was decided he should remain outside Italy in order to continue his anti-Fascist efforts. He wrote Ruth Draper on December 21, 1930, from Paris (the day before the trial): "My friends were ready to [face] this as well as I, and I am only sorry not to share the full glory with them. If I were not sure that I can wage a good war from here I would take the first train to join them. I pray heaven with all my heart that I may receive a Condemnation of Death. It would be such a feather in my cap! I hardly dare to hope for such an honour."

Though aged 66 and already suffering a nervous collapse, Signora de Bosis conducted herself with great pride, dignity, and calm, taking upon herself the entire blame. Finally transferred to a clinic as a concession to her health, though still under guard, she was reported to be "happy and serene and reads Dante." However, for fourteen days she was prevented from seeing anyone except the police and a lawyer whom she too blindly trusted. This man told her that Rendi and Vinciguerra were free, not under suspicion, but that all her own family were in prison. Seeing the situation as merely a family matter, therefore, she was persuaded, in order to save them, to sign a letter to Mussolini refuting all anti-Fascist sentiments and action for herself and her family. In this way, she was assured, there would be no trial and the whole matter would be dissolved. Those who saw clearly the design of what was happening could not reach her with their warning. So Signora de Bosis was taken completely by surprise on December 22nd, when she was brought before a Special Military Tribunal for the Defense of the State. She was shocked and stunned to find Vinciguerra and Rendi, with the four men from Verona, guarded by soldiers with fixed bayonets, manacled together in an iron cage at one side of the courtroom, with five Carabinieri beside them inside the cage. They, with the two women, were charged with being members of a clandestine organization plotting the overthrow of the Fascist government. (This description of the trial is based on the New York Times reports published December 23 and December 28, 1930.)

The letter to Mussolini that Signora de Bosis had signed was read in court. This letter thanked him for his "extraordinary goodness" in allowing her to leave prison for a nursing home and assured him that everyone had treated her "with great kindness and consideration." It expressed "profound admiration for the wonderful work [he was] performing with titanic energy," and stated her regret for what she had done and her intention to spend the rest of her life in trying to make Italy and the Fascist Regime forget her "momentary aberration." An act of clemency on Mussolini's part would, he was assured, be followed by the sincere collaboration of herself and all her family. It was now too late for any stronger action, and under cross-examination Signora de Bosis said that she had acted only under pressure from her son Lauro and confirmed her letter. Lauro always felt that had his mother maintained her original position of pride and heroic faith in liberty the risk of permitting her to testify in a public trial would have been too great, but that by signing the letter, her trial was made certain as a vehicle of publicity for her "recantation."

Vinciguerra and Rendi admitted to their participation in the A.N. letters, *but on the advice of their lawyers denied they were working toward the overthrow of the Regime and Vinciguerra labeled the pamphlets "largely bluff," intended only to prepare a small body of public opinion in the event that the Regime might suddenly collapse. Both threw the chief blame on Lauro de Bosis. There was general surprise that not one of the accused made the slightest profession of anti-Fascist faith and all denied any thought of working toward the overthrow of the Government by violent means. The Prosecutor noted that all those on trial laid the blame on Lauro de Bosis, who was not present to defend himself. The Defense lawyer pointed out that while there may have been opposition to the government it was within the limits of the law. He then said: "This 'conspiracy' is limited to two men and an old woman—who are fools, not conspirators."*

After one hour's deliberation the Court, which consisted of six uniformed militia officers and a civilian judge in his robes, acquitted Signora de Bosis of the charge of inciting rebellion by means of clandestine pamphlets, but sentenced Vinciguerra and Rendi to prison for fifteen years each for participation, and Professor U. Gelmetti of Verona to three years for circulating the letters. The rest, who confessed to circulating the letters but claimed it was not their intention to work against the Government and that they did not realize the gravity of their action, were acquitted. Arnaldo Cortesi of the New York Times *wrote: "The eight anti-Fascists cut a poor figure at the trial. None had the courage to proclaim their views." Lauro's letter to the Ambassador was read in court and was, of course, doubly damaging.*

Lauro de Bosis was not *tried in absentia, though it had been announced he would be. He was bitterly disappointed, even humiliated at thus being ignored. He wrote on January 7th: "The movement [A.N.] is going splendidly [but] I think Fascism has grown stronger in these last months and I expect no quick solutions—am in fact quite prepared to a long exile." On Christmas Day he was able to telephone to Rome and spoke at length with his mother and sister Charis. Signora de Bosis was well although her nerves were "quite shaken." For many months she felt sure her son must despise her for her weakness and kept asking if he still loved her! As a protection to his family, Lauro sent them "a false letter" to give to the police, making clear that there was "no connection" between him and his family. Actually, he hoped that his mother could secure a passport and join him in Paris, but this visit did not, in fact, ever take place.*

De Bosis' letters to Ruth Draper at this period clearly indicate her emotional reaction to the arrests and to the trial. Her immediate impulse had been to cancel all engagements and join him in Paris. It appears that this was her first full realization of the involvements and potential of Lauro's political activities. It was a situation completely removed from her experience and in no way foreseen. She was fearful for his safety; her imagination ran free and she knew no peace; she cabled, she wrote. Repeatedly in his letters over the next four months Lauro cautioned: "There are here thousands of exiles protected by the Paris police. France protects emigrés in the most extraordinary way. . . . It would have been terrible if you had left everything to join me. Especially with the bad feeling against me in America. Don't hurry. Do everything as if I did not exist. . . . Do not come—there are so many unfavourable voices about me that we must be extremely cautious. *A hurried sailing of yours would be very compromising. Achieve your plans as if nothing had happened. . . . It is too dangerous. Come as late as possible for your London season—directly to London. I will join you. There are reasons . . . terrible to have somebody else getting in trouble for me! . . . You might curse a love that gives you so much trouble. . . . Your fears are* phantastical! *. . . Good gracious! Even kidnapped!! . . . Do* not *come yet. I assure you that there is no issue involved. No problem. No choice possible. Nothing!!"*

Still she reproached herself and could not understand; things were terrifying; now there could be no peace for them, ever; he was trying to soothe her with false optimism; was there a flaw in her love that she should remain at home? "I shiver when I think what a terrible entanglement I have thrown you in," he wrote, "I am mixed up in so many things alien to your interests—it must all seem so far and alien to your life." He attempted to put in perspective the things being said about him, the political calumny: "I am sorry perhaps to shock you—but in these six weeks I have matured ten years." To comprehend Italian political life, he urged her to read Thayer's book on Cavour. He tried to reassure her. He tried to set forth the magnitude of the national cause to which he was committed and the relative importance—or unimportance—of one family's tragedy. "God knows how torn I am by the grief of being free and by the regret at not having been at the trial instead of the others . . . the battle has just begun . . . something has been done; Italy is not entirely dishonored as it was a year ago. One must either not look at all or look at the whole." And he warned her not to send his anti-Fascist pamphlets to American friends, except those known to be sympathetic.

Typically, when someone she cared for was in trouble, Ruth Draper reacted with help. She sent Lauro a cheque—which he refused to use for himself but put "in the A.N. funds for future work." She wanted to help the children of Vinciguerra and Rendi, so he told her whom to see in order to send money; "my family needs nothing, absolutely." He told her he was writing some articles, French poems, and rushing work on his new versedrama Eros and Psyche; *so she sent him a typewriter, "a Rolls-Royce of typewriters." She sent two large cases of food. At her behest he spent Sunday with the Walter Gays, he saw her friend Bernard Fäy, had tea with Malvina Hoffman—then he wrote, "Please don't make me see people." It was wiser, he thought, to see only those who also were actively working for Italian lib-*

erty: Carlo Sforza, Francesco Nitti, Gaetano Salvemini, his A.N. contacts. De Bosis continued to work and plan. As soon as he had word of the trial he sent out 600 A.N. letters—mailed by colleagues in Spain, England, Holland, Germany, and Austria. On February 5th another letter (250 copies) went out. About this time he took a job as concierge at the Hotel Victor Emmanuel III, rue de Ponthieu. For this he received room, board, and 800 francs a month. He drafted anti-Fascist letters on the backs of old bills, and obsessively driven by the need to strike a blow against the government of Mussolini, he worked out his own secret and dramatic plan. "The A.N.," he wrote, "is the first serious political movement started in Italy in nine years. It cannot be had at too high a price." On March 14th he cabled Ruth: "Sacred anniversary blessing adoring." Finally Ruth Draper finished her New York season, her tour in Montreal, Ottawa, and the New York area. She sailed for France early in April, with three weeks booked at the Théâtre Daunou in Paris from May 4th to 24th. She would be near Lauro at last.

To Harriet Marple

April 18 [1931]
Hotel Lancaster
7, rue de Berri
[Paris]

Lauro and I are writing in my sitting room—very cozy.... [I've] arranged with [Lugné] for my season here: Théâtre Daunou May 4—three weeks. Seen Léa, Malvina, and I'm hoping to leave for Versailles tomorrow. Lauro was very busy and couldn't get away so I thought I'd try and start things. I hope we can have a little quiet in the lovely country but it's been raining and dull; Paris and a fire and comfort is better till the sun shines. No nice apartments available. I'll try and stay in Versailles or nearby until May 1.

Lauro met me at the station here, and it's all been perfect. We love each other more than ever, I think. He looks well, seems older, steadier, but no less charming. He is no longer managing the hotel; he is writing and full of ideas but it's better to say nothing and be perfectly ignorant. I count each hour of happiness—that's all I can say. It's all as if these five months had gone up in smoke—and we are so close; I feel less than ever worthy—he is so fine, so brave and so lofty in all his outlook and thought. He is gallant and full of hope and strong as ever. I know I was right not to come and feel completely free of any regret—thank heaven for that.

I got in an awful jam about clothes and nearly fainted with fatigue and depression at Vionnet's this afternoon. You know how I am about clothes and with neither you or Aileen to support me I was in despair—found nothing I liked for the theatre though their things are lovely.

To Harriet Marple

May 8, 1931
Hotel Lancaster

I opened Monday—all French people—'Répétition Générale' for press, authors, actors, etc. I was really scared, but seemed to make a good impression—for I've never had such notices anywhere—perfectly marvellous—too good really, they make me feel rather ashamed. Lugné is so happy and proud, and they've handed him lots of compliments for discovering and guiding me so he's very pleased and I'm so glad for him. The theatre is adorable—seats 450, and I've had fine audiences since the opening—of course mostly Americans and English, but lots of French too, and they seem absorbed. 'Les Cliffords'—'Cliffors' (with a marked pronunciation!) is tremendously appreciated—'inouïe' etc. buzzes thro' the foyer between the acts! I wish you were here—you'd be so amused—Lauro goes with me and I think Lugné has guessed already—he's got a terrific eye! He's so sweet and has worked *so* hard to make this a success; he is a wonderful friend and I admire him tremendously. He's not acting now, thank heaven, and seems to me improved and finer than before somehow; he's writing his memoirs.

Lauro and I went to Chartres the Sunday after Versailles and had a lovely time; he'd never seen the Cathedral, and tho' it rained the sun came out in flashes and shone thro' the glass and we spent hours of wonder in and out and in and out and up onto the roof, and it was a delight to see Lauro's joy in the beauty of it all. Then last Sunday we went to Fontainebleau just for the day, for I had a party at the Loudons' in the evening—a lovely party and I had a new dress, (chartreuse color) from Vionnet for the occasion. My theatre dress is a great success—from Chanel—very delicate sheer (brown) lace—terribly graceful lines and dainty and cool looking.

Lauro is more wonderful than ever; but his situation is terribly difficult and I find I'm deeply troubled by all it involves, and it's hard to cast off the shadows, and the ominous element in the future and the actual question of daily bread! One can hardly advise or criticise or suggest—where such a nature is involved—and such ideals at stake. I feel so far off from the vision he sees—so unequal—so unworthy.

Gosh, I'd like to see you—for a good long talk—this minute! There are moments when I feel that I must marry him—to have him more, and closer—and throw in my lot with his; but always comes again the reasoning that warns me, that shows the many dangers, and 'impasses', and the unlikelihood that I could make good and give any more than I give now. One thing I know, that if I lose him—not having married him—the anguish will be far greater. He continues to love me, as I am. His unfailing tenderness, and love of life and faith and humour, amaze me as when I first knew him. His disappointment, and the problems he faces, leave him unscathed and full of courage and hope and determination. I must stop and write a few more letters before he comes at six. We dine at 7:30 and then to the theatre.

The ominous shadows were darkening.

Immediately after the arrests of December 1st, de Bosis had conceived a plan and, since January, had been "entirely absorbed by the great dream"; possessed by his heritage of Shelley and of the Risorgimento, he was obsessively determined to strike back against the accusations and ridicule heaped upon him, to prove his spirit in the work of the A.N. had not been eliminated, that he would never make a retraction in order to win his return to Italy.

Inspired by Bassanesi's daylight flight over Milan the previous August, he planned to become a pilot, to purchase a small plane, and to fly over Rome dropping thousands of letters—to the King and to the citizens of Rome. "Naturally I am not doing it for my personal satisfaction" he wrote secretly to his mother on June 26, 1931. "I have much more grave, serious and, above all, sober reasons for making the attempt. It is first of all my duty because I am an Italian; then because I am the head of the A.N. and am free while my two friends are in gaol for having believed in me. And . . . I must confess to the joy and satisfaction I feel in having a fourth reason, in as much as I am the author of 'Icaro', I hope that no longer will they say it was full of rhetoric." In the dark of the moon he would fly over Corsica, gliding the last twenty kilometers, arriving over Rome in the early evening, scattering his leaflets as widely as possible. If the element of surprise held good he could get away the 163 miles to Corsica before the much faster Fascist planes could rise to bring him down. "What ever happens I shall have won. It is better to fall in the attempt of flying over Rome than to live for another thirty years as a peaceful bourgeois with utilitarian ideals. Even if the flight ends in a catastrophe, it can only further the Cause, because the dangers are all on the way back, after my 200,000 letters have been delivered. And once that has been done my life will have been justified. And the joy of those hours of flight are worth all the pleasure which might have been mine had I lived without making it. These letters will make an impression. Will they prick the conscience of my fellow citizens? Will they constitute a lesson in civic spirit? This is hardly my concern. I do my part. The others will do what they can." In mid-March he wrote Eric Woods: "I have found the plane, the money, and all the other paraphernalia." At the suggestion of his friend Ferrari, d'Arsac, the Editor of a liberal journal, Le Soir of Brussels, "a little old man with a heart of gold," had provided more than half the money, and Dr. Sicca, an Italian living in London, also contributed generously.

Twenty-four hours after Ruth Draper's arrival in Paris on April 14th, she learned for the first time of Lauro's plans. "After the first shock she was wonderful and never said one word to deter me." Two days later, near Versailles, he took his first flying lesson, under the name of Louis Russell, and worked almost daily until his first solo at Whitsuntide (May 24th). Then, his secret betrayed to the Fascists, he went underground, letting everyone— even his family who yet knew nothing of his plan—think that he was leaving for America. Actually he took refuge in England, with Ruth, changing his name as well as his flying field every week.

Ruth Draper had opened for a month in London on June 6th. Charles Morgan cabled the New York Times: "[Ruth Draper] is a unique genius. Her greatest strength arises from two sources. One, very fully developed and the origin of her present fame, is her power to make a general criticism of contemporary civilization by means of ironic portraiture; she compels us to criticize not only the characters she represents but our own attitude toward them. The other, as yet used but tentatively, is her tragic power. Her rivals provoke us to laughter; she alone can summon pity. [These sketches] are supremely beautiful and touching and profound . . . she is potentially a tragic artist of very high rank."

Probably it was at this time that Gaetano Salvemini came to occupy a special position in Ruth Draper's life, although as old friends of Bernard Berenson they may have met earlier at I Tatti. Of peasant ancestry, from the Apulia, Salvemini had become a professor at the University of Florence, where he found his intellectual home and where his peasant ways and Pugliese accent were accepted. His wife and five children had perished in the Messina earthquake of 1908. In Florence he escaped the cultural limitations of the South but yet avoided a commitment to the industrial North. More Christian than Socialist in his thought, distrusting theory or formal philosophy, he nevertheless worked with great understanding and concern for the poor and for universal suffrage. For a time he abandoned historical scholarship for political activity and in 1919 served a year in the Chamber of Deputies. Like so many Italian intellectuals, his eyes were opened to the true nature of Fascism by the murder of Matteotti. As editor of the first clandestine journal in Italy he became a leader of anti-Fascism in Florence, where in June 1925 the police, without a warrant, forced their way into the home of Aldous Huxley in search of Salvemini or incriminating documents. They found neither, for Salvemini and Aldous Huxley had never met. Finally arrested, tried, and acquitted, but knowing his life was in danger, Salvemini escaped into exile, resigning the University chair he had held since 1916 on the grounds that there no longer was academic freedom.

In England and France he worked ceaselessly to assemble evidence of what was happening in Italy and to expose the true facts with irony and humor. His book, The Fascist Dictatorship, published in London in 1928, was a brilliant polemic. The only effective attack, he felt, was to force the Western democracies to recognize this terror and by its own words to dis-

credit Fascism in their eyes. He never believed that Mussolini's regime would succumb quickly to internal crises. Inevitably de Bosis became associated with him.

To Harriet Marple

[c. June 10, 1931]
28 Chapel Street
London

I'm all alone, the room filled with flowers—it's 10:30 pm and I'm dead, after a long day in Steyning with Master. He's pretty well. I took [this] house from the owner, who lives in Paris, heard of it by chance: two adorable, peerless maids, and very quiet, cozy and central. L. has already been over for two days. The servants sleep in the basement and there are two nice spare-rooms over mine, so the arrangement is perfect. Paul Kochanski comes tomorrow for a week and I hope L. will come again and perhaps settle here very soon. I suppose in that case he'll find a room near by. No one even knew he was here before and it was perfect, but now that people know where I am it might be difficult to keep him here— . . . he's trying to keep his whereabouts unknown as far as he can. He's well and adorable as ever—too good to be true—and his gaiety and courage and thoughtfulness with the pain and the cloud on his heart are so marvellous. He can't stand sympathy, and his chief distraction and happiness seems to be in handling my moods and seeing my reaction to his love. If I let myself think, I should be crushed with worry and distress of various kinds, so I try just to live and enjoy intensely the hours we are to-gether and the rest of the time pursue my life—since I can do nothing for him. I wish I could find him a nice job here. The weeks in Paris are already a dream—the swift oblivion of each passing week is terrifying—one has already gone here— I've taken the house to mid July.

My season is "on" with a rush, packed houses, same old dazzling wonderful story. Fred, bless him, and the Rolls on hand, and the welcome of loving friends—all the same nice ones at the theatre. My Paris shows were really a big success—great fun—too long to write about. Lugné was pleased as punch and took one third of my profits, so no wonder. We had no contract but made a good sum and we're too friendly to make a fuss about it! I'm collapsing with sleep. [Paul Draper] I saw dancing on his table and it's *marvellous.* I went sad and hating it—my Paul's name and all, offended me; but the boy is *master* of what he does—supremely fine work of its kind and one has to admit it and give him great credit for terrific work and skill.

To Harriet Marple

June 19 [1931]

Last Sunday L. and I spent with Jane and Wilfred [de Glehn] on the River [Thames], and motoring, and had a lovely time—they love him. He is here with me, and so far not a soul knows. . . . He is supposed to have gone to America—at least in Paris and Italy that report has gone about—so you'd better not say anything.

It's awful not to be able to write more—but it's better not. I live from day to day in thankfulness. We have never been so close—our love seems to grow and grow.

Paul K. was here for three days.

Although experienced pilots most emphatically warned de Bosis that longer training was necessary (at least 600–800 hours) and that he had only a ten-to-one chance, he determined to make his flight after only five hours of solo work. Salvemini, in his book published in Milan in 1948, recounts that on July 11th the English plane that Lauro de Bosis had purchased was flown by an English friend from England to Cannes where Lauro waited. On the plane were 80 kilos of his Manifestos, printed at the last moment in a small English town in order to avoid scrutiny by the French police. As arranged, Lauro flew from Cannes to Corsica to refuel but when landing at his rendezvous in an ordinary field not far from Bastia, the wing of his plane was damaged. Lauro was unhurt but had to abandon his plane with its cargo. Now, of course, his secret was out and both the French and English police would be on his trail, so again he went into hiding—this time in Switzerland and Bavaria. Under the name of William Morris he arranged in Germany for another plane and, at Annemasse near Geneva, 400,000 letters, reprinted on India paper, were dated 8th year since the murder of Matteotti. Ruth provided some of the money for this second plane.

To Harriet Marple

[c. July 14, 1931]
[Paris]

I reached Paris Friday night. I'm hoping Aileen will turn up today. Say *nothing* to a *soul* of what I wrote you. It's all postponed—a temporary relief, but in a way the agony prolonged. I have been thru hideous hours thinking it was about to happen and have just had a wire it's put off—know nothing more. Don't bother to tell Ned unless already done—as I thought it might come off and be in the papers and I wanted you to know, and him, but now—not a word please till you hear from me again. I thought I'd be happier nearer—and dear Aileen will find herself at her old job of seeing another friend thru' a bad time—but I'll try not to be a burden. . . . It's hot and heavy. I've been in the hotel all day waiting for a possible call or wire. I'm writing in a kind of mechanical way—I'm sort of dazed—recovering from hours of agony when I thought L. was going, with very insufficient training—but such will and confidence I could do nothing. Now, evidently, he's decided for himself he was not ready. Old Salvemini has been very fine and helpful to me. . . .

I feel I have been very weak and stupid in not being firmer with L.—he's like one possessed, so impatient to be off and not realizing the gravity of it all and the necessity for perfecting the mechanical end. I wish I were high hearted, optimistic and courageous; it's all a nightmare to me, what is a dream of glory to him. I try so hard to see his vision—and, God, I love him so! We had lovely times in London and, thank Heaven, I had a sweet home to give him there.

To Harriet Marple

August 2 [1931]
Palazzo Josty—Madulein
Engadin

With my usual luck L. and I found the nicest, cleanest, quietest, cosiest place you ever saw and have had a perfect week of sunshine, hay and glorious bracing air that did us both a lot of good. Zosia and Paul [Kochanski] and Karol [Szymanowski] and some friends are at a ghastly pretentious "castle hotel" in the next village [Zuoz]. I gave one look and turned away, and we fled here and found perfection; such marvellous food, and only 3 guests, all Swiss. So we had a huge double room, 4 windows, all panelled; it's a beautiful old manor house, and cows go by the front door and sweet peasants. Stables and the post office and one store are all crowded to-gether, near a rushing river, and a great sweeping valley of hay fields. So I've been out working, and L. and I also played tennis, and walked, and sat in the forests, and read and slept and it's been too lovely. We started from Geneva last Sunday in a motor and were 2 nights and 3 days on the way, thru' the finest parts of Switzerland, the great passes and lovely rich valleys. We got here Tuesday afternoon after such a marvellous journey. One afternoon we drove near the Italian border, and took Zosia and Karol. I am supposed to be with them in Zuoz—if you see any of my family. My mail goes there, and I join them there to-morrow. L. left to-day for a few days. Salvemini feels we should never be to-gether for long in a place where we could be traced, for they undoubtedly know we are friends, and where I am, he may be. And naturally he must try [to] keep his movements rather hidden.

After a week in Geneva I left for 5 days in Paris. I had to get my luggage for I came away hurriedly with only a bag, and I wanted to talk to Salvemini and see Aileen and Mallie. It was a pretty desperate strain and I felt I must get away and leave him too, to collect his resources and not have me and my ill-hidden anguish and sympathy too great a burden. It was a wise move and was good for us both, and we have had such joy and profit out of this week. God knows what's before us—it is as if this respite was just to prepare me for the next terrible ordeal. I count on your having said nothing to anyone—and that you will of course say nothing now—but he means, as I wrote you, to try again. When and how I know not but he's making various enquiries. I'll let you know—I can't write about it all—but it helps me to know you will understand—thanks for your letter. I'm afraid my last one, and the long silence since I wrote it, have worried you. I'm all right now—and hope to keep my nerve. He is marvellous—but indomitable—and nothing could dissuade him from another attempt. I never dreamed there was such hell as I have known and I know I must go thro' it, and maybe worse—again. Aileen was adorable as always—and will come to me and stay with me when and wherever I want her. What a friend. *Do* go to Gertrude's [in Maine]—if all goes well we may come home—come up there too—too good to think about! I wish you were here to brace me up—in a situation like this—it certainly is destructive to be as pessimistic as I am. I long to take things easily, cheerfully and bravely and optimistically, and be full of confidence and faith and fervor. It's just what thousands of women endured every day in the war . . . but it's hard to try and soar alone to the heights one is capable of in a common emergency. Well—one is thankful for such interludes as this past week has been.

To Harriet Marple

August 25 [1931]
[Starnberg-am-See]
[Bavaria]

You wrote me such a lovely letter and it helped me very much. Of course I have been trying to be and do, all that you say I should—since 24 hours after I arrived in Paris on April 14th—when L. told me of his plan and his desire—and it has been a frightful strain—doubling in effort since the terrible defeat on July 11th and now soon to be doubled again! We've had two perfect weeks of rest and refreshment—'bicycling' in the Black Forest, and Bavarian Alps and are both very well and fit. I've thought of you a dozen times and recalled our trips—and wished for you—you would have loved it so. It has been very difficult to write. We are to-gether all the time and I can't bear to let the worry and emotion that assail me, the minute I let myself think, or communicate with you about it all—come into my consciousness, so near him. Even now—he's writing on the other side of the table—I feel my fears may somehow reach him. Everything is still very uncertain—delay has followed delay—and the demands on his patience have been incessant. Nothing would do but that he should try again and Germany was the only place—to buy, or train, and start from—so he came to Munich and found a perfect plane and all promised well and it was about to take place two weeks ago, when again delays, in adjustment of machine for emptying the leaflets—so it had to be put off till the next moon. Now he hopes to do it next week—about Sept. 7. I had the happy thought to bicycle—so being on the move, in wonderful country, has been a healthy, physical and mental activity for us both under the trying circumstances. Now—another week to wait around here—till he starts for France again. I can't bear to leave him—tho' at the last it's best he should be alone. What after? God knows. I've not told my family where I've been these weeks—I shall never lie easily or invent companions—they'll be full of wonder I suppose. God only knows what a price I pay for the secrecy and simulation that the life I've chosen involves. I hate it so—and it grows more painful—I knew it would—yet I can't say I regret not having married—and don't see how our love could be more lovely, deeper or more tender, nor his character and ideals finer. Life is too strange for words—I hope that you will run up to Gertrude's after Boston—you'd have *such* a lovely time. How often I've longed for the peace—beauty and air of that coast. Aileen is in Paris again, after her visit to the Sennis. She proposes to spend October in Paris with Agnes Milliken and November in Rome with Justine, not returning home until December! She will join me now and do whatever I want—but until this business is over I can't make any plans. I'd like to go to Paris and get a few clothes before returning, and perhaps to England to see Master and a few friends whom I missed in June—I don't know what I shall do. I have not written anything—not an idea—or any will or desire or patience, tho' I've tried several times. I certainly will not try a N.Y. season, the West only is open for work, yet I long to go back to my cosy flat and don't relish a tour. L's best chance is America I guess—but where? or what? God knows? I'm not very sanguine about the opening for lectures—but there is certainly no chance for work in Paris or England. I don't know what to suggest, or how to help him at all about that. I feel he'd be good in a boy's school—tho' slightly "revolutionary" and I wouldn't know how to go about it.

Good-bye for the present—I'll write soon again and, by the way, if anything should ever happen to me—I think I'd like my sisters to know—from you and Aileen and Zosia—how happy I've been and how perfect was the love we had.

To Harriet Marple

September 4, 1931
Starnberg
[Bavaria]

I wrote Ned the other day after at least two months silence, just a chatty letter—(it has been so hard to write)—and in it I said that if he cared to communicate with you—you might someday be able to go and see him and tell him all you know about L's venture, the failure and this new preparation. He knows something is going on about which (naturally) I can't write, and if he really feels he wants to know—I just left it up to him. Thanks—if it should so happen that he does ask you.

Here—it rains—one day after another goes by—I dare not say when I hope the attempt will be made. I've gotten so superstitious—fear and doubt so beset me—I can hardly write of it all. The delays and things that happen are fantastic and fate seems to mock us—rows in the club where he bought the machine, personal spite and animosity of members toward his teacher—the only one who speaks French so I must help him—mistakes in the adjustment of mechanical devices—illness of friends who promised to help—miscarriage of letters—fears of detection—bad weather—all added to my increasing fear and nearly exhausted patience. He is so wonderful—I bow before his spirit and his nerve—and I cannot leave him. I am desperate but I love him more than ever. I can't speak of the awful thoughts that nearly overwhelm me—I don't see why he isn't unnerved by the lack of faith and optimism and courage in me—I so fail in hiding it—but I still feel that my presence helps—so I stay. I have not been able to write—that would cheer him more than anything—but nothing comes. It's been impossible to write letters—for I can't make up my whereabouts and reasons, and who I'm with—I just can't—so I don't write at all.

I'm so ashamed of my weakness but it's been so long a strain. I don't see how he stands it—but he is upheld by his burning desire and his confidence—and he adores what he's doing—he really adores the flying. I don't see how these wives of flyers stand it. I'm in agony if he's late—when it storms etc.

Our bicycle trip was lovely, but these two weeks in this place—not doing anything but wait—when he expected to work all the time, have been very hard. We read Cavour aloud—it's a great book—a great story—and P. G. Wodehouse for lighter moments. I take comfort in washing, sewing and keeping things tidy, and he has been obliged to accept that all, tho' he hates it!—But it makes us laugh.

I had a fine lot of letters yesterday—tho' they made me terribly homesick—a nice one from Aunt Nin, saying she'd loved your visit and you looked so pretty and were in good spirits. My letters are awful I know—my moods change like the weather. I hate to write in such a depressed frame of mind. Don't worry—I'm all right we have heavenly times to-gether and I know I'm a help to him and I cry 'shame' to myself when I have waves of self pity and think what *he* has endured and what he is facing! If only I'd been strong enough and inspired enough to use these dreary hours of waiting in producing something I would be all right—but there it is—that's me all over—and the circumstances are not to blame. I did nothing last summer when I was mentally at peace, in divine surroundings. I just don't feel any urge to work—have no ideas—no faith. I have scribbled some things—but they're no good. I hope to see Aileen next week—if all goes on as we hope—I'll wait at Geneva for L. and can run up to Berne to see [her]—I'm hoping for a letter to-day. I hope to get a few clothes in Paris and perhaps go to England but I know nothing of course of what the next weeks will bring forth! How I have needed you—God—I re-read your letter and it helps me—if only you could be near me for the terrible days—I dare not think of them. I know your thoughts, your love and faith are with us. One thing is supreme comfort—he is happy—and I have made him so—with all my fears and falterings I still can be sure of that. As I finished this L. returns unexpectedly—we're just off to lunch—life is couleur de rose!!

To Harriet Marple

September 10 [1931]
Lake of Geneva

I'm nearly wild with apprehension and terror and the long strain of waiting. I can't write more than to say we parted Saturday, I to wait here, he to go to Marseilles, join the machine (flying from Germany with a pilot) and hoping to go on the great journey Sunday. The machine hasn't yet come and he's there waiting. I long to go but I believe it's better not—each day he hopes to do it. Weather is not very good there and the pilot wired it was too bad to start from Munich—but I suspect more than that. Something may be wrong with the plane. A thousand terrors assail me but I can do nothing—he is confident, courageous and calm. I am terrified of my thoughts getting across to him and taking his nerve and concentration. I really feel I'm better out of the way in these terrible days. The [Ernest] Schellings are kind and it's peaceful and beautiful here, but I'm wild inside. Two nights ago I felt sure he was doing it and I never closed my eyes—only to learn the next day that he hadn't yet got the plane. There was a delayed telegram—so otherwise I would have known. . . . God I wish you were here—Aileen is taking the cure at Berne—I can't ask her to leave it.

I must go for a walk and try [to] work on a new sketch. I started three new ones and lost the book of mss! But now I've got a better idea. I long to succeed for L. so wants me to—and not feel that the strain of these months has taken all my creative strength. If only he succeeds—that's all that matters. Love me—and pray for us—if you can. I hope I don't fail—or ever regret what I've done.

After this disappointment de Bosis returned to Geneva to wait again for dark nights. On none of these visits to Ernest Schelling did they sign the guest book. They spent ten days there and in Taloures, Chambéry, and Annecy. "He was wonderfully patient and calm though inwardly restless and eager to get it over with." Then they left by way of Avignon for Marseilles. There, at about four o'clock on the afternoon of Friday the 2nd of October, they parted at the railway station, Ruth Draper taking a train on to Cannes and de Bosis going to the Hotel Terminus. Later that evening he posted a letter to her saying "Bohning [who, with Rainer, brought the plane from Munich] telephoned at seven—excellent trip but too late to continue and he spends the night in Cannes and will be here tomorrow morning early. I burn to go and be through with this thing. I feel absolutely sure of this success and am not even excited about it."

During that night he wrote, in French, "The Story of My Death," and posted it to his friend Ferrari in Brussels, with the request that his "story" be published in the Press if he did not return. With it he enclosed a letter addressed to Ruth Draper in Paris, to be sent to her if he was not heard from. The Marseilles postmark was 3 P.M., October 3, 1931. At 3:15 on the afternoon of October 3rd he made an excellent take-off from Marignan airfield near Marseilles in an 80 h.p. plane (150 km. per hour), with eight to nine hours of fuel, and the repeated, very apprehensive admonishments of Max Rainer not to forget to pump fuel from the wing tank into the main tank before that supply was exhausted. De Bosis had seemed alarmingly nervous, had only seven and a half hours of solo experience, and had not flown for three to four weeks. At eight o'clock that evening he silently glided in over Rome and for about half an hour flew very low over the city, swooping on the Palazzo Chigi (Mussolini's headquarters), dropping 400,000 leaflets in the streets and squares, on café tables and the laps of spectators in an open-air cinema, so low that the plane appeared to be mounting the Spanish Steps. In places it appeared that snow had fallen, the leaflets were so thick. Eyewitnesses reported that copies were quickly shoved into pockets for private reading and later furtively passed to trusted friends. The atmosphere in the squares "changed." It was said that many were impressed by the sense, education, and simplicity of the Manifestos.

Not long after the plane had gone from the sky over Rome there was a "spontaneous" demonstration—a parade of Fascists in the streets—upon order of Mussolini, who was reported to have been "hopping mad." The

Roman air defenses were taken completely by surprise and de Bosis got away before pursuit planes could take off as was admitted several years later by General Italo Balbo, Commander of the Italian air forces. But Lauro did not return. No trace of his plane was found nor was any face-saving claim ever made by the Fascists. The Italian press kept silent. Icarus had fallen.

On October 6th, in Paris, Ruth Draper received Lauro's last letter, forwarded by Francesco Luigi Ferrari. "I could not have wished for a happier solution of my wish to serve my country and my ideals. . . . If I had lived you would have done thousands of things for me. Won't you do only one more? My last and deepest desire? Be happy and continue your glorious life not as if something had been taken away from it but as if something had been added.

"Be happy, 'sta allegra', and work. You will have given me then your crowning boon. If you do that I will feel that my love continued after death to protect you, otherwise my soul would never have peace. Never until you are again happy. And please *love somebody else. I will consider [it] indirectly as love to me. I embrace you with all my adoration."*

The Story of My Death *appeared in the* Soir *of Brussels, in the* Manchester Guardian, The Times *of London, and in the* New York Times, *all on October 14th. Largely uncut, it appeared also in the Press of many European countries. In an editorial,* The New Republic *said on November 25, 1931: "Behind [his] act lies the Mediterranean genius for finding the great symbol, which can both express the idea and satisfy the imagination, and by doing so takes on to itself its own life and powers."*

Many years before, Rodin had said to Malvina Hoffman: "To live is nothing, but to sacrifice life for an ideal is what gives to man his veritable quality."

Ruth Draper was prostrated. She had returned to Paris on the 3rd to keep her agonizing vigil, finding a haven at Léa Dessay's house on the Avenue Wagram. For a week or more she seldom left her bed, seeing only Aileen Tone, Salvemini, and Dr. Bardi. Her young nephew Bill Carter had arrived on the 5th en route to the Institute of International Studies in Geneva. For the first few days they waited and hoped. If the Fascists had captured de Bosis, shot down his plane, or found any of its wreckage, it seemed certain to be announced as political capital. It was possible he had made for Yugoslavia across the Adriatic, for Corsica, or even Sardinia, and, especially in largely anti-Fascist Sardinia, he might well be hidden and unable to communicate. The Italian Security Police watched Léa's house, and the French Police watched them both. Ruth Draper went to the local Préfet of Police for questioning. She frankly spoke of her love for Lauro but disclaimed any part in his political activities. The Préfet, greatly moved by her story, tears in his eyes, came from behind his desk saying, "C'est un amour extraor-

dinaire!" and kissed her on both cheeks. Bill Carter, as the person least familiar or likely to be identified with Ruth Draper or Salvemini, and under instructions of complete wariness and secrecy, went to Rome for just forty hours—to talk with friends of Salvemini, to learn what he could of the impact of the flight and of Lauro's fate. He found it was generally felt that the "raid" had made a significant impression and that the Manifestos, so clearly and simply stated, had carried their message. One witness said: "There was something different in the atmosphere, in the attitude of the crowd. Coming into the square was like coming into a new world." The heroism of the gesture greatly affected those who witnessed it. Psychologically it was a complete success.

To Harriet Marple

October 13 [1931]
65 Ave. Wagram
Paris

I've written Ned a long letter, and I've asked him to have either you, or George, read it to him so, if he sends for you, you'll get all there is to say at present, and I haven't the strength to write it all again. I wrote at length to Chester Aldrich hoping he might be able to get someone to write something nice in the papers still. Thanks for your cable—I would love to have you— yet I can't bear to ask you to come. I have no desire to come home—my only comfort is to be near friends who knew and cared for him—to go over his papers—to work for as wide a publicity as possible. At home I'd feel so cut off from sympathy with his ideals. Dear old Salvemini is like a loving old uncle to us both—so proud and full of tenderness it comforts me. Léa is an angel—I've *never* seen such devotion and solicitude—this little house has become my haven—and [this] sweet room—I feel I never want to leave. Dr. Bardi is one of the rarest, kindest souls—he comes in all the time—for breakfast and the last thing at night; his philosophy and wisdom and clear fine point of view, his enthusiasm, perception of L. and his superb courage and idealism, is a joy to see. Aileen comes—and these friends have saved me and been everything that was helpful. And Lugné like a rock—keen to protect me from any possible annoyance of police or papers—he is wise and kind, and will help me later with articles and translations etc. which I want done. He *is* such a fine friend. Jane and Wilfred [de Glehn] have been in and that is all. A few others who knew L. and have helped—there's been lots to do—and that has been a god-send. You speak of hoping still—others do too—I try to—but dare not really—there are still mysterious rumors and speculations—but—

I think I'll just stay on here; I feel no desire to move—I feel arrested— afraid to touch the earth—afraid to really hope. Bill Carter has been adorable and a *great* help. He went to Rome and got fine first hand impressions, reports that thrilled me so that last night, in my pride, I rose completely above suffering, it was a strange and exalted sensation. I've had it for moments from the first—but last night I lay long—just thinking and almost happy—and fell asleep in peace. I dare not write and get emotional.

I don't feel sure enough of my plans to urge you to come—and am too unwilling to 'détraquer' your life. I cannot even think of my own life or work—tho' ultimately I must begin again—if only for his sake—who loved it so, and urged me so—and with his last perfect message bade me work. I might go to England if I can best see to translating and go over his papers there. Irene [di Robilant] is trying to come from Italy. His family knows— except his mother—they've not told her yet. Complete silence in the Italian papers—making nothing of the raid of course. Cortesi of the N.Y. Times will probably write rather lightly about it and minimize it. I doubt if the Times will publish the very strong message contained in a unique and beautiful document he left to be published in the event of his death. They cabled it over from the office here—but I fear it will be deleted or turned down when they see it. The head man here jumped at it when he saw it. The "Soir" of Brussels and the "Manchester Guardian" publish it to-morrow—a very daring thing to do—but they are the only two frankly anti-Fascist papers on the Continent. So you see, all these considerations have been a tremendous help and forced me to conserve my energy—which I found was being alarmingly spent in the first terrible days of shock. How I laugh now at all that I ever thought was suffering in my life before— If you by chance should come—if I should beg you to—if you decide you want to— I would like you to bring all his letters—Miss Brewer has the key of my private drawer—but look all thro' that top drawer. There are bits in there—regarding his principles and ideals that I might want to assemble. Good-night— I'm very weary. Bill is just off to Geneva—a dear boy and really moved by all this. I saw dear Amey Aldrich just before she sailed on Wednesday—*do* go and see her— and nice old Gretchen Green before she sailed for the East—They were both so full of understanding for they loved Lauro. *So* glad you are in my flat. Love to Aunt Nin—and do make her realize how fine L. was—who need be told that now!

To Harriet Marple

October 16 [1931]
Château d'Héricy
[near Fontainebleau]

My whole state of mind has changed now about the possibilities that Lauro is safe. These are the hypotheses: 1—that he flew East, was picked up by fishermen in the Adriatic and is being hidden, or got to Jugo Slavia.

2—that he was picked up in the Mediterranean and is on a vessel bound for a far off port, and can't communicate with anybody. 3—that he got to Algiers and that the French police are hiding him until Italy is less angry and stops pressing the government for some accounting of his activity and the origin of the whole affair. The police have strongly hinted that he is alive—but have told me *not to tell*, save to my close and *trusted friends*. They won't say where—how—or how they know. At first I thought it was a trick—but now I'm told they wouldn't say so unless it were true. It's desperate not to be able to give this news to his anxious friends and family—tho' God knows how I could get a message to them—but the very clever French lawyer has told me I *can't* tell. There must be some good reason for this silence. No trace of the wrecked plane has been found; this adds, people say, to the probability that he was rescued and hidden. Lots of people think he may be safe. I'm writing you and please read all this to Ned. Bernard Fäy said to Aileen—"I hope none of his friends will do anything to search for him—he knows what he's doing—and to make an effort to find him might mean his death." You know my nature—how I *would* despair from the first instead of hoping. In those first days I couldn't hope—it seemed so likely—that with so little 'essence,' so little experience, and after the terrific tension and strain of his great accomplishment—that something might go wrong. I feel ashamed now that I didn't trust him more and trust his skill and his lucky star and everything.

I hope you've saved American newspaper notices. I only saw the "Times"; 1st—the two inch notice on an inside page way at the bottom, (with murders, suicides, scandals, etc. in the leading columns!). Then a 2nd in a slightly better place, but a very brief notice. It shows how terribly careful our papers are. The London "Times" and "Morning Post" and "Telegraph" and "Manchester Guardian" all had long detailed leading articles on the foreign news page for three days running—and on the 14th The Times and Manchester Guardian published his entire "Story of My Death" as leader with big title on the "Foreign and Imperial News" page—a full one and a half columns! Tho' the N.Y. Times man here was crazy about it, and jumped at it—I don't believe for a moment the N.Y. Editors would print it—at least not all of it—I long to know—it was very strong—but so fine. The publicity given it will make Mussolini boil; it's terribly important for the "Cause", and a newspaper correspondent of Rome told me the British papers had never given such prominence to such a thing before.

I've had many cables, and everyone has been so kind. I felt I must write Doro and Martha and Alice, and to the latter I spoke of our love for each other. They all, I know, realized it and it seemed too obvious to conceal. I knew the time would come some day, and, in their distress for me, it seemed too unnatural not to be frank. I am sure they'll be discreet. Those things seem to matter so little in the face of the anguish and strain of this experience.

It's amazing the way I've 're-acted' to the hope that he is alive and that we shall see each other again. Tho' the doubt and worry are enough to still keep me in a tormented state of mind, the contrast to the ten days of certitude of his death, seems to find me almost happy again, and able to enjoy life and it's as if nature commanded me to make use of this 'pause' to recuperate my forces. I'm sleeping and eating well, and feeling normal and serene and sane—yet if I face the situation as it is—God knows it's bad enough—is he in prison—ill—wounded—suffering—for how long, where—and when? A dozen questions come into one's mind. And what next anyway? I realize the futility of asking—I want to be as strong and steady as I can for whatever the next shock may be—so I'm just living from day to day.

I left Paris yesterday. I'm in one of the most enchanting places you ever saw and who do you think with? Linzee's first cousin, Miss Alice Cushing, about 60, with a girl friend companion of about 50, and—you will of course laugh—but I asked myself! (Thought it would give them *so* much pleasure!!) Not really so bad, she begged me in May to come—anytime! I knew it was best for me to leave Paris for a few days and get away from the 'ambience' I'd been in, and from possible Fascist spies; don't tell the family this—it will worry them, but I have an admirable lawyer, close to high-up Government and Police officials, and am doing what he advises. Lugné helped me to this, and I feel it's been so wise to let my French friends help me, and not Americans, in this delicate situation. They've been wonderful and so understanding and considerate in every way. Aileen motored down with me yesterday and longed to stay, it's so lovely. Such beauty and peace you never saw—by the river—woods—garden-walks—lovely house—*heavenly food,* and such a bed, and a sweet maid, and books and old prints and sunshine and autumn leaves; and my hostess—purest Boston (Miss Cushing has not been back for forty years!)—knowing nothing about my state of mind.

The forest is golden and green—and we've been driving for hours and now I must have a bath and change for dinner. It's like a dream—I wish you were here—should I have asked you to come? I don't want to break into your plans or possibilities for a job—and who knows, if Lauro should call me up perhaps from Spain, or South America, or Egypt— It's so hard to know what to do, where to go, but my instinct is just to stay here and wait and be ready for anything! What a drama—love takes one into strange places—I sometimes wonder if I can keep it up—I who was never made or trained for adventure. Garbat sent me such a wonderful cable "Love and patriotism have no basis in reason we must be brave to accept the results of both", and dear old Barie—she always can be depended upon to understand—said in such a lovely message "Keep your courage at his level."—I was so grateful for both those thoughts. Good-night—dearest friend. I'll write as soon as I know anything more. I told Lucie Schelling to speak to Dorothea about most of this—but with care. She understood that it's only for our personal comfort. Nothing is certain and is only hypothesis. It must never be known that the police hinted it. Please be sure that Dorothea, Martha and Alice realize this. There are Fascist spies everywhere.

To Harriet Marple

October 22 [1931]
Paris

Ask Dorothea to show you my letter to her—[letter no longer in existence]— I simply can't write again—tell Ned—it has been a devastating experience—this crashing of my hopes again—this "improved certainty" coming from the highest source! I was terribly broken—but I'm better this morning and am off to the Ministry now, with my lawyer, to beg them to give me the sources of the report so we can pursue its origin etc.— I wish you were here—but I can't quite bear to ask you to come. You know I'm so uncertain what to do next— I cling to the few who knew and cared and understood. Irene is trying to come from Italy and I must wait—give what comfort I can to her—to take back to his people.— I went to the country for two days, when I was hopeful and confident, and had a rest from the anguish, and physically too— I may go to the Gays' for Sunday with Aileen— she is an angel, of course, and Léa and Lugné and Dr. Bardi, and Salvemini and Philip Monod— I have all I need— I couldn't stand seeing more and these all understand. I feel I must not suffer—it would be an agony to him; his divine courage and joy in life and his love should be all I need to make me live—but, oh Harriet— I can't write—one must surmount this human pain— I will— I will.

It is possible that the Paris Police had spread this rumor of Lauro's safety as bait in the anti-Fascist centers in the hope of further news about him. Nothing came of it.

Malvina Hoffman, with her husband Samuel Grimson, was on her way around the world on a commission from the Field Museum in Chicago to sculpture The Races of Mankind. *Gretchen Green, who had spent many years in China and India, had preceded them in the capacity of advance agent.*

To Malvina Hoffman

November 2 [1931]
Paris

That amazing communication from the middle of the Pacific Ocean and your pencilled words, came a few days ago; it seemed so strange that the news should be flashed across space like that, and reach you on your way to distant lands.

The destiny that I foresaw—has fallen on me—to overwhelm me with intolerable grief—and lifted him to glory. I try and catch the light in my darkness—I struggle to believe the sacrifice has not been made in vain—to feel the pride and happiness I should in his achievement—but it's as yet a losing battle with the human need and the heart that bleeds. O Mallie—how I need his courage and his will and his faith and his love of life to lift me from the horror of this suffering. The hell of thoughts of what might have been, obstructs the memory of the beauty I had, for which I should be so grateful that even the price I'm paying now is small. I know time will help—I know resuming my work will help—and the hope that I can do something to make the significance of what he did—and was—known. And that if I am worthy—I can give something of what he gave to me. But all these things are only thoughts and hopes—intangible substances and abstract strength—as yet of small avail.

I enclose the London Times of October 14th. You will not have seen it, and it tells his gallant story. He left it with an exiled friend, a well known writer—in Belgium—(written in French and much more beautiful in the original) and all the papers seized it and gave it great prominence (even the New York Times had the courage, which surprised me). Spanish—German—Austrian and Belgian papers gave it the front page—with fine forewords—so all this publicity was a help to the cause and made me thankful for him.

The mystery of his death has never been solved. The Fascists in Italy—and agents here and in England spread the news that he was rescued by waiting friends and is safe in France. Their one desire is to minimize the heroism of the act and not permit admiration and emulation of the sacrifice.

High up people in police and aviation feel that had he been caught—alive—or discovered dead—secrecy would be maintained. They want to suppress even knowledge of the raid as far as possible—and knowledge of his tragic fate—sensing foreign and even national sympathy and admiration. He was pursued and possibly shot down. No wreckage has come to light—but if it did on the Italian coast—it will not be known. Airplanes went in search—various enquiries were started but nothing has been discovered.

I've lived in alternate despair and hope—for five days was sure he was alive—told by the Ministry of the Interior who based the announcement on unfounded rumors that he'd been picked up by Algerian fishermen! It was Machiavellian in its cruelty—they expressed regret etc.

I only hope he was drowned quickly—without knowledge perhaps and without pain. I love to think of the ecstasy he must have felt when he saw the lights of Rome—and flew over the city. He flew low they said—dropping to 2,000 feet or less—right over the Corso and Piazzas and the

Duce's palace itself—so he tasted, thank God, the glory of achievement and the fulfillment of his desire.

But—oh—he loved life so—he was sure of coming back—quite fearless—and quite confident—and he had *so* much to give, and to achieve; such beauty and such enthusiasm—he'd been so hurt—so terribly hurt—and lived to cast off the burden he carried in this one gesture—and then face life again, a free man, and gloriously equal to the struggle which he loved and believed in with such passionate sincerity.

Someday you will let me talk to you more of him—you saw us in such a strained moment. His mind was a storehouse of knowledge and beauty, his soul without a stain—and life had no more to teach him in the sense that most of us need tests and experiences to purify and strengthen us. The love he gave me in those three and a half years has been a revelation and must be a source of life until the end—but I had so much still to learn—and had leaned so much on his strength and drunk so deeply of his tenderness—that I feel completely lost and in darkness.

Gretchen came a few days after the blow fell and she was dear and hated to leave me. But I have good friends—and all that sympathy can do to help. Splendid men friends—who are wise and strong and have clear vision and tenderness too, and who counsel me and have helped me throw out wires to get information etc. from Rome—but it all takes time and one has to be *so* careful.

I can't bear to go home—and am looking for a little flat here. Aileen Tone will stay with me for a while, and Harriet Marple is free and will come over later. I've been with a dear French friend for this month of anguish—but am moving to a hotel to-day in order to be with an Italian friend who is coming from Turin—and who will bring news perhaps of his mother—I can't communicate with her, and to think of her suffering—almost makes me forget my own—she adored him—and she'll probably feel her action of last winter started him on this venture, even as I feel that my love also is responsible—for sending him to his death, i.e. in making it possible. I wonder if the torment of these thoughts will leave me? Added to my grief and loneliness is the burden of regrets and questionings. I suppose it's always so. I was terribly aware always of the beauty of what we had—aware of our happiness—of its poignant and constant reality—but I did not suspect that the regret that I had not married him—and *had* him more (and made a situation that would have absorbed his thoughts and interest along other lines—so that this desire would not have developed to such a degree) could take such possession of my mind. I know our love would have been strong enough to overcome the obstacles my 'reason' used to find—his nature was so perfect—but I failed—thro' fears of various kinds—and a constitutional baulking at committing myself to any bond. O well, I must grit my teeth and know one can't recall the past, and have a second chance—with all my weaknesses and failures he loved me—and regretted nothing—that I know.

Forgive this long letter—full of myself—but it helps to release these burning thoughts that fairly burst to be released—one smile from him—one touch of his hand—could make them vanish—but this silence and this darkness makes them grow. Dear friend of my childhood I cry out to you in my pain—send me a word. My dear love to you both. Keep well and take care—I shall think of you often and hope for news thro' Helen now and then.

To Bernard Berenson

December 26 [1931]
Paris

My dear B. B.

Only last night in writing to Mrs. Wharton I asked her to someday tell you of what this tragic and beautiful story meant to me. I wanted you to know for I felt you would be one to appreciate its significance, and that you would remember the afternoon we came to-gether to I Tatti. This morning comes your letter showing me that the story in "The Times" had not escaped your notice and it comforts me to feel that you were touched by its beauty—and that you can guess what my grief—and my pride—must be. I can't write more—and I can't come. I could not look at the sea—or feel the warm sun and the beauty of the south that he so loved—without unbearable pain. It is dear of you and Mrs. Wharton to want me—to offer me your affection, and the rest, and solace of beauty—but I believe it is better to work—hard as it will be—and I've decided not to travel, as I told Mr. Norton I thought of doing, but to go to England, and do a tour through those cold and grimy towns! It will be ghastly but it will be hard work—and I shall make people laugh and forget their troubles, and, perhaps, feel deeply the pitifulness of all of us; and I shall make money—and that at least is the measure of work; and it is my duty after all to go on. I cannot hope for anything but the satisfaction that I am doing my best not to fall short of his faith in me. Don't pity me—I have known the perfect, if brief, realization of the best life has to offer. Unlike most of us, he needed nothing more to lift up or purify his soul, or to strengthen his character—he was a knight—"sans peur et sans reproche" indeed—and we loved each other. Now, I must pay the old, old price. That's all. Dear B. B. Thank you—I know you are sorry—help me only to be proud and grateful.

Your affectionate
Ruth

Shall we ever see the end of the "thing" that drove him to this sacrifice? Like Shelley—he had a passion for freedom and for beauty—and he couldn't bear the betrayal of his country and his ideal.

1932

All my wealth
is in my memories.

Ruth Draper to Alice Carter
March 25, 1932

After spending Christmas in France, apparently with Aileen Tone and Harriet Marple, Ruth Draper crossed early in January to England. Both financially and emotionally it was essential she get back to work; and besides, Lauro had laid this upon her as a charge. But the emotional strain was almost unbearable. She opened in Brighton on January 11th, in the first of a series of twelve one-week engagements throughout Great Britain.

To Harriet Marple
Berne, Switzerland

[January 15, 1932]
1st Avenue Hotel
Hove
Nr. Brighton
Sussex

A lovely sunny day here—glorious air. Ball [stage dresser] is such a comfort. My, I wish I could have her always, she just suits me. My work is very uninspired, just mechanical—they seem to like it but it means less than ever to me, and I can hardly wait to get home [to the hotel]. I don't know how I can face two and a half months of it. I begin the "Cliffords" to-night and I'm really scared, there's so much to remember. It's been terribly hard doing the Railroad accident, the end nearly finishes me. Too many of them have bits in them that bring [Lauro] back suddenly—lines he loved and quoted etc. A friend has just sent me some lovely jonquils. The sale of Master's things is Feb. 11th 12th and 13th. Don't you want the red parlor 'suites' and carpets etc.? I must write some letters—appeals come in every post now people know I'm here.

I wrote Lauro's mother and sisters to-day—Reggie Temple will take letters thro' to Vittorio [de Bosis] and I have been so terribly depressed. I can't rise above this tragedy—only at moments do I feel what I ought to feel, of pride and thankfulness, so overwhelming is the pain, I think it gets worse. It is a blow too, to realize that the help I hoped for in the work—which was such a terrific effort to resume—is not there. You can't think what it means to be on the road again: this hotel life—entering the old shabby theatres, making up—returning, weary,—the old story of so many years,—at it again—with this scorching pain in my heart—and the laughter and applause—. I had such a fight with myself this morning, walking by the sea. I'd so gladly give it all up—make an entirely new life—adopt several babies—have a sweet house in the country etc.—yet I know it would hurt him so, if he thought love and grieving had really broken my spirit, and made me hate, rather than love my work more. It's such a fearful challenge to go on—I don't know—perhaps I've forced myself too hard—perhaps I'm just not brave enough—I suppose that's it. I'm looking forward to tea on Sunday with my dear old ladies [the Misses Mudie, friends of the de Bosis family]. They will help me, I know. Good night—much love to you and thank you for all your letters and for the wire, and your loving thoughts. I don't know what I'd do—without you and Aileen over here. I'll try and not be so sad—I know it's no use—

To Harriet Marple
Hotel Beau Site
Berne

[January 17, 1932]
First Avenue Hotel
Hove, Sussex

I'm lunching with Mrs. [Yates] Thompson, who found out I was here—I dread so seeing these old friends. Thank Heaven I avoid most—by not being in London, but now and then I can't help it. I long so to be brave and re- served, but you know just how good I am at concealing anything! My own instinctively expressive and emotional nature, with the added long training of expression, is not the best combination for stoical control. But I shall try and hold myself in, yet there are so few to tell his beautiful story, to make his character known—and where people are worthy, one feels one has given something so inspiring.

I'm longing to do the "Icaro" myself. I'm thinking of trying to get an Ital- ian woman to travel with me, to talk and study all the time, and work at it. It would be such a deep satisfaction—do I dare? I can but try—and see how it goes. I had the sweetest letter from John Carter about "Italy To-day"; he is so moved by the beauty of the letters and Lauro's heroism—just the lovely young ardent response that would bring that heavenly smile to Lauro's lips and eyes. It draws me close to the boy. Thank you for telling me what Léa and Anxie said—those are the things that help me most—little remarks that show how his flame has touched other lives. My cousin Janet [Longcope]— from whom for years I've felt rather far apart, writes "the sheer beauty of it—and the triumph of the spirit puts one on one's knees!" My heart warms to her in such gratitude—one more to really understand—thank God.

I shall be glad to leave the sea tho' the air here has done me good. It's been terribly hard—the audiences excellent—much laughter and applause and a kind of reverence—as if they wondered—at the end. I wish I didn't have to bow—that's almost more than I [can] bear—I'd like to just run away and not appear at the end. Well—I feel he'd be glad—that's my only satisfaction, but *it* all means nothing—and the loneliness and longing seems to grow.

To Harriet Marple
Berne

[January 21, 1932]
[Boar's Hill Hotel]
[Nr. Oxford]

I had a long letter from Irene [de Robilant] last night. She is a grand person but she has a way of making you so disturbed and sad—I can't bear to think what her letters to Lauro were last winter. Of course in a way I want to know all that is said, yet one must close one's ears—or go mad—to the things said by the 'monde.' Countess [———], rank Fascist and black Catholic, is an oracle of gossip—and tho' she writes me I have "her prayers" she evidently talks and talks about all she gleaned in Paris; so it goes. [———] is ardently fascist, had a grand time in Rome, thinks it all perfect; I shudder at what he will take back to New York about things said against Lauro. Perhaps he will recall his old affection for me and be decent and silent—? On the other hand, I hear the 'raid' was an amazing success— frightened Mussolini to death and they have machine guns and lights on roofs of high buildings—and men on guard all night. Irene says many have read the 'Mercure' and been deeply impressed. One just clings to one's own faith, and the secret glory of my memories and my knowledge. I had a beautiful letter from [———], embarrassingly personal since I've never talked with her, and felt an antipathy toward her personality—much as I admired her intellect. Aileen must have written her, and she saw us to-gether once or twice. Anyway her comment is profound and beautiful and sincere.

It's not cold—lots of flowers are out—such a funny winter! Marvellous audiences here—they laugh *too* much. The taking the bows is what nearly kills me—if only I could run away and not face the crowd—out of character. Ball is an angel. I'm looking for an Italian to travel with me—to talk and study—I think it may distract me. I have never been so sad, it seems to grow worse—the moon and the birds and coming of Spring perhaps make it worse. But night does come, and sleep—the waking is always the worst. I am anxious to hear how you are, what the 2nd blood test showed—also Léa's—do write soon—wasn't Léa to return this week-end? I *do* hope there is some improvement for both of you.

I have begun to work a little on Icaro and it interests and distracts me. I lunched with Prof. Murray—*such* a lovely person—and his sympathy with the cause and admiration for Lauro are a great comfort. I'm staying in the country, near them outside of Oxford, and it's been much nicer. I must get up, walk, and then return to work a bit. I'm going out to lunch with a friend at a lovely place in the country—that will help—O, Harriet—I never dreamed of such pain—forgive me—I'm not very brave.

To Harriet Marple
Hotel Beau Site
Berne

[January 22, 1932]
Oxford

I'm nearly crazy—I have so much writing to do. I don't know why, but in England my mail becomes enormous and, so far, none of my friends know I'm here. The de Glehns I lunched with on Monday; I saw the French exhibition, which is marvellous, and I had a long tea with the old ladies—I love them.

I've heard of a young Italian girl and am seeing her on Sunday and if she seems possible I'll let you know at once. It will be very strange having a perfect stranger—I hope I'm not making a mistake. Ball has to leave me this week and I'll miss her. She's been perfect and the greatest comfort. I don't know if I'll take a maid with me for I suppose this girl in the capacity of Secretary will be expensive and I may just get a local maid in each place.

I'm enjoying the work on Icaro. But the hardest part is still to come—putting it into clear beautiful sounding lines without changing the sense. I'm just doing it word by word now.

To Harriet Marple
Berne

[January 23, 1932]
Boars Hill Hotel
Nr. Oxford

Just rushing down to lunch at Balliol with David Astor and then to my matinee.

I had a chatty letter from Aunt Nin—not one word about my concerns—nor the green pamphlet. How can she be unmoved by such a story—I confess I'm hurt—strangely so—Can she have ever loved me—to so dis-regard my grief—? or can she know anything of love? I am baffled—how can she be so cruel to pass her own judgement in opposition to what those letters show of what he was?—Well—one learns—one must be generous and forgiving—somehow I've never had such strange necessity for ignoring wounds before.

The green pamphlet was one of a series put out by Salvemini. This one was devoted to de Bosis' work and death: ITALY TO-DAY, *by Friends of Italian Freedom, November–December* 1931.

To Harriet Marple

January 25 [1932]
Canford Cliffs Hotel
Bournemouth

You say you hope life isn't too hard—it is—"but what are you going to do about it?" I find that doing something quickly with my hands helps most. I've just made a lovely fire, then taken a bath and I'm resting, and the waves are gently roaring on the beach below the cliff. I'm all alone. Ball's mother got ill, and she couldn't stay on. I'm hoping the little Italian girl will come on Wednesday. She speaks perfect English, French and Italian and is a stenographer as well, and started studying medicine and can teach Greek and Latin and she's only 23!! An ardent anti-Fascist—her brother has just been in prison for 9 months. She can't go back and ever get out again, so she's badly in need of work. She doesn't look very prepossessing—rather like a picked sparrow—a little like me—but I guess a little luxury and good food (to *her* good!) will build her up. It's a strange experiment, but I'll try it. I may get only local theatre maids, I don't know. I want to do 'Icaro' all myself—I have a good dictionary and Roget's Thesaurus—but now and again she could help with a very peculiar word or sentence. It *is* very agreeable work, but I don't know at all if I can make the English beautiful—so far it's just literal.

I'm delighted you're going to Mount Pelerin—That's where I went last year when you were just moving from your favorite Alpine resort! I expect you gathered from my cable that I did not want you to join me here, now that I'm trying this linguistic companion. God knows how it will work! Ball has been dear to me—simple folk express such deep tenderness in their dumb respectful way, and she picked little snow drops and primroses to put in front of Lauro's picture—and asked if she might keep the green pamphlet. She seems to love me and was terribly sorry to leave. I have bad moments, when I *long* for you to talk to, but on the whole I guess it's good to try and stifle my agony—the mornings are awful—I still wake so early and torturing thoughts still crowd into my mind. Going to the theatre and dressing and beginning is bad—the actual work helps—not the emptiness afterward—remembering him in the wings waiting—remembering lines he loved—gets me even on the stage—and the lonely return, weary. Taking the applause is perfect agony—the contrast of my feeling to the shouts of laughter (in Oxford those boys literally shouted) and clapping is simply fantastic and horrible. Fine houses everywhere. Kreisler plays Saturday Matinee, our posters are side by side.

The dear old ladies were adorable! The eighty-four year old was at the Duke of Wellington's funeral at St. Paul's [November 18, 1852]—aged four—taken to see the tomb, piled with flowers and flags and remembers it perfectly! She went recently with her sister to the unveiling of a Memorial Tablet to some friend, and said to her "Do you know when I was last here? to see Wellington's tomb after the funeral,"—and she hadn't been *since* and remembered where it was and guided her young sister of seventy to see it! We all roared with laughter! I feel Lauro is beside me there—he would be happy in our friendship.

To Harriet Marple
Pelerin Palace Hotel
S/Vevey

[February 2, 1932]
Glasgow

Croce can't do the preface—wrote Irene [di Robilant] a beautiful letter—definitely says no. Now I must try and see George Trevelyan—O, I *hope* he will do it! [Preface to *The Golden Book of Italian Poetry*, selected by Lauro de Bosis and published by Oxford University Press 1933]

[*From Edinburgh on February 9th, Ruth wrote a young nephew who was overstrained and disturbed in finding his direction:*] I've not been in your particular department of Hell, but I've seen others who have been, and I know another department very well, so it is easy for me to realize what it's like for, though the causes that send us to Hell and the conditions there vary, the effect of the atmosphere and the sensations we endure are very much the same. Of one thing we may be sure—we will know more about it all when we emerge than people who've never been—we'll know more about everything, and everybody; and the whole meaning of life, and all its values . . . so in a way, we can consider ourselves among the elect and hold our heads very high and reach out our hands to others who miss their footing, and get into blind alleys, or lose their way, or are scared by the dark, or to whom Fate sends a scorching pain or a shattering blow, or who never have been given the tools or the strength to build their lives. So we should be thankful, in a grim way, for being in Hell!

Don't be afraid that this will last—everything keeps moving and dawns keep dawning—and as long as we go on loving and working life is worth while. I wish you would go and see my beloved friend Ned Sheldon—he's perfectly delightful, and I always tell him it's just like talking to God, to talk to him. He's been blind for three and a half years, flat on his back for eight or nine years, and he's one of the most happy, sane, cheerful, wise, and good and understanding persons I know. He'd love to see you and it would give him pleasure to know you, so please go. Though you, alas, cannot have the inspiration of talking with him—I hope the thought of Lauro will give you a lift and bring a smile and a warm glow in your heart. He would have helped you most; if I can at all—it is his spirit working in mine. He had a genius of healing and of life, and of happiness in its deepest sense. He loved life in its entirety—even suffering he welcomed and endured gladly because he knew it was part of the whole.

Punch, *in its issue of February 24, 1932, said: "There has been no publicity, no interviews in the newspapers, no biographical details . . . not one poster . . . only a few small paragraphs in small type to say that Miss Ruth Draper will appear for one week at the King's Theatre, Hammersmith . . . this small whisper goes round the town like wild-fire, and all the town appears at the King's Theatre."*

To Harriet Marple
Paris

[February 24, 1932]
Manchester

This is an awful hole, but the audiences are splendid—nine shows a week and all packed! I go to Dublin next week, then Belfast, then Liverpool, Bristol and Birmingham—that takes me to April 3rd. I have no definite plans after that. It depends somewhat how I get on with Icaro—it goes rather slowly, and I may not be at all satisfied with what I have done and want to work over it. Do you think of going home? I don't know when or how I'll get the desire to go—? When does Aileen plan to go? Are you nicely fixed there? How is she? I dread returning to Paris in May, to be there at the time I was last year—I may not come over at all. Whatever I do will be hard—I know that—any change—any decision. I've got in the traces of this work now and it seems natural to go on. I see I am giving enormous pleasure and making enormous money—but it's three hours a day (six hours two days a week), the rest of the time I'm alone—writing mostly. I see a few people. To-morrow I'm going to the criminal courts and lunching with two old Chief Justices—that will be interesting. I shall go to the Picture Gallery and to see a babies hospital on Friday. I must have my hair washed. So the hours pass—there is little leisure——sleep is best. I was in Cambridge Sunday and I think Trevelyan will do the Anthology Preface; I'm still not quite certain and the relief when I know will be very great.

To Harriet Marple

[March 3, 1932]
Dublin

I can think of nothing but the Lindbergh baby—that poor mother (apparently about to have another baby too!). Isn't it too awful? I feel their anguish and the most wild indignation. How can anyone be so devilish as to steal a little sleeping child—and he had a cold—and is old enough to be frightened and lonely—poor lamb—O, I hope they'll give the money and not hunt the man till afterward—if they frighten him he's so likely to hurt the child—they must do whatever he asks. It makes one shudder.

Many agreeable people have turned up here—too many. I'm lunching with the Gogartys today. Francis Hackett is coming to see me tonight; I knew him in America so many years ago. Tom Monteagle came last night—he was in Dublin to buy a bull. He's living at Mount Trenchard now and has left the Foreign Office. He's such a dear person. I'm going to Hove Castle to-morrow—there they have Tristram's Sword! I never knew that Iseult lived between Dublin and Belfast and it was from here she sailed with him to go to King Mark in Cornwall! I'm taking a drive this afternoon with a cousin of Miss Somerville.

I've finished the literal translation of 'Icaro' and now the hard work begins. I'm terrified. It will be hard to make it at all consistent—parts can be left literal—parts must be considerably altered. There are many lines, purely beautiful and simple in Italian, virtually "unsayable" in English. It will be so difficult. Valéry has also refused to do the French preface because he recently asked a favour of Mussolini in regard to some young man in whom he was interested, and feels his lips are sealed where any political reference is involved. I don't know what to do now. I've written Edith Wharton to ask her advice. Trevelyan is inclined to accept to do the Preface for the Anthology—but say nothing yet. He wants to see it first—so that will delay matters again.

No news from Italy—tho' letters I sent went by hand of my dear little Reggie Temple who saw Vittorio. I hunger for word but I suppose they are afraid to write. My friend Helen Spicer gave me such a beautiful passage in Ecclesiastes to help me. "Weep bitterly and make great moan and use lamentation as he is worthy, and then comfort thyself for thy heaviness. For of heaviness cometh death, and the heaviness of the heart breaketh strength. Thou shalt not do him good but hurt thyself. Be comforted for him when his spirit is departed from him."

"He being made perfect in a short time fulfilled a long time. For his soul pleased the Lord; therefore hasted he to take him away from among the wicked." and many other lines—same old wisdom—I struggle to use it—to hold to it—but, oh, the waking in the nights—and the mornings——I keep on being very well—the time passes quickly and, amazing as it seems, my regular task, and the hours all filled, and writing in between accomplish that. The little Italian is very helpful—typing apparently all day. I don't know how I got on without a secretary before!

I don't know if I can bear to come to Paris this Spring—I don't know what to do—I dread stopping work—I dread any change—and going home beyond everything. Yet they all love me, and I them. Someday I must go.

To Malvina Hoffman

March 10 [1932]
Belfast

I would have written before—many times I've longed to, but you never gave an address—I am just guessing at this—Calcutta—but I never got from you or Gretchen an inkling of your dates or route!! I got your lovely letter from Peking, and it helped me to know you were thinking of me, helped me with what you said . . . then a little word I think from Bali—and several cards from Gretchen. Thank you so much! I follow you on your great journey in my thoughts and often wish I were with you. I considered going far away on a long journey—but in the end decided a return to my work was best. It seemed dreadful to take only my grief to the beauty and wonder of new scenes—and I knew just from trying to enjoy seeing things in Paris—what agony it was. The pain mixed with all beauty now—and the longing for his enthusiasm—his knowledge in looking at things was and is, all too intense, so I decided to come to England and work.

I began January 11th—and this route continues till April 4th. I'm not sure yet how long I'll go on. Any change or new decision is desperate. I dread terribly going home—yet suppose someday I must. I dread so seeing those I love and who love me. I long to keep my anguish secret, but I am so weak—always I've suffered from tears coming too easily—it's a curse. It is all so sacred—yet sometimes I feel that I have so much to give in making him known, his story is such an amazing example of courage and idealism and spiritual triumph that if I can I must pass it on to move and inspire those who are worthy to sense its significance.

I have had much comfort, joy really, in translating his "Icaro"—it is most beautiful. I've only done the literal translation, and am now working over the phrases and verses—very much more difficult. If I can do something fine—I shall have it published. It is uncanny in its prophetic similarity to Lauro's destiny, and rings with all his ardent idealism and gallantry. O Mallie—I long to talk to you—try as I may I cannot crush my wild regret that I did not marry him—long ago—this paying the price of one's weakness, and one's own qualities is so bitter—this awful business of growing up—so slowly—it's a curse. The loneliness and longing increases with time, and I fight like a demon with reason and all that I have of spiritual force—

to overcome the human need and hunger and regret. The poignant memories of four perfect Springs make this season a kind of agony—and I wonder if ever again I can see and feel beauty without a pang that makes me wince. O I know it's an old, old story, but somehow the circumstances of this experience involve the most cruel torture—for it's all mixed with such lofty beauty, and raises one so high—yet being human, it is so hard to climb. I long to go to his mother, but it seems it would not be wise—and really I think the emotional strain would be too much for both of us.

I wonder when you will be back? I hate the idea of being in Paris just at the time I was last year. I'm probably going over in early April for a week or ten days to see about some things and I'll find out from your maid if I can when you are expected. My work goes with frantic and ridiculous success. Theatres packed, wild applause and laughter, and money pouring in! The irony of it all is fantastic—and I can hardly wait for it to end each night, and rush back to my quiet room, and all the reality that is gone, yet which is more real than life itself. I found a fragment of Shelley's which might have been written for us—and which serves me like a prayer. It's so beautiful—I must tell it to you:

I am as a spirit who has dwelt
Within his heart of hearts, and I have felt
His feelings, and have thought his thoughts, and known
The inmost converse of his soul, the tone
Unheard but in the silence of his blood,
When all the pulses in their multitude
Image the trembling calm of summer seas.
I have unlocked the golden melodies
Of his deep soul, as with a master-key,
And loosened them and bathed myself therein—
Even as an eagle in a thunder-mist
Clothing his wings with lightning.

Shelley has helped me so—Lauro was much the same nature, and had the same feeling—and the poetry is full of the vital beauty that I found in him. Forgive me—I knew if I started writing to you I could not refrain from unburdening my heart. I've been alone so long. I have a nice little Italian secretary, but our relations are purely formal tho' friendly—but I see no one to whom I can talk since I left Aileen and Harriet in early January. In a way it's best to be alone. I see a few pleasant people as I go along—but no one who knows—at home there will be so many, and I dread it fearfully for that reason.

All are well at home—save Ned Carter one of Alice's twins—he's better, but it's been a great anxiety, and poor Alice has suffered terribly of course. The unemployment seems to have kept everyone working [to help]—like in war-time, and latterly the tragedy of the Lindbergh baby has set everyone wild with indignation and pity. It's too awful to believe and grows in horror as each day passes.

Well, dear friend—I must close this long letter, so full of myself. I hope your trip has continued as wonderful as it seemed when you wrote and that Sam is well and not got any thinner! My best love to you all—your strength and courage spur me on when I think of you for you've always been so brave and valiant thro' your many sorrows. But in a grim way, it helps me to think of others whom life is lashing now with cruel blows and I go back to women in the war; but I was not made of heroic fabric—and I feel so unequal to my task. If only my work meant to me what yours does to you. It meant so much more to him than it does to me—and I try to love it for his sake—but all these efforts are so vain—

On March 9th, from Belfast, Ruth Draper wrote her nephew Bill Carter in Geneva asking him to join her for his week of holiday after her work ended April 4th. She would go anywhere, do whatever appealed to him for this short time, and counseled him to get away, for a bit, from a difficult job situation: "but learning is a lonely game in the end. One must be patient with oneself, and as honest as one can be, and above all never sorry for oneself. Don't think and analyse too much—that's the family's inheritance and danger; the 'locality' of our origin has much to account for!" [New England] She enclosed a cheque "in case it comes in handy for rail road fare."

When Ruth Draper reached Bristol on March 15th to begin a week's engagement, word came from New York of the death on the 13th of her nephew Ned (Edward C. Carter, Jr.), twin brother of Bill Carter. She was devoted to these two nephews, who as children spent many holidays with her. As always, her love and her need to give and to help surged uppermost. She wrote to Bill: "now it is your turn—you stood by me in my darkest hour—now I long so to be near you, and this miserable duty binds me here and in desperate sorrow I must stay and not go to you! I wish you would come to me—at once; that is if you feel like it." She discussed alternative plans and enclosed a cheque "in case you need a little extra ready cash. I wanted to give you a holiday trip anyway so this is just part of it." She suggested that if he wished to bring along one of his friends she would be "delighted to have him too as my guest."

To Alice Draper
(Mrs. Edward C. Carter)

[March 17, 1932]
[Bristol]

Last night—in the middle of the Bazaar [sketch *Opening the Bazaar*]—tears suddenly flooded my eyes—with my face grinning in the 'part.' I thought I'd have to leave the stage. I'd caught sight of a happy boy's face in the second row. Ned loved my things so— I'll never forget him last winter in Boston [early December 1930]—he came so often with friends and I was so proud.

Bill Carter joined her in London on the 20th of March and they motored to Liverpool, stopping at Kidlington, Oxfordshire, over Sunday with Mr. and Mrs. Lionel Curtis. Contrary to her usual practice, Ruth Draper took Fred and the Rolls on this part of the tour so that the traveling would be pleasanter and she could take her nephew for drives and sightseeing between her shows. From Liverpool Bill Carter wrote his mother that he was helping Aunt Ruth with the translation of Icaro: "*with the wording and the cadences of the sentences.*" *This added to his understanding of the depth of her relationship with Lauro and, particularly, the very great meaning and importance of poetry in her life. She referred constantly to her Morocco-bound notebook filled with quotations that for one reason or another had touched, or comforted, or inspired her. Shelley now held particular significance because she found in his life and ideals, his sensitivity and poetry, a likeness to Lauro. Bill Carter added:* "*Few of us, I think, realize what Aunt Ruth has been going through this winter; but now I can see the power she has found in having conquered sorrow and in living in a fine poetic memory.*"

To Alice Draper
(Mrs. Edward C. Carter)

[March 25, 1932]
Good Friday
Chester

Such a strange mixture of sorrow—and joy—that Bill is with me—such deep comfort and satisfaction that I can so help you and Edward and him (and myself, for he is, as I have *always* found him and Ned, the most cozy, stimulating and delightful of companions). It comforts me greatly to know now what it is not to be alone in grief, but to have others who need your strength and spirit, so that one can't let one's sorrow engulf one. I have a few dear friends—but accepting and feeling sympathy and love is not so healing as giving it.

We lunched yesterday with the Bishop [of Liverpool] and his wife, whom I knew, and went over the wonderful new cathedral—it is extremely beautiful. Then I rested and sewed while Bill read aloud G. B. Shaw and Ellen Terry's *enchanting* letters. After my show [last night] we motored here—the most lovely old town—and as I have no show tonight we shall motor to Shrewsbury and to the Welsh mountains today. We'll return to Liverpool for my two shows tomorrow and leave after the evening show for Phyllis Brand's, arriving there about 1 a.m. She has no party, just the family. It's a delicious place, tennis and walks, and her three nice children, and Bob is such a dear. I'm sure Bill will enjoy it. Bill and I have been having breakfast each morning by the fire in my room—and cozy high tea in the evenings— and we've walked the dreary Liverpool streets, went to one movie and went to see the great docks and storehouses. He seems to have enjoyed my shows and watching the audiences. Dear Ally—I envy you—you are rich indeed . . . all my wealth is in my memories.

At Liverpool In a Church in Italy *closed each performance with its silent, highly charged finale of the Italian woman, eyes closed, kneeling at the foot- lights in prayer—Ruth Draper, as always, sensing how long the audience, in almost unbreathing participation, could hold the tension before she opened her hands in the gesture that signaled the slow lowering of the curtain. Dur- ing all this week it seemed as though the audiences were gripped, intuitively, by depths beyond the character on stage, and their riveted attention held to an almost unbearable length—and held until well after the curtain was fully down, as though they themselves could not loose the spell.*

To Harriet Marple

[March 29, 1932]
Queen's Hotel
Birmingham

I was working on Icaro till 4 a.m. this morning with the most wonderful Italian woman—a Professor here—whom I've known for some time, and whom I've been waiting eagerly to see—knowing she was *just* the perfect person to go over it with me when my literal translation was done. Of course, as luck would have it, she leaves this morning on ten days holiday but she was so interested and anxious to help me that, after three hours yes- terday afternoon, she came back to my hotel last night after my show and we worked from eleven to four!

Now it's all being typed again, and I hope I can show it to Professor Mur- ray on Sunday. It's terribly interesting—parts smooth and easy—parts fear- fully difficult—and English seems so inadequate at times. Of course with my literal and too exigent demands on my-self I feel I have sought more help than I should have done [to] call the translation "mine"—but she laughs and Bill too, and they say that *all* translators seek help and comparison and suggestions from natives and other authorities and that I'm entirely within my rights. And poetry of course is very different from prose, and dictionaries are *far* from complete or satisfactory.

I'm only pleased with it in spots but I shall work on it again of course.

To Alice Draper
(Mrs. Edward C. Carter)

April 1, 1932
Friday 6:40 p.m.
Birmingham

It may be too much for me to go back to Geneva [with Bill]—a place of memories that burn with a mixture of ecstasy and anguish—but I suppose I'll find those everywhere for a long time still and one must not be afraid of places.

How I go back, and over again and again my years with Lauro—my selfishness, my fears, and my blindness and stupidity this summer. I have suffered such self torture in tracing and searching for hidden, unconscious motives, etc. that I am convinced it does far more harm than good.

To Alice Draper
(Mrs. Edward C. Carter)

April 15, 1932
Paris

I shall be in London to meet you and may have a little house. Perhaps I'll come back to France with you. I've not decided yet whether to continue work in England or return to the Continent.

Paris is lovely now but terribly hard for me, for it's just a year since I was here with Lauro, and all the beautiful spring blossoms and greens bursting out—the lights and wonder of it all are like swords in my heart—but so it will be in every place and before all beauty that we enjoyed together. It's so strange to think that always now, pain must be born with every lovely memory.

Last Sunday I took Bill and Harriet and a sweet young friend of Bill's to Chartres. It is *the* most satisfying 'monument' I know. So tremendously real and one comes away smoothed out and deeply nourished.

I [have been] very busy getting a few clothes—such a bore, but necessary. I've had nothing new for a long time. In England I wore only my suit and sweaters for I never went anywhere but to the theatre every night. In that sense a perfect life—never having to change or *think* of clothes.

To Harriet Marple
Hôtel de l'Université
Paris

[c. April 26, 1932]
The Connaught Hotel
Carlos Place, London

Thanks for your nice letter. I am so happy that you had good weather and have seen such lovely places. I hope the company and the car and chauffeur were all up to standard. I had three lovely days at the Brands' and one won-derful ride—alas only one because they didn't take the horses out on Sunday—but we played tennis so I got nice exercise. The country and the place were a dream of beauty and the children so refreshing and sweet. I came up to town yesterday, dear Mrs. Leslie came to lunch and we had a good talk. I also saw Cecil Sprigge who brought me some wonderful notes on Lauro written by the friend with whom he grew up (with the idea of get-ting to-gether material for a serious article). They glow with his qualities, and how these must have radiated in his boyhood! Always he was searching, his friend says, for a philosophy based on "poetry, thought and action—fused." He describes coming into Lauro's laboratory (he took his degree with a brilliant thesis on chemistry) and finding him alone holding a test tube over a flame and chanting one of the choruses from Euripides. It was lovely to read—but the joy those glimpses and memories bring mean such bitter suffering and longing. I seem to feel no real strength inside and am still just drifting—getting through each day and waiting for the oblivion of sleep.

I have another charity affair this afternoon and go early to-morrow to stay till Friday with dear Miss Eliza [Wedgwood]. That will do me good. On Friday afternoon I go to Dartington Hall to see the Elmhirst School, and stay for Sunday there; I have another charity on Tuesday afternoon, and Alice arrives, I hope, Wednesday a.m. I've made no further plans and expect I'll come back with her and reach Paris the 15th and perhaps go on to Geneva. I go to tea with my old ladies this afternoon and must also run in to see Mrs. Phipps and family.

After one recital in Lausanne and four in Geneva, where she joined Bill Carter and his parents, Ruth Draper returned to Paris for a week at the Théâtre Daunou.

To William D. Carter

[June 10, 1932]
[Hôtel de l'Université]
Paris

Your mother and I had a grand day shopping on Tuesday—We just ram-paged thro' the "Trois Quartiers" and found presents for everybody and it was great fun. They loved this hotel. They dined with friends in the evening and came to fetch me at the Daunou. They found several agreeable sailing companions at the station, and I think will have a good trip for the weather is lovely.

I've had two good evenings at the theatre, a charity benefit to-day at the matinee; I doubt if I play into next week—the audiences are good, but it's not filled to overflowing—very little advertising, Lugné-Poe is over prudent—a bit too stingy—he thought it wasn't worth while to spend for such a short run. Harriet is here, Aileen away, Malvina and Aunt Helen return to-morrow. I have Chauncey McKeon's motor and feel very grand. I'm lunching to-day with the Rossellis—he made that exciting escape from Lipari two years ago.

Write me soon—I think of you so much and know well the strange mixture of thoughts that race through your mind and heart, that oppress you and excite you and puzzle you all in turn. Just recognize them all, as life—so it must be—so we must face and grasp all these moods and emotions and problems—quietly accepting it *all* knowing we are going to work out toward growth and assimilation and wisdom. We must be patient with ourselves, kindly—slightly humorous—trying always to look at things in the large, not concentrating too much on any one thing. It helps often when one gets in a jam of introspection and worry to make little outward gestures—give a penny to a child—take a rose to Mrs. Thudicum—I remember once, more than once, giving some grass to a sad looking horse waiting with a load—and it made me so happy and somehow simpler and freer inside!

I know you'll cling always to the thought of Ned's simplicity, his smile, and honesty, and plain goodness; just as I cling to all the rare things in Lauro that I *need* and haven't got in my own nature—just the memory is an unfailing source, and thank God the depth and significance of such memories live on in us. Don't forget to keep in touch with all the nice friends you have down there—the Schellings want you to come out there one day—give my love to Mrs. Sams and nice Bessie Griswold whom I was sorry not to see again. Look up A' Prato one day—he liked you very much—he has some mss. articles of Lauro which I want, sent registered post, and as he's rather dilatory you might try and get them! Dearest love old thing, write soon to "Auntie."

To Harriet Marple

[June 10, 1932]
Paris

Arthur [Rubinstein's] concert was wonderful and I've had lovely talks with him—he remains the vital, faithful friend that one can find again after years of silence and indifference. He grasped at once the significance and beauty of Lauro; and all that enthusiasm and energy of life that I always found in both of them did me good to feel again in him. His music was like a torrent of sparkling sound—healing and strong—divinely beautiful in the andantes and wildly alive in the Spanish things—God—how he plays them! Aileen went with me and I went to a party at Mme. Sert's afterward, and recited and it took me back to Edith Grove days and Paul's delight in Arthur's genius. The Manet exhibition is *too* beautiful—I went with Arthur yesterday.

The Italian refugee has arrived and is going to Léa's. She's a sweet gentle little thing and the boy a darling. He's gone to the school and I hope the plan is going to work. Léa is an angel from Heaven; her face is cured, an amazing thing—a Chinese cure—a needle inserted and the pain vanishes—most interesting—ask her about it.

I saw [———] at Arthur's concert—a queer sensation. I can't see her—not so much that I am hurt—but that I realize with her intense Fascist feeling and dis-approval of Lauro's act—that any mention of him would involve a most painful contact. So does politics really scar friendship and I think it's better not to talk. I had a little note (we only bowed across the hall) saying she wanted to see me to "explain" her silence—she "felt I had not understood". Her only reason of course was *fear*—there's nothing more to explain, and that leads to the attitude about it all—and naturally I cannot find anything but suffering in talking to someone against the thing Lauro gave his life for. It's the first time I've felt I simply cannot break thro' the barrier—or be generous; it costs me too much.

It's hard to pack and leave—if only I could get over my horror of stations and trains. I think I miss him more and more.

To Harriet Marple
Le Hohwald
Bas Rhine
France

[July 29, 1932]
Friday
The Connaught Hotel
London

I'm playing to 2,400 people every night and not making one penny! [Golder's Green Hippodrome] I shan't make the necessary amount unless I stay two weeks more—so I'm at the King's Theatre, Hammersmith next week, and at Wimbledon the week after! That takes me thro' the 13th then, as I gather Martha [Draper] does not want to come to England, I'll go across to Paris again and see her a few days, and then sail about the 20th.

Arthur and Nela, his 23 year old bride, were married on Wednesday at a Registry Office, and had a lovely reception later at Lady Cholmondeley's. I saw a lot of them the days before and shopped and helped her pack, and was quite helpful! She is a sweet little thing, frail and flowerlike, very young (tho' already divorced), and loveable. We had wonderful music two nights running, before—at an old friend's studio—and it took me back to Edith Grove days. Arthur has never been so nice, it's brought out all his sweetness and I really think the chances are—at least—even! He's very serious, and really seems to want marriage and children. I was so happy to be there—only the

Ambassador—the girl's brother, two other old friends and I were present at the ceremony—which is, by the way, very nice—so swift and simple. I winced when I thought that Lauro and I might have done it—yet with his need of hiding last summer of course it is foolish to think of it.

You will be glad to hear I know, that the Oxford Press has accepted 'Icaro'. I am terribly proud and happy about it. They like it very much and will make a beautiful book, I think. It will not be published before next March—as the autumn lists are closed, and it would be rushed to get it out this Fall. The Anthology will be ready in October and it's better to have them separated by a few months, they say. I feel such a sense of relief and such deep thankfulness. I'm going to Mrs. Thompson's for Sunday and Bank Holiday. Germaine Tailleferre and her new husband are coming to supper and going to the theatre with me. She has a baby and has written a symphony and seems very happy!

Late in August Ruth Draper sailed at last for home—after seventeen emotion-packed months in England and Europe. Still she could not bring herself to meet family and friends in New York, but sailed to Canada, arriving in Islesboro on September 3rd to spend several weeks alone, and not reaching New York until early October. All through these five years of fire and turmoil, terror and tragedy, she had been almost continually on stage and before the public.

To Harriet Marple
in New York

September 4 [1932]
Dark Harbor

I wonder if this will catch you before you sail? I arrived yesterday afternoon about four and it's just too good to be true. Wilbur and old Mrs. Fairfield here to meet me and we all wept a little, one of the many Mrs. Hatchs to look after me. The Inn closed—only a few people here—and so far no one has disturbed my peace! The weather is perfect and the place looking lovely. I'm in the little house and it's very cosy and comfortable. I'm lying on a chaise-longue—gazing at the blue bay and the hills and the green firs. No sound but an occasional chip-munk springing thro' the branches and a little soft breeze in the birch trees. It's heaven—and I live over those two perfect days with Lauro—that crown the memories of 35 years [at Dark Harbor]. I see Paul and myself sailing in our little boat—and my last sail—with Lauro—in that same lovely bay. Now and then a sail passes between the trees—as I write. One cannot but be strangely moved, and humbled and strengthened all at once by the sublime and tranquil sameness in nature—that remains fixed in the background of our mutability. Nature everywhere of course has this quality and is healing—but I am thankful that there is this place that in its beauty holds an added value because of its intimate association with all these past years. I can't tell you what it means to look at it all now, and breathe this heavenly sweet air, and feel this familiar peace pouring over me—and it's wonderful to be alone—quite alone, with him. I realized last night, in the intense silence of the starry night, as I closed the doors and put out the lights, that I was not lonely in one sense—nor ever shall be again. If one can, even at moments, dis-associate oneself from the idea of physical loneliness, one tastes for a while the communion of the spirit. I say all this and feel and believe it—yet the pain stabs through me, in the midst of my thankfulness for all the beauty I have had.

Wilbur has come for the letters and I must close. It's best not to write more—I must not let sadness mar the lovely smiling beauty of this day, so like him—and what he would have me rejoice in.

To Mrs. Douglas Robinson

[c. December 27, 1932]
66 East 79th St.
New York

Dearest Mrs. Robinson—

Thanks so much for sending me the copy of your collected poems—I am so glad to have it and thank you for your loving message. I shall never forget that Sunday morning with you and Corinne at Avon—and how I felt your warm sympathy, and appreciation of what I had known, and what Lauro was—as his spirit was revealed in his poem. Thank you for your understanding of my grief—and of my pride . . . and my lost joy. Your verses help me and I'm glad he knew them too.

If you are by chance near here any time to-morrow afternoon it would be lovely if you would drop in—I leave my flat on Thursday; it looks so pretty, and is full of such memories that it is almost sacred—yet it's hard to be here——I don't know whether I'm glad or sorry to go. My dear love and gratitude to you always.

All her life Ruth Draper had close and devoted men friends—many suitors—and, over the years, a vast and varied host of admirers. But she had seemed unable to reconcile with reality her highly romantic, highly emotional, super-sensitive nature, demanding so greatly of herself and of one she could love. Was she a little afraid of marriage—of her ability to meet its demands—of its fulfillment to reach her ideal—and her dream? Her complex nature, as discernible in her letters, leads one to believe it was so.

The spark that flamed with Lauro was not to flame again, though it burned forever in her memory. From Paris, in March, while planning his flight, Lauro had written her:

After the chase, then dies the spark. . . . You are the only woman I have ever heard of that even after years can keep that divine sense that the others so quickly smother. You do even a greater miracle, you combine the loveliness of the two states which by their nature seem to be absolutely opposite. You give trust without habit—the charms of Peace and those of War without the disadvantage of either—the charm of the hunt and that of the prey without the inconvenience of either. I am amazed beyond description when I think that I feel exactly the sense I had in the Garden of Boboli or that evening in the Poderino. . . . This is supernatural. Nobody would believe it—I have nothing to do with it—I just stand and look in amazement. Swinburne says 'Our loves become corpses or wives.' He had not known you. You are a Paradox.

Enriching and ennobling her life, this love remained her unfailing beacon—lost—unattainable—untarnished—forever cherished.

1933 –1938

As long as we go on loving and
working life is worth while.

Ruth Draper
February 1932

To Alice Draper
(Mrs. Edward C. Carter)

[January 13, 1933]
The Connaught Hotel
London

I had a lovely long talk with Bill on the telephone. The Geneva wire is miraculous—one gets the number in half a minute and hears the voice as if it were in the next room! I was in the tiny suite at the 'Vendôme', beside a fire, with Aileen—Bill was beside his fire with his friend—and it felt so cosy, so safe and happy and we both enjoyed our talk greatly. I was sorry not to go to Geneva and have a little holiday perhaps with him in the mountains, but my work begins on Monday next in Liverpool and there was no time. I shall work for six weeks, and then probably plan some nice trip to Egypt or Morocco. I hope to make enough to pay my taxes on last summer, and my taxes on this tour, and save enough to live on and take a trip and come home with! The journey over was terrific for four days, like a summer sea for the first two. I can never thank you enough for getting me off so beautifully. Nothing was forgotten, and I found everything and had no trouble at the customs.

I came to Paris on Sunday for four days, and accomplished a lot I must say. I saw seventeen friends—of such variety that it makes me smile to think of them—and I saw them most satisfactorily too, plenty of time for good talks!

I dined with Mrs. [Winthrop] Chanler one night and I had a wonderful visit with [Jean-Julien] Lemordant, Mallie's blind friend—he is amazing—a Spartan hero of old and one feels like kneeling at his feet. It is a great experience to talk with him.

Paris was fascinating. I had a satisfactory time with Mr. [Ferdinand] Herold who has translated 'Icaro' into French and I saw the publisher and made all arrangements, and think it will be nice.

Tomorrow I turn over my work to the Oxford Press and I hate to see it go—and not fuss over it any more. It has been my salvation this year and a real joy and I am thankful beyond words that I had the courage and the presumption to undertake it.

I've seen all the old friends here and my beloved old ladies—the Miss Mudies.

To Harriet Marple

February 23 [1933]
Manor Field
Grantchester
Cambridge

I'm here—for my last week of work for the present—at Louis de Glehn's, and it's lovely and quiet—out of the town. I go to the Trevelyans' on Friday for the week-end—and there are many pleasant people to see here. I go to Paris Tuesday [February 28] and hope to go to Geneva at once, for I must see Romain Rolland about a few things I hope he will change in the Preface. It has just come and is perfectly beautiful—almost too beautiful—but a few things I don't like. It is almost more than I can bear, this asking these big writers to change things but somehow love gives me courage, and so far I've not been too tactless in my approach and do not feel that I've annoyed them. Anyway we're all on the pleasantest terms and I must say Mr. Trevelyan and Mr. Murray were very patient and tolerant—certainly my efforts with the former were worth while, and I hope Murray will fix certain things I don't like; and now to approach R.R. which is the most difficult—for he is the most sensitive, I guess—and it must all be done in French! He's said a few things that might offend the family, and anger too much the Government. I'm suddenly terrified at the risk I'm taking anyway—and torn in my decision to tell Elena [Vivante] or not—she is coming March 6th to Paris. In one way I know she'll be glad and understand—in another she may hesitate—and I'd be crushed if all I've done had to be held up now! This all brings out the awful force and fear that the Fascist Government has created and angers one to the very soul—that even across the border one can hesitate to speak or act for fear of its repercussion and effect. I long for a very wise person to sustain me in my decision—how often in life one longs for an all-wise person to throw oneself on in dark places.

I have been terribly grieved to learn of Corinne's mother's death—pneumonia—it is a terrible loss to so many people, and such a vital part of Corinne's life—they were very close. She was a remarkable woman—and her faults seemed a sort of overflow of her virtues. Her heart, her intelligence were so warm and alert and her sympathy and enthusiasm a torrent on which others lived and drew strength and inspiration. I shall miss her—we had a heavenly morning in Avon this autumn—she and Corinne and I in C's sunny sitting room—reading Icaro aloud—and she was deeply moved, and so understanding. I think of you waiting and watching beside your mother and life seems so cruel and such an end so inexplicable and so stupid. How can people believe in a merciful God? It seems to me so insulting and ironical to hold to that illusion, so much more honest and brave to face facts and just hold to beauty and goodness and all the abstract virtues which outsoar the hell into which we plunge from time to time, and which co-exist with the sorrows that are in evidence everywhere.

Gosh, what a world to-day—these wars, breaking and brewing. Such war talk in the air now—with Italy and France and the Balkans and Poles and Germans, not to speak of the East—it's never been more evident and terrifying. The poor old League not brave enough or quick enough to take action—no nation big enough and sure enough to stop loaning money and supplying arms to others who plan to fight. Well—we go on in our little orbits and only our minds and hearts are troubled and we seem so helpless. Millions are cold and hungry and spending days just waiting for the night and nights just waiting for the day.

Must get up—my hands are like ice—it's very cold—even in bed—tho' I have a fire and the sun is pouring in my window. Some old horses, all shaggy, and so gentle and happy are in the meadow and silly chickens— perfectly happy—pecking the grass—they help to teach us the great lesson and somehow lighten the load—bless them. So long—I hope you are well and still able to meet the long strain.

To Corinne Robinson
(Mrs. Joseph W. Alsop)

[April 30, 1933]
Eydon Hall
Eydon
Rugby

Returned from Paris two days ago and am here with Phyllis and Bob [Brand] and the children. To-morrow I move to a little house I've taken in London, 24 Carlyle Square S.W.3, for May. I have four weeks of work planned and as I've had two months of costly idleness it will be pleasant to see the gold pouring in again!

The book has now got to the stage of second proof and, as the first was nearly perfect, I think it will go forward rapidly now. The French edition too is nearly ready, and with Romain Rolland's Preface and the "Histoire de ma Mort" published with the " Icaro" will be a most interesting volume. I am only sorry now I did not have a prose translation of "Icaro"—the poetic translation tho' fine in parts, departs too much from the original in the Choruses. But it's too late now.

I think I wrote you from my lovely flat in Paris—it broke my heart to leave—it was so enchanting. How I wish that you might have seen it. It was a rare chance to be able to live that way in Paris even for three weeks. My little house in London will be nice, but like a pill-box after the great panelled rooms of the Rue du Bac. I wish you'd run over. How I'd welcome you!

All that you say of holding to your memories goes to my heart—how I understand. The significance of my loss grows, it seems to me, as I grow in realization, which is normal as one grows older if one continues to think and feel and observe etc. I miss him at every turn, and in these tragic days, for over here one feels intensely the German debacle, the retrogression, the triumph of 'anti-Christ' one might almost say. [Reichstag fire, February 27, 1933. Hitler and the Nazi Party were now effectively in control of Germany.] Last night a man who is staying here played divinely to us—Bach and Schumann—on and on—as I sat by the fire—all the noble and exalted beauty that they—Germans—have given to the world—and I shuddered to think of the contrast to the man they have set up as their God. The youth are all aflame with desire to fight, revenge and hate fill their hearts. Cruelty and brutality and lust for power are unleashed again. And I thought of my love—flying toward the stars—dying for his ideal—with his faith in life, in the universal, in aspiration—and the struggle and sacrifice that growth involves; one's thoughts get so tangled—one sees such triumph of materialism, such insoluble problems and blocks to spiritual enlightenment; then I think of him and I know he would still believe, still see beauty and be undismayed. I must go out and walk in the lovely Spring—blossoms, lambs and flowers everywhere—paradise save for the longing which makes it almost hell—

My dearest love to you. I'm so happy about the baby—do you feel older, with a grandson?

To Corinne Robinson
(Mrs. Joseph W. Alsop)

May 18 [1933]
24 Carlyle Square
Chelsea, London

I sent you to-day a copy of "Europe", one of the rather new and important "revues" of Paris. R. Rolland's Preface to "Icaro", the French adaptation of Lauro's play, is in it, also the original version of Lauro's last document. The force and simplicity of Lauro's style is an interesting contrast to the flowery delicacy of Rolland's article—but he has done it with fine sincerity and in a lofty tone, I think, and on the whole I am deeply satisfied and grateful as you can conceive. I will of course bring you a copy of the book when it appears—in a month's time I should say. My "Icaro" is to be published in the Fall [October 1933]. It is by far the best time to issue books—and get the Xmas trade. I'm impatient and to have to wait is hard, but it is going on well, and I think will be lovely.

I came over April 28—gave two big charity shows at Brighton and Northampton that week, and from May 1–7th gave nine for London charities taking in £ 4260. Since then I've been on my own—filling great theatres nightly—3,500 people last week [at] every show, 2,800 this week at Golder's Green, and next week at Hammersmith all seats are already sold! It is all quite ridiculous but there it is—

London is lovely—the parks a dream—and I have a darling house. *How* I wish you were in my spare room. I've not taken my passage yet but I expect to go to Islesboro by the end of June. I love it here, tho' it will never be the same, never free from memories that shoot thro' me like spears—that lovely June to-gether here—so clouded with fear—premonition and anxiety every day—and so mixed with joy. I think of Lauro and feel that in spite of the futility of making *such* a gesture before *such* a world—he would still have believed it more than ever justified.

My days are free—no parties—but many friends and work and time passes swiftly.

In May 1933 John Jay Chapman, an old family friend, wrote from London to one of his sons: "Lunched with Ruth Draper, where also the Spicers. Ruth is perfectly enchanting—handsome, gay, vigorous, beaming. Well, I wish you could see her. She is a perfected soul."

The façade, at least, had been repaired.

But she lived out the tragedy of Lauro's death—it would be with her always. A faded photograph—increasingly faded—she kept on her theatre dressing-table; in it he stood, a slight figure beside a small slight plane. No one backstage asked her about it—one did not invade Ruth Draper's privacy.

To Harriet Marple

[October 4, 1933]
22 Worthington Road
Longwood, Mass.

Islesboro was divine that last day—it nearly killed me to come away. I never longed so to stay anywhere—and kept to my decision to go! I longed for solitude and all that beauty for that two days particularly—but I do not think it right to indulge in morbid sentiment of anniversaries—it would be so against his feelings. I enjoyed the two evenings alone. I'm never lonely now—when most alone I can turn most completely to him—yet I realize it is a dangerous privilege and indulgence—for reading his letters, coming too close to memories still rips me up with pain—and it is best just to go on with life, thinking of him a little all the time, happily as he would have, mingling his spirit in all I do—but not letting myself look back too much.

In the Fall of this year Ruth Draper proposed to Harvard College the establishment of a chair in honor of Lauro de Bosis. Beginning in February 1934, her nominee, Professor Gaetano Salvemini, was appointed to "The Lauro de Bosis Lectureship in the History of Italian Civilization." This involved, in 1934, six public lectures, and a Seminar for students on the History of the Italian Risorgimento, thus providing an opportunity to set forth the historical origins and backgrounds of those liberal institutions in Italy that were abolished by the Fascist regime. It was made known indirectly that Mussolini was not pleased.

Ruth provided the honorarium for this annual Lectureship and in May 1939 a permanent endowment for its continuance. Salvemini occupied the post until his retirement in 1948, when he was appointed Lecturer Emeritus and held the post until 1955. Since then other noted scholars have lectured on various aspects of Italian Civilization.

In about 1949 the University of Florence reappointed Salvemini to the Chair he had resigned in 1925 in protest against Fascist control. When he returned, twenty-three years later, the only announcement was a notice on the University bulletin board which read: "Professor Salvemini's classes will resume on [such and such a date] at [x] o'clock."

To Professor John Erskine
Columbia University
New York

> October 30, 1933
> 66 East 79th Street
> New York

I have just asked Oxford Press to send you a copy of my translation of Lauro de Bosis' play, "Icaro". I hope some day you will find the time to read it, for I know you were fond of him, and I hope you will find my translation of his beautiful play worthy and satisfying.

My heart is very heavy these days, as I am spending most of my time with our dear friends Zosia and Paul. Paul is gravely ill. If it would be any satisfaction to you to talk with me, you can reach me by 'phone—Rhinelander 4-1562—or at their apartment, where I spend most of my time—Rhinelander 4-7760, and we could make an appointment to meet.

I know Zosia wants to talk to you herself, but she is naturally terribly preoccupied and in a really nervous state, and has not yet been able to call you.

I think everything is being done, but I feel you should know that his condition is very serious.

I am asking my secretary to sign this, as I cannot wait for it to be written.

Paul Kochanski had collapsed immediately following his concert in Pittsburgh, Pennsylvania, on October 20th, and remained gravely ill with an abdominal ailment. John Erskine was President of the Juilliard School of Music, where Kochanski headed the violin faculty.

Kochanski had made his debut in London when he was 19, and with the New York Symphony Orchestra in 1921. Its Director, Walter Damrosch, was greatly struck with the dignity, power, and beauty of his playing—"a kind of flame that burned within him."

He was to die on January 12th, aged 45. Fifteen hundred people attended non-religious services held at the Juilliard School. John Erskine gave the Eulogy and Félix Salmond, Ernest Hutchison, and Albert Spaulding partici-pated. Among the pallbearers were Toscanini, Frank and Walter Damrosch, Heifetz, Horowitz, Kreisler, Koussevitsky, Stokowski, Zimbalist. He left no Will and an estate of only $20,000.

To Dorothea Draper
(Mrs. Linzee Blagden)

[November 27, 1933]
En route to Dunquerque

I never meant to come to Paris! But Saturday night decided to come, on receiving a wire from Mallie that Elsie Hooper was very ill, and she wished I was there, and a letter from Claude Aveline (who published 'Icaro') saying he had many wonderful letters and articles about the book, and wanted very much to have me see them. So I hopped on the 11 P.M. train and got to Paris at 10 yesterday. I stayed the night with Marie Curtis and accomplished a great deal. I saw Luigia Nitti, an Italian friend—and Isabella Mallet, a French one; sat an hour or more with Elsie, went to Mallie's Trocadero show and to tea with her and Lord and Lady Reading. Aveline came to dine and we read and talked late. To-day I breakfasted with Léa, and saw Dr. Bardi, and went to see Nela Rubinstein and the baby—Arthur is in Spain—the *loveliest* baby I ever saw! Nela is a darling and I love her. I wanted her to know all I could tell about Paul for her to tell Arthur on his return in a few days. I lunched with Mallie, had a lovely talk, and went to the Bank, ordered some slippers and got some tennis shoes, gloves and stockings and had two hats fixed—went to see that Brentano's and Smith were carrying 'Icaro,' sat an hour and a half with Elsie both this morning and afternoon, bought flowers and writing paper; Léa came and she and Marie took me to the train—also telephoned Lugné! Such a full two days and I'm so glad I went. Elsie has had pneumonia and nearly died. She is going to get well, and is much better, and loved my coming—so I am thankful I went. She's a grand old thing. Mallie was on the job, and grand of course. She's done a beautiful head of Reading. Her show [of the original models for *The Races of Mankind*] has been a huge success but I like the big sizes in Chicago better. Paris was lovely and I hated to come away. So many other friends I wanted to look up.

I've got three busy days in London ahead of me—getting two *lovely* dresses, permanent wave—engagements daily for lunch, tea, and dinner—Friday and Saturday were busy, seeing friends and arranging tickets, money, getting orders etc. I haven't had time to feel lonely yet. Lunching with Phyllis, teaing with Dorothy Macnamara, and a dinner for me at Mrs. Thompson's tomorrow. Shall see Nancy and Irene one day and am getting letters for South Africa. The Clarendons have asked me for Xmas at Pretoria.

The voyage over was pleasant and easy and the Purser invited me to take all my meals in the First Class! I felt slightly ashamed but accepted and had caviar every night—the best caviar.

Forgive this boring chatter—the journey is long to Dunkirk, yet I can't sleep. Much love, me own, I hated to leave you all. I think of you so much and love you and bless you and hope you'll keep well and have a good winter.

To Alice Draper
(Mrs. Edward C. Carter)

[November 27, 1933]
To Dunkerque from Paris

You . . . helped me by your reassurance that I have not failed since I lost actual contact with Lauro's inspiring and ardent presence. Only at moments do I feel it burning within me—fleeting moments, but they renew my faith.

Those last hours in New York ripped me to pieces—leaving you more than the others—and saying good-bye to Paul and Zosia going through their particular hell of sickness and fear of doom. I hope the doctors may be wrong—but if he can never be really well and play again— I would beg for death.

Edith Wharton wrote to thank Ruth for a copy of the French edition of Icaro—*though she much preferred Ruth's own English translation. She said that "B.B." (Berenson), whom she had seen that Autumn, sent thanks for his copy, but thought it unwise to write himself. The Fascist police later confiscated it.*

On December 1, 1933, Ruth Draper sailed from Southampton for South Africa, beginning a series of overseas tours.

Three years earlier she had begun to record her "strange wandering life" on a large (9½ × 4 foot) decorative map of the world designed and painted by Stanley J. Rowland. It hung on the long wall of her living room and was increasingly high-lighted by gold stars identifying each place she visited, in most of which she had performed. This map now fills one wall of a special reading room for children of members of the New York Society Library.

There was a catharsis in travel, for every new country, new city, new landscape, all new faces and characteristics, new voices and speech held her concentrated, absorbing attention. Always, through her eyes and ears, her emotional sensibility, these new experiences entered the very fabric of her being. But equally effective in distracting her thoughts was the necessity for living in the moment, concentrating on her schedule, her work, the business of her tour.

Anne Lindbergh has written: "It isn't for the moment you are struck that you need courage, but for the long uphill climb back to sanity and faith and security."

(Introduction to Locked Rooms and Open Doors)

ITINERARY

1933

Fri.	Dec.	1	Sailed from Southampton
Mon.	Dec.	18	Arr. CAPETOWN, SOUTH AFRICA
		18–19	R.R. to Johannesburg, Transvaal
Wed.	Dec.	20	Arr. JOHANNESBURG
	Jan.	6	*2 weeks Performances* Empire Theatre
			Christmas in Pretoria with the Governor General, Lord Clarendon and Lady Clarendon

1934

Mon.	Jan.	8–13	PRETORIA
			1 week Performances Opera House
Mon.	Jan.	15–17	PIETER MARITZBURG
			Performances Grand Theatre
Thurs.	Jan.	18–22	DURBAN
			1 week Performances
Tues.	Jan.	23–24	EAST LONDON (with Lady Crewe)
			3 Performances
Thurs.	Jan.	25–27	PORT ELIZABETH
			3 Performances
Mon.	Jan.	28–Feb. 8	CAPETOWN (with Lord and Lady Clarendon)
			2 weeks Performances Opera House

Thurs.	Feb.	8	Fly to BULAWAYO, S. RHODESIA (with Jessie Cooper—sightseeing)
			1 Performance
Thurs.	Feb.	15	Fly to SALISBURY
			3 Performances
Thurs.	Feb.	22	Fly from Salisbury (via Imperial Airways)
	Feb.	22–23	Overnight at BROKEN HILL, S. RHODESIA
Fri.	Feb.	23	Arr. NAIROBI, KENYA
			1 Performance
Sat.	Feb.	24	Fly from Nairobi
	Feb.	24–25	Overnight at JUBA, E. SUDAN
Sun.	Feb.	25	Arr. KHARTOUM, E. SUDAN
Tues.	Feb.	27	Fly from Khartoum (delayed by weather)
Tues.	Feb.	27	Arr. WADI HALFA

Ruth Draper's theatrical luggage was strictly functional. In New York and in London she kept brown velvet backdrops, but on the road often made do with whatever was available. With her she carried a soft hat box, sometimes a square Vuitton hat box for the extraordinary hat of Opening a Bazaar, *and two large suitcases (a third case if carrying the costume for the* Court of Philip IV.) *These held her shawls, coats, jackets, semi-costumes, and few props. Always she carried her "kitchen": a 12" × 10" × 6" alligator-patterned, zippered case which held a folding cooking kit for Sterno, one using Meta fuel, small electric hot-plate, china plate with cup and saucer, asbestos mat, utensils, tea, coffee, sugar, salt, and pepper. This equipment came into service in hotel rooms, train compartments, berths, or for "clandestine cooking in the women's wash-room." Her letters tell of its constant use. She was prepared for all contingencies—even needle and thread for a fellow passenger's button. On long tours there usually were, in addition, a brief case, typewriter, and often a book box. Her personal luggage, through long experience, was compact and exactly suited to her needs.*

On this trip she had a total of eleven pieces of luggage.

To Dorothea Draper
(Mrs. Linzee Blagden)

December 19 [1933]
En route to Johannesburg

The train is swaying and bumping along, and writing is almost impossible, but I am anxious to get some letters off by the air mail, which closes in Jo'burg to-night. I only arrive at 4:30 and have to go to a tea party given by the American consul! So I shan't have time to write quietly on arrival. I dread the stupid social things that I shall have to be nice about. To-morrow is a luncheon of "The Press" and I have a letter from a friend of Alice's—the Johannesburg branch of the League of Women Voters if you please— (Why?) who want to give me a tea—and an old clergyman cousin of Beatrice Herford who played with her as a child (she must by this time be seventy) and therefore thinks he'd like to entertain me—isn't it awful. I'll choke him off, but suppose I must accept clubs and things.

The journey from Madeira on was lovely calm blue sunny seas—mild and lovely—two days before we arrived very rough. Cape Town *sweltering* hot! Dear old Mrs. Lindley and her daughter met me. She made me think so of mother. She's 80—bright and so charming and sympathetic. She's lived there for thirty-six years. The train left almost at once after landing so I saw nothing, but the entrance to the harbor is superb—great mountains rising out of the sea—jagged and rocky.

The railroad journey was frightful all yesterday and last night, but it got lovely and cool this morning, and the air is now like wine, 4,000 feet high—just like Arizona or New Mexico—barren, desolate, flat—what they call the 'High Veldt'—here and there a little Dutch settlement, a few thin cows or sheep, and little mounds of earth, where a group of men are sifting for diamonds. We passed Kimberley at nine—and it's all diamond country until ten o'clock. What they call alluvial diamonds—just scattered loosely near the surface. I suppose the mines are not to be seen. We've been coming steadily thro' [Boer] War country, as it follows the line of the R.R. more or less—and I can't get over the horror of fighting in the utter desolation of the country—it's ghastly—just one's idea of hell—mountainous for a while back of Cape Town—no green—exposed to glaring sun—rocks, flint, sand, sage brush and tracks for roads. I've been reading 'Commands,' a remarkable book on the War and it makes all so vivid. It does not make one love the English. I read two absorbing lives of Rhodes on the ship. One feels very far away—yet it seems very like Western U.S.—I don't believe I'll like it at all—but if my work goes well, that's all I ask. It will be pleasant going to Government House and I met some nice people on the ship and I have some letters, and I know people will be kind. I rather dread the heat when I go to the sea again at Durban and Cape Town. Jo'burg is 6,000 feet high, so the air is grand.

I hope you'll send me a cable about Paul—I think of them all the time and worry, and wonder if the doctors say what it is, and if they have decent nurses at last, and are getting into a more ordered regime of life. I hope George [Draper] goes in sometimes.

I read of the bitter cold at home, and think of the poor people and shiver, tho' here it's so hot. One doesn't get much from the papers about the financial situation but it still looks bad—I know how busy you are and how hard it is to write, but I hope you will just the same—for I shall be longing for news.

To Dorothea Draper
(Mrs. Linzee Blagden)

January 1, 1934 [Monday]
Carlton Hotel
Johannesburg, S. A.

Just a word, as I've so many letters to write to catch the post this week. It's costly but so worth while sending by air and they have to go off every Wednesday. It's so exciting getting a huge packet from B[rown] S[hipley] and Company each Saturday—nine days from England. They have to go from Paris to Brindisi by train, as Mussolini allows no foreign air planes to fly over Italy at all! I hope for a letter from you this week end. Ba and Ally wrote last and I long for more detailed news of Paul and the state of affairs there. I was most grateful for the nice long cable, and can imagine, from what you said, that the strain of uncertainty continues.

I have no news! You don't really want to hear about gold mines, kaffirs, race problems, politics, diamonds, flowers, sunshine, ugly houses, kind people, stupid people, gardens, luncheons, teas, the Zoo, animals, the heat, tennis, bathing pools, my hotel room and lonely evening meals on my paper-strewn bed—writing, reading, resting between shows.

People pour into the theatre, money pours into my purse; here is a hundred dollars, please use it for sweaters for the cold people at home. I shudder to think of the suffering and the windy streets and people seeking work.

What a mess everything is—it's so awful to think it will never be straightened out. Here politics is crooked and stupid, and laws unjust—and the suffering of the blacks, the degeneracy of the 'poor whites', and the general race confusion is rampant and insoluble! The sun shines and flowers bloom but culture and beauty is nil. The city is built on gold—purer than the hearts that dig it.

To Martha Draper

January 19 [1934]
Durban

This picture will amuse you, you might save it along with other clippings if you have them. In each town it's the same old thing—well-written reviews of lavish praise. Pretoria was a very intelligent friendly audience, and last night too. The truth is, these people get so little it's pathetic—and many have heard me in London, and others have been hoping for years I might come. My room is full of flowers from people I don't know, but the flowers are a great help. I feel I owe a debt of undying gratitude to pink! What I would do without pink in my lonely wanderings I can't imagine! The minute I arrive in a hotel, I whisk out my pink and lace bedspread—my pink soft shawl, and little pillow—arrange flowers, get out my pictures and books, and in two minutes I'm in my own room in my own world, even if the windows happen to be opening onto the Indian Ocean. My bed is littered with letters from people I love—the air mail brings me a fat packet each Saturday and I shall be writing all day to catch the air mail of tomorrow morning.

It's a lovely sunny day, the surf is roaring, and a warm wind blowing thro' my room and I'm sitting up in a little yellow flowered chiffon 'peignoir,' with heavenly roses, larkspur, lilies, a plant of blue hydrangea near me, the sea sparkling outside—a bunch of lichees near, delicious fruit they are. I'll go in swimming soon. I know several people here who are pleasant and kind. This is a very dull letter, but I have no news—here a week then three days at Maritzburg—three East London—three Port Elizabeth—long journeys between.

To Corinne Robinson
(Mrs. Joseph W. Alsop)

January 27 [1934]
On the Train

My heart is sad thinking of my darling Zosia in her overwhelming grief—after those ten weeks of strain, watching Paul go. I loved him dearly—and he gave me something I got from no one else, apart from the divine beauty of his music, as I had the privilege to know it for the past twenty years! Knowing her as I do— I can conceive her helplessness—her super-sensitivity, and my heart aches. I wish of course that I were at home but I know friends abound and she must find out her way alone—in the last analysis no one helps very much—but the person we've lost, and what they found in one, and made of one, and believed in. And the tragic thing is one finds one is not what they thought.

I've been reading books on this country learning all I can, and it's very interesting. I've met a few really delightful people—very few—and mostly old—they are by far the most interesting, those who remember the early days, and have seen the growth and the wars and the struggle, and the problems solved or increased! The native problems are of absorbing interest, the effects of Christianity and Civilization on the various tribes, is in many ways disastrous—yet having come—one must give them the best we have—alas—one hangs one's head in shame. In their native state they have such dignity—nobility—uncompromising loyalty to their standards and codes and customs, which shame our hypocrisy and lawlessness. *They* have no asylums, prisons, or prostitutes! The great Zulu tribe of fiercest warriors are now servants (those who have left their "kralls"), the gentlest sweetest creatures, whom everyone loves.

I'm going to stay with Lord and Lady Clarendon (Governor General) this week, and then with the [———], they are dears—but I hear are terrific "Oxford Groupers" and I dread that and hope I don't have to talk about it, for it's a kind of bête noir to me—Buchmanism. You know I seem to dislike religion more and more, but one shouldn't hate anything, I suppose, that helps people to be good.

My present plan is to leave Cape Town on February 12th. I'll fly from there to Bulawayo and see the Victoria Falls, Rhodes' Tomb, and strange Bushmen caves and native territory. Then to Salisbury from where I fly for three days to Wadi-Halfa, the second Cataract, where Irene will join me! I forget if you've been to Egypt. We'll go down the river from there to Luxor, and from there by train to Cairo. I think it will be a wonderful journey—if all goes well. I dread the flight—but if I die—it was meant that I should, that's all, and I often think that I've had all that life has for me, all that I'm capable of having—and giving. My only real sin, only real regret is that I have not made more of what I've had—of what I still have.

I hope to see Lauro's mother in April—somehow we must meet—in the Tyrol or Switzerland—or Italy. I must be brave enough to face the emotion it will be—it will be a fearful joy. The book has given her great happiness and I'm thankful beyond words for that. Well, my beloved friend—farewell for the present. I'll write soon again—and it would be too lovely, if you came to join me in London—what fun! My love to Joseph and the boys when they come to the farm—how lovely to have them now and them bringing their friends. I'm already looking forward to Islesboro and the youth that I can gather there. I hope you got my Xmas cable. I was thinking of you all.

To Dorothea Draper
(Mrs. Linzee Blagden)

[January 28, 1934]
Westbrook, Rondebosch
[Cape Town]

You can't imagine such peace as I am enjoying—at the moment, it probably won't last long, in fact a lady has just telephoned to say she is coming to take me out! They have morning tea in this country at eleven—and eat cakes and sandwiches, and ruin one's luncheon. I arrived yesterday and have a lovely room leading right out into the garden and there are masses of flowers—lemon verbena at my window—and beautiful trees. Birds and crickets and things making soft noises. I've just had breakfast—porridge, brown sugar and cream, sausage, bacon and eggs, and coffee, and figs to end up with! A wicked indulgence—but it's Sunday—after this I'll breakfast in bed, on my customary slim meal. My, but it's nice to get marvellous food and sleep in fine linen! I've lots of letters to interesting people here, and these two weeks will be the nicest part of my visit for here there is beauty— romance and charm—all the old Dutch settlers tradition: silver and beautiful furniture and East India Co. china etc., and lovely white farm houses! The whole story of the country is thrilling, and the problems of the day absorbing, tragic and insoluble.

From now on I shall be no more in hotels till I leave Rhodesia. I move to [———] next week, when Prince George comes here! The Clarendons are delightful and seem to like to have me. It was terribly kind of them to ask me, for Pretoria would have been enough. I am well and my clothes are exactly what I need, so far. Everyone is amazed at my compact luggage, and I must say it's very 'chic' and practical.

It's strange to think my tour is nearly over—only two weeks more. I'm waiting for a wire from Irene di Robilant to hear if she can definitely join me for the Egyptian journey, for if she can't I shan't go. I long to come back in many ways—since Paul's death—to help Zosia—but I know many friends are about, all offering suggestions and trying to help, and I'd just be one more, and she would probably be distressed if I gave up my trip, so I guess I'll go on. I wonder so about the fiddles. I wish Yehudi Menuhin could take the Guarnerius—I'd love to think a young artist had it, and he could make it sob and sing as Paul did. They both must go into the hands of worthy musicians. How he cherished them—I can't bear to think of what it will mean to Zosia to see them and hear them again, knowing how it would affect me. I don't see how she can listen to music again. I'm sure you have been a help to her. I suppose [D———] and others saw to any immediate financial needs. I dread the letters I shall get, yet long to know all they will tell me.

I was glad to hear all about the Xmas parties. You iss marvellous—to give the big luncheon—and I thought of you all. I lunched with a nice young A.D.C. who drove me from Pretoria, at the hotel, with a thunderstorm going on. He was away for the first time from his family at Xmas, so was lonely and I cheered him up.

Hope you got the money for the sweaters, and that the fierce cold is over. What *is* going to happen to America? *Everyone* asks me as if I should know, and I feel such a fool! Does anyone approve of what Franklin [Roosevelt] is doing?

To Martha Draper

February 15 (1934)
In air from Johannes-
burg to Bulawayo

I left Jo'burg at 6:30, down at Petersburg for breakfast, Bulawayo at eleven. I'll be there with friends—see Rhodes' tomb—give a show—see cave paintings and on Thursday 22nd take the plane to Egypt—four engines, two pilots.

I'm longing to see Abu Simbel—H. H. Hefter revealed it to me when I was seventeen and I knew all about it then! Irene will be a good Cicerone—she knows a heap and will have better shoes than Aileen in Morocco!

Had I known I'd make such good friends, and love the Cape so much, I would not have planned to do Egypt this year. However, it will be rather marvellous to go from Cape to Cairo and one never knows if a better chance will come. The Cape really is enchanting—I adored the Dutch houses and the rich valleys of fruit, and the two oceans meeting, and the superb mountains; lovely sun and air and many delightful people.

The audiences were grand, and all made a great fuss over me. I met General Herzog—Prime Minister—General Smuts and General Reitz—all the finest type of men one could find anywhere. I saw at last real Dutch people—because naturally the English predominated in the world I frequented. They don't get on very well.

We're down—I must rush to get this posted—to go on in this plane.

Now we're up again! I decided to wait and post this in Bulawayo. I had a nice breakfast in a clean hotel and now we're en route again. I will write Doro next—I was so rushed at the Cape I never got much time to write.

To Harriet Marple

February 26 [1934]
Somewhere in the Sudan
9,000 feet high
En route to Khartoum

I got both your letters of January 23 and 31st at once at Nairobi yesterday, as the week before I'd been travelling a lot, and feared to miss the weekly packages from London. As a result I got such a lot that I was quite overwhelmed reading them all as they were the first I'd had about Paul's last days, and the newspaper notices; so I was filled with so much emotion and feel so far away and absorbed I hardly realized I was flying over Africa.

Thanks for writing. I'd not heard for so long, and fear I've not written for long myself. What with Alice, and Bill, the family at home, friends and business and bread and butter letters, and post cards—I find it hard to find time enough. Well, it's all frightfully sad, and life is poorer indeed for me without Paul and his music. The service must have been lovely, touching and fitting indeed. I'm glad so many were there to give him what he gave my Paul—that he had such a tribute from his fellow artists. Edith Lindley wrote me all about it.

Smudge and Marcia sound deliciously young and happy. [Sanders Draper and Marcia Tucker were engaged.] I had sweet letters from both. I hope I'll be back for the wedding. I don't know my plans at all. I'll want to see Zosia when she comes—and Lauro's mother and family if I can—and I thought I'd wait and return with Alice, but I'd like to be back for the wedding.

We get to Khartoum to-night—we are a day late, as we were hung up a day with bad weather—at a charming rest house in the middle of nowhere. I did monologues to entertain us all after tea, and the hotel manager gave me a lovely little ivory bowl for a souvenir! It was great fun, and nobody minded the delay. I guess we'll stay [in Cairo] two weeks or so and perhaps go to the Holy Land. I don't know at all after that—I'm waiting to hear from Zosia. I wish I knew of some divine place in Switzerland or the Tyrol or Savoie where I could ask Lauro's mother to come, and have a little chalet or a really charming hotel. Let me know if you do.

I agree with what you said about [———] and that one should be able to give sympathy without fear of getting involved and I admire you for your skill. I can so understand [his] sadness—his sense of growing old, and disappointment at his defeated dream for his art—and his lack of real achievement and a longing to grasp life again—it must come to every virile man—and be so bitter to accept. I met a man in Cape Town who touched me deeply—a real spark was struck between us—but of course our paths divided and I could do little for him and I fear made him more sad—realizing he could still feel—and only to be left again, ships that pass in the night!

To Corinne Robinson
(Mrs. Joseph W. Alsop)

[February 27, 1934]
[En route from Khartoum
to Wadi Halfa]

The start this morning from Khartoum was so beautiful—quite dark when we left the hotel at 5—the aeroplane, as we approached the 'drome, like a phantom against the sky—the morning star over one wing—the wide desert all around in the dim light looking as infinite as the sky. Promptly at 5:45 the engines start, and we rush upward as the light grows, the desert mauve and buff, cut by the blue ribbon of the Nile, and the sky milky grey blue in the West, rose and amethyst in the East, melting into the desert, suddenly the red gold ball of the sun cuts thro' the mirage, and light rushes over the land. I shall never forget it. We follow the Nile all the way to the Second Cataract at Wadi Halfa where I leave the plane. It has been a marvellous experience. I've covered 4,500 miles over the vastest country you can conceive—wild, savage mountains, dismal wastes and swamps, Lake Victoria, and desert sands. The idea of a forced landing gives one the jibbers, but one gets completely calm and confident and it's as comfortable as an old arm chair. The pilots are thrilling, so young and alert and sensitive, but so calm and poised that one is inspired with confidence at once. Think of the responsibility they accept—it's very inspiring to see such men, and they're so friendly and courteous and visit us from time to time and chat. There are two—dual control—so at any moment one can take control from the other, a wireless operator in almost constant touch with the ground getting reports etc. and a steward. I've just had four slices of cold pineapple set before me! I think all the time how Lauro would have loved it—in moments of misgiving and fear I've only to think of him and my spirits rise.

I got a huge mail from home at Nairobi bringing me letters and clippings about my dear Paul Kochanski's death, and I lived through it all again. My poor Zosia—he suffered hideously; why can't they give them a little more morphia, it seems so stupid when they know there is no chance—to let them live in a coma, or suffer. I can't think where or how she'll live. Such concentrated devotion she's given him all these years—I feel all her agony—her regrets—and long to be with her——but I know many devoted friends are about and I shall be in Europe to meet her when she arrives. I imagine she'll bring his body back to Poland.

Irene di Robilant is waiting for me at Halfa—we start down the Nile on Wednesday [February 28] by Cook's steamer—that will be four days to Luxor—then we'll stay there several days, and go on by train to Cairo, and there stay several weeks. Beyond that I don't know yet. Irene will be a good companion I think—she's so intelligent and knows so much, and it will be lovely to have one who knew and loved Lauro, and she'll bring me news of Italy and the family. I have such lovely letters from his mother. I'm so thankful that the books have brought her great joy and comfort. I have so many beautiful letters and reviews—only one disparaging one in all. Such a beauty from the London 'Observer'—I'll show you some day.

I enjoyed my last two weeks in Cape Town, met many interesting and delightful people, and made several real friends. I'm thankful I came alone—one is more free. I stayed with several people, saw plenty, and was only alone when I was thankful to be. I've kept well, and made a heap of money, so the winter so far has been a great success. I've missed you all—often longed for your companionship and a good laugh, and a handclasp in dark moments, but I know you don't forget me—and love is an actual living force and transcends space. My dearest to you now and always—I am so thankful that I love you—

To Dorothea Draper
(Mrs. Linzee Blagden)

March 21 [1934]
Jerusalem

We had a lovely week in Cairo and were sorry to leave. Miles [Lampson] insisted on our moving there from the [Mena House] hotel and I must say it was awfully nice. He and Ann [Phipps] and Mary were all very busy, so we were able to be very independent, and were out to many meals, and on sight-seeing jaunts; but we had several very nice evenings—one, when my old friend [King] Alfonso was there and we had a nice time to-gether. Another, I gave Miles an 'evening' of monos. and all the 'elite' came and it was very "jolly"! and a big success. He has a palace on the Nile and my room had a balcony with a view I can't forget, and a crescent moon at sunset and boats going by. Miles asked affectionately for you and Linzee—he is enjoying his job—but is really very lonely and restless and wants to marry but can't quite bring himself to it. [Miles Lampson's wife, Rachel, younger daughter of Mrs. William Wilton Phipps and sister to Paul Phipps, had died in 1930.] He gets great joy from the children who are lovely—Mary a great help to him now—in many ways like Rachel, and very dignified and gracious in her bearing in a not easy position for a girl of eighteen. Little Margaret is very pretty and very like the Duncan side of the family, sensitive and with dark eyes and hair.

We saw some of the important 'diggers' [Howard Carter], which added to the interest of it all. The Museum is a treasure house and we went, I think, six times. I regret not seeing Abydos and staying longer in Luxor, and feel I made a big mistake, but perhaps I'll go back one day. Egypt is an experience, like the Grand Canyon, and one feels one has added something to one's small store of wisdom, just by passing thro' the land. It's quite lovely here, and moving, and I keep thinking of the people who ought to be here instead of me, to get a deeper thrill—like the Kents, and Aileen's Rose. The Mosque of Omar is too marvellous. We go on to Damascus and Baalbek in a day or so. I've not decided yet whether to sail or fly back to Marseilles. I shall not go to Italy, and I doubt if Lauro's mother is well enough to come out, so I'll probably go right to Paris and wait for Zosia tho' I've not heard yet when she's coming.

To Harriet Marple

March 28 [1934]
Palmyra

It's ages since I've written. Irene and I had ten lovely days, quietly moving down the Nile, seeing the tombs and temples and living intensely in the times of the early Pharaohs and strange Gods. We came on to Jerusalem and stayed four days and since then have been motoring in the Holy Land and Syria. This place is amazing, a 1st and 2nd century Roman city of great splendour, in the middle of the desert. We go to Baalbek to-morrow, and sail from Beirut on Saturday for Alexandria and Marseilles. Irene will go with me, as the ship does not stop at an Italian port. It will be nice to have her, for you can imagine it is not easy to go to Marseilles—yet I want to go, and I shall see the flying field and go to the hotel where Lauro spent his last night. I may see Marie Curtis at Grasse—she is going soon to Italy, and I want to send messages and some papers and letters. I shall not go—they can't get to Switzerland so I fear my plan must be abandoned. I am dreadfully sorry not to see Lauro's mother, but the situation and the reasons remain the same, and my doubts about it all prevent me from going without definite assurance. I've had lovely letters all winter, and the books have given great comfort and joy, so I am deeply thankful for that. I shall stay in Paris and get a few restorations to my wardrobe. Wish you were to be there—do you want me to bring you anything? I hear Smudge's wedding is June 9th and I want to be there, so I shan't wait for Alice as I had hoped to do, and return with her, but shall probably sail toward May 20th or so. I may give a few weeks in London, and a few charity shows.

I think I'll go to Islesboro' again, and hope you'll come for a nice long visit any time. I shall hope for some of the family and children. I long to know how everything goes with you—and what you expect to do?—Stay on in New York I suppose. Life is as uncertain as ever with me. The trip has been deeply interesting, but only serves to pass the time, and travel is a great indulgence. I can't see that it does anything to improve one's nature; does anything? I've had so much of beauty, success, sorrow, freedom, affection, love, and an ideal example—and I'm just what I always was—and, I fear, shall be.

I suppose I'll go on—faute de mieux—giving shows now and then. I always planned to stop when I was fifty—and I'm nearly there!

The thought of Smudge and Marcia and their youth and faith is good to think of! I wish I dared adopt some children—it seems to me they are the only things to make life worth while—just the fact of their innocence and need. One would at least have something definite to concentrate on—but I know I'm too selfish and too cowardly ever to make any decision that involves sacrifice———Can you wonder at my outlook.

Well, my love to you anyway—hoping all is well with you.

To Dorothea Draper
(Mrs. Linzee Blagden)

[April, 1934]
Hotel Vendome
Paris

I had a long, sad but infinitely satisfying afternoon with Paul [Kochanski's] family. Never have I felt that I had really so helped to bring comfort to anyone—his poor little old mother just broke your heart—he had adored her—supported her since he was twelve. She told me what a loving faithful son he'd always been—the light of her life. She and an unmarried daughter and son who plays the piano—and has a few accompanying jobs—live in a little flat, two other sisters and a miniature painter husband, 'round the corner. Heaven knows what they'll all do———

Arthur [Rubinstein] and Nela are on tour—the baby is in Warsaw—He is an adoring husband and father all say—and the baby, who looks like him, is a dream of beauty!

Jean-Julien Lemordant was a French painter. At the outbreak of the First World War he volunteered for the army, although over age. Seriously wounded, taken prisoner, and exchanged, he came to the United States in March 1917 with an introduction to Malvina Hoffman from the Director of the Luxembourg Museum in Paris. Although walking with two canes because of a shot in his knee, blind and with the bandages of his head wound covering his eyes, he had come to lecture and to receive the Howland Prize at Yale University. Forced to cut short his lecture tour he returned to France, where he was rushed to a military hospital and operated upon for a ruptured abscess in his head wound; this left him without speech and with a paralyzed left arm. After long years of laborious effort he taught himself to speak, regaining both voice and vocabulary, and began again to lecture and to sing the old Breton fishermen's songs. A few years later, in a taxi accident, he suffered a blow on his head that re-opened his old wound. The ensuing operation resulted in his regaining partial vision which, over the years, improved or worsened but never was completely restored.

This is the man about whom Ruth Draper now wrote in such detail to Malvina Hoffman.

To Malvina Hoffman

> April 24, 1934
> The Connaught Hotel
> Carlos Place
> London

I had a wonderful visit with our friend, Lemordant, the other day, and he gave me a quantity of notices of his recent tour. I have read them and hate to destroy them, but he didn't seem to want me to send them back, so I am sending them on to you to read. He seemed to me more wonderful than ever, and as usual faultlessly dressed, and looked extremely well, in spite of the fact that he was still suffering terribly from a fall in the train which he had about a month ago. The train had stopped suddenly while he was in the corridor and he had fallen full length, and remained ten days in the local hospital. He was very glad of any news that I could give him of you, and hopes that you are coming soon to Paris. I took him a big basket of fruit, and arranged to have some sent him every week for the next few months.

He had read the French translation of Icaro and Lauro's last letter, and spoke so beautifully of them. I was sorry I could not see him but once. I wanted to take him for a drive in the Bois, but his back hurt him too much to get into a motor. He spoke enthusiastically of his Tour: he had splendid audiences everywhere, and seems to feel that his Lectures are really helping people to value the things of which he speaks. I always come away shattered and uplifted and full of good resolutions and a stiffening of my morale, but alas, it doesn't last long!

I hope you are well and have had a lovely time in Mexico. I had two very busy weeks in Paris—seeing a great many people, getting a few clothes, and enjoying the marvellous new rooms at the Louvre. The Loudons asked admiringly for you. I heard that Paderewski was in Paris but that he will see no one. He seems to be completely broken by his wife's death. He never left her for a moment forty-eight hours before she died. I wish I could have seen him, but I did not know how to reach him.

I am opening tonight at the Haymarket Theatre for three weeks and then expect to rèturn to Paris for a fort-night before sailing, to be home in time for the wedding.

I shall be at home all through June, and hope you will not sail before I return.

To Dorothea Draper
(Mrs. Linzee Blagden)

May 8, 1934
24 Carlyle Square
Chelsea

Just to say hello! I'm very well and very busy and have no news. I sail on the 24th on the 'Washington.' My season ends the 12th.

It's cold and grey. I spent Sunday with Miss Eliza Wedgwood—how I wish you knew her. She is, I guess, the finest person I know—75—a pure delight, with the vitality of youth—with such laughter and wisdom and pity and tolerance and wit all merged—to be with her is like drinking some rich cordial that gives one new life. This house is sweet—I hope the children will enjoy it—perhaps they'd really prefer a hotel!

To Harriet Marple
155 East 38th Street
New York

May 8 [1934]
24 Carlyle Square
Chelsea, London

I have so much to write and see to, that I don't know where to begin. So I'm writing to you while I waste time thinking. I've just had breakfast and the cook is coming up now to get orders. She's pretty poor—and having offered the house to Smudge and Marcia, I'm rather worried they won't be nicely enough catered for—but the house is sweet. My work goes on furiously as ever—it is fantastic, and satisfying in a sense. I had a cold the first week, so have not seen as many people as usual, but the days are crowded now. Charis Cortesi arrives to-night, her first visit to London, and you can imagine how happy I am to have her. We had a perfect visit at Chartres together—but not half enough—and I am so glad she is coming here. We'll sight-see and I have Fred and the car, and have asked just a few friends that I know she'd find congenial and she'll see the dear old ladies [Mudie], who are fairly palpitating with excitement at the thought—and various other friends she has here. She's never seen me on the stage, only at the Tower, [Portonovo] before an audience of peasants at a wonderful harvest festival we had there. (She has many little resemblances to Lauro, and it's a kind of agony, yet joy, to be with her—certain tones in her voice—certain pronunciation of words—and her hands.) I spent a heavenly Sunday with Miss Eliza, and she asked so affectionately for you—'and how is dear Harriet?' My, but I love her—she's as vital and beautiful as ever—so keen about everything, and such a sense of humor.

The wedding now being June 2—I am sailing May 24th on the Washington. I shall go to Paris on the 19th to be with Zosia those few days. She's too ill to come here. She collapsed after the final effort of laying Paul to rest and is under some French doctor heaven knows who, or what the cure is! She seems woefully thin and anaemic and nervous, and says her heart is not right. I suppose if I were there I'd probably be able to do nothing but agonize over the atmosphere, and queer doctors and cures and general situation—knowing so well we don't look at things in the same way.

If you return in August I count on your coming up [to Islesboro] for a nice long stay. Dearest love—I'd like to see you this minute. I'm just the same—life piles up distractions, but the wound, if touched, bleeds. I dread the pain of being with Charis—yet there is no deeper joy than recalling all that her presence represents. You will understand—Bless you—it comforts me so to know you loved him and will understand always———

To Harriet Marple

> May 17 [1934]
> 24 Carlyle Square
> Chelsea

I've changed my plan to go to Smudge and Marcia's wedding. I can do so much good in London and earn a pile of money to help them here. My Haymarket season was a smashing success and I could have gone right on. It's nice having a little leisure and seeing a few of the plays.

My house is sweet and full of flowers. Charis Cortesi was here five days, and did we see London! Her first visit and she was thrilled and enjoyed it all so much. She is a wonderful person—more and more I realize what Lauro's youth and inheritance was—such an interesting family—such strength, stoicism, lofty clear thinking. She has many things that reminded me of him, and I hated to let her go. I am happy that we are such good friends—like sisters too—and no cloud between us. It is a great consolation to know how they love me and feel I am his.

I must dress now—going to 'Le Crime et le Châtiment,' they say beautifully done by a French company. Flying to Paris.

Ruth Draper played at the Haymarket Theatre all during the month of May and early June. Always she was thrilled to see her name in lights at the top of the Haymarket, and Fred would drive her in the Rolls the whole length of Charles II Street so she could enjoy a clear view on her way to perform.

Engagements in Brighton, Oxford, and Cambridge kept her busy during

May 8

24 CARLYLE SQUARE,
CHELSEA. S.W. 3.

Do you
know the
Lippi? ?
"John P.?"

Rarest Harriet,

I have so much to write & see to
than I don't know where to begin. So
I'm writing to you while I waste time thinking.
Lee just had breakfast, the cook is coming
up now to get orders, She is pretty poor —
I having offered the house to Mundy — Maria,
I'm rather worried they won't be nicely
enough catered for — but the house is sweet.
My work goes on furiously as ever —
it is fantastic, — satisfying in a sense.
I had a cold the first week — so have
not seen as many people as usual —
but the days are crowded now. Charis Cortés
arrives to-night her first visit to London,
& you can imagine how happy I am to have

represent — I will understand — Bless you — I conjole me so
I thank for him who understand always.... my dearest
love — God bless & keep.

the middle of June and her sister Alice, [returning from a round-the-world voyage], visited for ten days. To Harriet Marple, in Paris, she wrote:

> Smudge and Marcia arrived the 12th [June] and I've a gem of a house for them in St. Leonard's Terrace. I'm playing with the idea to buy and do over 24 Carlyle, or in St. Leonard's Terrace—another burden but it would give me much pleasure to have a home in London.
>   I shall sail the 23rd on the 'Berengaria,' tourist, to be with Alice. Going to Islesboro July 15th thro' September.

From Islesboro on September 24th she again wrote Harriet:

> This week as I recall my Calvary I'm glad to be here alone and the beauty he loved so in that brief but perfect visit will help me as I relive those last precious days.

Laurence Alma Tadema had written her in May: "What poise must exist between your wits, your heart, and your soul."

Existing records of the next three years are scanty. Letters partially carry the narrative during Ruth Draper's months abroad—otherwise she was touring in the United States or on holiday at Dark Harbor. "Diaries" and schedules sparsely furnish some clues.
    January 1, 1935, started out with a "party for Barbara [Longcope] and Ruth [Carter], 68 present—Restivo to play. [Ruth Draper performance] Ethel Barrymore Theatre 8:30. Dance till 3:15!
    "January 2 largely spent clearing up! 8:30 theatre."
    Then on the 5th she lost her beloved Cairn, "Jock," after an operation. That day she had both matinee and evening performances. Closing in New York the 13th, there was a week in New Haven, then three days each in Toronto and Buffalo.
    On February 9th Ruth Draper flew to Miami, spent two nights at Mrs. Wickes', and on to Havana for a week where she performed (once?) at the Campo Amor Theatre. Then to Mexico with Edith Lindley:

Diary:
Tuesday, 19,	Flew to Merida—lovely lagoon—Percy Madeira on plane—very agreeable
Wednesday, 20:	At Cozumel
Friday, 22:	At Merida—enchanting little town
Saturday—Sunday, 23–24:	Motored to Chichen Itza
	Dined and lunched with Dr. and Mrs. Morley

(Saturday)	Flew to Teheria
(Sunday)	Orizaba—lovely
Monday, 25,	Eight hours by train to Mexico City
	very hot, dusty, beautiful journey thro'
	mountains. (Staying with Mrs. Rincon
	Gallardo, 67 Calle Cordoba)
Thursday, 28:	Motored to Cuernavaca to lunch
	with Mrs. Morrow and Amey Aldrich.

After a short East Coast tour she sailed May 27th on the French Line
Champlain *with Barbara Longcope and Diana Draper. Zosia Kochanski*
and Jacques Porel also were on board.
She played a month at the Haymarket in London and remained abroad
into December.

To Harriet Marple
in New York

March 1 [1935]
Mexico City

I can't seem to write, it bores me as never before! And there is little time.
It's cold as blazes every morning and night, hot from eleven to four—very
strange climate. We had a lovely day yesterday at Mrs. Morrow's at Cuer-
navaca, about one and one half hours by motor from here. She has a lovely
house and garden and glorious view. Amey Aldrich was there and the young
son-in-law [Aubrey Morgan]—and Harold Nicolson and one or two other
agreeable people and we enjoyed it. The three flights have been wonderful;
the bathing at Havana lovely and some pleasant people; otherwise rather a
wasted week. Yucatan was fascinating and I could have done with a few
more days there. The markets and the types everywhere are interesting
beyond words, and one is puzzled and intrigued sorting out the features of
the races that make up this strange country; one feels one's ignorance to
a point of agony! It's terribly interesting and picturesque and very strange,
and so queer to think it's all on our continent—anything so remote and
foreign to us. But the tourists are pouring in and it will soon be ruined. It
makes me despise our civilization, or barbarism, it might easily be termed
the latter in view of its power of destruction!

We are taking two or three trips away for a few days to see lovely
places—the city itself I think is pretty unattractive, tawdry and full of *ultra*
modern little houses. There are, of course, very interesting things to see. We
have no exact plans for returning, but roughly I hope in three weeks.

Early in 1936 Ruth Draper sent, with the following letter, copies of Icaro *and* The Story of My Death—*containing Lauro de Bosis' Manifesto and the letters dropped on Rome—to colleges and universities around the world with which she had some contact.*

Lauro de Bosis conceived and carried out a plan to arouse his countrymen to the dangers of Fascism, to awaken their social conscience to the principles and traditions of liberalism and to the need of saving it from extinction. Lauro de Bosis was an idealist, who with a great love of life, risked death for his ideal. He has left a message, not only to his countrymen, but to all youth, and it is my hope that his ideals may inspire our young men.

These books have a peculiar significance at this time. For in the confused issues and conflicts of the day there is still to be found inspiration and a stiffening of moral sinews in this example of a young man who followed his convictions to the end.

To Harriet Marple

Sunday, March 15 [1936]
Bull Hotel
Cambridge

I'm writing on the train en route to Edinburgh. As there is nothing fixed on the Continent yet it seemed a pity not to take advantage of what is sure to be a wonderful week. They wanted me for two—but I'll only do one—as I want to get going abroad. Bright had done *nothing*. I'm rather cross—but I find I can get lots of lines out by inquiring on my own—and I have hopes of getting things going soon and glad I came. Will let you know as plans take shape. I've been awfully busy—four days in London—with several hours each day at the Chinese show [Exhibition of Chinese Art] and lunch, tea, and dinner with friends.

The week in Cambridge was marvellous. An exquisite new theatre, many adorable youths in attendance, pleasant friends for lunch and tea; Earle [Balch] and a friend and Lily Swann came one night and Mr. Keynes gave me a delightful supper party—I was made much of, and it's so beautiful there. I'm looking forward to Edinburgh, too.

My fur coat is a God-send! I nearly perish on the stage, but my velvet dress wasn't fit, so I have only my tulle, which is smart but frigid! I gave my velvet to a friend in London, as well as the little green striped wool. I hope I can get something quickly in Paris.

I had a lovely letter from Lauro's mother. I sent her, by Amey, copies of all the letters I'd received at the time of his flight and later, and about Icaro, and you can imagine what it meant to her to read them. I feel as far beneath her as I did of Lauro. She says there is no chance of a passport for her, or for

Vittorio. It seems so cruel and stupid, I hope very much Charis may be able to get out in May. I'd give so much to see them.

I saw the sweet little English girl Miss [Elman?] who was with Elena last summer. She met you she said. She is at Newnham in Cambridge. She had a very disagreeable time—was followed and questioned, and her letters opened. So eyes are still on that poor family and anyone connected with them. Irene writes: "the boss has never had greater prestige and power—thanks to Mr. Eden—how strangely things work out—and how rare really great men are."

It's very interesting here of course—papers absorbing—much talk—sentiment pro-Germany and an acceptance of the inevitable—her last step merely another plea for recognition. [Germany reoccupied the Rhineland on March 7, 1936.]

To Mrs. Yates Thompson

April 15 [1936]
Stockholm

You will have heard of my "hurry call" to Jessie to send my brown net dress! I had left it in London (on purpose but stupidly!) as I wanted a new and lovely dress for my Scandinavian tour! This I got in Paris, but it was not finished in the brief week I spent there, and it was sent on ten days ago by what is called "Service Rapide". On Monday I got in a panic lest I should not have it (I open to-night with Their Royal Highnesses present!) and so I wired Jessie to send my old dress by aeroplane, which she did, and it's safely here! The new dress is not, so my fears were justified, and I'm endlessly grateful to Jessie! I do hope the excitement and bother did not interfere with her holiday!

All goes well and Stockholm is beautiful. I give two shows here, two in Gottenburg, two in Oslo, two in Copenhagen, two in Brussels and one each at the Hague and Amsterdam. Then Paris, and I expect to be in London by the very last of May. I fear you've had a very cold Easter.

Excuse this scrappy note—I have many to write, and odd things to do before to-night. I had tea at the Palace yesterday and am meeting delightful people. It's very cold still. Much love and many thanks always!

To Harriet Marple

April 26 [1936]
[Sunday] Copenhagen

I had a marvellous evening here last night. Queen, Crown Prince and Princess, and all the Diplomatic Corps and a full house! Wonderfully quick and delightful audience. I go to Hälsingborg to-morrow and Malmo Tuesday; here again Thursday and fly to Brussels Friday, reciting there Saturday and Sunday. Fly to Hague Monday and have a big party there Monday and my recital there Wednesday. Amsterdam Friday, Saturday Brussels again— quite a strenuous week! My tour has gone too wonderfully, far better than I ever dreamed with the brief time for preparation.

A charming lady has accompanied me everywhere and made all arrangements so it's been most easy and agreeable. I've met lots of nice people, everyone so kind, friendly and *awfully* intelligent audiences. I can always come back, and I like the countries so much now. It makes all the difference knowing people of course.

Charis is coming from Rome for two weeks on May 10, and I'm planning to give her a lovely holiday, and looking forward to it. Shall probably not go to Paris—but motor and perhaps go to England. *Whatever* she fancies doing. Everywhere is lovely the last two weeks of May.

Ruth Draper gave a four-week season in June at the Haymarket Theatre, remaining in London through July.
Freya Stark wrote to Flora Stark on July 24th:

> *Ruth Draper was at the [Julian] Huxleys', and Jelli d' Aranyi and a most charming old couple, Lady Ottoline and Mr. Philip Morrell, looking just as if they had stepped out of Walpole's letters. . . . No one there had read my book: I can't tell you how nice it felt to be happy and friendly and liked without the assistance of a label. I know now that I don't enjoy the limelight. . . . I can't tell you how pleasant it was to sit in a corner and watch Ruth Draper being made much of. She has a very intelligent face which looks as if it had been sensitive in youth: I should think she must be a good and true friend to those she likes. She gave me a lift in her car and, as I told her I had never been able to see her as the theatre was always full, said she would see that I got in if ever I wrote to her—which I thought awfully nice.*

To Stark Young

January 1937
66 East 79th Street
New York, New York

My dear Stark—

I was so touched to hear from you at Christmas as you started for Texas and have thought of you many times and meant to write you before this. I can imagine the comfort you are to your sister, how she can live over with you so many precious memories. Do come in to see me some day, if you are back. I shall be here until the middle of February when I plan to go to the coast, where I've not played for 12 years.

You will be glad to hear that Renzo Rendi and Mario Vinciguerra have been released on parole [after six years of prison] and though closely watched and unable to get work, they are out of prison—which I suppose means heaven to them and their families. I feel a great weight off my heart. What a world we live in; but, alas, our capacity for indignation is not equal to the challenge.

My love and good wishes for the New Year and thanks again for thinking of me along with friends who can realize what Christmas and going home means to you now. There is something so tragic about youth to-day—perhaps those who have gone have a better chance—

Yours always
Ruth

February, March, and April of 1937 took Ruth Draper right across the northern States to San Francisco; she made a side trip to Honolulu, where she visited the Walter Dillinghams at "La Pietra" and gave two performances at the University, then returned home through the Mid-West and Virginia. She had given sixty-seven performances, all one- or two-night stands except for about a week each in San Francisco, Los Angeles, and Washington, D.C., and grossed over $61,000. Then she took a long summer holiday in Islesboro in expectation of her world tour.

To Dorothea Draper
(Mrs. Linzee Blagden)

[November 24, 1937]
Just leaving New York

I hate seeing the shore recede and my thoughts are with you all, going about your various tasks, and will be very often as my forces gather for the great journey and the long absence. We all follow some urge and must believe it is for the best, action springing from spiritual motives can't be unconstructive; all good things have a price and every pang reveals something worth knowing. The security of your love, and your fineness, is like a warm fire and an unfailing beacon—a cozy, secure anchor, and I bless you for all you are—and for your quick mastery of the struggle of the past year.

[Linzee Blagden had died in September 1936.]

To Martha Draper

[December 11, 1937]
70 Lansdowne House
Berkeley Square

It is as if eighteen months had not been, and I am just in the same stream of activity, acclaim and affection that London always carries me; it's moving—overwhelming at times—and I always wish I had more time, more strength to bear the burden of fame and good fortune and, I may say, love; and I feel it a bit confusing and difficult. Sounds funny, but it's so hard to fit everything in: see so many people, get things going in regard to my journey, and find time to rest, dictate tiresome letters, and still acquire a few more clothes. I'm playing to packed houses at every performance and they are enthusiastic as ever.

I've seen dear old Mrs. Thompson, and shall see Mrs. Rathbone on Monday. I'm going to Blanche Serocold's to-morrow. I've seen Margaret, Paul and Pamela. Tommy's wife has a son—to be called Wilton [all Phipps]. Charis Cortesi, Lauro's sister, is arriving from Rome to stay with me for a fortnight, I hope. This charming little flat has two bedrooms and two baths, sitting room, hall and kitchen, so it's delightfully convenient. If Charis leaves in time, I can take Mary Erdman here. If not, I'll get a room for her in the Connaught, near by.

I plan to go to Paris the Monday after Xmas. If you are all going to be any where to-gether at a given hour on Xmas, let me know, and I'll telephone! I suppose you will be very busy getting ready for Xmas. I'd love to send you all presents, but suppose the trouble with duties would be more trouble than they're worth. Do write me how everyone is— I hope Alice is getting some peace and pleasure from 66 [East 79th Street] and not doing housework! I've had no letters yet. I'll have Brown Shipley forward everything by air mail from London, so it will be safest and easiest to always address me here.

I'm getting quite cold feet about the trip—and wondering if it will be too strange travelling with someone I barely know! I hope Alice will ask her to 66 and that you may meet her, and, I hope, think she's nice. [Mary Erdman was coming from her home in Hawaii to accompany Ruth Draper as far as Singapore.] It's so hard to find anyone free and eager, and, I thought, attractive; I hope we'll get on all right! I'm seeing various people who will give me letters and advice, and as I stop work the 18th I'll have a good week free for friends and engagements, packing, etc. I think I'll stay in London for Xmas. I find many friends are staying. If I go to a house-party I'd feel rather mean leaving Mary. My love to everyone at home. I'd write more often if I had more time. I'm resting between shows now, and it's time to get up and go!

Dearest love, my dear Barie, I love you very much and wish you were here.

To Dorothea Draper
(Mrs. Linzee Blagden)

[December 26, 1937]
Eydon Hall
Eydon, Rugby
[Visiting Lord Brand but, apparently,
at Cliveden for Christmas dinner]

The telephone call was rather a desperate experience—I was *so* excited, and the rapidly changing speakers confused me! One can think of *nothing* to say and has the impulse to shout, and the emotion of hearing your voices and picturing you all about the fire in the library was shattering to say the least. However, I'm glad I called, and only hope you heard me, tho' I said nothing worth hearing and I'm sure my voice sounded like a cracked siren! You must have had a lovely lunch all to-gether—I couldn't seem to hear Alice, there seemed several voices at once. Ba I got—then Ruth, John, Di, Nelson, and Bill—you at first, only a second. Well, it's all mysterious beyond words, and the very mystery is an experience worth paying for. Nancy A[stor], at Irene's, had just called her four sons—first they rushed from the table—then I did. There were twenty-two—all family save me and three odd young men—Joyce [Grenfell] was lovely and Nancy and Alice Winn and families. No one is here, but Peter Brooks—it is terribly sad but I think I've helped a little. [Phyllis Brand had died in January 1937.] Bob is wonderful—thinking only of the children and their happiness; his face breaks your heart and he's so fine it is a privilege to be with him. I hate to go but I must get to London to pack and say farewells to various friends, [I'll] try and get off to-morrow—I may not till Tuesday.

It's almost as bad to leave London as New York. I'm so happy here and love so many people and life is so secure and full of affection and stimulating interest. But the long sea voyage will be nice I guess, and the strange lands I'm going to see. Mary [Erdman] went to Ireland for Xmas, so I was re-lieved to know she'd not be alone. I must go for a walk.

The girls and Jim [Brand children] are darling, thoughtful and sweet. We all had presents after breakfast yesterday and went to Church and to Phyllis' grave—Bob and I had a long walk in the afternoon.

Dearest love and Happy New Year. I'm *thrilled* about your cairn! Don't name him 'Wheatena'.

Ruth Draper, with Mary Erdman, arrived at the Hôtel Vendôme in Paris on December 28th, for two whirlwind days, shopping, seeing Mrs. Gay, the Loudons, Lugné, the Bolaffios, Yvonne Printemps in Trois Valses— *"perfection"—and visiting "the Louvre, Notre Dame and the Exhibition Grounds. Dinner with Dean Jay and on the train!"*

ITINERARY

1937

Fri.	Dec.	31	Sailed from Marseilles 3 p.m. M.S. Baloeran

1938

Thurs.	Jan.	13	Arr. COLOMBO, CEYLON (Galle Faci Hotel)
Sat.	Jan.	15	*Performance* Grand Oriental Hotel
Mon.	Jan.	17	*Performance* Grand Oriental Hotel
Tue.	Jan.	18	KANDY, *Performance* Empire Theatre
Wed.	Jan.	19	Motored to Nuwara Eliya (Grosvenor Hotel)
Thurs.	Jan.	20	Return to Kandy
Fri.	Jan.	21	Motored to Talaimannar via Pollonorna, Sigirya, Trincomalee, and Anuradhapura
Sat.	Jan.	22	Train from Talaimannar
Sun.	Jan.	23	Cross Channel by boat early a.m. and cont. by train (24 hrs.)
Mon.	Jan.	24	Arr. MADRAS, INDIA (with Governor and Lady Marjorie Erskine)
Wed.	Jan.	26	*Performance* New Elphinstone Theatre
Thurs.	Jan.	27	Picnic to Seven Pagodas
Fri.	Jan.	28	Motor from Mattipuliam to Ootacamund and MYSORE (at the Residency)
Sun.	Jan.	30	Motor via Seringapatam to BANGALORE (at the Residency)
Mon.	Jan.	31	Arr. BOMBAY (Government House with Sir Roger and Lady Lumley) *Performance* Taj Mahal Hotel Ballroom
Wed.	Feb.	2	*Performance* Taj Mahal Hotel Ballroom Ajanta Caves
Fri.	Feb.	4	UDAIPUR (Residency—Guest House)
Tue.	Feb.	8	DELHI (Viceroy's House with the Viceroy, Lord Linlithgow and Lady Linlithgow)
Thurs.	Feb.	10	*Performance* Regal Theatre, New Delhi
Sat.	Feb.	12	*Performance* Regal Theatre, New Delhi JAIPUR (Guest House)
Tue.	Feb.	15–16	AGRA (Cecil Hotel)
Thurs.	Feb.	17	Return to DELHI (Cecil Hotel)
Sat.	Feb.	19	BENARES
Sun.	Feb.	20	CALCUTTA (Government House with Lord and Lady Brabourne)
Mon.	Feb.	21–24	*Performances* Regal Theatre
Fri.	Feb.	25	Depart evening for Darjeeling
Sat.	Feb.	26	Saw whole Kinchinjunga Range in morning sun Arr. DARJEELING (Hotel Mount Everest)
Sun.	Feb.	27	Saw Mt. Everest at dawn from Tiger Hill
Mon.	Feb.	28	Drive to Kalimpong (lunch with Mr. and Mrs. Odling) Evening departure for Calcutta

1938

Tue.	Mar. 1		Fly from Calcutta to RANGOON, BURMA (4-1/2 hrs.) (Government House with Sir Archibald and Lady Cochrane)
Wed.	Mar. 2		*Performance* Jubilee Hall
Thurs.	Mar. 3		Evening departure by train for MANDALAY
Sat.	Mar. 5–6		to MAYMYO
			2 *Performances* for local charities and Radio for the 60th Rifles
Mon.	Mar. 7–9		By boat down the Irrawaddy to Prome
Wed.	Mar. 9		Overnight train to RANGOON
Thurs.	Mar. 10		Fly to BANGKOK, THAILAND (5:30 a.m. to 8:30 a.m.) (with American Minister and Mrs. Neville)
Fri.	Mar. 11		*Performance* Royal Sports Club
	Mar. 12–15		to Angkor (2 days) and return to Bangkok
Thurs.	Mar. 17		Fly to PENANG, MALAYA (with Mr. and Mrs. Allen/Mr. and Mrs. de Mowbray)
	Mar. 17		*Performance* Majestic Cinema
Sat.	Mar. 19		By train to KUALA LUMPUR (with British Resident, Mr. Jones)
Sun.	Mar. 20		From Port Swettenham by boat to SINGAPORE (Raffles Hotel)
Mon.	Mar. 21–24		*Performances* Victoria Theatre
Fri.	Mar. 25		Mary Erdman sailed for Hong-Kong and Hawaii
	Mar. 25		Dep. by boat for Java
Sun.	Mar. 27		Arr. BATAVIA (now Jakarta) JAVA
Mon.	Mar. 28		Djockjacarta—Borabadur
Tue.	Mar. 29		*Performance* at Kunstring
	Mar. 30		Motor to BANDOENG
Thurs.	Mar. 31		*Performance* at Kunstring
Fri.	Ap. 1		Flew to Batavia and on to SOERABAJA
Sat.	Ap. 2		*Performances* at Kunstring
			Flew to BALI
Sun.	Ap. 3–6		In Bali
	Ap. 7		Flew to Soerabaja, Java and sailed for Australia, S.S. Marella
Wed.	Ap. 20		Arr. BRISBANE, AUSTRALIA
Thurs.	Ap. 21–27		*Performances* His Majesty's Theatre
Fri.	Ap. 29		Flew to SYDNEY (Government House, Lord and Lady Wakehurst)
Sat.	Ap. 30–		Fri. May 13. *Performances* Theatre Royal
Sun.	May 8		at Mossvale
Sat.	May 14		NEWCASTLE (with Bishop and Mrs. Battege)
			Performances Assembly Hall
Sun.	May 15–16		weekend at Markdale (sheep station) (with Mr. and Mrs. Geoffrey Ashton)

1938

Tues.	May	17	Arr. MELBOURNE (Hotel Windsor)
May 17—June		16	*Performances* Comedy Theatre
Thurs.	June	16	School Children's Matinee (2000)
Fri.	June	17	Charity matinee Dep. in evening for ADELAIDE
Sat.	June	18	Arr. ADELAIDE (So. Australia Hotel)
Sat.	June	18—	
Wed.	July	6	*Performances* Theatre Royal
Sun.	June	19	with Mrs. Dutton—Analaky—Kapunda—Keith Angas—Angaston—Lindsay Park
Fri.	July	1	Special School Children's Matinee
Thurs.	July	7	Beaufort (sheep station) with Mr. and Mrs. Beggs (cousin of Eliza Wedgwood) Ret. to MELBOURNE
Fri.	July	8—10	weekend at Frankston with Mr. and Mrs. Russell Grimwade
Mon.	July	11	Special Matinee for School Children Dep. for Canberra after tea
Tue.	July	12	Arr. CANBERRA (Government House with Acting Gov. Gen'l. Lord and Lady Huntingfield) *Performance*
Wed.	July	13	Drive to Mrs. Rutledge's sheep station Dep. by train for SYDNEY (stayed with Mrs. Hubert Fairfax and Charles and Hannah Lloyd-Jones)
Thurs.	July	14—26	*Performances* Theatre Royal
Fri.	July	22	Special Children's Matinee
Tue.	July	26	Charity Matinee Farewell dinner given by Mr. Wilson, U.S. Consul Farewell Broadcast Sailed 6 p.m. for Auckland
Fri.	July	29	Arr. AUCKLAND, NEW ZEALAND
Sat.	July	30—	
Fri.	Aug.	5	*Performances* in WELLINGTON, Opera House weekend with Mrs. Riddiford
Sat.	Aug.	6—10	*Performances* in CHRISTCHURCH Theatre Royal
Thurs.	Aug.	11	fly to DUNEDIN
Thurs.	Aug.	11—12	*Performances* His Majesty's Theatre
Sun.	Aug.	14	Ret. to Wellington by train and boat and fly to AUCKLAND
Mon.	Aug.	15—20	*Performances* His Majesty's Theatre weekend with Mr. and Mrs. Douglas Neill—to Rotorua
Mon.	Aug.	22	Sailed S.S. Mariposa from Auckland
Thurs.	Aug.	25	SUVA, FIJI ISLANDS *Performance,* Town Hall (Broadcast)
Sat.	Aug.	27	Pago-Pago
Wed.	Aug.	31	Honolulu

1938

Mon.	Sept. 5	Arr. Los Angeles
Wed.	Sept. 7	Albuquerque (stop-over to see Diana and children)
Thurs.	Sept. 8	Arr. Newark Airport

To Corinne Robinson
(Mrs. Joseph W. Alsop, Sr.)

January 8, 1938
In the Red Sea

My month in London was *such* a *whirl,* I got no time for personal letters! It was a wonderful month, and of course I hated to go. Charis Cortesi was with me for two weeks, and it was such a joy. We saw delightful people every day, and beautiful things, and my little flat was perfect in comfort and cosiness, so we had lovely talks, and quiet little dinners by the fire before I went to work. She came with me nearly every night and we had one lovely week-end with my beloved Eliza Wedgwood, and the Cotswolds were white with snow, and the little villages nestling in the valley were so adorable with lights in the tiny windows and smoke rising into the sky at dusk. We saw several plays when my work was over, and did Xmas shopping and she left Wednesday before Xmas—a perfect visit. Every one thought her so charming—and I was so proud and happy taking her about. She is like Lauro in so many ways—same quick sense of humor and lively intelligence, and such a strong fine character; you can imagine what it means to me to have her and we are close as sisters.

My London season, as usual, was a fantastic success. I played to 'sold out' houses at every performance and broke the record for capacity as I have also at the Haymarket, with more 'standees' than they've ever had. I was almost reduced to tears by the welcome I got and by my farewell show. Did I tell you I got flowers on my first night from the Haymarket manager and stage hands "To *our* Miss Draper." It was very moving. I had my darling maid and chauffeur, both more perfect than ever in their respective capacities, and as rare human beings—I *wish* you knew them—in fact I often wish you could be with me in London. It's all so heart-warming, and I'd love you to see and share with me the thrilling and happy days and the wealth of affection that surrounds me. It was cold and grey and foggy, but I love it in all weathers and leave a great piece of my heart there always.

My dear old Miss Mary Mudie—90—died the day after I left. I hoped she would not linger. I saw her several times, and was thankful I got there. Her love for me was a lovely link with Lauro, whom she'd known always, and I loved her dearly. Those terrible months in 1932 were made endurable by the sanctuary of her home, and her tenderness. Every Sunday I'd come back from the provincial cities where I was working and spend the long afternoon with her and her sister, talking of Rome, where she'd spent fifty winters, her vivid memories of Mazzini and Cavour and Risorgimento heroes, and exciting adventures. Her memory was fantastic and I never tired of hearing her. She spoke Italian like a native, and knew Greek and Shakespeare and all poetry, and was an angel of goodness, with humor, and vitality amazing to see. She'd known the de Bosis family always, and had a wealth of memories of all the children, and Lauro whom she adored chiefly. I will never know anyone quite like her again; and I am rich indeed in my friendships with remarkable older women. I pray you may know Eliza Wedgwood still. Somehow I must manage to get you to England with me once!

Mary Erdman is a perfect travelling companion—quiet and quick and neat and responsive and charming—a grand sense of humor and very intelligent. We laugh a lot, and sleep a great deal, for this warm sea air is stupefying. Rather a dull ship's company. A few charming people we've collected for after dinner talks and coffee. It's very warm and I already hate the black evening dress—(exceedingly smart and nice)—and wish I had nothing but flowered silks and cottons. I'm sure we have too much luggage six bags each! but it's hard to do with less, as we've been told it's cold in Northern India, we land in the tropics in Ceylon, then go north, and in Burma shall strike great heat again. We went ashore at Port Said and motored to Cairo for the day and motored back to Suez in a wild sand storm. It was a terrific adventure—we had to go very slowly to even see the road—and arrived at 2 A.M. The ship had been delayed in the Canal by the terrific wind, and we had to spend the night in Suez and rejoined her at 10 next morning. It was an exciting break in the trip.

It's quiet and cool in my cabin—we have a lovely bath and fans—and with the door open between our rooms get a fine draft. It's a great temptation to stay in bed all morning and again for a nap after lunch. I'm busy reading books on India and am already practically a Buddhist! It's the bloodiest history possible to conceive. Hordes of plundering conquerors keep sweeping down from the North and West and East—most confusing—and I'm mortified by my ignorance and the muddled state of my brain after reading! I shall depend on the good old eyes and try not to understand too much!

I can hardly wait to reach Colombo where I hope for letters by air mail, and to see my manager, who is wandering thro' India now, arranging my shows. He is returning to meet me at Colombo, where we also have an Indian 'bearer' meeting us, who will accompany us for the rest of our journey. I am armed with letters to all the Governors and Viceroy, etc. and I'm sure it's going to be difficult to keep to our schedule, for pleasant things to do will undoubtedly turn up to upset our plans! But time is limited, for Mary has to get home by mid-April. I may have to go to Java and Bali alone—which is hard—but it's a question of ships and dates and connections. If we decide to fly I suppose we could manage much more. I'm still vague about Australia and New Zealand but imagine I'll go—being so nearly there.

Tell me all the news, tho' I shall be looking at strange sights and trying to remember Akbar's dates, or reciting 'Maine Porch' to a Maharajah.

To All Three Sisters

January 19, 1938
Grosvenor Hotel
Nuwara Eliya, Ceylon

Dearest Davil—Ally—Ba,

I meant to stop at Davil, but realize I'll not be writing more than one letter from here, so I address it to you all, tho' the last should be first! I've not written since the ship, and the days have been crowded since I arrived a week ago. Our arrival was superb: a private launch, reporters, photographers, our bearer 'Mariados' with two garlands, my manager with a bouquet, the hotel managers from where my shows were to be given with another bouquet, our baggage was rushed thro'—a lovely run to the Quai through the moonlit harbor and my name in electric lights over the Grand Oriental Hotel (Alice will know the hotel, just by the pier) the first thing to greet my eye—it was about 10 P.M. It was *so* funny—Mary was highly amused—and we went at once to the beautiful hotel on the sea, the 'Galle Faci,' and had two lovely rooms and bath right on the ocean with warm wind pouring in.

My three shows were all sold out, and tho' they were in the ball room of the hotel with a stage built in—which I dislike—it all went very well, and everyone seemed to enjoy them very much. We had lunch with the Governor and Lady Caldecott one day—friends of Christopher Chancellor—and saw a few people we'd met on the ship, and saw a few sights—but a few days were enough and we were glad to get up to Kandy—an enchanting place. I gave a show there last night and the Tea and Rubber and Cocoa planters motored from miles around, and I had a packed house in the local theatre—awfully amusing.

To Martha Draper
(Written on both sides of six
memo pad sheets, headed:
For His Excellency
For Her Excellency
For Comptroller
For Surgeon to His Excellency
For A.D.C. in Waiting
For Military Secretary)

February 6 [1938]
Udaipur

I guess it's about your turn for a letter but you might send it the rounds of the family, for I find it very hard to find time to write letters. I found, on my writing desk at Government House Bombay a long line of little pads, from which I tore one sheet each. I thought it would amuse you to see the variety of people to whom one can send a message! Masses of lovely writing paper but these pads amused me. The British Government do their "Upper Servants" very well! Never have I tasted such food, nor had more luxurious care and comfort! I must say it's very agreeable after long, hot, dusty journeys to be met by a charming A.D.C. in a swift clean car and rolled to a lovely cool room with punkahs whirling, enormous bath rooms and all the fixings at hand in the line of soaps and bath salts. Our hostesses have been charming, particularly Lady Lumley in Bombay—a perfectly lovely person.

Well, the great journey goes on swiftly and easily so far. We've kept well, and tho' the dust and dirt and length of the journeys is trying, what we find at the end makes up for any fatigue and discomfort. I am fascinated of course watching the crowds at the stations, and as the trains stop every half hour or so, the journey is entertainingly broken. The country is like our Southwest desert, or the bleak ugly parts of the Northwest—like Nebraska and Southern Wyoming—dry, arid desert, parched, forlorn, with poor trees struggling to find enough moisture to make them green. Here and there vivid emerald patches of rice where they have drawn water from deep wells, pulled up in great leather buckets by patient white oxen. We've passed thro' a lot of cotton country and seen mills with mounds of cotton like piles of lime under the sun. The poverty and dirt is really frightful, but every where the lovely moving figures of the women in their Saris carrying brass jars, clay pots, baskets or loads of sticks, or green fodder for cattle on their heads. The whole pace and rhythm is soothing, and their grace and gentleness is the essence of feminine repose and charm. Even the lowest of them all have what the "highest" of us so painfully lack in general!

Ceylon was rich and green—quite different—and the people seem healthier, happier and better fed. The jungle was fascinating to see for the first time—such a neat jungle—yet the depths of wildness—miles and miles stretching ahead with about 20 feet of grass and wild flowers on either side of the road, before the tangle of shiny leaves and beautiful interlacing trees and creepers and shrubs began. It was all rather like the avenue in a great private place, yet beyond the edge, one knew that snakes and leopards and elephants and panthers roamed at will. We saw lovely birds, wild cocks, lots of monkeys, but nothing more exciting. In the night in a Rest House in the middle of the jungle I was sure I heard a leopard snarling, and the door was open and I went thro' all the charming state of panic that I was hoping to have, but in the morning found it was a buffalo—who makes a peculiar savage noise!

The old buried city of Polanarna was mysterious and lovely (with the quality one finds in Greece) evoking the soul of the people who built it and worshipped Buddha there. I find I cannot stir up any emotion, aesthetic or religious, for the Hindu cult and art but Buddhism, contaminated as it is

with Brahminism and the distasteful symbols and forms that one finds every
where, has a message of beauty and enduring example that one is glad to
feel. Udaipur is the loveliest thing we've seen yet—from point of setting, and
romantic splendour of the past—but the inside of the palace (and I hear
they're all alike) is something to give one a nightmare! The worst type of
furniture—French, English, Victorian—any old style—hat racks such as
you'd find in a 3rd Avenue boarding house—bibelots such as [———]
might have had—quangle wangles and corner cupboards, red jardinieres
with calla lilies growing around them, glass beds, chandeliers, tables and
chairs, dreadful brocades and golden horrors of chairs; life size photographs
of the Maharajah mounted on heavy cardboard so you are startled as you
come into the room, thinking it's a man; stuffed tigers walking about, a
commode with elephant's tusks for the arms—not one beautiful object did I
see! But the setting and the views and the floating palaces and gardens in the
lake were enchanting. The bazaars are always alluring, but don't compare to
the Moroccan, Constantinople or Jerusalem bazaars. We have a nice
servant—the one Mallie had—and are well cared for.

To Dorothea Draper
(Mrs. Linzee Blagden)

March 7 [1938]
Burma

You would laugh to see me—in pale blue flowered pajamas, on the shady
deck of a river steamer, moving peacefully down the Irrawaddy from Mandalay to Rangoon. I've just had a bath after a nap, and am imbibing a lime
squash. Mary is still asleep. We're the only whites on board, one high class
Burmese family with three little girls like flowers, and about 150 travellers in
the second class—sitting silent for the most part on mats, in pretty colored
clothes and little muslin jackets, smooth black hair coiled, with jasmine or
some sweet flower stuck in the side, or on top. Everyone looks clean and
smiles if you do—and there is no smell—they bring their own food in little
lacquer trays and bowls—it's like a scene in a play. We go to little villages
along the banks, first one side and then the other, turning up stream to face
the strong tide sweeping us down. The houses all on stilts built of matting,
bamboo, and thatched roofs, look very airy, and everywhere are little coni-
cal white temples rising from the trees. I would *really* like to fly back to England for the spring and return [home] in June, but I've decided to go on to
Australia and New Zealand and work hard and have that off my chest! I'm
not getting any younger—the world is so crazy—I've come so far, and a
tremendous season awaits me there. Also I've got Merica [manager], and
am more than half way, and will never want to go so far again for Australia
alone! We had two perfect days in Darjeeling—saw the mountains in their

shining splendour—they knock you flat—and, as Alice will tell you, had the greatest luck in seeing Mt. Everest at dawn!

We flew from Calcutta to Rangoon and stayed (as usual!) at Government House—then came to Mandalay. Martin Charteris—Violet Benson's second son—and one of the most enchanting and lovely people I've ever met—is stationed there in the hills above Mandalay, a big Regimental H.Q., and he'd arranged to show us everything, put us up at the General's and have me give two shows (and radio for the 60th Rifles). We had a lovely time, spent last night at a charming Captain Trotter's bungalow, and sailed this morning at seven.

Never have I conceived such hospitality and kindness as we have had—it's been very demoralizing in a way—but lovely!

To Dorothea Draper
(Mrs. Linzee Blagden)

April 3, 1938
Bali

This place is idyllic—really so—but fiendishly hot. As I write a lovely breeze blows over me so I shouldn't complain! I flew here from Java yesterday—over a blue sea, and this Island of rich forests and mountains, rice fields in perfectly curved terraces under water, so they look like a lovely design in greens reflecting clouds and sky. The natives have enormous charm, sweet smiles, gentle ways, graceful and beautiful; to watch them passing with their baskets of fruits and vegetables is endless pleasure. I saw wonderful dancing last night, and longed for Paul to see it. The *accuracy of the rhythms* rivals his; all rather slow, studied and perfect—*completely* satisfying—and tho' one cannot understand, one knows it is high art, come down through ages of sincere and intense devotion; and I love the music! The young boys and girls are incredibly mature in their mastery of gesture, poise, and expression, and become almost rapt in the intensity of the smallest movements; yet they do not seem tired, or breathless or bored, and each motion has a freshness and significance that leaves one moved and admiring.

To Mrs. Yates Thompson

April 10 [1938]
On board SS Marella
On the Java Sea

I've resisted sending you picture post-cards because I felt you deserved a letter, with the result you've had no word these many months which is perhaps worse! I've gone so far, and so rapidly, that dealing with my family alone has taxed my leisure for correspondence. And I've thought of you so very often, during the long journeys—seeing the beautiful and interesting places and the strange people—and would dearly love to look in on you and tell you all about my wanderings! I am homesick for England and the Spring, and all my friends, and wish I were flying in that direction instead of sailing toward Australia! I tried to give up my Australian tour, and cabled Mr. Bright asking how far I was committed. He replied, "Consider you morally bound"! Such cruel words to a Puritan, for I could not then change my mind. My coming had been announced in Australia and New Zealand and it would have been a great disappointment I suppose—so I'm on my way. I expect I shall be there seven weeks and in New Zealand three weeks, and sail for home about mid-July. I am sure I shall enjoy my tour once started tho' I am rather dreading the social end of it, for I'm told the Australians 'kill you with kindness' and I'm afraid they'll insist on newspaper interviews and be dreadfully offended if I'm not 'matey' and willing to 'say a few words' at large luncheons! It's a pity I've never learned to love all that side of my professional life—the truth is I'm only a professional when actually on the stage and dislike all that is expected of me off it! I can't say my work has been very arduous up to the present—so I'm really ready for some weeks of steady hard work, where there will be little of great beauty or interest to see during the days—I mean in the way of 'sight seeing' of historical interest. I've no doubt I shall be shown things by the hour!

Everywhere the heat has been terrific and it has been a real trial to perform—but the public seemed to enjoy my work, and I had splendid audiences everywhere, and was urged to give more or to return—so that has been a great satisfaction. But I'm sure I never shall go back, at least to work, in those hot countries, it's too trying and the theatres are very bad—often cinema houses—too big and the acoustics and lighting rather dreadful. Mr. Merica has flown to Australia ahead of me to prepare everything—he, poor man, got dysentery in Madras, and has had a very bad leg as a result of the Serum injection, and I was rather handicapped in India for he couldn't move much, but he's better now. It was very bad luck. Mary and I have kept splendidly well, and none of the grim warnings we received have given us cause for worry. I've not seen a snake, scorpion, or other unfriendly or unpleasant animal or insect, and tho' mosquitos have bitten me in malarial localities, I've had no fever yet! We've lived a most luxurious and sheltered life, because everywhere we've stayed at Government Houses! Delightful welcoming telegrams reached me everywhere asking us to stay at the next place! The Erskines in Madras, the Roger Lumleys in Bombay, the Viceroy and Lady Linlithgow in Delhi, and Lord and Lady Brabourne in Calcutta. Sir Archibald and Lady Cochran in Rangoon, the American Consul General and Mrs. Neville in Bangkok, the C.P.O. and Mrs. Allen in Penang—he a nephew of dear Eliza Wedgwood, so he and his wife kindly put us up there. Raffles Hotel in Singapore, and the Cecil Hotel in Agra and Delhi for part of our visit there (we returned for the [Viceroy's] Ball and polo) were the only hotels we've been to! So you see how I've been spoiled! Mary was perfect as a fellow guest being young and very attractive, and all the A.D.C.'s rather lost their hearts to her. We made many delightful friends. Lady Lumley is the most darling person, and Lady Cochrane—the finest type of Englishwomen—so charming and simple and intelligent, with their jobs so tremendously at heart. I loved them both. I was impressed by all the Governors, Lord Brabourne I think the cleverest, most alert and ambitious, and perhaps his job is the most difficult. Their grave responsibilities seem to me overwhelming—the Viceroy's of course the greatest. I liked him and Lady L. so much and it really was thrilling staying there, so magnificently carried out—the whole picture—tho' the House is superb, it's all a bit too big and grand between you and me, and they are kept so terribly aloof, and I do not feel have a chance to see interesting and important people in an informal way. The houseparty of some twenty-six people including the very young and charming, (but quite uninteresting) A.D.C.'s and three attractive daughters, was gay and delightful, but had no relation to India, and I should think would tire their Excellencies rather than refresh them. They work awfully hard and it's all so complicated and difficult to understand; the vastness of the country, the barriers of religions and races and prejudices, and the poverty, keep one in a state of perplexity. I could never be happy there. Of course the things and places of beauty stand out like oases in a desert. The Ajanta Caves—great Buddhist carved and painted temples 3rd to 6th century—the Fort of Akbar at Fateh-pur-Sikri, the Taj Mahal by moonlight, the Forts and Palaces of Shah Jehan at Delhi and Agra, the Himalaya Mountains, stand out with shattering significance and wonder. And they are all worth coming far indeed to see and have stamped in one's memory forever. Rangoon, the Irrawaddy, down which I sailed from Mandalay, had enormous charm. Bangkok and its gay colored temples was bewitching; and Angkor, stupendous, mysterious, and satisfying. I take a deep breath, just writing these names, recalling the wealth of impressions I've received, wishing that I'd brought greater knowledge with me to help me assimilate such wonderful experiences. I've met a few delightful people along the way and had good talks with some Indians, and people who know India well, and was impressed with several of the older Civil Service men. What lives of sacrifice and devotion—and the sad separation from children and the loneliness, I should imagine, when they return to England with responsibilities suddenly removed.

You must be exhausted reading all this, and I realize I've said nothing of Java and Bali! The last a real Paradise. I'll spare you now, but someday try and describe it! I've never seen such beautiful country or such beautiful people and such unspoiled, untroubled lives. It was moving, and thought provoking, and one trembles to think it will not last if tourists and merchants and missionaries are allowed to come in too great numbers! I hope this finds you well—all the family at home and in China, well—give my love to everyone—if you have time some morning do send me a word of news—*How* I wish I were driving up to the door with 'Fred,' seeing the top of your head at the desk—greeting Dade, and rushing in—for a long talk and a quiet luncheon—happily the thought of it is enough to make me feel the warmth of your affection and the reality of what it means to me. My dear love always.

In her Diary of March 1, 1939, Anne Lindbergh describes a visit to Mrs. Yates Thompson:

> *. . . an old lady in a wheelchair in a house reeking with associations—pictures, books, whatnots, mementoes; another age. One does not notice the wheelchair or her age. She seems to come out to meet you, in the warmest and most heartening way. You feel her life is full—that it was always full but that unlike most elderly widows (and lame also) she does not live entirely in the past but is spiritually interested in the present and future too. It makes one not dread old age. I should like to see her again.*

To Martha Draper

[April 17, 1938]
Easter Sunday
S.S. Marella

I am thinking of you all to-day—and was reminiscing to myself while I rested after lunch, thinking of the thrill of Easter as a child! Getting ready for church in 47th Street—the new suede gloves, the hats with corn flowers, the challis dresses, and 'covert [cloth] coats', and other 'new articles'—Miss Hyett and Miss Luzzini's fittings of things "to be ready for Easter"; the lovely whiteness of the flowers, the smell of the church, pushing thro' the crowd at the door, the squeeze in the pew, the choir and hymns, the throb and soaring of the Gounod Sanctus—how lovely it all was—and the gay walk uptown, everyone gazing at each other's clothes! I wonder will memories of later years ever quite equal in vitality and significance the memories of childhood—untouched by cynicism—lit by novelty and the thrill of innocence and unanalytical observation. Speaking of the last quality, I'm reading Aldous Huxley's *Ends and Means*—it's marvellous—profound and full of truths one recognizes and wishes one could keep readily on one's tongue to use in arguments and awaken dull minds. It's stiff reading but terribly interesting.

This trip has been a lovely rest. I've wished for you—it has been *so* calm and blue—lovely clean little ship, delicious food; and such dull people—but not disagreeable—so one can do as one likes and be alone. I've read a lot: "Pepita"—fascinating.

To Dorothea Draper
(Mrs. Linzee Blagden)

April 21 [1938]
Brisbane

I arrived here yesterday morning after a most lovely restful journey. I found at Cook's three big envelopes of mail covering three weeks of postings from London. I'd managed badly in not giving intermediary addresses between Singapore and Brisbane, so it had been accumulating here. You can imagine what a feast I had—thirty-seven letters to read—quite overwhelming! I retired to a bench in the lovely Botanical Gardens opposite my hotel, and under a huge pine, looking at yellow roses, with birds gently chirping above my head, I had a feast of news and affection, and felt quite a wreck at the end. Letters are terrible in a way, they pull one so close, over thousands of miles, over time that has passed—and then one snaps back to the lonely actual present. Your cable was a joy to get this morning—such a quick reply to mine and I'm so relieved to hear George [Draper, nephew] is on his way out [of Spain]. I hope you'll wire again when he's really safe and say how he is. I wonder what such an experience will have done to him—one feels very humble before the boy—in our sheltered lives we have never tasted of the kind of human anguish he has seen. One's heart breaks thinking of the Loyalists' losing fight—of all the mockery of Italy's promises to withdraw and Chamberlain's acceptance of them. What a business—the whole ignoble story—but one is tormented by the thought of the alternative to perjury; fighting, unfittingly prepared, to preserve one's honor and ideals? I am sure the Government can't be happy to have acted as they have—they're just scared—and unready and temporizing before too dangerous odds; poor Austria [*Anschluss*, March 12th]—the Jews again, and all the proud thoughtful older generation whose hearts must be broken. I have longed for good newspapers—it's been so difficult to get news—except scraps—no articles—no way of knowing the trend and point of view of the nations—no Dorothy Thompsons or Walter Lippmanns to illumine the darkness! Well, it wouldn't have made any difference, one agonizes and does nothing anyway! That's what's so awful.

To Corinne Robinson
(Mrs. Joseph W. Alsop, Sr.)

May 1, 1938
[Sunday]
Government House
Sydney

Thanks for your last lovely letter, *undated,* but it gave me lots of pleasant pictures of friends and your activities, and the view from the 'budwar' window and late patches of snow, which by now are tulips and crocuses, I suppose, and lovely apple blossoms and young greens! Here, trees are turning to autumn shades, and it's sparkling cold at night and early morning—lovely and warm by day. Yesterday we went on a heavenly picnic, and cooked chops over a eucalyptus twigs fire, and ate our lunch under a mimosa tree on a hill looking over miles and miles of rolling country and blue distant hills and sunny galloping clouds! Lady Wakehurst is one of the most charming people I know, a darling 16-year-old girl and boys of 13 and 11, whom we picked up at their school for the day's outing. We had such a cosy delicious day—lying on the hill, walking, and motoring home as light and stars came out over this glorious harbor. I 'opened' Saturday night to a packed house, and it promises to be packed all fortnight! Wonderful alert keen audience. I suppose I'm stupid not to stay here—I could make a fortune but I hate to miss the summer at home.

This country is thrilling in many ways—very like our own, the people like our Westerners. But I must say it's nice to be with a sophisticated, intelligent and sensitive friend to whom one can talk of everything and laugh at much with no fear of offense. My week in Brisbane was killing, for there I met only Australians of the Women's Club, Elocution teacher variety, and I felt I should scream if I were asked once more "what I thought" of:

"OUR"

sunshine
blue sky
climate
fruit
gum trees
koalas
oysters
'billy teas'
river and bridges and roads
views
accent
moonlight and stars!

Sydney is much more of a city, of course, and the harbor is superb. Thank heaven there are good newspapers here, I've felt so out of touch (since Singapore, end of March) with news from Europe. It's all so complicated and tragic—those poor Jews—hounded again—and all the mockery and hypocrisy which England is forced to indulge in. One understands but hates it none the less. The Huxley book [Ends and Means] is indeed a bitter poignant challenge and leaves one hopeless for one knows humanity will not rise to it. The message he gives seems as futile as the symbol of Lauro's flight—to germinate in the stupidity of our brains and the egoism of our moral consciences. Our spiritual progress is so bound up with technicalities and mechanism, outgrowth of our genius and material needs. It all can be simplified in the old adage "one reaps what one sows" after all, we are all responsible—unequally equipped for all the various responsibilities and demands of life, and Hitlers and Mussolinis will come and go, I suppose, as long as there are such needs and such opportunities for men of their type. It's all so terribly sad. Meantime, I carry in my heart the knowledge of my personal failure; and proceed with the contribution I have to make— knowing that politics, religion, causes, discussion and argument, intellectual pursuits, bridge, golf, gossip—civic influence and efficiency and public service are not my sphere or strong points—but knowing you love me, and laugh with me just the same and, more important, that I love and admire and cherish you close—and forever—

To Dorothea Draper
(Mrs. Linzee Blagden)

May 8 [1938]
[Sunday]
Sydney

I've had *such* a lovely day in the country [Mossvale] with some nice people, and now I'm all cosy in bed, at 8:30 looking out over the starlit harbor, with hundreds of little riding-lights of small craft reflected in the water. I moved yesterday, as the Governor and Lady Wakehurst and the children, secretaries, A.D.C.'s and servants moved to the country for three weeks. I had a delightful week there but I've found a charming little quiet hotel [Windsor Hotel], with a superb view over the harbor, so I'm quite comfortable, tho' it's lonely after the lovely week in a happy and luxurious house, with a darling boy of four running about. Lady Wakehurst is a rare and enchanting person and we really became great friends—for I'd known her only slightly in England. (George was quite taken with her sister Nancy Tennant in England when he was with me years ago.) It was a joy to be with a highly intelligent sensitive person; after Mary left me in Singapore, it was lonely in Java and Bali, tho' I was most kindly looked after in Sourabaya and Batavia by the Dutch Governors and wives and a nice American Consul and wife.

In Bali I found an interesting German artist, living in a heavenly 'nook' in the mountains, and I spent a night there and swam at dawn in a pool, with orchids hanging from the trees—it was lovely. I forget if I wrote you of Bali, and *how* I wish I'd stayed longer, and had the gumption to fly here! It remains the most enchanting memory of my whole great journey, unique in beauty, mystery and unsullied charm. Something to dream about always, when striving to forget the complex and sorrowful mess of our times; and civilization's problems.

I am facing another nasty decision about staying on here! Never have I had a more fantastic yet genuine reception. The poor things get nothing but movies, and are mad about my shows. They have fine music (Tibbett is here now and is having a big success) but few plays; anyway they are wild—no seat at any performance, many turned away, appeals on all sides for me to stay! I really want to come home. I'd planned to sail July 12th but it's hard to leave when I'm making over a thousand dollars a day; when by staying 'till August 25th I could make twenty-five or thirty thousand dollars more! Now don't talk about this—but I'm telling you as a good argument! By the time you get this I shall have decided, I suppose. I know you'll be disappointed, but summer is so quickly over and so distracting anyway. I *long* to come home, but I'm thinking of all I could do with that money! And the pleasure I appear to be giving here is persuasive, and the pressure hard to resist. I'm hoping for letters from home and perhaps they'll help me decide—when I learn how everyone is, and plans and general news.

To Harriet Marple

> June 9 [1938]
> Having hair dried
> Melbourne, Australia

It has been a terrible struggle to make up my mind to stay on but all reasoning led to a decision to remain—in view of the uncertain future and the now 'destructive' passage of time! I'm really tired, and longing for country and leisure and home—but never before have I so clearly sensed the reality of my job in life. The response here has been overwhelming—from all kinds, ages, and social categories. My taxi-driver came in last night—I got him a nice seat—he arrived all dressed up—but when I came out he was waiting for me and gave me a free ride home! He used to sing in a vaudeville show, so we were comrades. It's all very touching and gratifying, but I long to be sitting under a tree sewing and talking to people I love. There can never be anything like it again—unless I return—for I can't expect such wholesale hunger and childlike delight and spiritual and intellectual yearning in any of the old countries—here one feels the immense potential qualities of strong, unsophisticated people. What I bring them of types they've never seen really seems a revelation, and they eat up every thing ravenously, and pour out their gratitude. I've met some delightful people here and in Sydney, so I'm surrounded with kindness and pleasant distractions.

I've just had a marvellous oil shampoo—a nice Frenchman, but I'm depressed because he thinks Italy and Germany are perfect now and admires what has been done (cleanliness, order, etc.) yet he lives in and loves this *very* democratic free country. People are so illogical and prejudiced and it's so hard to talk convincingly in support of a principle which seems to have failed. Oh, if only I were eloquent and well informed enough to argue convincingly—if only I could use my talent to arouse people's consciences and indignation, and stagnant egoism and blindness, to the dangers. My heart breaks sometimes thinking how I've failed to carry on Lauro's vision and sacrifice.

I've seen a few attractive men—always married—but have had no thrill and realize one must make one's life without it—being thankful for having had a brief but perfect experience and live on in its memory when the distractions of living this crazy life leave one cold.

I've had a sort of funny digestive trouble—in my 'tummy' (so English I can't say stomach!). Had X-rays—no sign of anything—I guess it's fatigue. Anything I eat gives me a little pain—I'm trying to be sensible but it's maddening to have to be conscious of such a thing.

To Dorothea Draper
(Mrs. Linzee Blagden)

> June 19, 1938
> Analaby-Kapunda
> [Near Adelaide]
> Australia

I finished in Melbourne with a matinee for charity at which L600 were realized—and another for school children—2,000 of them. A most remarkable audience and a really thrilling occasion. I couldn't help contrasting the attitude of the teachers who rushed at the chance of having their pupils hear me for the educational value of it all and to see something of the various types etc., with Miss Noland of Foxcroft who wouldn't let her girls come to see me, because the horse show was ten days off and they had to practice stunts!

I'm having a lovely peaceful Sunday on a beautiful 'station.' It's cold and bracing, and I must leave my bed and fire and flowers and go for a walk before lunch. Mrs. Dutton, my hostess, is a very beautiful woman, about our age and frightfully nice, and motored me out after my 'opening' last night. It promises to be as delightful in Adelaide as Melbourne and Sydney. I could stay on for weeks more—and pack them in! Needless to say, I'm enjoying Australia enormously and meet really charming people. I always seem to find a few rare ones everywhere, who are cosmopolitan and superior, or have the universal elements that draw one to human beings anywhere, elements of brain and heart and character, sensitivity or charm; often I wish you could enjoy them too and regret they can only be additions to that mysterious group of 'friends' that always puzzles you! The horde of mediocrities are everywhere too, but I don't let them bother me—tho' I try to be decent and have succumbed in each city to a ghastly reception by the Lyceum Clubs or Forums! You know the ordeal.

Mr. Merica continues to be invaluable and he's found a paragon of a banker, a perfect dentist, devoted taxi drivers, an A 1 tailor and several ardent admirers to even up the sexes!

To Corinne Robinson
(Mrs. Joseph W. Alsop, Sr.)

June 29 [1938]
Adelaide

I'm having my hair washed, greased, heated, rubbed and waved, so if my writing is a bit jerky I'm sorry! I get so little time for writing, and I have so many people I long to write to; I think of you so much, and often wish you could share the amusing and interesting days that happily fly by, bringing me nearer home. It seemed wise to stay on—where the business was so good and crowds, really hungry for what I have to give, strange as it may seem, were literally storming the doors! It was irresistible. There is something very touching and stimulating working on this virgin soil—people so eager and with an unjaded point of view—generous, outgiving and really intelligent and quick to understand. It is as if I brought them pictures of human beings they never saw, or probably will never see, and it seems to interest them deeply, even the languages they've never heard and do not understand! The 'Porch in Maine' and 'Vive la France' go extraordinarily well, which amazes me. People are very kind and friendly, and every where, as is my good fortune, I meet a few very sympathetic souls—who seem to talk one's language—who have travelled, read and thought, and have a sense of humor and are sensible and real.

It's cold, but sunny and bracing air, and the flowers are lovely, and seem to bloom all winter—regardless of season—roses, poppies, stock, wallflower, narcissus—nearly everything all the time. I've been to lovely country places or big sheep stations for week-ends, and got nice long country nights, and walks over windy sheep paddocks—the country is beautiful in its way—and the prevailing tree, the gum, or eucalyptus, is everywhere—beautiful, strange, and many varieties of it.

To Mrs. Yates Thompson

August 30 [1938]
S.S. Mariposa, Oceanic Line

Your lovely long letter of some months ago was so very welcome. I read it and reread it, and was so glad to have all your news—and your views—and it made me long for a quiet talk by your fire,—and to tell you all my impressions of this great journey, which is now nearly over. I've been going at such a pace, seeing so many people, that I've had little time for letter writing or reading, and this long sea voyage is a perfect and restful finish to these active and delightful months. I forget when I last wrote to you—but Australia and New Zealand have been my 'scene' for the last four months! With the exception of Sundays, and three days of rest in Melbourne, and a few days out for travelling, I've been working eight times, sometimes nine times, a week ever since I arrived! Mr. Merica and I calculated, roughly, that over 120,000 people heard me—and hundreds were turned away! I kept well all the time, and even in the frigid theatres never caught a cold. The faithful Mr. Merica was perfect as usual, and sailed home to England the day I left. Altogether everything went wonderfully and I don't think I've ever had a greater triumph, or a more convincing sense that I was really giving delight, and stimulating pleasure to so many people, literally starved for entertainment. I found them most responsive, and with the exception of the minority who have travelled and have a normal experience of the world and culture, I was amazed that the general public were so appreciative and intelligent in their understanding of types they've no knowledge of at all. I gave two matinees for [1700] school children in Melbourne, and [2000] in Sydney, which were packed, and I thought it such a tribute to the intelligence of the teachers to send the children—fourteen–seventeen years old, and such fine young people. The reviews in the papers were always so discerning and well written, and everything seemed to be enjoyed and understood. They loved the little woman in Maine, and 'Vive la France' and the English ones of course—but really all went well. I was most pleasantly surprised by my enthusiasm for Australia. I met so many agreeable people, and went to lovely stations for week-ends and saw quite a lot of the country. Its peculiar quality grows on one tremendously—at first I found the 'gum trees' terribly monotonous but they have a haunting charm and beauty all their own, and the colour of Australia is unique and fascinating—a sort of blue grey light over everything. I love the vastness of the land, and really preferred it on the whole to New Zealand, which is more obviously beautiful, familiar, rich and green. My visit there was too short—and I missed seeing the famous lakes and glaciers and mountains, but I loved Dunedin and Christchurch and had wonderful audiences there too. I'm sorry I never got to Perth in Australia, but I hope to go back someday! Little did I think I should ever say this!

I've had very exciting news from home. Dorothea is marrying Harry James! I'm perfectly delighted. They've been friends for years and I think he's really loved her a long time—and he's been so lonely, and so fine, and now will be so happy—it's good to think about. D. was terribly lonely after her husband's death and as Harry was his friend too, it's all most natural and understandable. Mr. James [uncle, Henry James] would have been so pleased, and Mother too. They'll be married the 1st and are coming to stay with me in Islesboro' as soon as I get home. I shall only stay in New York long enough to re-pack, and rush to Maine. I hear good news of all the family. Helen wrote me she'd seen you, and will relieve you of my trunk! Thanks so much for keeping it. I long so to come to England again before next Spring, that I may not be able to resist running over—before Xmas—

just to see you! I hope Christopher and family are safely out of China—and for good! How awful is all the news—terrifying and tragic. I wonder what is going to happen?

To Edward Sheldon

[August 1938]
[Australia]

I shall have so much to tell you—so many things, places and people. My thoughts leap to my chair beside you—and the silence and intimacy of your room, and I hear you laugh and see you smile and know that you will understand and feel everything as if you had been with me everywhere. . . . I'll book my first evening with you when I land.

On August 25th the S.S. Mariposa *called for several hours at Suva, in the Fiji Islands. A matinee had been scheduled for the Suva Town Hall and promptly sold out—a month in advance. As there was no time for an additional performance, Ruth Draper, on arrival, was asked by the Director of the Fiji Broadcasting Company if she would permit a broadcast of the performance. This was an experiment—from the center of the front beam over the stage a microphone was hung and at the noontime news broadcast it was announced that Station ZJV would not close down between two and five o'clock that afternoon but would stay on the air to carry Ruth Draper's matinee. She was heard on isolated coconut and sugar plantations, in the gold mines at Tavua, on remote islands, on ships and yachts more than 500 miles at sea, and in Tonga, 1600 miles away. Those listening heard her clearly and remarked that the sound of men's laughter predominated, marveling that so many men had deserted their offices on a busy mail-ship day!*

After Islesboro, and visiting her sisters, and Corinne Alsop in Avon, Ruth filled engagements in New York and on the East Coast for several months. But she was eager to get to Europe.

1939 –1945

We must go on and not fail.
So only can one prove one's love.

Ruth Draper
1932

To Harriet Marple

> March 1, 1939
> Tryon, North Carolina

Paderewski made me so sad—a real farewell of an old and broken hearted soul and brought back a wealth of treasured memories. I can see him in his God-like beauty and pathos fifty years ago! A sad and exquisite creature— twenty-eight years old—his wife had just died and he adored Paul who was like his boy and I can see him still looking at Paul with emotion and playing to us all and I surrounded him always with the aura of his effect on me as a child of five—one of the most tremendous and lasting impressions in my life.

To Alice Draper
(Mrs. Edward C. Carter)

> June 6 [1939]
> 58 Avenue Foch
> Paris

I couldn't resist Paris and decided in the middle of the ocean to land at Havre instead of Plymouth. So I wired the Jays (who'd asked me to stay in N.Y.) and here I am! Never have I seen Paris more lovely—heart-breakingly lovely—and all along this glorious avenue they are ripping up the soft green lawns, and digging trenches zig-zag among the great trees, so as not to hurt the roots if possible. It seems like a horrible insult to beauty, and one shivers with indignation. The trenches seem so ridiculously inadequate too, tho' I'm told they are doing it all over Paris, in the parks, etc.

I've had full days—shopping and friends, and on Saturday we went to Fontainebleau, drove and walked in the fairy forest, lunched with the Bunny Carters at their beautiful house at Senlis on Sunday; saw the cathedral with a group of little girls in their clouds of white muslin in the choir; went to the races at Chantilly, and a tea party—garden or cocktail (I saw no tea)—at the American Ambassador's—an enchanting place overlooking the lakes and lawns and forests of the chateau. So I've had a taste of every thing and am off for England to-night in the ferry train, (for the first time for me). Never was I more reluctant to leave and I'm *furious* that I booked Oxford and Cambridge otherwise I could have stayed here till Sunday. I perform in Oxford to-morrow at 2:30, also Thursday, and Cambridge on Saturday. I shall go to Margaret's to wash to-morrow morning and leave at eleven by car for Oxford. Fred will meet me. My luck prevails, and I've got a lovely house, all new and fresh—belonging to the Hubert Howards (he, I know well). It's a darling little green quiet place, not far from all my Chelsea friends, and I'm told the cook is wonderful! I had massage on the steamer; but food here has been my destruction. Last night we dined at Armenonville—the trees flood-lit, the sky brilliant blue as the day-light changed to dark—such a gay, beautiful Paris picture—and I nearly cried at the thought it might end. Such beauty in such danger—all the beauty—the whole meaning of Paris—expressed at that moment in that frivolous aspect, but none the less poignant. I am very tempted to return here immediately after London and give a short season. I know I shall hate to leave London by that time, but I feel I must see more of this—in case. Eve Curie, Zosia and I had such a lovely crossing. Divine weather and calm all the way. Such a lovely ship, quiet and the right size and not too grand. Flagstad was on board, but rarely appeared. I had a brief talk with her, and she is as lovely and simple as she appears on the stage—not a bit like an opera star—and *very* young. I met a few agreeable people and 'assisted' at the concert—and the days passed all too fast.

I think of you and Molly at Islesboro now, and hope you're having sunny days for the work and have not found it too bothersome. I realized I'd forgotten how shabby the old red chintz in the big spare room was, and I hope you got something pretty and durable—that having done service for some thirty years! I'm afraid that will have made a lot of extra work for you both. I long to hear of your sojourn there, so please write. Did you see Irene and any native ladies. I'm *so* sorry I neglected to give you a list of their names as you asked, but I guess they all loved seeing you—and can't expect you to remember at such long intervals. Hope you saw Mr. Osgood—and dear Mrs. Blanche Hatch (Del's widow). Well, I must get up—Léa is coming to fit some underclothes—and then I'm off—bank, shampoo, slippers, hats, lunch with Jean Ciechanowski and Zosia, etc., and a full afternoon— Arthur and Nela's children are *dreams* of charm, personality and beauty, exquisite and darling. Her mother is an angel, and the atmosphere is charged with all the things one loves to find in a house. Little Paul grabbed my hand and pulled me upstairs to see his toys—never having seen me before—so dear and frank and friendly and gay with humor—and to hear them chatter Polish and then French to me was intoxicating—those baby lips framing the words of those two languages—with equal ease. You'd adore them!

To Corinne Robinson
(Mrs. Joseph W. Alsop, Sr.)

June 15 [1939]
11, Alexander Place
Thurloe Square S.W.7.

My London legend goes on—repeats itself—in all this lovely summer radiance, that only England—of cruel dark grim winters—knows. I have an exquisite little house, three perfect maids—my beloved Ada at the theatre, my beloved Fred and the Rolls—my beloved audiences packing the Vaudeville—my beloved friends on every side—every hour filled with interest, beauty, and affection. It is intoxicating, so warming, so vital and real, and *so* dear. The streets, the policemen, the smells and sounds, and lights, the glory in the parks of greens and flowers and enchanting children. War seems very far away—one's thoughts can't dwell on it, with life so normal, and so full. No one talks about it much—they've put it out of the surface of thoughts anyway, and go gaily and gallantly on their way. The same in Paris—one feels a deep thrill there—it is heartbreakingly beautiful—always a more emotional beauty than one gets in London. France, and Paris, are divine—the country, the city, the spirit of the people—all move one to tears. I had five perfect days there and *hated* to leave, but work is good to combine with the thrill and charm of life over here and I'm so at home, so secure in this beloved old town.

I'm going to see Queen Mary on Saturday—she sent for me and I was so touched. She is rather bored, convalescing from the accident, and I shall do her a few monologues, and I hope make her laugh. It will be fun, and I'm glad the old dear wanted me to come!

I've written this while resting before my show, and have just had my little supper of sole and asparagus, strawberries and coffee; the room is filled with flowers, the quietness is audible, a Sir Joshua hangs above the mantelpiece—of a lovely young man in grey satin and fur—the house is charmingly furnished, fresh and luxurious in the best possible taste—and I love it.

I find moments to contemplate my good fortune, and see the wonder of it all—now I roll thro' the Park to my theatre, full of laughing, eager people and give them all I have to give, in thankfulness, humility, and in pride and joy—and they fill me again with energy—and love—. And I feel my Lauro near me somehow—he saw my life here—and once sent me a wire from Rome on my opening night, which I carry with me always; "Close to your heart and glory."

To Alice Draper
(Mrs. Edward C. Carter)

June 20 [1939]
11, Alexander Place
Thurloe Square S.W.7.

My case is desperate. I have no time to write you all! My days are so crowded—my mornings a rush of dictation and telephones—I mostly lunch out every day—two matinees—tea generally here—an attempt at a rest—a little supper at 7:30 and off to work! I'm playing to wonderful houses (only three theatres about, and we have full houses!). Fred and the Rolls whisk me about—to and from the theatre, to Oxford, Cambridge, Broadway, Pangbourne, Surrey. I had three invitations last week-end—three next— and I'm nearly crazy fitting everyone in! I sold roses at Harrods this morning! [charity]. I've seen Mrs. Thompson twice—Winnie Mudie, old darling, I've seen twice. Margaret is adorable as ever—Paul too—Bill and Pamela and Michael are coming to tea to-morrow—Joyce I've seen here—not yet on the stage—she's a great success. Mrs. Thompson is wonderful but she does seem a bit older this year. London is lovely as ever, I wish you were here. I may broadcast and 'televise.' Zosia may come for a few days soon. Elena Vivante, Lauro's sister, is here—her thirteen year old boy passed 'Top Boy' in the scholarship for Worcester School. Paolo the older one is coming to stay with me—he's just taken his 'matric' and is going up for Oxford.

One is baffled by the situation here. All seems normal—gay and calm. The news is terrible—but people can't any longer be actively and desperately concerned. *All* younger men are training—women too—but in a quiet way and life goes on as usual. They have air raid drills—sham battles and gas mask, trench, and Red Cross drills—one in Chelsea yesterday—wonderfully carried out—onlookers much amused. The weather is cool, the country too lovely for words. I'm just going to have my supper—the sun is pouring in on my bed—a lovely room and huge bed. I'm going to give a special matinee for school children for a Children's Charity. I could go on for weeks more and have turned down lots of offers in suburbs and other cities. I may go to Paris and come back and work some more. I'm torn in my desire to return—I love it so over here! I long to hear how Islesboro was? hope you didn't have much trouble. Many friends from 'parts visited' last year are turning up and it's lovely but adds to my already large circle. I'm lunching with Lady Antrim to-morrow, she's 84 and going strong. I had a lovely afternoon with Queen Mary, and she gave me an aquamarine pendant—she was sweet and laughed hard at 'Doctors'. I must go to work—the time between shows just flies—

Queen Mary's Lady in Waiting (Lady Margaret Amphrett) wrote on June 24th: "Queen Mary commands me to thank you for your letter and to try and tell you again, what pleasure you gave Her Majesty last Saturday. Her Majesty enjoyed every minute of your performance (as indeed we all did!) and is most grateful to you."

To Martha Draper

July 27 [1939]
Connaught Hotel
London

I am having a wonderful additional [three-week] season at the King's Theatre, Hammersmith. The tickets run from 1/6–6/ so I get rather a different audience though a great many smart people come too and it is a very interesting mixture. They express themselves more freely than a West End audience, and the silences are incredibly charged with emotion and understanding, and the applause a spontaneous roar. At the end they shout, and it is a heartwarming and inspiring experience. The house is always sold out and it is great fun.

I feel rather sulky and discontented in this comfortable old hotel, after the luxury and peaceful privacy of my darling house. Harriet came over from France with me to see relations in Lincoln and Kent and is spending a few days here next week before returning to Paris. I had a heavenly two weeks there and the dazzling beauty of it all went to my head like wine. I saw lots of lovely things and, though one is full of hope, one cannot suppress a horrible fear that one may be looking at them for the last time. The danger seems to enhance the beauty, and I felt like crying about five times a day. The French are perfectly wonderful—completely united and [one] senses, as always, their fundamental character when their ideals are threatened.

I have decided not to come back—anyway not until the end of August—largely because Lauro's sister and her husband and four children are here, having left their lovely home in Siena in order to give the children a good education, that being denied them in Italy now because the father is a Jew. I am very fond of them and feel so sorry for them, and I think I can help in giving the children a happy holiday and driving them about the country in search of a place to live next winter. I have found a lovely house in the village of Stanton near my beloved Eliza Wedgwood, which in itself is reason enough to stay on an additional three weeks. I cannot but think seriously of staying on or of returning here anyway. My work becomes such a very vital thing over here, with no need of publicity or effort of any kind. I believe I could play to packed houses anywhere in the British Isles, and you will agree this is a great temptation, as I cannot have many more years of it, and I lazily prefer to work where I have to make so little effort to plan performances. Even if war should come (and I don't believe it will) I think I could help by amusing people!

I don't know why [———] got a step-up in the Legion of Honor, but I am very glad if it gives him pleasure to wear the rosette. Lugné-Poe, I discovered, was making tentative efforts to get it for me, and I nearly took his head off for doing so and insisted that he stop everything immediately!

**To Harriet Marple
in Paris**

[August 1939]
Stanton, Gloucestershire

The situation is very tense here—I'm torn what to do. I want to stay and help if I can—on the other hand there is much to settle and arrange at home and as I still have the passage on 'Champlain' I feel perhaps I'd better go. It's still hard to imagine the approaching horror—which seems inevitable now. How is the feeling over there? Wire me if you are remaining. I suppose we'd both better go—and return if we decide we can be of any use. I can work and make money in Canada easily, and would not be causing anxiety to so many.

This has been a rare and lovely interlude. [The Vivantes] lift me up to a plane of such fineness it seems I touch Lauro's hand again and feel the re-assurance of his nobility of spirit and greatness of heart and mind.

One is in anguish to see these people preparing. I can see my dear Fred's distress and hopelessness. My love to you—hope it's as lovely weather with you as we are having—

Diary:
"Spent my last afternoon and evening with Guy and Sis Dawnay at Long-parish. Margaret Phipps went with me—Fred and the Rolls took her back to London after seeing me off at Southampton."

Ruth Draper sailed in the French Liner Champlain *on August 29. On September 1st Hitler invaded Poland and on the 3rd England and France were at war with Germany.*

Many years later she was to say, publicly, in England: "I often regretted that I was not here to go through the War with you."

To Mrs. Ernest Schelling

[December 1939]
66 East 79th Street
New York

My heart goes out to you in deepest sympathy. You will take comfort in the thought of the happiness you gave to Ernest in these past months, and the new life you brought him. He was an old and dear friend of mine, and I had so hoped to see you both and rejoice with him in his happiness.

The world is so full of sorrowing people now, and personal grief must teach us to understand. I am so very sorry you must learn so soon, but I hope your memories and all Ernest taught you will give you the courage to go on.

Ernest Schelling's wife, Lucie, had died; he remarried, but died suddenly on December 8, 1939.

Harriet Marple, in New York, was determined to return to France. Fearing nothing on land or sea, though passionately hating the sea, she sailed in mid-January 1940 from Providence, Rhode Island, to Lisbon on a 4000-ton Portuguese freighter with some half-dozen other passengers. It was a ghastly three-week trip, drifting for days in mid-Atlantic with disabled engines. After considerable delay in Lisbon, she got through to France, and Ruth quotes her, "Harriet writes Paris is wonderful and one isn't afraid in the streets carrying one's flashlight in the dark, 'all the obscure figures seem to be friends and not in the least ominous.' She says twenty-three years seem to have dropped away and she sees her blessés again in the faces of the permissionaires on the streets! She is happy to be there and is going to work among the refugees in Central France."

Harriet appears to have been at a hospital in Etretat when France fell. After that she worked with a Quaker group at a camp for Spanish refugee children in Southern France, and later went to Malaga to assist a Frenchwoman who cared for some of these "lost" children as her own.

For many years after the war Harriet Marple continued to work in various capacities with Relief groups and other Quaker projects. Although she was intensely philanthropic and deeply involved with the Friends, she never felt herself "fine enough" to think of becoming a Quaker.

The August 1939 letter from Ruth Draper appears to be the latest one Harriet Marple preserved; in war-time Europe undoubtedly all letters were destroyed. After the war it is probable they were much together and communication may well have been more often by telephone than by letter. Their close friendship continued to the time of Ruth's death.

Immediately, Ruth Draper's war work began in earnest. In January 1940 she carried out a month-long cross-Canada tour for the Red Cross—23 shows in 27 days in 15 towns. The Governor General, Lord Tweedsmuir (John Buchan), wrote on the 26th to thank her for her admirable personal service in undertaking such a tour in mid-winter—no light task. Only a few weeks later he died in Ottawa, where she had stayed with him and Lady Tweedsmuir while playing there.

After performing on the West Coast, she worked her way back to New York by April 8th, to prepare for her South American tour of three months.

To Martha Draper

[February 25, 1940]
The vista del Arroyo
Pasadena

I've just wound a ball (inside wind) of wool equal to yours in even winding and lovely lemon shape! Never cease to be grateful that you taught me to knit so beautifully, and all your standards of neatness and order—like Aunt Edith's—will always be my ideal—not always reached, alas, but ever before me! It always distresses me that Doro and Alice never wear a 'combing jacket', for that's something Mother taught me and I rarely neglect. It's so funny the little things one does at times that give one a pleasurable sense of faithfulness—tho' one fails in so many and more important ways!

A "combing jacket" was a light, loose jacket worn by ladies while combing, brushing, and dressing their hair, which, until the First World War, was usually long and abundant.

To Martha Draper

[March 13, 1940]
Arizona Inn
Tucson

I stayed in Phoenix in a charming Inn on the desert. The colors at sunset are really lovely, and it's wonderful to see so far; like my Rosie "ye see an awful lot of land and an awful lot of sky." I had splendid audiences in both Phoenix and here—lots of Eastern tourists and a good many people I know, so that was pleasant. Los Angeles was interesting—a weird world. I went to a Hollywood luncheon on Sunday at the Edward Robinsons (the great gangster actor)—[he] with a strange gentle quality that struck one at once, and when he took me into his house and showed me his pictures I suddenly saw the man's soul, and, in that horrible queer place, I realized beauty could still flourish. There were Renoirs, Cézanne, (one of his greatest) Manets, a Daumier, a Forain that made one's heart wince—Pissarros of Spring in France, as only he can paint it—Monet, Gauguin, Berthe Morisot, an early and marvellous Picasso, and so on. My eyes fairly dropped out of my head—and the man really adored them. We lunched in a canyon out of doors—at a week-end bungalow—I sat next [Felix] Wildenstein, the [art] dealer, and a Hungarian, and there were two French servants, and an Italian composer, and others who talked French, and we had wonderful wines and delicious food, and it was so funny talking of Vienna and hearing French in that place—with the warm sun on our plates and red wine! I was dizzy with the humor of it all—and from having felt at sea in a group of movie people, I suddenly felt at home—and nearly cried thinking of the real places, and the real beauty evoked by the language and the sun!

ITINERARY

1940			
Sat.	May	4	Sailed from New York/S.S. Uruguay
Fri.	May	17	Arr. RIO DE JANEIRO, BRAZIL (Hotel Copacabana)
		17–22	*Performances* Teatro Casino Copacabana

Fri.	May	24	*Benefit for British and French Red Cross*
Mon.	May	27	Fly to BUENOS AIRES, ARGENTINA
			(Alvear Palace Hotel)
	June	3, 7, 14	*Performances* Politiama Argentina
Sat.	June	15	Arr. MONTEVIDEO, URUGUAY (by boat)
Mon.	June	17	*Performances* Solis Theatre
Thurs.	June	20	*Red Cross Benefit* Metro Cinema
Fri.	June	21	Ret. to BUENOS AIRES
		21–24	*Performances* Politiama Argentina
Thurs.	June	27	ROSARIO, ARGENTINA (Hotel Italia)
		27	*Performance* Odeon Theatre
Fri.	June	28	Ret. to BUENOS AIRES
		28	*Performance* Teatro del Pueblo
Mon.	July	1	*Performances* Politiama Argentina
Sun.	July	7	*Charity Benefit* Politiama Argentina
Mon.	July	8	*Red Cross Benefit* Politiama Argentina
Tues.	July	9	Fly to CORDOBA, ARGENTINA
Wed.	July	10	Fly to Mendoza (bad weather)
Thurs.	July	11	Continue flight to SANTIAGO, CHILE
Wed.	July	17, 18, 19	*Performances* Teatro Municipal
Sat.	July	20	*Red Cross Benefit*
Mon.	July	22	Fly to AREQUIPA, PERU (3 days rest)
Sat.	July	27	Fly to LIMA, PERU
Tues.	July	30 &	
Thurs.	Aug.	1	*Performances* Teatro Municipal
Fri.	Aug.	2	*Benefit British Red Cross*
Tues.	Aug.	6	Fly to QUITO, ECUADOR
Wed.	Aug.	7	*Benefit British Red Cross* at British Legation
Thurs.	Aug.	8	Fly to CRISTOBAL, PANAMA
Fri.	Aug.	9	Fly via Barranquilla and Miami
			Arr. New York 7:30 p.m.

To Martha Draper

[May 5, 1940]
12:50 a.m.
S.S. Uruguay

It's so late and I'm a little shivery with weariness—having stood on deck watching the receding shore—I hate to go off and yet know it is my destiny to wander and work—a wonderful combination of effort and reward. The first hours are hard but I'll get into the mood soon and I like to realize how terribly I care for those I love, and you are very precious to me and my thoughts will be with you all along the way.

To Martha Draper

May 14 [1940]
On Board
S.S. Uruguay

First letters from a steamer are always alike, and dull! The trip has gone so fast, and we are all sorry it's over! It has been made utterly delightful by our meeting Professor and Mme. Focillon. He, of the Collège de France, has a chair at Yale and is going to Buenos Aires to lecture and then returning to France. We foregather daily and nightly, and talk and talk and talk. Such wit and wisdom, such humor and philosophy and charm I've rarely seen; he is the essence of France in its most noble and enchanting qualities—and in the anguish of these days his courage and faith in the future is strengthening and uplifting. He has the 'long view' of a really great person who accepts sacrifice as a necessary price of what one values, and quietly goes on with his work, and delights the minds and warms the hearts of all who know him. I can never be grateful enough for the privilege of being with him. Aileen and Mildred [Bliss] spoke to me of him, and Charles Boyer raved of him to Arthur and Nela, so we are all so grateful.

Many Germans on board, and the stewards, and one suspects them all. One's hate of the whole race increases as the incredible news pours in. We sit about the radio several times a day and it is more than one can bear, the blind fury one feels and can do nothing about.

[On May 10th the German Army invaded Holland, parachuting into the Hague and Rotterdam, and onto Fort Eben Emael in Belgium; Churchill became Prime Minister. On the 14th Holland surrendered.]

The Focillons and Rubinsteins and, I must admit, I, all felt the great indifference among Americans all thro' the West. No re-action at the horrors portrayed in cinema 'news'—little comment or expression of disapproval. Admiration rather for Hitler's skill and success. The parachute landings are amazing, but when Arthur asked the Captain if he didn't think the wearing of fake uniforms was dreadful, he said: "Well, they got away with it"! It's all so terribly sad—but I do hope that the attacks on Belgium and Holland have aroused the country. We *must* do more to help—and I don't see how we can possibly change Presidents now. No new one would know so much about the European situation and our own defense preparations, etc. What a ghastly mess wherever one looks.

But the stars and moon and these calm blue seas, and the two enchanting children who come to my room every morning on their way from breakfast, are a great comfort. They are perfectly adorable, and correct my French, and run to me whenever they see me—with radiant faces. Nothing is so healing as the innocence and gaiety of children.

Quickly reaching South American audiences, Ruth Draper very much en-joyed this tour in spite of being in constant anguish at the devastating news from Europe where Belgium, Holland, and France were being overrun. She was in great anxiety for friends in England, and in France where Dean Jay was in Paris and Harriet Marple and Elsie Hooper at base hospitals. Her expressions of hatred for Germans are significant of the intensity of her feel-ings for she was not a person who hated—"It is terrifying how bitter and angry one grows—when can we ever forgive people such wickedness?"

She wrote from Buenos Aires: "I think in my small way I'm helping a little to make something of our country more sympathetic to [Brazilians and Argentines] and they've given me the warmest kind of welcome." Every morning she was on the beach with the Rubinstein children, "the bathing is the best I have ever seen"; she liked the people, found in Victoria Ocampo (Argentine writer and Editor of the literary journal Sur) a most sympathetic friend; she was widely entertained, lunched and dined at Embassies and Le-gations, in most of which she had friends or friends of friends; and she crossed and recrossed the paths of the Rubinsteins and the Focillons. She "had a delightful time."

In each city she gave shows for a local charity and for the Allied Red Cross. Everywhere her houses were sold out, the enthusiasm enormous, the reviews splendid, everywhere she could have stayed longer.

To Martha Draper

June 4 [1940]
Buenos Aires

I want to do all I can to promote friendly feeling—naturally for the Al-lies. It is all too heart-breaking and desperate—but there seems nothing one can do. I imagine you get a certain comfort out of rolling bandages as I do from making money—but why—oh, why, can't our country do something? How much longer must we wait to be *human,* apart from being *wise*? Surely it is *our* battle now, can't we see? I've just read Churchill's speech ["we shall fight on the beaches . . . we shall fight in the streets . . . we shall never sur-render . . ."]. I sent a lot of cables last night to give some relief to my sad heart—to Eliza—to Harriet—to Margaret P. and Lauro's mother. Surely to know of our love and thoughts will help a little. I think of so many wonder-ful boys I know in the midst of it all—[Dunkirk Evacuation completed]—Blanche Serocold's two—Cis Dawnay's two—Anne's husband—a Scotch friend's three sons—Lady Howard's four sons—Letty Benson's Martin Charteris, and others in the 60th Rifles who were at Calais (I recited to them in Mandalay!) and many others. I can only hope Harriet is safe—think what that Etretat Hospital must be? If you can get any news I know you'll let me know. Loulie Thoron may know something of Elsie Hooper at Etretat. I worry for her safety too.

I am very well—meeting dozens of charming people—enjoying the interest and novelty of it all—lovely weather, not cold. I'm going to a beautiful old "estancia" for the week-end, which will be lovely, I know, and with such a beautiful person, a great friend of Mildred's, Senora Sanchez Elia. The women are lovely—so smart and such hair and teeth—smiling and charm and beautiful manners. The young are delightful and so sweet to me it's very flattering. Everyone wears black and I feel rather conspicuous in my colored clothes! It's not cold enough for a fur coat and I'm sorry I brought it. I must get up now and see my manager and get my hair washed. There are lovely things to buy, but one feels one shouldn't spend money with all the terrible need abroad. O, those poor refugees caught on the roads. The Focillons are here, I see them daily and love them and their courage—with breaking hearts they go about their work—and are always delightful.

To Martha Draper

> July 10 [1940]
> Cordoba, Argentina

I'm so behind with letters that I don't know how I'm ever going to catch up. I'll begin with you and tho' Mother told me never to start a letter with apologies or regrets—I must express them both! The fault is all the newspapers! The moment one awakens, one starts—tries not to look while one is actually eating—and then the horror begins. [Hitler's invasion of Great Britain appeared imminent.] One feels indeed just a helpless drifting weed on the great tide of history which can't be stemmed. And one feels somehow the price of our failure as human beings—the punishment for the sins of the privileged—is being exacted from the innocent and ignorant. It's *all* so wrong. One doesn't dare write to France now, and one doesn't know what to say to English friends—I feel so ashamed of my idle, luxurious, peaceful life. I gave a show for the Red Cross both in Montevideo, where I spent a week, and in B.A., and I shall do so in Santiago. I think of you every day, and picture you making dressings on your terrace—your third, our third, war. How different—how increasingly terrible they've been.

I really loved Buenos Aires, for I found such good friends there. Arthur and Nela came the week before I left, and some friends of theirs, and I found them a nice flat. Toscanini had an absolute triumph, and I never heard the orchestra play so well—it was superhuman. The Argentines went mad—they're very musical. By far the most exciting and interesting audience I had was at the Teatro del Pueblo—1300 people who only pay .30 (about 8 cents) to get in. I did the Three Generations, Actress, Vive la

France, and the Church. They were wildly enthusiastic, got every point—
laughed or were silent. I was never so moved and thrilled! *Such* intelligent,
warm and unspoiled people—thoughtful, and deeply interested. They adore
the theatre, and give one all their ardent attention. I couldn't but compare
them to our dull, movie-paralysed, small town audiences. It is so thrilling
measuring a people's intelligence and heart and qualities by such a group.
One gets reality and can judge their potential capacity so clearly. I was uplifted by the experience and more convinced than ever that one must never
play down to an audience—and if only leaders in government and politics,
and any group, would appeal to the finest in people they'd find it. If only
they'd be fearless and trusting, as I am with the audience; you can't think
how wonderful it is—to be sustained by a great wave of good emotion. I
wish you'd been there. It speaks well for their general education—the
younger ones all take English in the schools and colleges now, and many
speak French. My Spanish is awful—I'm really *very* stupid—and this false
reputation of being a great linguist makes me squirm!

To Martha Draper
1001 Park Avenue
New York

November 25 [1940]
Bermuda

I'm sitting in a low chair on the grass, and from where I sit I see bananas,
roses, hybiscus, violets, onions, geraniums, cedars, rocks, orange trees (not
blooming now)—the strangest mixture, but all green and lovely and many
birds coming to drink at a little fountain. The sea is close, many islands that
make it look strangely like Islesboro, and the blue open sea beyond. It is
quite still, a bicycle bell, or a gentle little wagon and the patter of hoofs on
the road near by. A little train passes every two hours, rather pleasant and
cosy, otherwise the wind in the cedars is the only sound. It's very mild. I am
going in to town soon to see about my show to-night.

I am so happy, because I found Smudge here! He sails to-night, or flies
to-morrow, it's not yet certain. In any case I shall see him. He sounded fine
over the phone—you were away when [his mother] called to tell me he'd
gone to enlist in the R.A.F. I feel very proud of Smudge. I believe he came to
the decision and made all his plans alone, and he must know what lies before him.

I have four shows here and am playing 50/50 for the War Relief and it
promises to be very successful. The Focillons are in my flat. I get back the
morning of the 5th and leave at once for Albany. Hope you'll be all settled
when I return.

The years 1941–1945 were a separate war-time entity in Ruth Draper's career. She remained entirely within the United States and Canada, incessantly on the move, criss-crossing both countries nearly at random, performing almost exclusively to benefit the Red Cross, for British War Relief, and for the entertainment of troops in Army Camps, hospitals, and Air Force Bases. It was an enriching, exhausting experience, personally unremunerative. In no way did she spare herself.

The events in Europe were obsessively in her mind. The fighting, the bombing, the privations, the loss of friends were a constant anxiety. Privately, she did what she could, opening the Islesboro house each summer to family and friends, and children from England; and sending, with the help of Grace Martin, countless packages of food and necessities to friends in England, a kindness that they kept up for many years after the War. Gilbert Murray reported that the green jersey Ruth sent him was considered highly becoming.

The Vivante family had, of course, remained in England. Immediately upon the entry of Italy into the war (June 10, 1940) as Hitler's ally, Mr. Vivante and the two elder sons, although anti-fascist, were arrested as "friendly enemy aliens" and interned because German invasion was threatened at that time and "incidents" were feared. Mr. Vivante and his eldest son, interned on the Isle of Man, were released six months later. The second son, Arturo, aged 16 and at school, was interned for two weeks near Liverpool, then, in the haste and confusion of the time, shipped to Canada in a group of 2000 "friendly aliens" swept along with a large number of Prisoners of War, who were considered dangerous and sent out of England for safe custody.

As this deportation was admittedly an unfortunate blunder, Ruth Draper hoped that Arturo could enter the United States, where he had relatives and where she offered to assume complete responsibility for him. Due to a misunderstanding of the true status of these "friendly aliens," the U.S. Immigration Department could not, under the then existing agreement with Canada, admit him. In April of 1941, while on tour in Canada, Ruth Draper wrote on his behalf to Mackenzie King, the Canadian Prime Minister, regarding his release, and to Mrs. Franklin D. Roosevelt regarding his entry into the United States. Some weeks later Arturo Vivante was released in Canada, where Ruth found a friend to sponsor him and where she financed his living and tuition while he finished his schooling and medical education at McGill University in Montreal.

To Mrs. Franklin D. Roosevelt

April 25, 1941
Rideau Cottage
Ottawa

Dear Eleanor:

Little did I think that one day I should be writing to you to make an urgent appeal for help in a matter that concerns me deeply, and at the same time is an effort to right a great injustice. But this war brings up strange situations and I venture to put my request before you, relying on your forbearance and generosity, and on your prompt intercession, if you are willing to help. Will you be good enough to read the enclosed statement and then proceed with this letter.

A few days ago Lord Halifax went with Mr. Patterson, the [British] Home Office representative, to talk with Mr. Hull, who expressed interest in the plan referred to, but said he would have to see the President about it.

It so happens that among those innocent boys who are being detained in the Internment Camp, is one Arturo Vivante, aged 17, who is as dear to me as a member of my own family. His grandmother, Lillian Vernon, is an American, descended, I believe, from a sister of President Monroe. His Uncle was Lauro de Bosis, who flew over Rome in October 1931, dropping leaflets appealing to his compatriots to rise against Fascism. He was lost on his return flight. He foresaw the doom of Italy and offered his life in this gesture of protest and warning. He left a very remarkable letter stating his purpose, called "The Story of My Death," which you may have seen, and a beautiful play called "Icaro," which I translated from the Italian. His family have always been violent anti-fascists and his sister, Elena Vivante, mother of this boy, with her husband, three sons and daughter, left Italy, settled in England in 1937, because they were so unhappy under the Fascist regime and wanted their sons to grow up in a free country. The eldest son won a scholarship to Oxford, the younger ones were at school in Worcester. When Italy entered the war they were arrested. The subsequent story is that which is described in the statement which I have enclosed. The father and older brother have been free in England for the past six months and had Arturo not been sent to Canada he, also, would have been free in England now.

The impasse between Canadian and United States laws seems to grow worse rather than better. It is my desperation over this condition which moves me to write you, hoping that the President and Mr. Hull will agree on the scheme which has been pressed upon the latter by Lord Halifax, and thus enable innocent refugees to be admitted to the United States.

Dr. Lewis Perry, of Exeter, is interested in the boy and is holding a place for him at the school. He is sponsored by an Aunt and Uncle in Reading, Mr. and Mrs. Vernon, and he has many other responsible and devoted cousins. He is a splendid boy of the finest character, scholarly and intelligent and the whole de Bosis family are the most remarkable and superior people I know anywhere. They were intimate friends of old Moses Ezekiel, of whom your Aunt Corinne and dear Mrs. Leavitt were so fond. The George and Charles Trevelyans, the Gilbert Murrays, the late H. A. L. Fisher, the historian, are the Vivantes' friends in England, and all wrote letters to the Home Office in their defense. I vouch for his innocence and assume complete responsibility for his support and education. He will make a splendid citizen.

I hope you will forgive my taking this much of your valuable time, but I have been waiting and hoping for ten months to get this boy out of confinement. I hear now that the American Legion and certain members in Congress are definitely working against admission of any person of foreign birth into the United States who has been in internment camps, in spite of the fact that many have the highest recommendations and affidavits proving their innocence, and I am impelled by my great desire to see justice done these boys, particularly the one of whom I am so fond, and I therefore approach you and beg you to intercede in their behalf.

With grateful appreciation for any help you can give, I am,

Affectionately yours,
Ruth Draper

These war-time summers at Islesboro must have brought Ruth closer to her childhood joys, and for longer periods, than for many years—particularly with the comfortable, high-ceilinged, grey-shingled old house full of children and young people. Here she seemed most truly herself, with her humor and tenderness, her deep love of the natural world, and her intense delight in her friends—of whatever age—constantly demonstrated.

The living room and dining room, and the partially covered, open verandah outside all faced west, overlooking Gilkey's Harbor, with its islands, far below. On the wide verandah, in good weather, the entire company gathered for lunch, and rests after lunch were the strict rule. In an alcove at the north end there was a daybed heaped with cushions, where Ruth often rested and read in the afternoons. All small visitors, family or no, found it a good place to go for a cuddle and a story. When she read aloud to the children, poetry, The Wind in the Willows, *her marvelous voice rose and fell, making them laugh at Toad's pomposity or weep with Mole as he yearned for home; she could not always get through "The Piper at the Gates of Dawn" without weeping herself. She never hid from the children her own emotion and response to beauty, and an invariable rite was the wonder and enjoyment of sunsets over Penobscot Bay and the Camden Hills. The evenings were full of talk by the fire, and games with Ruth and Salvemini participating as gleefully as the children.*

She gave herself endlessly to making the summer a delight to everyone: a bountiful table, conversation and hilarity at meals, swims, walks, picnics, sailing. She taught many of the children in Islesboro to sail in Gilkey's Harbor, where she, as a child, had sailed her own little "Flickamaroo," exploring every rock, inlet, and small island. But with all this activity, she had her deeply private times: quietly out in her canoe in the dawn stillness of the harbor, disappearing for long walks on foggy mornings, or scrambling down to a secluded cove on the East beach to swim nude, always invigorated by the icy Maine water.

Before the war the tennis court was much in use. Penelope Draper remembers watching Aunt Ruth, Mrs. Charles Dana Gibson, Mrs. Dudley Howe, and another friend play doubles. It was the "ultimate in hilarity."

> *Mrs. Gibson wore a large Gibson girl straw hat with a veil to protect her beautiful skin. Mrs. Howe wore long white kid gloves which she moistened at the outside faucet in order to grip the racquet and Aunt Ruth sometimes tucked her dress into her bloomers for swifter action—quite unselfconsciously. Their game was mostly lobshots, gentle, but dirty, if one ever played with them, and the conversation was superb. They never stopped gossiping as they played and a particularly devastating comment would be accentuated by the whack of racquet on ball. We used to sit, hypnotized, with aching sides.*

During the war the tennis court, neglected, became a hay field and was never remade. Once a summer it was mowed. One perfect Maine day Aunt Ruth and Penelope were raking the hay, each in her own corner, preoccupied with private thoughts and the rhythm of raking. Suddenly Aunt Ruth said, "When you come right down to it, I don't like talking"; there was no reply, and after a while she added, "or even thinking." They continued to rake in companionable silence.

Undoubtedly these were her happiest times with the children of family and friends she gathered about her, for her love of children and her joy in them was intense. Yet she wrote, in 1934: "I guess it's lucky I had no children—their imperfections would have hurt me so—and my disappointment would have hurt them so." As Joyce Grenfell said, "We had to be on our best behaviour with her—but it was worth it."

The English children who came in 1941 were: Anne and Venetia Murray, Oliver Gates and Nana, Sallie and Tessa Marris with Nannie, Pauline and John Rathbone with Nannie. Various family and friends also came and went: Aileen Tone, Anxie Gamble, Salvemini, Grace Martin, Justice Frankfurter, the Félix Salmonds.

All the war-time summers were much the same, filling the house with the young, the adults in need of a rest, those she loved having about her. Except for 1946, the year of her return to Europe, this summer pattern of several months at Islesboro was to continue for the remainder of her life. Even at the end of her last summer she wrote: "I love having this old house full of young things, and I love feeding them and planning for their pleasure and well-being. It is indeed a contrast to my London life, but equally absorbing."

Ruth Draper completed very few new sketches after 1930, but when the children had left Islesboro, and while sitting waiting for the return ferry, she outlined in her mind the sketch that was to become Vive la France—1940. *Then she set forth again: "2700 ladies laughed in Detroit at 11 a.m.; and my three shows in Canton, Ohio, went awfully well considering I'd not been for 7 years." In October she reported to Martha Draper: "I had a lovely letter from Harriet—she said Churchill's speech had been dropped from the air, causing intense excitement and then salvaged from the police, selling for 100 francs! She was in touch with Léa and had ordered some slips, and was sending her food! It is all so crazy. H. hinted she might come home in the Spring—that morally and physically she is feeling the strain of her work. I hope everyone will write a line to Smudge—he is probably fighting now, and in such danger."*

To Corinne Robinson
(Mrs. Joseph W. Alsop, Sr.)

November 14 [1941]
Minot, North Dakota

I'm well and happy and it is fun. We go to such funny places, and now and then to a friend and luxury and comfort, and in spite of the bad hot air I do like trains! I have superb audiences everywhere, and the response is terrific. New people, young people, alert and keen and warm, and it's very gratifying. That is the advantage of this kind of management [concert tours]. No worry about advertising, no risk, an assured packed house every night with the "best people" in each town and, what I love, the youth! The high school and civic auditoriums I simply *hate*, but that's where concerts are held, so I have to bear it, but the audiences seem wild with delight, and it's a wonderful satisfaction. The jumps are fantastic. It is as if I went from Paris, to Rome, to Warsaw, to Bagdad and back to Vienna, in a week almost! Josephine [maid] is going home on the 24th—so I'll have only three weeks alone—I just can't pay those terrific fares.

She kept on her way, "amused by dreary hotels"; grounded in Grand Forks, North Dakota, in November: "two nice young men in the hotel lobby who'd heard me the night before, offered to motor me [to Winnipeg]—140 miles . . . . Such fine fellows—one with Swedish grandpar-

ents and one with Russian grandparents—emigrés of sixty years ago. We had a nice time and good talk, and the wife of the Lieutenant Governor, where I was staying, asked them in for tea on our arrival." So it went: "41 shows in 34 towns in 62 days! I start off on my next tour on January 10th [1942]."

When she was home: "three sailors came to supper last Sunday, and six are coming next. I cooked and we had a lovely time. Margaret was with me." But she preferred "the road"—it made her feel she was doing something worthwhile. "Fussing about at home doesn't defeat Hitler."

The entire year of 1942 was very much the same; then, over the Christmas and New Year's holidays, she gave a short season at The Little Theatre in New York, writing to Grace Martin: "I've not worked for so long, I've somehow lost faith in my work—but I must 'go to it' again!"

To Martha Draper

[February 9, 1943]
Jacksonville, Florida

You would laugh if you could see me—I'm sitting on the step of a parked car in front of the station. It's a lovely day and I'm in the bright sun. There are no seats, tho' it's a grand station and hundreds of boys are standing about the sunny portico, waiting for trains. It's crowded and smelly inside and so in despair I seized a sheet from a [news]paper and walked out into the great parking space, chose a nice car and am very comfortable! I arrived at 8:30 this morning from Birmingham and as my Miami train is late, I went to a hotel and after trying three got a nice room. I had a lovely bath and then made myself a *delicious* breakfast—ordering my milk and toast 20¢! I had an egg with me and honey, and made wonderful coffee, heated the milk, re-toasted the toast and had a feast. Then I dressed and came to the station for the train which was supposed to be in at 11:30—now it's not due till 12:40—hence my resort to a sun bath and this letter to you. The crowds are terrific—but so far I've had no difficulty—and last night I got the Drawing room which was not sold, and a soldier took my lower, so I was in great luxury and had cocoa and crackers and an apple in my room—as there were three shifts in the diner and I wasn't very hungry. This place is a great junction for Navy, Army, and Air forces, so it's jammed. I am so impressed by the men—so fine looking, so patient and courteous—they just break your heart—and the farewells at stations, and the young draftees going off from small stations, and the young mothers and their babies, following, or off to join their men, rip you to pieces with the pathos and courage they show. Fine boys carrying their babies and luggage, waiting interminably. . . . The porters and station personnel are awfully nice to them. Such a fine older man at the Information Desk here answering so kindly the endless inquiries. What a world—I suppose you saw it all in 1898 and probably passed thro' here.

To Grace Martin
(Mrs. David Terry Martin)

[April 14, 1943]
Goderich, Ontario

[This work] has a special significance to me now—apart from the deep feeling I always have for aviators—because my beloved nephew, Paul's brother Sanders, was killed on March 24th in an accident due to engine trouble, in Hornchurch, England. He did a heroic and skillful thing just before he crashed. He avoided a school in which were 1000 children, turned rapidly and managed to crash in a field. His Spitfire loaded with gasoline and bombs would have caused a hideous tragedy. We read in the papers that he stayed with his plane and controlled it till he crashed. The tragedy is exalted by his way of going—keeping his head as he did to the very end. I am terribly sad tho' I'm very proud. I longed to see 'Smudge' again in his beautiful Flying Officer's uniform—made such a man by his two and a half years faithful service in that glorious R.A.F.! He was a fighter pilot in a Spitfire. He seldom wrote, and couldn't say much, but I think had recently been on 'operations'. He had been doing a lot of Instruction and found that tedious, as they all do, but it is none the less important. I suppose the tragic story will come soon officially from his Squadron Leader.

So far, we've only had the Cable with the actual announcement of his death—and then the thrilling story the Radio and Newspapers carried. It is a comfort to know it was given wide publicity over all the U.S. and Canada. It was on the front page of the Toronto paper. No one knew he was connected with me. They got his name wrong, which was unfortunate. He was named Raimund Sanders Draper, but never used the first name, and the papers carried the first name only, and spelt it Raymond. It was too bad, but in the Memorial which the School is making to his memory, we'll see it's put right. 1500 children and parents of the village attended his funeral, and he will always be remembered there, and someday little Anne can go and see his grave, and where her heroic father died.

God rest his brave young soul, with all the other thousands who've given their lives in this awful war. It is only one of millions, and when I realize the suffering of the people who loved them all it makes the whole thing so gigantic, so real, and so hopeless to heal in your time.

To Martha Draper

[mid-April 1943]
Hamilton, Ontario

A letter from my friend Lorna Carew, who was my secretary in London, has just come, enclosing a clipping from The Times and I am weeping with pride and gratitude. How rightly and beautifully the British and the old Times value the meaning of an incident like darling Smudge's death. It says:

DRAPER—SANDERS (Smudge) Flying Officer R.A.F. To the most proud and glorious memory of an American who was born in London, England in 1914 and was killed on active service in March 1943.
"Per ardua ad astra"

That's the Air Force motto. It was signed D.P., so perhaps some one of his squadron or a friend put it in. I am so glad it was done, I am sending the original to Muriel and have written to The Times asking for another and to know if possible who D.P. is so we can thank him.

My tour is going beautifully and it is thrilling going from one Air Force Station to another. Some are R.A.F., some R.C.A.F., and I can learn so much of the life and work that Smudge had these past two and a half years. I read with enormous interest, poignant and thrilling, a little book called "Squadrons Up"—a story of the R.A.F. in the early part of the war. Toward the end, it gives a list of forty-three dials, buttons, etc., that the Fighter Pilots have to memorize and work—and I felt so humble and amazed to think that Smudge had mastered all that, and taught it! I had a lovely letter from Dicky Aldrich and was so touched. I am with a dear friend here, but go on to-morrow to the next station—a very nice flying officer motors me from point to point, and it's the happiest way I could spend my time, working with these splended aviators. Strange I've had it in my mind for so long to do—and it's working out so beautifully and they seem so grateful.

To Malvina Hoffman

[Martha Draper had died on June 19th.]

July 10 [1943]
Dark Harbor, Maine

Dearest Mallie—

You wrote me the loveliest letter and we were all so touched by your sending the lovely white gladioli. Thank you very much for your tribute to Martha, and the thought, and loving loyalty that made you go to her place and think of her, and gather the little pansies on the day of her funeral, since you could not be with us. I was awfully touched by that, and she would have been.

Well, another chapter is closed, though I don't like the phrase. The beauty and meaning of her life and character will be significant always in our lives. Never was there a more self-effacing and selfless soul; witness the account of her activities, which surprised many people. She never talked of herself or anything she'd done. I'm glad our daily papers gave so much space to such a worthy and modest person—who really had served long and faithfully. Sam [Grimson] sent flowers, and I thought it so sweet of him. He always had a great feeling for Ba I think.

I got here on Monday and it's simply heavenly. I have Felix and Helen and little John Salmond, Anxie Gamble, Zosia Kochanski, little Bill Coleridge, and am hoping for little Anne Draper next week. I hope you are feeling better, and will have a restful summer. I feel very self-indulgent taking such a holiday—but I can give such a healthful rest to others too, that I feel justified!

Lots of love old dear; one feels the bonds of the past so strongly when the blows fall, and you belong in the wonderful circle that made us all what we are, and what we must still strive to be worthy of—

By an anti-war coup d'état *in July 1943 Mussolini was overthrown; this led to the entry of the German armies into Italy. It was not until the 3rd of October that the Allied forces of liberation reached Naples—and at long last the Italian people were to be freed from Fascism. A few days later the* New York Herald-Tribune *published an editorial noting that October 3rd was the twelfth anniversary of Lauro de Bosis' flight over Rome, when "he offered up his own life in order to prevent the catastrophes which have since taken place," and quoted him as saying then: "The new oppressors are fiercer and more corrupt than the old, but they will also fail." Elsewhere on the editorial page the* Herald-Tribune *reprinted in part* The Story of My Death *and noted that the letters he dropped in 1931 "might have been written this spring."*

It was another eight months, exactly, before Rome was liberated, but in that German-occupied city Charis Cortesi, Lauro's sister in Lauro's old home, had received in secret meetings the "shadow cabinet" of the Roman Committee of National Liberation. This was a dangerous and daring thing to do in any case, but also it was just around the corner that a bus-load of German police had been bombed—leading to the infamous ten-for-one reprisal massacre of 335 Italians in the Ardeatine Caves on March 24, 1944.

To Grace Martin
(Mrs. David Terry Martin)

November 16 [1943]
The 1811 House
Manchester, Vermont

I have *no* jobs (after three, end of November). Hurok has let me down *flat!* I've a new manager named Harold Peat who is trying to fill up a few weeks here and there, but it is doubtful if he gets anything. Going as far as Chicago, I don't think I'll return. I want to go to the coast to see my other nephew in Seattle, and his wife and boys in San Francisco, so I'll work where I can in camps, and get a few pay jobs when and where I can. I rented [my apartment] to economize, so I'm foot-loose and free, which I like, but it's sad not to have any work. Hurok's only explanation is that they can't sell me any more, as I have nothing new. There may be *some* truth in it—but more likely it is that they have new and bigger draws like the Negro dancer and her company who plays to $30,000 a week in New York! However there is the truth; youth and glamour and novelty are what is wanted—none of which I can claim! I'm here for a week, in this beautiful country, sparkling air, sun and snow. I thought I might find leisure and solitude conducive to work—but so far I've not been inspired!

To Grace Martin
(Mrs. David Terry Martin)

April 18, [1944]
With Miss Wilks
Cruickston Park
Galt, Ontario

I wish you could see the house I'm in. The old lady who owns it, and some 2500 acres, is 94 years old with a memory far clearer than mine! She walks with a quick firm step, tho' she uses a cane, in a gay sort of way, and is only a little deaf. The house is full of old deeds, books, furniture, objets d'art, and souvenirs that keep living in a past of dignity and humor, opulence and peace. There is actually an old tin bath tub under my huge bed (tho' a perfectly appointed bath-room is adjacent to my room!) A fire is crackling in my grate and I look into a forest of beech trees all lit up by the morning sun, against a blue sky. It is a most beautiful place, and she runs a great farm so I'm swimming in cream, butter and fresh eggs, her own bacon and ham, and beef! It is so cosy, and I adore hearing the gossip of seventy years ago, and her life as a girl.

I've just had three jobs up here—Quebec to a big French Canadian audience, (and one to Air Force boys in a Navigation School) in Montreal at the Theatre, and one at the big hospital, and one in a factory, and a big Benefit in Ottawa, for the French refugees in England. I stayed at Government House, and it was great fun. I had a wonderful letter from Miss Mudie.

To Grace Martin
(Mrs. David Terry Martin)

April 10 [1945]
Robert Driscoll Hotel
Corpus Christi, Texas

[The German army was crumbling and on May 4th surrendered.]

Thanks for forwarding my letters. *Such* treasure as that envelope contained: three from the boys in Germany, one from Lauro's mother in Rome, one from a dear friend in England, one from a friend in France, three from my sisters—and a cable from London from my old stage manager, saying he could get a theatre, and please to come! My heart is bursting with pride, and love, and longing, and confusion—so many thoughts merge, and race, and vanish, and quicken and delve,—reading all these messages from thousands of miles away—while I sit up in bed looking out on the Gulf of Mexico! My life is an orgy of color and action—and I'm too small to digest it all—and use and coordinate, and create some beautiful evidence of my rich possession.

Thanks for both your letters, and all your affection! My heart is sad for the frozen blossoms, and fruit that won't go in your jars,—it must be awful to stand and watch the cruel destruction of nature; and how one can apply those same words in a larger sense to what is going on every where? Yet we hold passionately to our ideas of justice and mercy and wisdom and goodness and purpose and hope and faith—and our greatest creation—the idea of God.

·To Harley Merica
[stage manager in England]

April 16 [1945]
Chicago

I was thrilled to get your cable but I couldn't answer at once in the affirmative, for the same reason that I have not come to England before this! I have no new sketches! Indeed, I should have loved to reply at once, saying "Take theatre"—but there are a great many considerations.

First, let me tell you how glad I was to hear from you. I've written several times, in the early part of the war, and never heard from you after I left in '39—or whether you ever got a silver cigarette case I sent you with a map of our great journey to the East? I wrote Mr. Bright's office for news, but never could get a trace or rumor about you! I am glad to know you are alive, and well, and I hope you've written me in more detail about your suggestion of the theatre. You can imagine I've often longed to return and the very thought of facing again the beloved English public moves me deeply. But how *can* I come back with nothing new? I have one new French number—a 1940 sequel to *Vive la France 1916,* and it is very exciting and moving, and

I do the two to-gether. Then I have a very slight and silly piece called *Glasses*—but it doesn't amount to anything. The *Church in Italy* is too dated, and too sad to do in the light of the turn of events; the *Houseparty* I've dropped entirely, and forgotten; [the] *Italian Lesson* and *Cliffords* seem dated; and all the rest *so* inappropriate that I'd hardly venture to make a program, what do you really think? I'd love to raise money, and give benefits everywhere, and go to hospitals if I were wanted, as I've been doing here. I've just returned from a three-months tour—thirty-eight engagements and twenty-one camp shows—great success everywhere—but all new places, so my old programs were all right. I don't play in New York any more—the critics are too critical of my old material—not of my work—and theatres impossible to get.

I had a cable from Curtis Brown Ltd. in the Spring of '43, and a letter from Joan Ling (to whom I'd written for your address) begging me to come over—but my excuse was the same I give you now. Were I to come—what shall I do? Your cable is not explicit enough of where and how I should go about coming. Curtis Brown has all Mr. Bright's data, accounts, reviews and programs, I gather, with names and places where I've been. Should I let them manage me? I'd thought of writing Myra Hess to suggest letting her organization arrange a Benefit tour. I just don't know how to start, about getting permission to come over etc. I must have a good reason and evidence of work, I suppose, for the authorities both for permission to go from here, and permission to enter England. So there is *much* to be done before I can say that I will come, and therefore I could not answer your cable.

What have you been doing these five years? I expect you've been in the Army. I've been on long tours—to S. America and, since 1941, only in this country. I have engagements thro' May, but I could sail, or fly at the end of May. I return home this week and will be at 66 East 79th Street from now on. Let me know as soon as possible what you think is the best thing for me to do. A season in London?—brief visits to other cities? Edinburgh—Manchester—etc.? I suppose my old stage things are all right to use, but should I travel about I would use whatever I find in local halls or theatres, for travelling must be very difficult and I shouldn't attempt to carry more than a suit case of shawls etc.

Hoping to hear from you soon, and that possibly something can be arranged.

To Harley Merica
in England

[October 14, 1945]
Birmingham, Alabama

I received your cable this summer, but expected it to be followed by a letter, for which I have waited all these many weeks. The cable referred to your letter which "explained everything." I had received a letter from you in the Spring, which I answered, saying I did not like your idea of my giving a "benefit to honor the British Navy." I could not see that that was an appropriate thing for me, as a private citizen, to do! Nor did I like the idea of using that as a means of getting into England. So I wrote you accordingly—also to ask [about] working with "Curtis Brown" as managers? I know no other agents, and as they have all my data, etc. from G. Bright it seemed the simplest thing to work with them. I did not write them, but recently, Spencer Curtis Brown wrote me, having heard thro' Myra Hess, that I wanted to come over.

Had you answered my letter things might have been different but having heard nothing further from you—I was at a loss to know how to proceed, and I have answered Mr. Curtis Brown asking him for further details, and to get in touch with you. I should certainly want you to manage my tour, and look after everything as in the past, and I am quite prepared to pay more for your services, realizing that all salaries must be far higher, and expenses of living greater. It is so hard to arrange things from so far away— and you must admit that not hearing from you again left me very uncertain what to do! Work turned up to do here, my passport has not come through yet,—so I could not come anyway. This I feel would have been best, to come over and make plans when I arrived, but that is out of the question with no passport! I am hoping daily to receive it, then get my visa, and sail in early January. Meantime it seems best to try and get a theatre, and start in London with a regular season. Once there, I can arrange benefits—and go on a tour with C.E.M.A. which has been proposed by Mr. Curtis Brown. I have written him however, that I think in all the big cities, in England and Scotland, I had best give seasons of my own. I asked him to get in touch with you—as you know so much about my work, and where I've been, etc. and can go over all Bright's material, and see what I need to send over.

I can't imagine doing a tour without your management, and hope you are not committed to other work that will prevent your co-operating with Curtis Brown and handling my return appearances.

**To Harley Merica
in England**

[December 8, 1945]
Evansville, Indiana

Thanks for your letter of some weeks ago, telling me of the 'lost' one of the summer. I was waiting to answer it until I heard from Mr. Curtis Brown and Miss Ling. Dame Myra Hess had spoken to him, and he'd taken a lot of trouble, conferring with C.E.M.A. about a tour—but after seriously considering their proposal I feel I'd be happier on my own, working with you and Miss Ling—now that I know she has a firm of her own with H.Q. in London. I could not visualize you on the road with me, and running the business end too! I've written her that I'd be glad to start by end January or early February if a theatre is available. I feel it would be wiser not to go at once on a strenuous tour under the present conditions, and in mid-winter. I must admit that we being used to normal conditions (I feel to our shame) I shall probably need to get used to the diet, and the cold before I do much travelling, and I'd rather be in London, or one of the large cities, or possibly Oxford or Cambridge.

I am, of course, very happy to know that you want to work with me again, and that you can leave your present position with the Repertory Co., tho I expect they'll be furious! I do hope C.E.M.A. and Mr. Curtis Brown won't be terribly cross with me for throwing them over. I did not commit myself but before hearing from you or Miss Ling—I felt quite hopeless of getting anything started, and I did answer their very nice letter, proposing that I come over under C.E.M.A. management. I may want to do some shows for them sometime.

I am sorry for the long delay in getting plans under way and do hope things can be amicably arranged. I wrote Mr. C.B. that my long association with you and Miss Ling made it easier for me to resume my work in England, than to go under a new management. I hope they will understand.

It will be wonderful to come back, and I know the warmth of the welcome will make up for any difficulties I may have. I wish I could get that darling Adah [dresser] but I fear she'll not leave her husband and girls. I wonder if Fred is still about? I think of the wonderful old days—and know how different everything is—but if I can still give pleasure with my work I shall be so happy. I know the emotion of facing the public that has endured so much will be tremendous. I shall probably be made quite speechless, with humility and awe—for it moves me even to think of it—and has done all these years. I shall hope to hear soon that work can be arranged. Best wishes for Xmas and the New Year.

In November Ruth Draper had written Grace Martin: "I'm not working—and feel rather desperate being idle and forgetting my sketches, and not caring much, alas—they seem so dated and out of harmony with the world to-day." But early in December she wrote again: "I have a new sketch—The Return—about an English prisoner coming home. It promises to be good—thank God!"

This problem of new material was a continuing worry to the end of her career. "The same old bag of tricks" was welcomed with love and en-

thusiasm and nostalgia in Great Britain, but in the United States it had begun to be a handicap. When the necessity of new work was urged upon her she would say: "Yes, that is true, but the old ones acquire a patine—a patine" and smooth the back of one hand with the other. Constantly refined, changed, tightened, some of the sketches gradually were re-done over the years; if long in the repertory, she said, "They are unrecognizable as I do them now! They change all the time; I should never be satisfied with a final written form."

Between January 1942 and January 1947 she did not appear in New York, partially because of the cost of the Union requirements for stage crew, but largely because of the apparent apathy of audiences and drama critics and the need for greater promotional effort—something she had no need for in England.

With their long tradition of theatre and love of being told a story, the British audiences responded, from the very beginning of her career, to her powerful story-telling—stimulating their imaginations. Joyce Grenfell, in talking of this, says: "She never played down—never explained. It was all so clear in her mind that she simply projected the outline and we all saw it, completed it; she took us miles away to the Church in Florence—we believed! This was her great gift—making the audience do the imagining too. And British audiences are notoriously loyal—once you are in you are in forever." The rapport, in January 1920, had been instant.

1946

Walked ....
looked .... wept
Remembered .... all wonderful.

Ruth Draper in Diary
1946

Ruth Draper sailed in R.M.S. Queen Elizabeth *on February 28th arriving in London March 6th. The Britain to which she returned has been described by Sir John Wheeler-Bennett:*

> ... a Britain tired and war-weary, yet compelled to face the severities of continued wartime shortages while deprived of the continued wartime stimulus. I shall never forget the dour drabness of those years, the greyness of one's daily existence, the seemingly endless nightmare of a Labour Government struggling manfully to solve the inevitable problem of post-war reconstruction, yet electing to embark simultaneously and precipitately upon the completion of the Social Revolution which had begun with Lloyd George's 'People's Budget' of 1909.
>
> Food was scarce, scarcer than it had been in wartime. Bread was rationed for the first time in our national history, and had it not been for the food parcels which [were] so generously sent us from America we should have been hard pressed indeed. As it was we were able to share our blessings with our less fortunate friends and neighbors. One still queued for nearly everything, and coupons were required for most commodities, including clothes and petrol.

To Dorothea Draper
(Mrs. Henry James)

[March 13, 1946]
[Hyde Park Hotel]
[London]

Everything goes superlatively well for me. It is really like a beautiful dream instead of a nightmare—this return. I feel I should not have it all so easy—but it would be an effort and a stupid one, I think, to try and change the lovely welcome my friends and fate have designed for me. To have Fred and the Rolls waiting for me at Waterloo (darling Margaret not being there with her delicious chuckle and large embrace was the first thing I missed) seemed to start a series of incredible happenings that have made me gasp with wonder and emotion. Lorna [Carew, secretary] had engaged the most beautiful 'suite' overlooking the Park and the Kensington Gardens, Serpentine, duck pond and lovely old trees and the Row, with riders and children on ponies going by every morning. The rooms were filled with flowers, and messages lay on the desk, and the telephone began and the first morning Anne and Joyce and Pamela Dawnay and Rosemary (Chancellor) all arrived, and I doled out presents from my trunk, and it was a heavenly happy gathering. Paul [Phipps] came and lunched with me—much older and rather sad he seemed—Margaret Stanley came to tea, and I dined with Bill and Pamela [Phipps]. Each day I've lunched and dined with friends—always taking them something from my store of food.

I've been to the National Gallery—a moving experience to see those beloved and familiar pictures back—after being buried and hidden for over six years. I've driven to the City and seen St. Paul's, and all the devastation—gaps where buildings were—the rubble all neatly cleared away now. The churches are tragic evidence of the horror, yet strangely enough the lovely steeples stand, and much of the walls—the roofs and insides all gone. I've still much to see. The old church in Chelsea is completely levelled, and *all* that block near the bridge where the de Glehns' house stood. It is so sad—I was near to tears those first days, and still am. London somehow is like a beloved person, with a soul—and one feels exactly as one would toward a friend who has been tortured and scarred, but remains undaunted, valiant and calm. I am surprised how good the food is—far better than I thought it would be. People are thin and faces look worn and strained—but less than I imagined they would—of course I see my friends smiling and most faces, everywhere, in repose are rather sad; what you don't see is the hard look, the assured, well groomed, artificial look of the faces in New York. People look just plain and natural and suffering has left its mark, in character.

I've seen one most interesting play with Irene Ravensdale, and enclose the program. I'm going to Hampton Court this afternoon with little Anne Balfour (who stayed with me last year) to see Lady Isabella Howard, and Ros Coleridge's mother and sister who live there. To-night I'm dining with Bill and Pamela again to meet Rachel's Margaret, and her fiancé Jameson, and Nicholas Phipps. I shall take some tinned bacon, a box of chocolates, a lip stick, a few handkerchiefs, a box of Lux and a lovely pink gardenia (Bloomingdales!). My mail is terrific, but Lorna is a grand help. I hoped to go to the de Glehns' for the week-end, but I have to speak on the B.B.C. Saturday night—an awful bore—so must give up going.

My dear Ada is with me again at the theatre and is going on tour with me, so I'm very happy and I have the same stage manager, Mr. Merica, so, tho' I can't have Fred on the road, the same faithful group (of twenty years!) surround me now. My manager is a very able and enthusiastic gentleman, and is assiduous and considerate and showers me with flowers, as does everyone, so my lovely room is a bower, and I give a lot away. I've been dictating letters all morning and must now get up. Lunching with Pauline Clay.

B.B.C. Broadcast

March 16, 1946
6:45 p.m.

I am glad to have this opportunity to come before a larger audience than I face four times a week in the theatre, because I feel that I should like to convey to as many people as possible who know me in Britain, my deep emotion at being here again. The welcome I have received this week has been overwhelming, and it is difficult to express just what it has meant to me.

At my opening performance I was moved to say a few words—very inadequate—yet I hope their sincerity made clear my meaning, that the gift of my talent, which you so generously acknowledge, seems a small return for the great gifts of the spirit, which I, and countless thousands throughout the world have received from you during the past six and a half years, that the debt of gratitude will always be heavily on my side.

In the twenty years of my happy annual visits before the war I came to think of all my listeners as my friends. Now, I am not only happy, but very proud to have such friends. London seems more wonderful, more dear to me than ever, and I am so glad to be here again; so glad to greet you, and thank you for your loyalty and your welcome to me, who have loved you for so long.

Apart from this personal gratitude, I can't refrain from thanking you as an American for your great kindness to my compatriots during these past years. I am sure they will take back most happy and lasting memories, even as I hope your men will hold the same, of their brief sojourns in my country. England is a second home to me, and I am thankful that so many Americans have now experienced something of its character, its beauty, and its heart warming, kindly and inspiring qualities. For the tangible and intangible things that you have given to them, and to me, I thank you, with reverence and humility, with pride, and with most true affection.

In closing there is one thought which I should like to leave with you. Please think of me more than ever before, as an American—understanding and fraternal. One of the old links—a small one—among the many new ones in the chain that binds our two countries, but none the less a symbol of endurance, of confidence in the future, and abiding good will.

To Alice Draper
(Mrs. Edward C. Carter)

[March 16, 1946]
Saturday, 8 p.m.
Hyde Park Hotel
Knightsbridge

I am sitting in front of a *lovely* fire, in my *lovely* sitting room filled with flowers. I've just had a *lovely* hot bath, sweet with rose geranium (from N.Y.), and I'm about to have my dinner on a tray—and later dress, and go to a small dance of Mrs. Geoffrey Dawson. I've just come from the B.B.C. where I broadcast a greeting to Britain! I nearly died of nervousness and emotion. I enclose a copy of what I said. I almost cabled you to listen but don't think you get short wave. They say it was very good, and my voice didn't break thank good-ness.

Well,—I am overwhelmed by my welcome here. It is perfectly terrific! In my wildest dreams I did not anticipate anything like it. The theatre was sold out at once for all twelve performances. It holds about 800, a perfect place for me, and hundreds are turned away. It is with the greatest difficulty I can get two seats now and then for particular friends. I got two for Winnie and Con [Mudie] (84 and 87) for the opening, two for my beloved Lady Antrim (91) on Monday, in the front row. Queen Mary (my fan) and Princess Elizabeth have been—she is *lovely,* far prettier than her photos—the most perfect skin I ever saw—and a beautiful expression. She and the Queen roared, and liked it all. The new French sketch brings the house down every day and is the biggest triumph I've ever had. "The Return" goes very well, but not *as* well as I should like. It's too new, and doesn't compare, naturally, with the fluid, easy authority of the old standbys. Some people are crazy about it, and some (the more critical of my friends) not so. I think it's by contrast that it is less good. Of course I'm disappointed, but it will improve I know. They roar over "Doctors", they adore the "Cliffords," and they shout after "Vive la France," and are mute in grave silence that is thrilling to feel. I love it so myself, that I'm happy they love it too, and I feel I'm doing something to uphold the glory of France, in these days of confusion, and the shameful behaviour of the upper classes, or rather, of the few who one hears of.

I'm *nearly crazy* with mail! Lorna takes dictation for three hours every morning, and I've no time for personal letters and endless things I want to do. It was a week before I even got to 123 Pall Mall [Brown Shipley & Co.] but a grand re-union when I got there, with the clerks and Mr. Johnson. He was very fond of Smudge and we had a nice talk. My friends are all so dear—so welcoming and loving—several have come from the country to see me and hear my show. I am so filled with emotion and gratitude and wonder and humility. It seems like a great and overwhelming gift that one can barely sustain. I only wish you were here—you would understand, and weep and rejoice with me. I can't grasp it—and feel so unworthy and yet so 'charged' with the love that's given me that I know I shall not fail.

Anne [Holmes] is having a family and old friend sherry party for me on Monday—for me and Margaret Lampson! She is *perfectly beautiful,* and has a splendid looking and very sweet fiancé. Margaret Stanley is having another, of her family and friends on Thursday. Lyulph, her boy, (whom I've held on my knee) introduced me on the B.B.C. to-day—a dear young friend. I'm so touched by them all—sons of people I've known—asking me to lunch and for a week-end, etc.! I'm going to the de Glehns' next Sunday and long to go. I am distributing all the clothes I brought, but wish they were all wool! It's bitter cold—I *live* in my mink coat!!! Send any warm things you can to give away. Some chocolate and cheese is always nice to have. I wish I had more but food is really very good. I'm too comfortable for my conscience but must take every care for that big job I have ahead. My darling Adah and Fred are with me. Too good to be true!

On Sunday March 10th, four days after arriving in England, Ruth Draper drove to Hornchurch to find the grave of her nephew "Smudge." Seeing only a little girl in the street, Fred stopped and asked if she knew where they could find the airmen's graves, as they were looking for that of Flight-Lieutenant Draper. "Yes, I do," she replied, "as I always do the flowers on that grave myself." She got in the car and directed them to the cemetery. Then they drove the child, Sheila Connally, home to her mother, who invited them for tea. Ruth always kept in touch with the Connally family.

To Corinne Robinson
(Mrs. Joseph W. Alsop, Sr.)

[March 29, 1946]
Hyde Park Hotel
London

I finish my twelve matinees here to-day. To-morrow I give a show at the school in Hornchurch where Smudge was killed. Then I go to friends for a quiet Sunday, begin my great tour of fourteen weeks on Monday. Every seat has been sold already. There were hundreds turned away here for each performance—a tiny notice in the theatre column appeared in the papers and the theatre was sold out for all twelve matinees in three days. The storm of applause that greeted me was nearly overwhelming—and I had to make a speech at the end. I've never had more wonderful response—so warm and loving and happy an audience. It seemed like waking from the nightmare of the war and finding my old audience still there. Such interesting people wait in the Pit and gallery queue that I pass thro' as I roll up in the Rolls to the stage door. Such smiles greet me, I feel like crying: old and young, poor, simple, shabby, weary people—clerks—soldiers and airmen. I get about thirty letters a day and dictate by the hour. Friends pour in and I'm out for every meal and cocktails and tea and I'm nearly dead at times—but uplifted always by the warmth and sincerity and beauty of the affection I feel pouring over me. It goes so deep, and is so heart warming. Such letters of welcome and gratitude—such words of thanks I could fill a volume, and I feel how much I can give them and only regret I never came before.

Before leaving London, Ruth Draper sent to the Actors Benevolent Fund a gift that Laurence Olivier, in thanking her, termed "heroic open handedness . . . a truly noble sacrifice."

To Dorothea Draper
(Mrs. Henry James)

April 6 [1946]
Cambridge
University Arms Hotel

You can imagine my sorrow about Ned. Never again to talk with him, seek his counsel, delight in his beautiful mind and spirit and feel the warmth and wisdom and beauty of his soul. He was a unique being and somehow the symbol of immortality—cut off from the material and the dross—one felt removed from the havoc of the world in his quiet room. I used to say it was like going to heaven and talking to God in a cosy way. I shall not find his like again and never thought that he might die.

Well, I must get up and go to work. It's hard today—two shows! It's wonderful to hear the laughter everyday and the terrific silence in Vive la France—which everyone adores. I do myself, it's great fun to do it, and I feel as if I really were a woman of the Resistance and I pay tribute with everything that's in me.

To Mary Sheldon
(Mrs. Alfred MacArthur)
(sister of Edward B. Sheldon)
(From typed copy of letter)

[April 7, 1946]
Cambridge
England

I have been so shocked and saddened by the news of Ned's death. I cannot realize it yet. Somehow I never thought that he might die—he seemed so a part of things that never die—the things by which one lives, believes in, clings to as secure and beautiful forever. So I shall always think of him. That I, and all his many friends, will miss beyond expression, the wisdom and counsel, the understanding and sympathy he poured out to us—goes without saying. We can only go on, remembering with pride and tenderness, all that he gave to us these many years—hoping to recapture the magic of his spirit, his mind, and the warmth and goodness of his heart.

I only know from the papers that he has gone. I can but hope that he did not suffer—that the end was swift and merciful. Perhaps a friend will write me. As so often happens I feel a deep sense of reproach that I had not written him since my arrival in England. I was waiting for a chance to write a long and full description of the overwhelming welcome I'd received. He'd foreseen it and wanted me to come to England again. I spent my last evening in New York with him, and shall always be grateful for those wondrous hours and for his blessing. I send you all my sympathy and love. I hope to see you when I return—keep in touch always—for his dear sake.

Ruth felt deeply the loss of Ned Sheldon—Ned who had said: "When Ruth Draper performs, a Holy Ghost descends upon her shoulder."

Helen Hayes wrote that Ned's nurse told her he died at seven o'clock Monday (April 1st) suddenly, without pain and, apparently, without premonition. She added "our world is a little less lustrous, and a great many of us are feeling a little lost—as if we had suddenly lost our conscience and our strength. He gave such meaning to everything we did or hoped to do."

The following letter is inserted at this time in order to preserve its context. It was occasioned by the publication of a biography of Ned Sheldon, The Man Who Lived Twice, *by Eric Woollencott Barnes.*

To Mary Sheldon
(Mrs. Alfred MacArthur)

September 27 [1956]
66 East 79th Street
New York

I have just received the book, and though I've only glanced at it, I am sure it is going to be a moving and wonderful experience to follow the account of Ned's life, and to recall my memories of the last wonderful years. The last quotation (p. 357) from a letter I must have written [April 7, 1946] to *you*—not 'my' sister, as the book says, but 'his', (I hope this will be corrected in another edition) revived what I felt and still feel. I never forget him, and often when I am acting—a picture of his room comes back to me, as I gave my sketches for him, and I know a special emotion is conveyed to the audience. I hope you and your brother are happy about the book. I talked to Jack Wheelock about it and he seems very satisfied that it is worthy, and will be widely read. I am so glad it has been done, and that you waited to do it. I always think it is best not to hurry with such a work, and publish it at once after a person's death. I hope to be in Chicago toward the end of November, and I shall try to see you if you are about.

Thank you and your brother so much for giving me this precious record of Ned's life. I appreciate deeply your ranking me among his friends, and I love to feel I gave him pleasure with my talent.

To Dorothea Draper
(Mrs. Henry James)

[April 20, 1946]
Burley Grange
Near Ringwood, Hants.

No show yesterday, so Thursday night, Lady Sybil Middleton, Margaret Stanley, and Vera Grenfell, (Lady S's niece) motor'd to my show in Bournemouth and brought me back to this dream place. Lovely wood fires, supper and heavenly bed waiting, stars and clear cold air as I opened my window against roses and wistaria—not yet in bloom—but young and green, and in bud. A flood of sun in the morning, and breakfast, and a long lazy day mostly lying in the sun; and later a drive thro' the New Forest to see the great old oaks and beech trees breaking into green—their mossy trunks luminous greys in the low golden sunlight of late afternoon. The blossoms and flowers, all sorts of bulbs are too beautiful now, and there are great blue wooden tubs of gay shaggy tulips on the terrace. The house is small but charming, and full of pretty things and cosy. Lady Sybil is Lord Grey's (of Canada) daughter, niece of my beloved Lady Antrim. She [Lady Antrim] stayed here last summer and did a lot of sketching; someone complimented her on her work and she said: "You know I never painted till I was 80, but I've done a great deal since." She's now 91. She does (tapestry) needlework too!

I finish Bournemouth to-night and move on to Brighton. I love the sea air, but B. is an awful place—marvellous packed theatre, but too big and rather boring people—many very old. Old Mrs. Keppel, all lacquered and dolled up with an ostrich plume sticking up in front of her hat, and fluffed out grey hair—an Edwardian in more ways than one! The de Glehns motor'd over to my show, and I was glad to see them, but I've rather enjoyed knowing few people, and getting more chance to read and rest. One kind lady brought me eight eggs and Octavia Wilberforce sends me butter, as Mrs. Thompson used to do, so I fare very well, and there is more milk now. I'd love a jar of honey, or jam or marmalade, all that is very short over here. If you have *one* old slip I'd love it—I've given away all but two. Ada does all my laundry so I manage all right, but three would be nice to have. They only have one kind of common cheese and not much of that. If you could send a variety of cheeses it would be *lovely* to have some to give away! I like to take or send something wherever I visit. Do get the Siegfried Sassoon book (Siegfried's Journey)—now I'm reading a short "Portrait of Churchill"—wonderful. I'll send it to you.

I don't get enough American news—you might send me a weekly. People ask me so many questions I can't really answer! Are people responding to the appeal for saving food—the difference of views of Truman and Lehman are rather embarrassing—how can the President say "the food crisis will be over in ninety days! Will [Mayor Fiorello] La Guardia succeed in stirring the conscience of the country to give more to Europe? These are my queries, not theirs—they are very polite, and avoid painful subjects. I met a brilliant young woman, Barbara Ward, thirty-one, writes foreign news for the Economist and is a director of the B.B.C. One is so impressed by the way women have worked over here, and the conversation is so intelligent, unhysterical and mature; and the young I've seen have such nice thoughtful manners. The boy (twenty-three) in this house (only son) is at the B.B.C. and reads the news, and sometimes poetry and short announcements etc. Lyulph Stanley does the same. Both have beautiful voices and cultivated speech. It is interesting that the public does not resent this as they would at home—but perhaps there's no way of knowing if they do! The policy and management of the B.B.C. is so totally different to our radio, it's very interesting to hear about it.

To Corinne Robinson
(Mrs. Joseph W. Alsop, Sr.)

[May 13, 1946]
Blackpool

It is so wonderful over here, and of course the opportunities for work are unlimited, constant and most tempting. I realize more than ever, in the thrill and 'sense of action' of my present life, how short a time I have left, and how much time I have wasted—or lost! I remember once, when I was on the road, working hard, I wrote Ned telling him how happy I was—inwardly happy and content—and he wrote back such a simple analysis: that 'the natural state of an actress is to act'. It is so plain that exercising one's highest faculties, and seeing the effect, expressed in the delight of thousands, is an experience to be grateful for and enjoyed as long as one can. That my profession is far *easier* to pursue over here, for many reasons too complicated to go into, makes it clear that I am tempted to stay on and on—and feel only a deep regret that I didn't return long ago! I am no longer young enough to fight and struggle in the publicity and managerial morass, and risks, and delays at home. Long and interesting tours I can have, but the dates must be made a year ahead! Here I can find endless work anywhere, any time, with no fuss, no interviews or publicity—and an enormous public waiting, eager and loving. It is a deep and moving satisfaction. The welcome has been overwhelming, the letters I get so touching—from all kinds of people of every class, and the queues for gallery and pit in London made me want to get down on my knees and cry. I would roll up to the stage door in my 'Rolls,' (with my beloved Fred driving) and the smiles and words of welcome from the people who had endured such hell for five years, standing in the cold and damp, waiting to get in, nearly killed me. That *they* should so honor me—and in my mink coat, warm and well fed, I felt ashamed.

You can imagine my sorrow at Ned's death. Somehow, I never thought that he would die. I used to tell him that going to see him was like going to Heaven and talking to God and he seemed as sure and eternal as that dream. Helen Hayes wrote me and said what I, and all who loved him, feel that we have "somehow lost our conscience and our strength." He never failed to give one a sense of both—as we bade him good-night. He was a Saint, vital and aware, humorous and deep in his understanding, his vision and philosophy. I shall never again have such a wise counsellor—so loving and true as friend, and such an example of selfless living, and enthusiasm in other's lives and interests, and the problems of the world. That quiet figure, in the blue covered bed—that fine head with the black eye-mask and amazingly expressive mouth and sensitive nostrils—remains a vision of a triumphant human soul who warmed us with his flames of spirit, mind and heart. I hope he knew how we loved him and depended on him.

Well, darling I must get up, and walk in the sun! I started this letter just before I went to work last night, now it's 11 a.m., the tide is rushing in, and I shall walk in the wind and watch the waves, and wish for all the people I love to share the beauty of the scene. A friend in Dorset has just sent me a dozen eggs, and a friend in Sussex a half pound of lovely Jersey butter. I'm spoiled by everybody.

To Grace Martin
(Mrs. David Terry Martin)

May 31 [1946]
Glasgow, Scotland

One parcel, the first, has come—no tobacco in it! Did you, at the last minute, leave it out? If not, I hate to tell you it was stolen! Lots of parcels are broken, when they arrive. Your parcel of rice was scattered, the peas were also opened, and only three bits of chocolate in the package. Were there more? I am dreadfully sorry—but I've had other parcels damaged—one—*all* the rice was gone—and ½ lb sugar box *empty*! Things get frightfully shaken aout and paper cartons are dented and broken by force of throwing about. But your dried fruits travelled beautifully and they and the rice have already gone to friends who will be so terribly grateful. The rice, apples and peaches I sent to Winnie Mudie, whose eighty-eight year old sister (merry as a cricket) has just had a slight stroke and they longed for rice and fruit. The peas, apricots and apples (there were two packages), and chocolate went to a dear young friend with two children and an invalid father. I kept the Sultanas myself and am enjoying them enormously, also the soup, which I use on long journeys in my thermos. Thanks a thousand times. I'd love a pair of nylons for one of Mr. George Wyndham's nieces, who knew [Wilfred Scawen] Blunt! Thought you'd be pleased. I've just been spending a week (holiday) with her, and her sister, in one of the most beautiful places I've ever seen in Westmorland. One night she talked enchantingly of her childhood at 'Clouds', Mr. and Mrs. Percy Wyndham's home (her grandfather's and grandmother's in Wiltshire), and described a visit with her mother (Mrs. Adeane) to W. S. Blunt's. I wish you'd been there to hear her—it was so vivid—I saw it all—and his Arab clothes and his great beauty—the fantastic setting and the Arab horses—four galloping down the country lanes and up the grass road to the house; and he recited his poetry, in a most beautiful voice.

I resumed my great tour here in Glasgow last Monday, and it has been a thrilling experience to find such a welcome after fourteen years. *Such* intelligent responsive public; the big theatre is packed to the doors every night, the laughter is glorious, and the applause thunderous! Workers come from Clydebank—and last night in the small Post office where I stopped to send a cable, all three women clerks had already been, and were so keen and appreciative, and wished me good luck! The standard of education is very high in Scotland and it is the most genial, democratic atmosphere. I simply love it, and hate to leave—but Edinburgh next week will be probably even more wonderful. . . . . . People over here are so grateful for everything. They never forget, and their manners are so warm and sincere.

The Black-out must have been absolute Hell. Two charming women I met were describing it last night, (I gave them a lift home—for they'd come back stage, as we had mutual friends) how ghastly it was cooking at night because they could never open any windows at night where they cooked or ate or sat. I never thought of this aspect. It was impossible for lights not to show if curtains blew or parted at all. So they choked with the heat and smells sometimes. And the black streets must have been so awful, and it lasted so long.

My beloved Eliza Wedgwood has lost her memory, she is not sick or suffering but lives in the past and knows no one anymore. It is so sad—I've not seen her and think I won't try, it would be so painful to see that *brilliant* mind gone.

On June 3rd Ruth Draper noted in her Diary: "Edinboro opening. Adorable city! Marvelous audiences! Art Gallery—Raeburns!!" She gave benefits for French Sailors and Orphans and for the County Council.

Afterwards she often told—giving full value to the two broad accents of Scotland—of the two taxi drivers taking her to the Railway Station; the burly Glasgow driver saying: "Miss Draper, I've not seen ye but ye've given us a great deal of pleasure and I hope ye'll come again"; and the very precise

Edinburgh driver: "Miss Draper, I've seen your picture in the paper, and they say you're without a flaw—without a flaw."

To Bernard Berenson

June 16 [1946]
Manchester

My dear B. B.

It sounds strange to say that for years I have wanted to write you, but such is the case! I've heard news of you at rare intervals from Sibyl Colefax and other mutual friends—rumors only, during the terrible years—and finally, long after it occurred, the news of Mary's death. [Mary Berenson died at I Tatti in March 1945.] I have failed in friendship for six long years—but not in the loyalty of thought. So often I wondered, and hoped, that all was well; so often I turned in memory to your lovely hill, and the house, and terraces and gardens and cypresses, the view and the serenity. And now that the danger and tragedy is over (alas, the last is *not* over) I hope that peace broods again within your walls, and that your wisdom gives you peace in your heart, in spite of the confusion in the world. And that the pictures remain.

I have been in England since early March, and am on a long and arduous tour of the provinces, receiving a great welcome everywhere, and loving it all, of course! I hope to fly to Switzerland in August, and later go to Siena to see Lauro's mother and sisters.

I hope this finds you well. My love and warm rememberances to Nicchi [Nicky Mariano], and if she would send me a line—I hate to bother you to write—I would love to hear how you are. Professor Salvemini is well, and happy at Harvard. I think he would love to go to Italy but he can't afford it I'm afraid. His step-son Jean Luchaire was executed for treason—a grim irony, and I'm sure it was very tragic for S. His poor wife lives on in Paris, heart-broken. I hope that the Republic will gather strength, and succeed in quelling the rebellious elements, and bring peace and unity at last. But one has misgivings about using those words- - - My love to you—and many thoughts—

Ruth Draper

To Dorothea Draper
(Mrs. Henry James)

[June 17, 1946]
Midland Hotel
Manchester

It's some time since I wrote. I am waiting for my breakfast—here it is—porridge and a bit of fish, very good coffee—which I make piping hot on my little stove, and cold soggy toast which I make likewise crisp and hot! It's a great comfort. I have on a pale blue flannel wrapper—Aunt Fanny's cashmere shawl—dyed pale pink—it really once belonged to Mother's old beau Mr. Fay's sister! I gave half of it to Aileen, it was so enormous—and she loves it as I do. It's the softest warmest thing in the world, and a most comforting possession. Barie's bed-spread covers my blankets every where, and I dress up in a lace cap that Alice made her once. I feel she would love to have me using these things on my lonely journeys, and they do add to one's self respect in these dreary hotel rooms. Then I have all my pictures and little boxes and Bunny from Batavia (1000 years old, Sung) on the dressing table, and I'm all set for the week! The *most* beautiful bell has just struck nine—it's so lovely a sound I eagerly wait for the hours to strike. I wish we had more bells! This is a grand old hotel—famous—and full of character and very comfortable. I have my own bath, which I don't always get, and it's a great luxury.

You know my beloved maid Ada left me—an awful loss—but her husband had a stroke, and she had to go back. So now I only have a 'dresser' at each place, and she has to be instructed, and told things, and watched, and I have to do the packing on Saturday nights, and it's not so easy! But Mr. Merica is ever helpful, and I manage all right. I'm on my eleventh week— five to go after this. Hull was a grim place—frightfully blitzed, but I played to packed houses, and tho' Yorkshire people seem heavy and stiff, *after* the brilliance and warmth of Edinburgh and Glasgow audiences, they seemed to enjoy the show, and two or three evenings were marvellous. It will be thrilling here. I've always thought Manchester perhaps the best public in the world—and musicians and actors all agree. I have a pleasant week-end to look forward to as between here and Leeds, lies the place of young Lord Shurtleworth (at whose other place I spent my holiday) and his mother is coming over for the Sunday with him, to fetch me Saturday night after my closing, and take me to Gawthorpe until Monday when I go on to Leeds. So it will be a lovely two nights in the country. This is a dull letter—so personal—but I thought you'd like a cosy chat.

To Grace Martin
(Mrs. David Terry Martin)

June 23 [1946]
[Manchester]

The food situation is bad, but in the country, easier, and I have been spoiled—a friend in Sussex sends me a little butter each week which I have for my tea, and everywhere people have given me eggs, one for every day at tea time, for the theatre hour is 6:30 (too early to dine, so I have a good tea at 5 and something at 9:30–10 before I go to bed). At the hotel I've had *nothing* but cabbage and potatoes *every* day at lunch—my main meal—and generally fish, meat perhaps twice a week (and a small portion), chicken *never*, except at private houses, and I think I've had it six times in four months. I got *desperate* for vegetables in Manchester last week (they're lovely in market now, but very expensive). I bought a bunch of asparagus for 7/ one day and cooked the tips in my room, (gave the rest to my grateful 'dresser') and had a feast, with lovely butter. Another night I had peas at 6/ a pound and another, carrots at 2/ a bunch—tiny ones. But oh, so good! My kitchen is a joy! I have a darling tiny sheffield tea pot I bought for £ 1/—/— in an antique shop in Bristol and I make my own tea (some China I brought over), save a little milk from breakfast, and with my own bread and butter and egg and jam, I have a perfect meal. I hide my stores and have not been discovered yet.

To Corinne Robinson
(Mrs. Joseph W. Alsop, Sr.)

[c. July 11, 1946]
[Cardiff]

It has been a triumphant progress. The quality of the public has varied interestingly—the quantity never! Packed houses have greeted me in all sixteen cities and the seats have generally been sold out long before the opening. A minimum of advertising, no "build up" or "photos" or "interviews". I just quietly slip in to town and the full theatre is ready for me. It is fantastic and heart warming. If only you could hear the laughter and the silence—the applause. Eager young things wait to see me go out; most of the people have never heard me, but I've become a sort of legend and all classes flock. The queues for the pit and gallery are in line before I arrive to dress; working people, old people, soldiers and airmen, maids and waiters at hotels where I stay, shop people, and taxi drivers often tell me of friends who've gone. And of course people who've heard me seven and fourteen years ago (my last tour of the provinces) have all come again. Nearly everywhere I know someone, and I've had lovely week-ends—and lunch or tea out or supper after the show, which is over at 9 or 9:30! Most start at 6:30! The country is too beautiful and flowers in their glory—and I drive a good deal so am refreshed each day by beauty of scene, and often in the art museums and collections in these smaller towns—and in the lovely old houses. I stay sometimes in lodgings as I'm doing here, and really prefer it. The pleasant landladies give me good food—and I have a cosy sitting room full of flowers. Yesterday I lunched with Constance Morrow Morgan. Aubrey, her husband, is Welsh, and they and three children are visiting his mother in her lovely place. He is very agreeable, and has shown me beautiful things and places. They are going to settle in Oregon—on a farm. I told him he should see Woodford Farm and talk to Joe. He'd like him, so I hope it might be possible, before they start for the West. The Lindberghs have bought a place near Darien, and the Morgans might motor to Avon some time. They're going home in September. I hop to go to Siena to see Lauro's sister and mother—if—I get my visa! I plan to return to London by mid-October, and have a six-week season, and then sail for home. Of course I could stay here indefinitely. It's a great temptation, when I think of the years I've lost, not lost, because I've enjoyed life at home, but as I realize my age, I know that there isn't much more time for work like this—and my, it's fine and satisfying. How I wish you could see my "Vive la France"—which bowls them over—and the "Return" is another thing from the "try-out" you saw at 66!

The following letter was sent to the Lord Mayors of sixteen cities Ruth Draper had visited on her tour in England: Cambridge, Oxford, Bournemouth, Brighton, Sheffield, Bristol, Blackpool, Glasgow, Edinburgh, Hull, Manchester, Leeds, Liverpool, Cardiff, Wimbledon, and Birmingham.

28 July, 1946
London

Before leaving England for my holiday, I am anxious to make a gift to Welfare Organizations in the cities which I have visited on my recent tour, in token of my friendship and admiration for the people of Great Britain, and as a gesture of goodwill.

As an American I should also like this gift to express my appreciation of all the kindness and hospitality shown to my compatriots in the armed forces stationed in this country during the war; and as an individual, my heartfelt gratitude for the overwhelming welcome that has been given me and my imaginary company, after an absence of nearly seven years.

In sending you the enclosed cheque I am leaving to your judgment and discretion the disposition of my gift among the organizations best fitted to serve the needs of people in any or all of the following categories:

Civilians who have suffered most from the effects of enemy
action
Children and young people who need protection, guidance
and training, and—the Blind, the Aged and Crippled.

I realize that I am adding to your many responsibilities in asking you to take charge of this money, but you will appreciate the impossibility of my choosing beneficiaries wisely, as I pass rapidly from place to place. So I beg to express my gratitude to you and your colleagues for enabling me to distribute this gift where it will do most good, assuring you and the citizens of my great happiness in making it.

To Dorothea Draper
(Mrs. Henry James)

July 30 [1946]
[Geneva, Switzerland]

I simply hated to stop my work—I am not a bit tired. It was hard to see the curtain go down on over 2000 laughing happy people, and know that I could go on for 365 nights a year—anywhere in England, and thrive on the spiritual as well as the material reward! I calculated I'd talked for about 315 hours—126 shows at an average of 2000 a time = 252,000 people! Well—it's been a wonderful four months.

I hope you don't mind letters written in pencil as much as I do—but all the ink in my pen leaked out in the air—and I haven't got any to refill it yet. I had a lovely flight—left London at nine—and Joe Alsop was on the plane and we had a wonderful trip to-gether, and *such* interesting talk, as far as Paris. There I changed to another plane and got here for lunch. A perfect day—Harriet got here the day before, and we met as usual, with a burst of laughter, and have talked steadily—over a lunch of thick juicy steak—lovely vegetables and fraises de bois with whipped cream—looking at the blue lake and the gay, neat, city, bright flower beds—sails and flags, and well fed people strolling under the clipped trees. It is a staggering contrast from dingy brave old London—and one feels every sense alive with aware-ness and feeling, and thoughts disturbing, and calm and happy at the same time. My room is in full view of Mt. Blanc—dazzling white against the morning sky—and I had crisp white rolls, wads of butter, foaming milk with my coffee and the familiar dark jam of luscious cherries! It is like Paradise, and stepping back into the world we were lucky enough to know. We had blue trout and artichokes for dinner, then strolled under the heavenly green blue evening sky with the golden lights of the town twinkling and reflected in the lake, and the dark mountains rising to the stars. We start on Thursday for the country and hope to find a perfect spot.

Harriet looks well—smart as ever—thinner and of course a little older, and is very interesting about her work and the tragedy of France. Joe said Paris is like a beautiful piece of fruit—with worms eating the core—London—drab and worn—but there are no worms. Little as I know—I cannot feel hopeless about France—as I flew over its wonderfully cultivated farms and fields and adorable tiled snug villages; I only had a glimpse of Montmartre and the Eiffel Tower against the sky, before clouds hid it all—but the emotion of flying over the Channel, and seeing those two coasts, and imagining D. Day—and all the progress to Paris—was great as you can im-agine.

Diary

Week of August 4–10, 1946
Switzerland

Too lazy to write any more—one perfect day succeeds another and time is only night and day—peace and beauty—awareness and oblivion; cowbells—church bells—gentle, sweet, smiling peasants; long walks, gentle and strenuous, hard climbs, and rests in hay fields in the sun or on rocks in the cool shadows of trees with a refreshing breeze always blowing down the valley.

To Harley Merica
Westcliffe
Essex, England

August 2, 1946
Hotel de la Dent Blanche
Valais, Switzerland

I want you to have the enclosed cheque in token of our happy association during the wonderful tour just ended. I send it with my heartfelt thanks for all your care and devotion to the company and properties of what I know you consider "the greatest show on earth"—the term always applied at home to Barnum and Bailey's Circus! It certainly has been great fun and I hated to see the curtain go down. I miss the bursts of happy laughter and the heart-warming applause.

I hope you will have a nice rest and find some interesting work, until you rejoin me in the autumn.

P.S. Switzerland is Paradise!

To Dorothea Draper
(Mrs. Henry James)

August 16, 1946
Evoline, Switzerland

I'm glad Alice was around and was with you [through illness]. She is a rock of strength—unshattered by her own fierce trial. I cried when I read your thoughts, and hers, of Ba—and what she would have been and done for you both. How blessed we are, to have had such a close and warm love binding us all—we four sisters—for so long, and that we turn to Ba still, as the surest and tenderest source of strength and the model of selflessness and behavior (for want of a better word).

To Dorothea Draper
(Mrs. Henry James)

August 30 [1946]
Milan, Italy

I seem to have had little time for more than post cards since my holiday started. The weeks in Switzerland were lovely, and the very different beauty of Italy is intoxicating in quite another way. The consciousness of man's mind and spirit, and their supreme achievements in this country sweeps me into a realm that one touches so rarely, and it is like realizing one was very thirsty, when coming on a clear cool spring, or very hungry, with a feast suddenly spread before one. I'd forgotten how lovely it was, how rich in beauty. The light and color and the Tuscan villages and roofs and towers and bells, white oxen, and grapes and red carts, shrines, and doorways and glimpses into courts and gardens, and girls leaning on window ledges, and the frescoes and marbles and bronzes! Gosh—it's good to feel beauty pouring into one's soul again—and all this in a defeated tragic country. As a matter of fact, the people are working like beavers with their hearts broken and their pride in the dust. Over 2000 bridges have already been rebuilt, and walls and houses of rubble are being cleared and tidied, and fine buses help the disabled train service. I came from Florence last night in one—across the Apennines where all the long fighting before Bologna took place. Horrible destruction, but the road building is quite stupendous, and young trees are neatly planted all along to replace those destroyed and cut down.

I only came here to bring the book about Lauro that the family had been correcting etc. and I shall leave it with the publisher, and go back to-night for ten days. Elena Vivante's place is lovely—a huge old villa on a hill, with beautiful views. They have twelve farms, and it's interesting to understand the Mezzadria system. They live *entirely* on what they grow—even the wheat that makes the flour, that makes the bread we eat; and the oil from their olives, and the wine from their grapes. Adorable peasant household, who never stop working, and can't do enough for you—sweet loving good people who make one love mankind again, and have hope for the world. There is little enough, God knows, but nature and art and simple human goodness restores one's faith.

To Dorothea Draper
(Mrs. Henry James)

September 14 [1946]
Casa Al Dono
Vallombrosa

It seems I've not written for some time, but the days fly by, and visiting does not leave me as free to write as when I'm on the road alone. I'm here with B.B. and it's wonderful. At 82—his mind clear, incisive, his vast knowledge, radiating his undiminished passion for beauty, his beautiful speech and voice make him a stimulating companion and it is a rare privilege to be here. High up in wonderful hills, and pine forests, the air is delicious and the comfort and good food add to the general sense of well-being. Mrs. [Otto] Kahn is the only other guest, besides a charming elderly lady, Countess Ritter, great-granddaughter of Fénelon, French and exquisite. [Baroness Kiki Ritter de Záhoney (née Salignac de Fénelon), mother of Marchesa Gilberta Serlupi, whose husband, the Ambassador of San Marino to the Holy See, under his diplomatic immunity, cared secretly for B.B. during the year-long occupation of Italy by the German Army.] Nicky Mariano, B.B.'s devoted 'Egeria', is a wonderful person—runs the house, and the lovely household—and is an angel of selfless devotion, but terribly intelligent and a free and delightful person full of tact, humor and understanding and charm. B.B. is vain—but he does know more than anyone in the world about his subject, and one sits gladly at his feet. The war and the horrible problems of the world seem far away—in these ancient hills and blue distances—in this serene atmosphere, and I'm drinking deeply at such a source.

I shall have five days in Florence when I go down and seeing the beautiful frescoes and paintings and sculpture there will be another joy which I wish I could share with you. The wealth of beauty in this country is staggering. The Siena gallery was a dream—to turn from the gold and heavenly colors of the pictures on the walls, and look out over the roofs and towers of that lovely city, and below onto the terrace of a house with grape vines, and a chicken and a kitten and a child, and a copper jar and terra cotta pots, and a girl in a window, and washing on a line, and blue smoke curling into a blue sky!— intense quiet—with the serene Madonnas and the glow of ancient gold— stirring one's heart after six hundred years—the past and present merged—one suddenly feels that the simple things of life, and the human spirit, are what count most and what will survive.

I had two lovely weeks in Siena—living on a great farm—where one eats only what the soil yields—a little meat, once or twice a week, is all they buy. It was very interesting—the fruit was fabulous, and a large part of one's diet—*such* figs—great straw trays of them—several varieties—peaches, pears and grapes. I learned to make tagliatelle and ravioli. I motor'd Lauro's mother back to Rome—and stayed three days. It was frightfully hot, but I saw some of the things I most love—and am glad I went. I thought of our visit there with the boys, as I bent over backward looking at the Sistine, and its colossal conception and achievement remains supreme. The quiet intensity and beauty of the 'Pieta' is all I want to see in St. Peter's—there it stands in its corner, saying more than all the grandeur and the power of the Church founded in the name of that limp marble body.

I must get up now and go out in the fresh morning air on a terrace looking down the lovely valley—where the Allies blasted the road and villages in pursuit of the Germans retreating. It's awful, and I fear the new houses will be ugly and modern with no more real tiled and stone roofs to harmonize with the colors of the land. The rebuilding of the roads and bridges is fabulous.

To Bernard Berenson

[September 20, 1946]
[Florence]

My dear B. B.

I am so grateful for all the beauty I gathered in my four days on your lovely hill-side. So many pictures will often swim before my eyes—those exquisite colors and smoky distances and folds of the hills and valleys, the peace and timelessness, the silence and grandeur of it all. And the human element, of course, that is of unfailing interest, and holds us poor mortals to-gether, enabling us to enjoy and ridicule and console, to teach and reveal and inspire, according to the mood, the moment, and the gift. How fascinating it all is! And you—with your undiminished passion for beauty, and your vast knowledge, which burn like beacons in the darkness of our times, gather us about you, and make us happy, and remind us how all-important are the things of the Mind and the Spirit, and how, with Nature, they outlive the tragedies of our failures—our Wars and "mortal strife."

Thank you for your friendship and your welcome. It was lovely to be with you and Nicky, whose beauty and character are a delight to find again. And I loved the peasants and the servants and the whole co-ordination of life and comfort and contemplation and peace. Thank you for all.

Your affectionate
Ruth

To Dorothea Draper
(Mrs. Henry James)

[September 21, 1946]
[Florence]

I'm writing in bed—very busy cleaning up papers and packing—hiding silk stockings in shoes. I long to bring more, but I only have a suit-case. The leather things here, and the shoes are enchanting. I never saw such lovely workmanship—they've lost none of their skills—whereas in England the work and materials are *pitifully* deteriorated—tho' I believe good things are exported. Thanks for your last lovely letter. I saw the moon and stars over Tuscany and thought of it in skies at home. The change each night was so exciting and gave me such a sense of our planets all swinging thro' space at such a rate. Barie always said she thought she could feel the earth spinning! How she loved the stars, and knew a lot of them. I wrote you recently and there's nothing much to say. Florence is so full of lovely things to see, and the color of it all is so satisfying, the *strength* of the old Palaces, the purity and grace and tenderness of Angelico's frescoes in San Marco are absolutely shattering in their loveliness. And yesterday I had a wonderful experience. Ghiberti's great doors—thick with the dust and grime of 500 years—are being cleaned, and I went to the workrooms in the Uffizi where they're being done, and watched the men working, and talked to the very wonderful foreman—a beautiful Italian, about sixty-five, with sensitive keen intelligence, and love of his métier (friend of Bertelli, and the greatest founder and metal specialist in Italy—Mallie would have been so thrilled to hear him talk and watch him work). The Reliefs are all in gold (gilded bronze) on the dark brown bronze, and the detail, unseen thro' the dirt of ages is simply incredible! There they are, as Ghiberti made them and saw them; it took him eight years to model and cast them, and twenty years to finish. It seems all the exquisite detail was cut in the bronze after casting. You can't believe how beautiful they are—they will create a furore when seen again, in about a year or two. The other two pairs, one by Pisano and the other by Ghiberti are the same—pure gold relief, and such a soft rich gold.

To Corinne Robinson
(Mrs. Joseph W. Alsop, Sr.)

September 24 [1946]

Who do you think has been my almost daily companion for several hours of trotting about or a drink, or a meal?—Reggie Temple, and at 82! He is as dapper and young as ever—terribly funny and so brave and gay and sweet. He asked specially for you and the boys, and Stewart whom he particularly liked. He remembers everyone and of course wanted all Marie's news. Neither she or I had ever received his letters and I was *sure* he was dead! So when I ran into him on the corner of Via Tornabuoni and the Strozzi Palace, in a white linen suit, blue tie, green goggles and a dapper Panama hat, and a cane— I cried out "Reggie" he looked at me as one from the dead, and we embraced dramatically, to the amusement of the crowd, who took a most sympathetic interest and seemed quite delighted for us both. He's as amusing as ever, lives in his same enchanting little house, with the same devoted maid who's the only one he's ever had in forty-five years. He was in Montreux during the war. I felt I must give a show for him—he so adores my work—so an English lady who has a villa, a mutual friend, was very happy to have a small gathering—about twenty people—and I gave a show and Reggie did enjoy it so, as well as the others, all rather starved for entertainment. Florence is lovely, but rather 'triste'—these places that depended on tourists for life are sadly empty and need people to buy the enchanting things in the shops. I've *never* seen such lovely purses and bags! I longed to buy a dozen, for presents, but travelling in a suit case, I just can't collect more stuff.

Paris, indeed Europe itself, is described in Janet Flanner's Journal *early in 1946. These are the conditions that Ruth Draper found on her return to Paris:*

Paris is struggling back to what looks and feels something like subnormal, at least. In other words, Paris is now like a thin, ill, handsome old woman with some natural color flushing her cheeks as she fumbles to her feet . . . still possessed of her remarkable habit of survival. The strictly European countries cannot aid one another. All of Europe, France included, is sick, weak, and physically and morally hungry in varying degrees. It is precisely in her stomach that Paris has recovered least. Parisians can now lunch off a legal menu in a very modest restaurant for three hundred francs, if they can afford it. The white-collar and the working classes cannot. . . . There are now five thousand taxis in Paris, and they are available even for healthy or unimportant people. Last month, you had to be pregnant, ill, or on top-level official business to get a taxi, and you had to apply first to the nearest police station. . . . Twenty-seven more of the closed Métro stations have just been reopened. Some of the antique green autobuses have lumbered back on the job, all with new routes and numbers, thus mixing confusion with satisfaction. Now that Parisians are off their feet more than they have been for six years, a ration ticket for having shoes resoled is to be distributed. The Galeries Lafayette and seven hundred and ninety-nine other Paris shops have just placed on sale the first postwar men's, women's, and children's shirts, pajamas, and underwear. The garments were sold one to a customer, under the category "Articles Utilitaires." There were not nearly enough to go around. . . . The inflated banknotes that have been appearing in steady volume are gloomy reading for the French. Despite the upward swing of business, another new banknote is just out—a fancy, five-hundred-franc note stamped with a portrait of the melancholy poet Chateaubriand holding his head, as well he might.

[From *Paris Journal 1944–1965*. (Atheneum, by Janet Flanner. Originally in *The New Yorker*.)]

To Malvina Hoffman
In New York

October 21 [1946]
Paris

I think of you every day here, with a kind of reversed envy and longing. I feel *you* should be here, at least sharing with me the poignant beauty and fascination of this place that you know and love so deeply. I walk about in a kind of dazed delight, mingled with sadness and fear and bitter disgust of my fellow men—I mean all the elements of mankind that defeat the good and betray the beautiful. I have had such perfect autumn days, of soft air and sun, and the colors of the trees and the gay and ridiculous and adorable flower beds in the Tuileries are all as you remember them. The children, and the family groups with their 'gouter' baskets!—the pony and goat wagons, and Punch and Judy, the lovely boats and the fountains and piles of burning leaves.—Yesterday afternoon—Sunday!—I strolled in the Luxembourg Gardens and bought hot chestnuts and sat on an iron chair by the balustrade overlooking the pond and fountain, and watched the happy throng. The late afternoon sun, all golden on the flying spray and sails of the tiny boats, the children with hoops, and lovers strolling under the trees, the emerald green 'pelouse' and that beautiful green bronze group of a stag and does!—the superb trees and the fruit garden, the old men playing cards—croquet and tennis and small merry-go-round! I never saw such a happy, quiet crowd, enjoying the peace and beauty, part of it all—owning it, creating it and living it profoundly. What is it that so makes life seem so complete and so real over here? The flowers were a glory—pale yellow chrysanthemums, dahlias, salvia—all mixed with blues and mauves and oranges that seemed a riotous harmony in the pale golden sun and grey shades. I stood by the grave of seven heroes of the Resistance, buried (three still alive) where they were shot, under trees where perhaps they played as children (right to the left of the Palace) and hot tears filled my eyes.

I walked to the other side to see your group, and it was not there, only the pedestal [*Bacchanale Russe,* Pavlova and Mordkin, bought by the French Government and placed in the Luxembourg Gardens in 1919]. I spoke to a 'Sergent de Ville' who was talking to another man and asked him if he knew what had happened to it, and he said the Germans took it in 1941 and, with several others, it had not yet been recovered. I was on my way to tea with friends in rue Monsieur le Prince, and it was then five, but so interesting was the policeman, that I stood for thirty-five minutes talking to him. One of those terribly intelligent, sympathetic men—with deep honest eyes and keen alertness and beautiful speech; he had sheltered 145 American and English parachutists (and had seven ribbons of the last war on his uniform), he was so interesting about the occupation, politics of to-day, and so fine a type that

I couldn't bear to stop talking, and I very reluctantly turned away. I took his name and address. [She sent him a large box of food.] He's received a 'Diploma' and formal thanks from the British and U.S. Governments, but no material reward, and something should be done. I met a couple who keep a Brasserie in Brussels, which was the center of information for R.A.F. and parachutists who fell in Belgium, and had a wonderful chat with them when I was there last week. So in many places I've wished for you to share the thrill and pathos and beauty that you love.

I went to see Lemordant and it was tremendous, for his vitality and fervor are all the same, and his handclasp crushes one's fingers. He's as neat and trim as ever, apologizing for keeping his hat—on that brave head! I shall go again. The studio is exactly the same; he told me most blood curdling stories of being watched and followed, of escapes in the boat, in Brittany, and terrible journeys. He spoke of letters, never received, both to and from you, and was so glad of all my news, tho' it seems letters are all right now and he'd heard fairly recently. He looked very well, but has had bad attacks of pain in his back. He wanted to come down and see me out, but I persuaded him to stay in his chair. I shall go again. He wants to come to my show, but I am at the 'Comédie des Champs-Elysées and the lift is not working. I may be able to get him in the scenery 'ascenseur.' I'll try. I open to-night and I'm quite excited as you may imagine.

I'm trying to arrange to get to Normandy just to see the sacred ground of the Invasion. I somehow feel I must grasp that tragedy and glory and heroic vision—as well as the untouched wonder of Paris, and the material charm of the rue St. Honore! It is undeniable that one thinks of clothes and food and things to buy, along with all the rest, in this distractingly lovely city. I've seen lovely exhibitions, and been to the Louvre, of course, and walked my feet off on the 'left bank', and along the quais and over the bridges—and bought flowers and grapes in the street! I've ordered two dresses and a hat and a few underclothes, and have busy days ahead. I'm staying now with Dean and Anne Jay in their beautiful flat in the Ave. Foch—a quarter I've not often frequented, but it's very comfortable, and near my job and since they so kindly urged me to come, I couldn't resist.

My months over here have been charged with happiness and interest and emotion and beauty!—but it's all sad too, terribly full of problems and insecurity. Switzerland and Holland seem on the surest basis—yet the Dutch Empire is hardly secure, and soldiers are being sent off to fight, and guard far-off places where people are fighting still.

Enough—too much—I must get up, and go to my theatre and set my stage—work is best!

To Bernard Berenson

[November 10, 1946]
Hyde Park Hotel
Knightsbridge
London SW 1

My dear B. B.

I have so often thought of you since I left your lovely hillside, and have been grateful again and again and wanted to tell you of my doings, and the beauty of things I saw, in which the thought of you played a part. The Ghiberti doors took my breath away and I lingered long talking with that wonderful man in charge of the work!—and felt the Renaissance living again in his feeling about his work, and his fellow workers, and the patient and exquisite labor involved in revealing all that dazzling beauty. It was a joy to see I Tatti again, and walk thro' the rooms and remember my last visit, and see the pictures and books and garden, and I wish you had been there too. I saw many beloved things in Florence, and then came on to Paris. There I was dazed anew by that rich and wonderful city, so throbbing with romance and life and I saw the marvellous Tapestry Exhibit—and the pictures returned from Germany, and the Louvre all rehung and very much easier to digest, and a lovely Exhibit of choice Masterpieces assembled in the Petit Palais to help the public renew acquaintance with treasures so long hidden away. After a week I went to Holland and there I gave 7 shows—! 2 in the Hague, 1 in Leiden, 1 in Rotterdam, 1 in Eindhoven, 1 in Hilversum, and 1 in Amsterdam. There I called on Dr. Friedlander, and he took me to the Rykse museum and it was lovely to see those great pictures with him. Only a selection have been rehung, but it's very satisfying not to see so many at a time. He seemed frail, and rather sad, but he has a nice little flat, with his books about him, and a faithful old maid whom I took for his wife! She offered me tea, and seemed very much in charge, so I stupidly made the mistake. He was very kind, and was glad to hear news of you. It was lovely to see the Mauritshuis again and I loved Holland. I gave 1 show in Brussels, but did not stay long enough to see anything there and tho' I talked with Mrs. Stoecle [Mme. Alphonse Stoclet] on the telephone I could not go there, as she was not well. She also was glad to hear news of you.

I then returned to Paris for two weeks, and there I gave 4 shows and had great success at the Comédie des Champs-Elysées! I went to several good things at the theatre and enjoyed myself very much—and also had the great privilege of going to Normandy, and seeing the Invasion beaches and roads and ruined towns and villages through which our army passed. It was all heart-breaking—horrible—but very moving and revealing. One has no conception, until one sees it, of the stupendous plan, and the ghastly sacrifice necessary to get the Germans out. The ruined houses and the lovely churches, the awful cold and misery that will go on for so long don't bear thinking about.

I reached London a week ago, and began my 4 weeks season last Monday. It is all sold out, and the same old welcome was awaiting me. It's very thrilling and very wonderful.

I saw poor Sibyl [Colefax] yesterday. She's in hospital, but she looks well and seems amazingly cheerful. She was delighted to hear your news but she can't bear to think of all she missed by this awful accident! She hopes to be out in 2 weeks, but she hasn't tried walking yet. The room was a bower of flowers and books, and people crowd in every day. Mr. Agnew and I were there at the same time. It's lovely to be in dear old London, shabby and brave and vital as ever. The King's pictures are stupendous—like a new gallery—I *wish* you could see them. I'm sure you've been sent the catalogue or I'd send one. How I'd love to see them with you.

I'm broadcasting to-night "On the Porch in Maine" and the "Garden" and must go now and close this long letter. My best love to Nicky, and greetings to the Anreps, and much love to you. I think so often of those peaceful days on your hill, our walks and talks and evenings, and I am so grateful for all that you gave me, of welcome and friendship and beauty and the satisfying exercise of the mind! I hope you are well and will have a good winter. I sail Dec. 7th on the "Queen Elizabeth", and shall hate to leave I know—but I have so many I love at home and my sweet flat awaiting me—full of memories, of comfort, and bits of beauty gleaned from my rich life of wandering and work. So I'm drawn back, but already dream of my return to Europe.

Your devoted Ruth

On November 27th, ten days before leaving for home, Ruth again visited "Smudge" Draper's grave in Hornchurch.

To William Adams Delano

December 18, 1946
66 East 79th Street
New York

These are strange and baffling days—and peace is far off—and rejoicing a mockery. . . . Beauty is the great comfort that holds one to a belief—beauty in human souls is the highest and most inspiring—and happily one knows a few people who have it—you are one of them. Bless you.

To Grace Martin
(Mrs. David Terry Martin)

December 29, 1946
66 East 79th Street
New York

I am enjoying the lovely honey every morning, and the nuts were more wonderful than ever! I had my Christmas party, about twenty-two—and it was great fun. Life is difficult as I have no maid!—and I love fussing in my flat, but it takes too much time. I never open a book, or read the paper, and seem busy all day! It's taken time to get settled, and I've decided to give a season here—four matinees and Sunday nights, for six weeks, opening January 12th, so I have lots to see to, and shall be quite scared! It will be at the Empire Theatre, where the Lunts are playing; a fine atmosphere and under the best management I could have!—too good a chance to miss, as I've been out of the running in New York for so many years. It remains to be seen whether the critics will roast me again for having nothing new!

I'm trying to get a maid, and have odd help for a few hours each week. To-day Dora came, cooked a lovely dinner, and I had Paul and Heidi and little Susan, and my precious Anne—who came in for the week-end. She's a darling and strangely like me as a child.

I have so many letters to write I'm nearly crazy!—with papers, etc. and publicity stuff to sort out: I wish I had more system and was a more orderly person. I've just made chicken soup out of this noon's chicken, and am 'nodding by the fire' so I must go to bed. I'm going to the country for over New Year's if an ice-storm makes the roads passable. Grateful thanks and Happy New Year!

1947–1956

Courage, enthusiasm, awareness—
if only one can keep these to the end.

Ruth Draper to Dorothea Draper
February 13, 1937

To Grace Martin
(Mrs. David Terry Martin)

[January 5, 1947]
Sunday Evening
Empire Theatre
[New York]

Well, I'm packing them in!!! I got your dear wire and I laughed, and felt your loving thoughts and wishes near me on my 'opening' night last Sunday. It was a great welcome—beyond anything I dreamed possible—and both shows to-day are "Sold out". I'm resting between shows, and I must get ready soon—having had a lovely rest, finished the 'River'—a beautiful book—and had a nice cup of tea. I am in Lynn Fontanne's room, as their show is closed! [Alfred Lunt] had to have a sudden operation so, tho' I'd expected to play four matinees and one evening (Sunday) while they went on, I can now have the theatre for a regular run! So next Friday (it took time to reprint tickets and notify papers, etc.) I start to play every night and Sunday matinees until they return, then I'll resume the matinee and one evening schedule. It is all a perfect arrangement and a great break for me.

To be playing at the dear old Empire where all the great ones have played, where I came as a child to see Peter Pan and other Barrie plays, and Irving and Ellen Terry etc. It is quite an emotion and a matter of real pride. I know Terry and you will feel it so, too! My beloved Ned Sheldon wanted and expected this for me. His last words, almost, as I left for England: "Go to your triumphs over there—and then come back to New York, take a theatre and sweep them off their feet." The critics have been so generous and genial and the public is on the run! It's all so interesting—the psychology of it—with Hurok, I was not "of the theatre", it was not of interest to the Dramatic critics. Here at the Empire, under John Wilson—the most brilliant and prominent young producer—with the Lunts' friendly co-operation (for this doubling-up has never been tried in New York before) I'm off for a really good run I hope. God grant I keep well, and full of pep—which I now am. My flat is a haven—I have a lovely Scottish maid who takes good care of me and all is lovely, I know you'll be glad to hear. I had fabulous reviews in all papers and it's like my triumphs in 1928 at the Comedy!—except that Lauro is not here, or Ned to talk it over with. But I feel how happy they would be!—and my beloved Paul—and before I stepped onto the Stage my heart spoke to my 'cloud of witnesses'. The French sketch knocks them over, as it did in England, and I'm glad of this.

To Grace Martin
(Mrs. David Terry Martin)

September 19 [1947]
On Board R.M.S. Queen Elizabeth

Lovely to have your letter to greet me in my cabin. The old days of excitement at a departure—steamer baskets, telegrams, letters, books, presents, fruit and food and flowers are things of the past! I slip away as a matter of routine with no one paying any attention! So your sweet letter and God speed were very much appreciated. I'm going off at once to Paris for ten days and when my work starts I have so little time. I go first to Brighton, where I open October 6th—[then] Edinburgh, Glasgow, Newcastle, Aberdeen, and London November 10. I sail December 19 on *Queen Mary* and work in London until I go. Newcastle and Aberdeen will be new. I don't relish N. but A. will be lovely as I adore Scotland always. I'm not going to Italy—there is no time, and it would be too hurried, and tantalizing to have only a few days there after a tiring and expensive trip. Work is after all my reason for coming, and I can't really enjoy, or feel justified, in a 'dolce far niente' trip these days. I'll write from Paris.

By the way!—I wish you could see the broken cup! [The Martins had spent August in R.D.'s apartment.] The handle has been shaved off and I have a perfect sugar bowl which I needed. I'll look for an odd cup, or a few new in old shops in Paris as I adore that china and want more anyway. So don't feel badly any more! I did a superb mending job myself this summer of which I was proud; a broken vase I loved had four small pieces out of the rim—only three were saved. I put Ivory soap in the gap—a sliver about (1/2 inch)!—covered it with clear liquid cement painted a green stem and rose leaf over the seams and it's as good as new!

I have a lovely cabin, and am writing in bed, both ports open to a blue sky and calm blue sea. It's so restful and so lovely and I feel more and more what a terrific debt I owe to life—one I can never pay. If only I could make new and better sketches!—but I never think of my work—except when I'm working! I had a wonderful summer—twenty-two friends! All gained pounds as I did, alas! And we had *such* fun, *such* laughter and *such* beauty.

To Malvina Hoffman

October 5 [1947]
[London]

I saw my policeman in Paris (now retired) and he told me they were planning to put up 'copies' of the stolen statues in the Luxembourg! I said: "How will they make copies?" He said: "Oh, they have all the photographs"! This filled me with horror, and I knew it would you, so I'm writing at once to tell you. The name of the man to communicate with is:

> Monsieur[———] Architecte en Chef
> Palais du Luxembourg
> *Paris VI*

He is the "Réprésentant direct des Beaux Arts" and will know the plans about reconstruction and replacement of lost treasures. Do find out about it. I'm so glad I discovered this and hope it will be helpful.

I went to see Lemordant and took many messages from you. He seemed well to me, and full of fervor and action, planning to start soon for ten conferences in Brittany and Le Midi. He has been very bad this past winter and spring and total blindness came back; and he couldn't write and was very low, I gather, but he's much better and was eager for news. He sent you messages to say he was full of ideas, plans for work, and hopes to have a model and paint again! The studio was cluttered over with drawings, drying because the paper was damp! *Superb* nudes for his "Last Judgment" he said. *Such* fine drawings of twisted bodies in action, and exciting poses. The place was alive with his great effort and achievement and I could hardly bear not to have others see them. Portfolios everywhere, all damp he said; all had to be dried on fine days. Weather has been superb, and he's taken advantage of it. I asked about the winter, and he had four sacks of coal! All that he has been allowed! His overcoat looked very mended and thin. He has no sweater, but Bill Carter has an extra one he will send at once. His 'femme de ménage's' work-basket was near by and I offered to mend the hem of his coat but he wouldn't let me. He was thin but looked well and vigorous and seemed glad to see me. I did my new 'Vive la France' for him and he was deeply moved. He said the simple conversation and little things I talk about are so exactly right for a Bretonne peasant, and so of course I was pleased. He wanted to know all about you, and sent his love, and regrets for his long silence. I wish we could get him a good warm overcoat; he wants shaving soap (a stick) and sugar and cigarettes. I took him some cheese, all I had, and saw potatoes and apples on the floor and he assured me his 'bonne' comes at noon to cook his dinner, but I left at 12:30 and she hadn't turned up. He was 'bien rasé' and clean and his dyed hair under his hat looked a bit odd at the back—but his face is so alive when he talks and his voice and diction superb. I begged him to talk on the Radio—but he said they don't want ideas or 'principes'!—they only want 'distractions' and 'vulgarité'.

France is tragic—Paris incredibly beautiful in divine September golden light and color. I thought of you and wished I could share the old heart breaking thrill—so utterly heart breaking now—for one feels the sense of shame and moral defeat, the fear and chaotic disturbance under the familiar aspect of the scene. I paid 6000 francs for the luncheon at Prunier's I gave the policeman, his wife and son. But *never* did I spend money more joyfully. They had rescued and succoured eighty-five of our flyers (and British boys too) and have had no recompense whatever. It is awful. The Americans bombed and completely destroyed their house at Dreux, and the Americans destroyed her family's home at Vire. Such fine people, such manners and *such* intelligence and integrity. They risked their lives and gave all they had for France and to our boys. Do you wonder I was proud and happy to pay $50. for two hours of happiness for them! My, how they enjoyed that lunch!

I'm starting my work to-morrow. Eighty nights of work. Five weeks on the road and five weeks in London. I hope I keep well! Brighton first, is a grand place to start. Lovely weather.

Charles Draper had died in February 1947.

Ruth wrote Grace Martin: "I bought a beautiful Chinese vase!–bronze!–with some money my dear brother left me. It's a beauty and about 3,000 years old–wonderful colors from being buried in the earth. I'm thrilled by it, and love it. It's on the center table."

Although not a collector in the usual sense of the word, Ruth acquired many precious objects in her wide-ranging travels. The Chinese bronze vase to which she refers was cherished in constant memory of her brother Charles, as well as for itself–its long history, the skills and art that went into its design and making, about all of which she was thoroughly informed.

Her appreciation of beauty, of paintings, seemed to be entirely an emotional response. Actually she had read and listened—and looked—and was far more knowledgeable than her self-depreciating attitude made apparent.

On the piano in her living room stood a head of Nefertiti, the Egyptian Queen. Often she would give it a companionable pat as she went by, remarking: "There was a wise old girl!"

To Grace Martin
(Mrs. David Terry Martin)

January 25 [1948]
66 East 79th Street
New York

I've had an envelope addressed to you for weeks—with a few others—alas long neglected. I posted twenty-two letters this morning. Now I'm at the Empire—between Sunday shows—resting, reading. I have two sheets of paper, and will scribble this to you. My dresser is making me tea, and a boiled egg; then I'll turn out the lights and try and get a nap. This cold weather is not too good for audiences, but a fair number came this afternoon. The Radio says: "People are urged to stay at home—don't take out cars—don't go into the streets!—more snow is on the way"! So the theatres have all suffered a bad slump. My Sundays have gone well, but the Tuesday, Wednesday, and Friday matinees are not good. So I fear I've lost money this venture. I'm going on a big tour, but not your way, alas, and to few interesting or important places. I rather dread it for some reason—perhaps it's once too often. The cost is so great. I make very little anyway. I've not been clever about managers. I *should* make Peat pay the R.R. fares, then perhaps he wouldn't send me chasing all over the country from Miami to Ottawa and three times to Chicago, and missing all the big towns; he only has small places. I'm too humble, too lazy, and too indifferent and have only myself to blame I guess. I didn't realize he was booking me such a tour, and now I have to stick to it—leaving here February 3. I'd like to hang around here!—be near my sister who is very sad—but I can't change now.

To Grace Martin
(Mrs. David Terry Martin)

[February 18, 1948]
Des Moines, Iowa

Isn't S———'s [letter] a touching and gallant British thing—they go on having those village fetes, trying to get some fun for the children and village people. It's so sweet and pathetic, and so *real*—all her enthusiasm about what you send. You are an angel to keep it up. I fall off terribly but my wandering life doesn't make it easy! This tour has been very tiring, and *not* very interesting jobs—all in colleges—and youth is always interesting. And I love to give them what I have (and what perhaps they need!) but I'm not doing any major cities or important audiences—in other words, the same type of job I had twenty-eight years ago! It's sad at the end of my career that I'm not more highly regarded and wanted. New York season was very poor—of course awful weather, and matinees only, were against me. The Sunday audiences, matinee and evening, were grand.

On May 26, 1948, Ruth addressed the members of the Council of the New York Academy of Medicine. She expressed pleasure at returning to the Academy, which she often had visited with her father, and her gratitude for the standards learned in her childhood from the medical profession as exemplified by him, by her eldest brother and their distinguished associates—for all of whom she held an affectionate and high regard; and she spoke of accompanying her father in his carriage while he called on his patients. Then she said:

In November 1946 I was playing at the Apollo Theatre in London. One day I received a letter from a young doctor on the staff of St. Mary's Hospital asking me to give a performance for the staff, the nurses, orderlies and servants of the hospital, as well as those patients who could attend in wheelchairs and beds moved in from wards near the library.

It was a remarkable audience, and though tired after my matinee performance, I enjoyed the evening enormously. When it was over a nurse handed me a bunch of roses and a young doctor made a speech, expressing the staff's appreciation of my visit. He said he would like to give me a small token as a souvenir of the occasion and handed me a little black glass-covered disk, which I at first thought was a brooch to pin on my coat. It appeared to have a pale petal of a flower on a black ground. Slightly perplexed, I turned it over to see how it could be attached—I saw some words written in red ink. I read:

> To Ruth Draper
> Penicillium Notatum
> From Alexander Fleming

My heart thumped, blood rushed to my head, a great emotion swept over me, knowing I held in my hand this frail fragment of the miracle, given me by its discoverer.

I soon realized this fragment was far too precious for me to keep—a thing of such interest to scientists and to the world should not be left in the hands of a "trouper" like myself. So I thought: Where would it be safe? Where valued and cared for?

I thought of the Academy of Medicine. I called my friend, Dr. Malloch, and asked him if the Academy possessed a specimen from the original culture of penicillin. He said no and he felt sure they would like to have it.

So I had my little medallion mounted, I think worthily and securely by Tiffany, in a box which Dr. Malloch told me would be the most acceptable form for safe-keeping and showing to interested visitors to the Academy's collection of treasures.

I have stood before many audiences as an actress, but I assure you, gentlemen, I have never felt a greater pride than appearing here as my father's daughter before you, members of the profession which he loved and ennobled in a long life of service.

Dr. Behr, I give this penicillin to the New York Academy of Medicine in memory of my father, Dr. William H. Draper.

To Grace Martin
(Mrs. David Terry Martin)

August 31 [1948]
On board M.V. Britannic

Here I am—on my way again! I meant to have written before I sailed, but the last weeks were so busy, and the last days—only three in New York—were hectic! I had my guests up to Saturday a.m. in Islesboro'—and I left Sunday p.m.! Flew down in Winthrop Aldrich's plane—such a lovely flight over that wonderful coast, and we circled around over our Island after taking off in Rockland, and saw our place and my boat and the beach where we bathe, from the sky! My summer was happy but not too restful—opening both houses (I'd hoped to rent one, but didn't, or give it away, but couldn't find anyone!) and having people staying all the time is not restful. I got a marvellous cook, which was a God-send—had old 'Nannie', seventy-two, Penelope's old nurse for a housemaid and general—two native girls, pretty and darling—but they had boy friends. They did well washing dishes, and were nice girls, so it helped—but I was endlessly on the go—fixing flowers, tidying, planning, on tap all day, so to speak—and there is so much I want to do and enjoy doing, anyway—boating, and sailing and walking—I got no tennis, alas, and time rushed by. I had no cook and did all the cooking for a month. I was never alone—which I hate anyway—that big house must be full to be really happy. My guests all gained pounds and got such peace and relaxation—and were so grateful and happy—it was pure joy to see. They are hard working people and the two who don't work are delicate, and could not get such rest and care and sense of home in any other way—so it's a deep satisfaction. I really love doing it, but I am the kind that can't spare myself much when I'm doing a job—and like to do it well; just as you would.

These eight days at sea are heaven, I rest and relax all day—know no one, and have nothing I have to do! A smaller and slower ship than the 'Queens' but more agreeable to me. I land in Liverpool and go on to Edinburgh for one week. There I meet my sister Dorothea and Penny [Penelope Draper] which will be fun. D. had to go to see about [Henry James' Lamb House] in Rye, as I told you she owned it now. She plans to let the National Trust take it over and had to see lawyers etc. about that. It's Penny's first trip and she's having a glorious time. They go to Paris the 7th so I'll catch them in Edinburgh over Sunday. My friend Harriet Marple is flying on September 4th to join me in Edinburgh for the festival. I'm so sorry I'm not 'in' it, as I'd hoped to be, but I was too late in answering, [the] program was made up. We'll enjoy the week I know and go to London the 12th and fly to Italy the 16th. I'll be at Lauro's sister's for two weeks in Siena, then a few days in Florence, then I hope for some jobs in Switzerland, then Holland, then Paris and back to England to begin my 'season' November 15th and stay on as long as I feel like it!

To Bernard Berenson

[October 11, 1948]
Hôtel Vendôme [Paris]

Dearest B..B.

I can't realize that a week has passed since my peaceful and restoring hours with you. You feed one's mind, quicken one's spirit, and warm one's heart, and your friendship means more to me than you could surmise from my neglect of it! Thank you for letting me come again and enjoy myself to the full for that brief visit; I was indeed sorry to make it so short, but I had made engagements it would have been impossible to change. I also just managed to catch the last place on the Milan-Paris "plane" on Friday by booking it that day! I had a miraculous flight over the Alps and was in my hotel here after 4 quiet hours in the sky.

I went to the Louvre yesterday afternoon, and thought how wonderful it would be to have seen those pictures with you, (it was lovely to go back to Italy, even having left it so recently!). The new hanging, and the clean walls, and splendid light in the long gallery and the Italian rooms, are a great improvement but there is still much to be done. It is wonderful to see the crowds that come, and feel the interest, curiosity, and faithfulness to tradition undiminished.

A soft autumn Sunday in Paris, with the sun on the crowds and bright flowers and yellowing trees, and the misty sweep up to the Arc, and the incredibly lovely light on the bridges and old houses, and the towers of Notre Dame and the flèche of Ste. Chapelle, overwhelmed me as always with penetrating emotion and wonder. In spite of the uncertainty and political confusion, and the qualities one hates to observe, there is a splendid vitality and sanity and a stubborn sort of wisdom for life, to which one clings in these old races, when one feels despairing and hopeless. I find I rather dread going back to England, after this lovely draught of beauty and sunshine, and the rich fruits of the soil, which feed the spirit as well as the body! One is so upset by values put on moral qualities (as well as aesthetic ones)—not in oneself, for one remains true to one's own—but in general, as one sees them changing, distorted and doing grievous harm, and making much confusion in the world.

I'm getting out too deep for a letter written after my petit déjeuner looking over the roofs and chimney pots in the sun. I only want to send my love, and endless thanks to you and Nicky for your care and affection and the happiness you gave me.

Ruth

Before she closed her London season in April, the Archbishops of Canterbury and York came to the Haymarket and sat in the wings, for there were no other available seats, just as Paul Claudel and his staff had done in Washington years before.

The Prime Minister, Clement Attlee, was given a birthday treat at the Haymarket—a family party—and wrote to tell her he was particularly appreciative of her study of the village postmistress (Mrs. Hancock in The Return*) in which he found every point exactly right—the very essence of English village life.*

To Bernard Berenson

April 30, 1949
On board
R.M.S. "Mauretania"

My dear B.B.

At last—hours of lovely leisure, no appointments, no interruptions, time to let one's thoughts dally and rest in far off places, conjuring up lovely places and dear friends. So I am sitting beside you in the garden at I Tatti, telling you all my winters' tales, and hearing your's and Nicchi's.

I look back on seven months since I left you at Vallombrosa, crowded with work and people, and wandering too. Tho' I've given you no proof that you were often in my thoughts—you were—always, when I see pictures—and at the Hague, Amsterdam, and Paris, and in London, Glasgow and Edinburgh, I seemed to feel your familiarity with the pictures that moved me deeply. Somehow you did not come to my mind as I wandered past the "Chantrey" collection pictures, tho' the "little girl" in me even enjoyed some of those! I hated to leave England, and stop my work—I wonder when I shall have the courage to stop? It *is* such fun! Besides my 104 performances in London, I had a week in Cambridge, with an audience of adorable laughing youths, a week in Stratford, filling the Great Memorial Theatre and blushing at the review in the local paper headed "Worthy to Walk with Shakespeare"! Then a week in Brighton—by the lovely "bracing" sea—and a fortnight in Glasgow (such intelligent warm audiences), and a week in Bath playing in a gem of a theatre where Sarah Siddons played, Garrick and Kean and where "The Rivals" and the "School for Scandal" were first played! It was thrilling; and Bath (in Holy Week) a dream of blossoms and flowers, and sunshine on that soft golden stone, and the lovely harmonious architecture, set in those green curved hills. It is an enchanting place.

I am headed for home now, after 8 months absence, and shall be in my sweet flat at 66 East 79th Street for May and June, and then go to Islesboro, Maine, for July and August and September. After that I don't know—I may stay in New York until the new year, and then come over for the spring, and to work perhaps on the Continent, which I've not done for some time. I hope of course to be inspired with some new ideas, but haven't much confidence in my ability and will-power to work up new things. I feel so safe with the old ones! I recently passed a night at Katie Lewis' in Broadway, on my way to Stratford from Bath to see Macbeth and Much Ado. We had a happy time to-gether on a perfect spring day (Easter) and spoke much of you. I've seen brave Sibyl—eagerly looking forward to her visit to you. I wish she had a travelling companion or maid. Her courage is stupendous. I should be overwhelmed by the illnesses and crippling accidents she's had. I do admire her, and her kindnesses, and thoughts for other's pleasures, go on.

I hope this finds you well. Give my love to dear Nicchi. I expect you are busy as ever, receiving streams of visitors, interesting, and some loved ones, I hope. I Tatti must be a dream of beauty now, and I wander from the sun-light in the garden, and the cypress trees into the cool library, the dining room, the hall, your room, and feel the quietness and the beauty you have brought to-gether, expressing your mind and your spirit—and the sanctuary they are in this crazy troubled world. My love and gratitude to you always.

Ruth

To Bernard Berenson

June 24 [1949]
66 East 79th St.
New York City

Dearest B.B.

I have thought of you often since Addie Kahn's sudden death, and realized the shock and sorrow it must have been to you. You will miss her devoted and faithful friendship. I imagine she was happy in the prospect of her visit to you and lovely plans for her summer in beautiful places, seeing lovely things she cared for so deeply. She will be greatly missed by her friends here, and all the visiting artists and literary folk who always foregathered in her hospitable and enchanting flat on the river. I remember so well the pleasant days I spent with you at Vallombrosa when she was there, and she was going over the MSS. of your book [*Sketch for a Self-portrait*]. I have read it with great interest; it is rare that people are so hon-est about themselves, but being honest is not necessarily being fair, and it's a pity that readers can't sometimes speak out as they read! I had a card from Sibyl, so I know she had her dream come true again—*how* brave she is. I hope she has kept well and been able to carry out all her plans for the summer.

Salvemini is planning to sail the end of July—and he is sad to leave these shores, but I'm sure he'll be happy to be in Italy again and I hope he will find a nice place to live in Florence, and keep warm when the cold begins. We all worry about that, as he had pneumonia three times last winter. His mind is vigorous and clear as ever, and he is great fun—*so* stimulating! He is more gentle and philosophic in his attitude about the piled up confusion and wrong in the world, tho' he will fight to the end for his convictions.

I am off to Maine next week. I've been busy seeing family and friends after my 8 months absence and, much as I love seeing them, I'm already thinking of my next journey abroad—because I love to work more than anything and find such a response to what I have to offer in the old world, besides everything else it offers me! I may be very blind to certain things here that one seeks and loves, but one's vision is clouded somehow by so much that one can't enjoy or be content about. My best love to Nicky. I think your plans are wonderful,— I hope you can carry them all out, and get to Paris in the lovely golden autumn. My love always and gratitude, even if I am such a very poor correspondent.

Your devoted Ruth

To Grace Martin
(Mrs. David Terry Martin)

March 17 [1950]
On Board S.S. America

I'm off again, happy to go, yet sorry to leave too. I've hated not working but it's been lovely being able to enjoy my sweet flat at such leisure, and see my sisters and friends. It's a double life—a two sided person I am—and I don't feel I'm living really unless I'm working, yet trains and hotels, and others' houses are not home either! But just the same, some latent fire is quenched when I'm static and comfortable, and lit again when I'm alone and wandering, and putting on make up in a dreary dressing room!

I'm lucky to have both, and turn to either as I choose. How I wish I could give some of my freedom to others. Life is so sad when we lose our powers and become burdens, and hurt others' lives. I dread the thought of what I'll be should my wings be clipped! I've been spoiled by freedom and opportunity, tho' I haven't used it enough.

I'm on my way to Paris, then Switzerland, and Florence and Rome for most of April. I dread always going back to Rome, and reliving after twenty-two years, the Spring I met Lauro there. But I must go to see his mother as long as she lives—and I am going to give three Benefits there for charities, and that makes my effort worthwhile—and after all—what a privilege to go to Rome—even with lovely memories warring with sad ones at every turn. I have friends there and in Florence, where I'm giving Benefits, too.

To Bernard Berenson

May 10 [1950]
Montreux
[Switzerland]

Dearest B.B.

The days have flown since I left you—and they have been so full of activity—really perpetual motion—that I've found no time to write—you will understand. I also wanted to tell you and Nicky what a happy meeting I had had with Baroness Pilar [a Baltic relative of Nicky's]. *What* a dear person—and I only regretted there was so little time for a long talk, and to hear something of her life in that beautiful life before the world went mad. She came to see me, and I was so touched, and I walked back with her across the bridge and through the pretty flowering park—and another day I went to her flat to tea and met her son and another lady. Alas, there was no time to meet the Bodmers and go to see Merlingue—nor did I have the temerity to write the Contessa de Sarre—and the Queen did *not* come to either of my shows! *Her* loss, for I think she would have enjoyed them! Everyone else did, and both evenings in Geneva the theatre was *packed,* with laughing happy people. I went to Vevey on Saturday and had a beautiful drive, and dined and spent the night with Marguerite Horton in her charming old house. We talked of you and Nicky and other mutual friends, and of course I remembered I'd met her often at the Schellings. She came to my show last night, with the Queen of Spain, and is coming to fetch me to-day and drive me to Lausanne, where I play to-night and to-morrow. I leave for Paris on Friday and shall be at Hôtel Vendôme. I hope Nicky will let me know if there is anything that I can do before you arrive [on May 28]. I had a splendid audience here last night, and am enjoying this week in Switzerland. The snow peaks are dazzling in the morning sun, and the lake is blue, all the apple blossoms and lilacs are bursting with sweetness and vitality—flowers everywhere—order and cleanliness everywhere—only the Soul of Man seems strangely not in evidence! I went to Coppet and was moved by the thought of all the brilliant minds and fantastic characters that had once filled those rooms, and walked in the lovely wooded paths by the rushing brook. I lunched at the United Nations and wished all the poor creatures at Lake Success could be in that beautiful spacious park, breathing real air and looking at Mont Blanc, instead of dumps, and the hideous ugliness of their present abode!

I must end this too long letter. The large blue page invites meandering along, saying little, and I would like to say so much—of all that my brief moments with you gave me to enrich my thoughts and memories with beauty and wisdom and affection. Thank you dear B.B. for all that you have given me always. It's lovely to think we shall meet so soon again. I hope your journey will be easy and happy and that the sun will shine on all the lovely places you pass through. My dearest love to you and Nicky, and so many many thanks for my happy hours.

Your loving Ruth

At this time Ruth was "deeply disturbed by Paul's cruel plight." In joint appearances with the harmonica virtuoso Larry Adler, Paul Draper had had eight very successful years dancing nation-wide in concert tours. Then, he

*and Adler were accused in a Hearst newspaper of being Communists and, in
an attempt to clear their names, jointly brought suit for libel, the trial ending
in a hung jury. But their careers were effectively halted and, when it became
impossible to obtain engagements, Paul, late in 1950, took his family to
England, later going to live in Switzerland.*

    *In no way politically minded, unable really to comprehend the nuances of
the situation, Ruth staunchly stood by Paul with all the support and comfort
she could muster. She wrote to Grace Martin:*

**To Grace Martin
(Mrs. David Terry Martin)**

May 24 [1950]
Hôtel Vendôme
Paris

    Paul's case drags on—a horrible business—I'm glad I'm not there. I am
so unhappy and confused by the whole situation at home—the power of the
press, and those writers who can sway thousands of readers. I'm afraid he's
finished forever in U.S. He could find work here—or in Australia. It's all a
mess, and I think of his father whom I so loved.

    *Evidently Ruth was to report to Berenson on how she found Sibyl Cole-
fax. Born in 1872, she was the widow of Sir Arthur Colefax, a prominent
English jurist, and was herself a legendary London hostess for many years.
B.B. was in Paris, but not strong enough, at the age of 84, to cross the
Channel. Lady Colefax, aged 78, was determined to visit him, therefore the
Duff Coopers invited them both to their château at Vineuil (Oise). B.B.'s
diary tells of the meeting:*

June 30th, Chateau de St. Firmin

At death's door as her friends thought for months, Sibyl Colefax insisted on
coming over to see me, as I could not go to London, and Diana Cooper
offered to fetch her from Dieppe and lodge us both. I wonder whether, if
she reflects, Sibyl was not disappointed. She did not realize how exhausting
in her state of health the journey would be, how tired she would find me,
how little either she or I was in physical condition to enjoy each other's
conversation. Let me hope she really cares enough to be happy to be in the
same house with me. She was brave enough to accompany us to see the
pictures at Chantilly. All the time she would talk in such a clipped, mumb-
ling way, that neither Diana nor I understood half she was saying, and
coughing as she talked. Nevertheless she may recount and recall this outing
with zest and joy.

To Bernard Berenson

June 27 [1950]
Edinburgh

Dearest B.B.

I have neglected to write you since reaching England and I'm sorry. I found Sibyl [Colefax] away the Sunday I arrived, but I saw her on Tuesday last and found her full of her forthcoming visit—full of her old spirit in spite of what she has been through. By now you've seen her and passed the moment you dreaded. I do hope the journey, and the venture of such an exciting expedition, and the emotion of seeing you again has not been too much. In her case, I'm sure it will all act as a tonic, and she is ready to pay any price. I hope you will have enjoyed the week-end, too—the lovely place— the lovely Diana—and all the affection and beauty that seems to be the ambience in which you move thro' life.

I've just been to the Gallery here— I wished you were with me—there are beautiful things—a new Blake that is soul stirring—God in a whirlwind talking to Job; the Ellesmere Collection from Bridgewater House—*such* beautiful Raeburns, two perfect Guardis, and superb Franz Hals. I like small galleries, with a few treasures, and I love this town, and the great hill-castle and the grim old buildings that have housed such brains and such character! I have wonderful audiences—faithful and warm—and am enjoying my week at the theatre. Last week I played to full houses in Wimbledon. I am going to the Highlands and to Skye next week—and then to London to fly home. Dear B.B., thank you for such happy hours, and for your affection. My love to Nicky and to you always, and many thoughts and wishes for your homeward journey—

Your loving Ruth

To Grace Martin
(Mrs. David Terry Martin)

July 15 [1950]
Dark Harbor, Maine

I'm in my little house and it is packed during all August. I expect to sail for Europe September 18th for a season in England returning about Xmas time. It is always hard to push off and leave the easy routine of life here, and family and friends and flat in New York, but I know I have a greater 'sense of action' abroad, and give pleasure to those weary worried people. I've not many years left when I can pick up and go so easily, so I must gather my forces and make plans to go—my manager in London is waiting to hear from me now.

I must go and cut dead twigs, and tidy things up generally—work is endless in a place like this!

Sibyl Colefax died on September 22, 1950. In his diary for September 24th, B.B. notes his memories of her:

September 24th, Vallombrosa

News yesterday of Sibyl Colefax's death. Knew her since she was eighteen, when she looked like a young begum. Something un-European in her looks always. Strange, for both her parents were ultra-Nordic. Became a great London hostess, and in last thirty years or more one of the few most prominent, and latterly the only one furnishing a meeting place for political, artistic, literary, and theatrical people. A godsend for stray visitors like me, who in a little time wanted to see their acquaintances. The soul of generosity, and, most generous of generosities, her sharing of friends with friends. So many otherwise dear people keep them in water-tight compartments.

To Bernard Berenson

October 28 [1950]
Dublin [Ireland]

Dearest B.B.

I have had it on my mind for weeks to write you about Sibyl—but the pressure of life has been so constant, and letters that take leisure and thought are somehow put aside. I enclose the little "order" of her Memorial Service—perhaps other friends have sent it. The words are always worth reading, and the music was lovely, but it was a strangely cold and unmoving occasion! Friends were all crowded at the *back* of the church, and Michael and his wife had rows of empty pews behind them, and stood quite alone. People are strangely shy, and there seemed no warm and united impulse to crowd forward, and express a common feeling of loyalty, and gratitude for the wealth of kindness we'd all received at her hands. I had expected a mob of every kind of person whom she helped and befriended and encouraged in their particular "line." Many were away perhaps—some missed the notice of the service—however, one did not get what one expected from such an occasion—a great tribute to her generosity and unfailing enthusiasm for people and what they contributed to life. The letters in the papers were fine I thought. I missed H. Nicolson's in the *Spectator* and hear that was excellent. I had a sweet letter from Mrs. Grey, her cook, and she and Daker [maid] adored her, and their tribute is good to have—and revealing of her essential kindness. You will miss her faithful scrawls—showing her really constant thought and love for you. There will not be anything quite like it again—what she did in London for her friends—I don't know of any rallying place, and one feels they will all be scattered now, and never brought instantaneously to-gether, as was her wont, to surround a new discovery, and help him or her on their way! What taste she had—that little North St.

house [19 Lord North Street] was a gem of quiet comfort, and charm and color—with the atmosphere of the gracious past and the exciting present strangely mingled and not inharmonious.

I have just finished 4 weeks at the "Criterion" with packed houses—and hundreds turned away. Now I am in the midst of a 2 weeks' season at the Gaiety Theatre here in Dublin—crowding the house (which holds 1400)—with wild applause at the end of every show—and fabulous reviews in all the papers. It is a gay and attractive city, lovely old houses, and I spent an hour yesterday turning over the pages of the Book of Kells and getting a great thrill touching that dusky vellum 1200 years old, and looking at the loveliest colors imaginable in that amazing and intricate design of letters. I could imagine how you would have enjoyed it again.

It's cold now, but the sun is shining and I must go out for some fresh air. I have 2 shows to-day, and it's very hard work—harder, alas, than it used to be! They love my "County Kerry" and the "Vive la France—1940" and the "Church"—they seem to love everything. They're all actors and it's fun playing to them, for as well as being the greatest talkers, they're good listeners too! I confess to enjoying the good food—lovely nourishing meat every day—which one so misses in England—and cream and butter galore! So I'm storing up strength for the next weeks. I go to Holland Nov. 7th for 7 shows in different cities,—then to Stockholm for 3 (unless the King dies, and everything is stopped!) and Oslo for 2 and Copenhagen for 3, and back to London Dec. 1st when I am going to do *Records* seriously, and not play in the theatre while I'm doing them. I hope they'll turn out well. Decca, said to be the best, is going to do them.

My dear love to Nicchi, and to you dear B.B. I hope this finds you well, and that Rome was warm and lovely for your visit. Forgive my long silence—I think of you often, and "ti voglio tanto bene!"

Ruth

To Dorothea Draper
(Mrs. Henry James, Jr.)

[November 12, 1950]
The Hague

I had a delightful time last night at Eindhoven, the town that *is* The Phillips Co., corresponding to our General Electric. An amazing concern, the biggest factory in Holland and wonderfully well run. They have a beautiful building for the employees—every possible recreation, and a wonderful auditorium and theatre. It's the third time I've been there, and the audience is extraordinarily intelligent—all the young engineers, electricians, research people. They have concerts, etc., of the best artists and orchestras. All pay for their tickets, but it's all so well run and gives everyone a chance to get first class entertainment. I stayed, as I have once before, with the Loudons (nephew and niece of my old friends John and Lydia Loudon) and their eight lovely children—six at home—I never saw a lovelier group of beautiful, intelligent and happy young—from sixteen to six—the older ones away at school. They begin French, German and English very young, and later Latin and Greek as well! They're all musical and their manners and looks are enchanting, natural and friendly.

I came back in time to lunch at [a] lovely place. Philip Nichols, the British Ambassador, an old friend of mine, motor'd me out, and we had a cosy pleasant lunch and good talk. The other man was an American, our Counsellor, a Mr. Coe, nephew of Mary Rogers and he's just been ordered to Korea. I feel sorry for him leaving this adorable country, so comfortable and serene.

I must get up now and get ready for my show. It's raining, but yesterday was beautiful and sunny. All the world is coming to-night—place sold out as usual. The mourning for the King in Sweden will prevent any attendance of Royalty in all three capitals; very inconvenient of the old gentleman not to wait until my season was over!

To Bernard Berenson

> December 20 [1950]
> 37, Chapel Street
> Belgrave Square, SW 1
> [London]

Dearest B.B.

I am still here! I suddenly decided to stay over Christmas in order to keep my nephew Paul, and his wife and children company. It is their first Xmas in a strange land, and as I am living next door, it is happy for us all to be together. I am sailing on the "Queen Mary" on the 28th. I shall be thinking of you all on Christmas Day and wishing I could be with you, too. I am so thankful that the Professor [Salvemini] is to be with you, and the care and affection you and Nicky give him must be the greatest comfort and help. I know he must feel very defeated, to have had to abandon his work. It seems the return of diabetes added to his weakness and depression—not only was it the result of his bronchitis, which is well over. I am glad that he has decided to go to Sorrento, and I hope his friends there will take good care of him, and that he won't have any more attacks of bronchitis which seems his particular danger. I bless you for all your generous friendship and kindness, for you give him so much that no one else can and, besides your loyal friendship of so many years, the warmth and beauty penetrate his loneliness, and revive his spirits. He loves you and Nicky, and has often told me what a haven you have given him since his return to Florence.

I have had a wonderful 3 months—here—in Ireland—in Holland—Stockholm, Oslo, and Copenhagen. Everywhere I could have prolonged my stay, and repeated my programs again and again. Such fine intelligent, warm and responsive audiences. I wish I could be in many places. I am drawn toward home, and those I love there, toward work—anywhere; this cold and grim old city I love with a deep tenderness, and Italy is always like a dream and when one goes to find it—it is true. I hate the great ocean, and the fear of war that always hangs over our thoughts these days—and that perhaps I can't return—but if all is well I will come in the spring. I'll try and write more often. Thanks for your letter. Many wishes for the New Year and my love and thanks always.

Ruth

To Grace Martin
(Mrs. David Terry Martin)

February 7 [1951]
66 East 79th Street
New York

I *thought* I'd written you! I *have* been rather rushed since my return January 2. I was only at home four days and I was so busy unpacking, and seeing my family, I don't think I wrote one letter during those days—then I left for a two week tour in the South. I'm home for a while, and *shall try and write down my monologues.* I've said this every year for at least twenty years—but I hope my character is strong enough to fulfil my plan in 1951!

I'm reading Jane Austen and am simply *fascinated.* What delicate irony, satire and humor! "The business of her life was to get her daughters married; its solace was visiting and news." (Mrs. Bennet) I've read *Emma* and *Mansfield Park* and am now on *Pride and Prejudice.* I have so many books and it's hard to find time to read them.

To Bernard Berenson

April 3 [1951]
66 East 79th Street
New York, New York

Dearest B.B.

I am in a place called Marshalltown, Iowa, and return home to-morrow after a short "tour". It is so funny to be writing from this small mid-West town. I'm looking down the Main Street from my window with farm land and corn fields stretching to the horizon beyond the edge of town. And in my mind's eye I can see the cypress trees and your garden and the distant hills, or sit beside you and the marble lion on the table, and the pictures and flowers, and Nicky, and feel all the exalted quietness of I Tatti, and your insight and understanding; and it is all as present, and as alive as my sordid little hotel bed-room, and the view from my window as I write. Imagination and memories—what gifts from the gods!

The winter has rushed by—I only returned from England in early January, and I've been in my darling flat almost continually, with jobs now and then—in Florida, Pennsylvania, N.Y. State, Connecticut and Chicago and out here. But no continuous season. They are "after me" for Television, and I may consider it—largely for the money that it may mean—and to "keep up" with the "Times"! I'm told I should, if only to raise the standard of the "stuff" now given on this miraculous device, to bring pleasure to millions. I had not meant to come over this spring (I was abroad 8 months out of last year) but I don't think I can resist coming now that spring is approaching, and I may sail in May for three months. I still so enjoy the summer in Maine, and sailing my boat, that I plan to go there again by mid-July. The Professor says he wants to come again, so I must be there to welcome him! I hear he is in Florence again, and I hope he will not fall victim to bronchitis after having the warmth of Sorrento. I think he had a happy winter there, working as he always does when he is well, and not getting to tired. I hope he will be prudent and that you will see him soon, for I know how he loves to be with you and Nicky.

Do you plan any journey this spring, and have you had a good winter? I saw Daisy Chanler recently and we spoke of you of course. Laura and Larry [White] have taken a flat just across the street from me, and are so happy to be in New York. I see the dear Hands sometimes. Amey Aldrich has been to Mexico with Betty Morrow and I shall see her when I get home. Forgive this brief note, my paper gave out—but I wanted to send you my love, and say I often think of you—tho' I am such a bad correspondent.

We have all been sunk in the revelations of crime and political scandal, literally floundering in it, and horrified! And the war news is bad as ever, and the future dark and full of fear and confusion—but one's little life goes on, and our usual cheerful re-action to spring and sunshine serves to keep our spirits normal. My best love to Nicky—and always grateful loving thoughts and wishes to you.

                                                                        Ruth

On April 22nd Ruth Draper received a letter from the British Ambassador in Washington, informing her that His Majesty the King had been pleased to confer upon her the Insignia of Honorary Commander of the Most Excellent Order of the British Empire in recognition of her extremely generous support of philanthropic institutions in Britain over a period of nearly twenty-five years.

To the British Ambassador in Washington
Sir Oliver Franks

April 24, 1951
66 East 79th Street
New York

Your Excellency:

In addition to my formal letter of acceptance I can not refrain from telling you that I wish the honour were not being given me in recognition of my "extremely generous support of philanthropic institutions in Britain." I am sorry that this should be known and published in the papers as the reason for the award.

I like to think that there is more than recognition of mere financial help to charities that has prompted this expression of appreciation. To me, my long friendship for England, Canada, and other countries of the Commonwealth and Empire, and my love for British audiences for over thirty years, have a spiritual significance far beyond any consideration of a reward for any gifts in money that it has been my pleasure to make through the years.

To me the honour will be a symbol of what England has given me so generously from the heart as I have given from mine, and I am proud, as an American, to feel that my affection is reciprocated.

If in my work I have helped a little to interpret the fine qualities of each country to the other, I am glad. And the inspiration I have received during my many visits to England has been cause for gratitude that I cannot find words to express.

I hope you will forgive my frankness and understand my feeling, and believe in my deep gratitude for this moving tribute.

On April 26th the Ambassador replied, regretting that a routine form of words should have been used in her case. He continued:

> The affection in which you are held by a very large, widespread and loyal following in Britain is only a measure of the manner in which you have stimulated and at the same time responded to that warm feeling. The complex Anglo-American relationship is always extremely difficult to define, but in a London performance when you have drawn your audience close around you, the interchange between you and them embodies the very best of that relationship. To every one of us who has felt that magic this award can only have one meaning.

To Grace Martin
(Mrs. David Terry Martin)

April 29 [1951]
66 East 79th Street
New York

I'm so excited for you both. You must come *here* and stay before you sail, for as long as you want. The flat will be empty and ready for you. I am sailing May 12th on the "Liberté" and my address will be Brown Shipley & Co. as I'm not sure where I'm staying in London.

Two *amazing* honors have been conferred on me!! The University of Edinburgh is giving me a Degree of LL.D.!!!! And the King is awarding me the C.B.E. (Commander)!!!!! Can you imagine such a thing? I simply can't get over the shock and surprise. The latter doesn't involve any ceremony, but is a very great honor—the next higher is Dame but of course that is not given anyone except a British subject. I am moved and proud and feel very unworthy of the LL.D. That is almost funny—but touching, and inspired too! For a great University (and I'd rather have Edinburgh's tribute than any in the world!) to give an Honorary Degree to an actress! It *is* sporting of them and I am deeply touched and moved.

To Bernard Berenson

June 3 [1951]
Venice [Italy]

Dearest B.B.

I'm sitting on the terrace of the Grand Hotel, gazing at the Salute in the morning light, and watching barges of vegetables, gondolas of travellers and the crowded vapore pass by. I've just had a delicious breakfast and feel fresh for another day of delight and wonder. I was *so* sad to miss you in Florence, but my days are very limited, alas, and this was the only time I could manage to come to Italy. My visit was quite unexpected anyway. I had given up all idea of coming when the summons came from Edinburgh. Then a few weeks later, I had the announcement from the British Ambassador, that the King "had been pleased to confer on me the Insignia of Commander of the British Empire"! So I am to go to Windsor Castle next week to be decorated there by the king himself!! So I could only fit in these two flying weeks, after my arrival in England, before returning there for the two great honors. I flew to Nice, and spent 2 days at Cannes, with Lucien Monod (do you know his great work on gravures?) a dear friend—who gave me sanctuary the night that Lauro flew to Rome [October 2, 1931—the night *before* the flight]. It is nearly 20 years ago, and I'd not seen him and his wife since that October night so long ago. I flew from there to Rome which was a great emotion, looking down on the city, and following Lauro's path. I only lingered there long enough to walk along the Pincio, and take the evening train to Florence, where an English friend was meeting me. We went to Siena for the week-end and then had 4 days in Florence, and darling Luisa, and Nicky's sister welcomed us at I Tatti to see the garden and the library and pictures. I knew you wouldn't mind, and I so wanted my friend to see the beauty of it all, and to have myself the nostalgic pleasure of seeing it again. It was dreadfully sad to me to be there without you and Nicky. Thank you nevertheless for the pleasure you unknowingly gave us! I saw Salvemini several times, and my beloved Signora Rosselli, and heard all about that moving ceremony. I saw Reggie, and Flavia, and Nannina and her mother, several other friends, and many of my favorite places and churches and pictures, and saw San Gimignano on the way to Siena, and dined at Henry Clifford's at Villa Capponi and heard a Verdi Opera, superbly given! It was all perfect and in lovely weather. I missed you very very much, but it was good to drink of all that beauty again. We motor'd to Ravenna for one ravishing day and night, and came on here for 4 days. Venice is of course all one remembers, and dreams to find again!

We had *such* a happy visit yesterday with your sisters, a really good long visit because it rained after tea, and we sat on till after 7—talking about many things and we all enjoyed ourselves. It was quite funny, because when I telephoned and asked if I might come to see them, I evidently didn't make Miss Berenson realize who I was—so they really didn't know who they were going to see, and it was delightful to see their surprised pleasure, and the warm welcome they gave me and my friend. We had a lovely time, and I thought them both perfect dears. We leave to-morrow for the day in Padua, and in the evening leave for Paris—going ovr to London by the ferry on Saturday night. I have taken a flat in London at 8 Curzon Place W.1 until July 3—when I go to Scotland.

Dear B.B. this is a dreadful tourist's letter, which will leave you breathless and really I only want to send my love and my thanks for your last letter, and so many hopes that you are better. I have been distressed to hear of your miserable affliction and hope the sea air and rest has dispelled it, and that you will return refreshed and free of asthma. I can't think why the Doctors haven't tried all these hay fever serums that seem to help people at home. My dear love to Nicky, and to you always.

Your devoted Ruth

To Dorothea Draper
(Mrs. Henry James)

June 14 [1951]
8 Curzon Place
London, W.1.

[Dinner at Windsor Castle on June 11th and "overnight with the Gowries in the Norman Tower"]

It was a glorious sight! Thirty-six at a beautiful mahogany table, the famous gold plate—*everything* gold—pink and mauve sweet peas in showers—nectarines and strawberries, peaches and muscat grapes—the loveliest colors—real candles, lovely high (epergne?) dishes and candelabra and baskets full of sweet peas or fruit—lovely clear soup in gold plates—the trout, chicken and strawberry cold soufflé on lovely china—dessert on gold again. I never saw such splendour! The Queen a dream in pale grey and silver and diamonds, Princess Elizabeth in blue taffeta, Princess Margaret [in] white satin, Princess Mary in pale blue crepe, Duchess of Gloucester [in dark blue taffeta, me in yellow chiffon often worn at Greenleaves [D.D.'s country house], all I had that was long—my smart blue lace was short! I never dreamed I'd be asked to dine at the Castle—fool that I was—my pompadour would have been exactly right—but I didn't bring it, being bulky to pack. But I looked all right and did six monologues; they howled with laughter—it was a young party—not a bit stiff as in 1926—just a lovely gay and happy group, and *lovely* looking women. A superb piper piped after desert—twice around the tables—the food was wonderful—I had two very agreeable men; the servants in knee-breeches and scarlet coats all covered with medals—all had been soldiers. The King ill at Buckingham Palace—too bad—(for I would have been given my decoration). Frankly I prefer to get it later if he's better. It would have been rather embarrassing before the party! I had a lovely chat with the Queen and with Princess Elizabeth. They're "just *lovely*" people!

The evening was a huge success but at the end a ghastly incident occurred. As I ended the 'Immigrant' (which luckily was the last piece) my feet slipped on the floor which was like ice—so slippery—and I fell on my back and thought I'd broken it! You can imagine my feelings of mortification and distress, mixed with pain, and fear of an injury—it was not an awkward fall because my legs remained neatly covered by the full soft skirt and were toward the wall—my back and head toward the audience. I managed to get up rather gracefully considering the shock, and the first persons who came forward were the Queen and both Princesses. I was so touched—they were so human and dear and solicitous I could have cried. I got very white I guess for a moment but of course said it didn't hurt at all—and lied smiling and unconcerned. I moved with the others casually into the next room and got some whiskey as well as orangeade—and every one was charming and behaved as if it was the natural thing to do to fall. The Queen had done it at Easter. The floors are too clean and quite glassy—I ran—and had on tiny sandals and suppose lost my balance when I threw up my hands. As far as I can recall I've never fallen before—and it is quite a record to have one's only fall in front of the Queen, and at Windsor Castle!! I had an Xray and a Doctor examine me the next day, and nothing was broken, and the soreness is nearly gone. I was lucky to fall as I did on the strong part of my back, not on the end of the spine itself—so there was less jar.

I opened the Barge in the afternoon, and felt quite Royal myself. It is charming!! [This was a charity benefit arranged by Gretchen Green on a barge on the Thames.]

To Dorothea Draper
(Mrs. Henry James)

June 22 [1951]
8 Curzon Place
London, W.1.

Alas, the King can't give me my Insignia—he's in the country, ordered a complete rest. He was going to give them to me himself and "much regrets" etc. I had a letter from his Secretary yesterday. (Sir Alan Lascelles) Too bad because the Public would have liked so much to read the announcement in the Court Circular! I discovered that foreigners are never in the Honours List—the C.B.E. is rarely given. I now hear the dinner party was to have been the occasion and I was the only outside guest besides the House Party. My tumble was certainly a poor alternative. I'm quite sore but the bones are improving according to the Xray—I go to the hospital for heat and sit in Epsom salts! It's not bad, just annoying when I move or turn or sit and get up, etc.

To Sir Alan Lascelles
(Private Secretary to the King)

June 28, 1951
8 Curzon Place
London, W.1.

My dear Sir Alan—
Thank you for your letter of June 25th. As I wrote you, I shall be in London between July 14th–21st and again, possibly in the autumn—during October and November. In view of this possibility, and the fact that His Majesty has so kindly expressed the desire to give me the Insignia personally—I would far prefer to wait His Majesty's pleasure and convenience, than to receive the Insignia in Washington. I am not thinking entirely of my self in this matter—but of the many people throughout the U.K., Commonwealth and Empire to whom this great honour will give so much pleasure. Lady Gowrie will always know how to reach me.

To Dorothea Draper
(Mrs. Henry James)

1951]
[Scotland]
[with the Alexander Maitlands]

Well, the excitement is over—and I'm thirty miles from a R.R.—in the heart of the Highlands—with snow on the high peaks—feasting off the fattest reddest strawberries, and the thickest yellow cream, (and porridge!), roses such as I never saw, in great bowls on the tables—sheep and cattle, rushing clear brown rivers and brooks and grey rocks—heather and broom—a lovely garden, and air from the Atlantic sweeping down the Loch. The other guests are off to fish for salmon; I have so many letters to write, I'll stay at home—the peace is heavenly. Scotland is really unique— people living the most civilized lives miles and miles away from civilization. It is the vastest, loveliest country, and the shepherds and crofters live as they've lived for a thousand years. I'm moving to Hector [Munro-Ferguson]'s to-morrow and returning to London to the Connaught on Saturday and sailing the 21st.

The Ceremony was terribly impressive. It was lovely having Sylvia there and how sweet of her to come all the way just for one night. It was a lovely sunny day and after the Ceremony at the University and St. Giles, I lunched with the Vice-Chancellor—*such* a charming man, Nobel Prize winner— having discovered some frightfully important thing in the nuclear heavens! He knows Conant well—and was one of the atom bomb boys. He's full of humor and charm—one of the nicest people I ever saw. The cap they use to hit you on the head is made of George Buchanan's trousers! It is over 400 years old, and has been used on all the heads honored by the University! George Buchanan was a famous scholar and historian—a martyr of the Reformation; having his head cut off, and he was tutor to Mary Queen of Scots' little son (James VI and Ist of England). The University also owns his skull! Just why they made a cap—(brown velvet—round and flat) of his breeks—I can't say—but so it has been used! I was calm, but very moved, and so thrilled by the men with me, and their citations—all with such great achievements—made mine seem very small and intangible. I got tremendous applause from my loyal public who seem to have been well represented in the great hall.

I'll bring you the citations. I was rather disappointed in mine because, believe it or not, they dragged in poor old Henry James!! I suppose they got their information from the newspapers and some interview I may have given once. It bores me to have anything made of that silly monologue he wrote for me! Some of it was very nice, and when they quoted Keats' lines I nearly cried. But there was much they might have said that was more interesting. However—it was all thrilling beyond words. It is a very great honor, because they never give to more than one woman a year and sometimes none. Last year there was none. It was lovely to know so many family and friends were thinking of me on my great day. The robe was beautiful soft thick fine wool, scarlet faced with grosgrain and the hood black faced with sapphire blue. The black velvet cap quite becoming. I wore mine all the time, but the men never put on theirs at all, just held them.

To Bernard Berenson

July 24 [1951]
On board
R. M. S. Queen Elizabeth

Dearest B.B.

You will be amused to see this picture, poor as it is. The ceremony was very impressive and thrilling. I was the only woman—Edinburgh only gives to one—or none,—and I was mis-informed about the other ladies I mentioned in another letter. Freya [Stark] got hers at Glasgow—Edith Evans and Rose Macaulay at Cambridge.

I had *such* a happy visit with friends—and after the excitement and parties of 3 days in Edinburgh I fled with them to the remote and wonderful Highlands for a rest. Then I returned to London for a hectic week and sailed on Saturday. Unfortunately the King's illness prevented him from giving me the C.B.E.—but that is only postponed. He has expressed a desire to give it to me personally, so I plan to return to London in the Autumn anyway to give a season (not having worked at all on this visit) and I hope to get my honor then.

The Myron Taylors are on my ship and yesterday we spoke of you—and at Edinburgh I spent a lovely afternoon at Balcarres, and saw David Crawford's marvellous pictures and books; he was in London, so I missed him, but his wife showed me about. I saw Freya Stark at a cocktail party and at the Royal Garden party and spoke of you also with her. I hope your various visits to the Exhibitions were not too tiring and I think of you now in the peace of Vallombrosa. Do remember me affectionately to your sisters. They are such dears, and my friend Blanche Serocold and I had the happiest afternoon one day in Venice—when it rained—we sat on and on chatting, and found them *so* delightful.

I am on my way to Maine for 2 months. Salvemini is coming and other friends—and I shall have a busy time—and then return to England. It was a great disappointment to miss you and Nicky in Florence,—thanks for your letter—Luisa [Vertova] and Alda [Anrep] were very kind in welcoming me and my friend, but I Tatti seemed strange without you. I hope you are well, and that the miserable Hay fever has abated. My dearest love and excuse this scrappy letter. The news of the world is more disturbing than ever and my understanding grows dimmer. The sea and the sky and nature and art seem the only steadying consolation,—and friendship! Dear love to Nicky and I'll write again from Maine.   Your devoted Ruth

On July 14th Ruth Draper flew back from Scotland to London; she attended a Royal Garden Party at Buckingham Palace on the 19th and that evening dined with the Drapers Company at Drapers Hall. On the 21st she sailed—"a lovely quiet passage"—in R.M.S. Queen Elizabeth, *and went at once to Islesboro with family, friends, Salvemini, Zosia Kochanski, Aileen Tone; "all the family of nations together again—such happy days."*

Three months later she again embarked for England, in R.M.S. Mauretania, *for a nine-week tour in joint appearances with her nephew Paul Draper, going from Brighton to Scotland, visiting en route at Stanway, with the Duchess of Roxburgh at Floors castle, with the Braggs and other Cambridge friends.*

Still she had the same warm appreciation from English audiences, the hosts of friends, the flowers, the constant activity. From Cambridge in mid-November she wrote: "my mornings are lovely and restful—yet I never stop catching up with my letters, my bed covered like drifting snow!"

To Sir Alan Lascelles
(Private Secretary to the King)

October 14 [1951]
The Connaught Hotel
Carlos Place,
London W.1.

When you wrote me last June, asking me to let you know when I should be in London again, I intended of course to write you as soon as my plans were made. But when I learned of the great anxiety about His Majesty's health, I naturally did not write, not wanting to burden you with any concern of mine. I was lunching yesterday with Angus McDonnell—a very old and dear friend, and he asked me if I'd got my decoration yet? So I told him my predicament, and he urged me to write you quite frankly. Having seen in the paper the other day, that the Duke of Gloucester is holding an Investiture in November, I thought possibly I should tell you that I am to be in London from October 29th to November 12th. For the following fortnight I shall also be within easy access of London, and could come up any morning or afternoon, except Thursdays or Saturdays when I have matinee performances.

I do hope this will not add to the burden of all the arrangements you must make, in the changes involved in my receiving this great honour, and please be assured that whatever is decided I shall be happy and most grateful.

To Dorothea Draper
(Mrs. Henry James)

November 14, 1951
Cambridge

I'm lunching at the Trevelyans' to-day and having tea with some under-graduates at Jesus College. Tomorrow I'm lunching with the Prof. of Economics—an old friend at Trinity. Friday Paul and I are lunching with Sir Lawrence Bragg and seeing the Cavendish Laboratory. I'm teaing with the wife of the Master of Jesus—who was a niece of my dear old Winnie Mudie. Saturday Paul and I are lunching with the Master of Clare—so it goes. He is doing some sight-seeing and we're going this morning to see Lydia Keynes—the ex-ballet dancer and sweet adored wife of Lord Keynes. Last week was a triumph at Golders Green—packed houses and great en-thusiasm. Paul was thrilled and so happy. Our dear dresser Maud is knitting Paul socks and keeping him very tidy! We went to tea on one of our matinee days with Geoffrey Keynes, a great brain surgeon (knows and admires George), who has a wonderful collection of Blake drawings and very beauti-ful books. Another matinee day I went to lovely Kathleen Ferrier's. She has had a serious cancer operation (breast) but is recovering well. She told me quite calmly and I felt shattered. She is so brave and so beautiful; she had to give up her American tour this year.

To Dorothea Draper
(Mrs. Henry James)

[November 20, 1951]
Brighton

The exciting telegram came yesterday and you can think of me trembling with emotion next Friday at 12:30!!! I will be thinking of you all, and all the others who are gone, as I always do on big occasions, realizing all I must be worthy of—to keep me calm!

To Dorothea Draper
(Mrs. Henry James)

[November 24, 1951]
Brighton—Saturday a.m.

Thanks for your wire in reply to mine—it came so fast—I sent mine late, when I got back from the show, and yours came at breakfast. It is all more complicated as the public [will] wonder why it's not been in the papers!

Many people are waiting for the presentation of honours, and many have been given theirs by the Duke of Gloucester. My C.B.E. is a very 'special thing', and is given very rarely by the King himself—[usually by] the Ambassador in the recipient's country. It seems the King very much wanted to give it to me himself, when it was known I was here again—I was told the Queen was to give it to me, (and she did receive me first). Of course the wide-spread pleasure it would give readers who've known me in far off places is now ex- or precluded and I'm sorry—I was really thinking of them, when I hoped the Insignia would be given me in London and then announced in The Times etc. This disappointment does not however lessen the thrill and simple beauty of my moments with the King and Queen. It was moving and lovely and I just can't get over her beauty and the gentle radiance of her face and voice and manner. (She, like the Princess, is *much* thinner, the terrible anxiety is I imagine what's done it.) One feels absolutely at ease with her, she is intensely human, sensitive, warm, and with infinite charm. We talked, alone for ten minutes I should say, in a small cosy sitting room, and then the door opened from an adjoining room and the King walked in, with the little box in his hand. He stood by the fire, talking pleasantly for another five or ten minutes and gave me the medal, and said he was sorry he hadn't been able to give it to me at Windsor in June—and something about how few had been given (meaning the C.B.E.) to any but British and how well I deserved it etc. I was strangely moved, at the simplicity and sincerity, great gentleness and frailty of the man, he has a winning charm, and no pomposity, or aloofness. He looked better than I expected, and seemed alert and interested. She had the look of someone who had been thro' a terrific strain, but always a look of health—and such a complexion! Of course I go back and think over silly things I said—one can't feel content, ever, with the way one talks at great moments—but fortunately other people are less aware than oneself, of what one says. I looked very neat and fittingly dressed—my good Worth black satin dress and velvet hat with my Royal brooch in it—and the wings on the dress, and little old mangy fox. I left my cape in the hall; dear Fred took me, wearing the Scarf pin the Duchess of Kent had given him, the car absolutely shining. I sent some flowers to his wife and to the old ladies who gave him up for [my] drive to the Palace, and stopped at Brown Shipley & Co. on the way home—to show my medal and send on Paul's profits. Then I returned to Brighton, after calling at our Embassy. I thought it was nice to tell the Ambassador myself, and he and Mrs. Gifford were so nice and thrilled and glad for me. I got home pretty tired by the emotion of it all, (I had come up the night before to the Connaught, after two performances on Thursday, thinking I'd rather be in London than take an early train), and then after my return from the theatre, I wrote a letter to the Queen. I was told by the Secretary who happily I've known for years, to address it to H.M. the Queen—Buckingham Palace—!—initialed in the corner—and she'd get it herself. I don't think it was a masterpiece, but it was straight from the heart and that is a pretty good starting point for almost anything!

Paul and I are debating whether to do another week here—I mean in England, if a very good theatre can be found, or a few shows in Geneva. He is very well and happy—is *probably* going to do a tour with B. Lillie, which should be wonderful for him tho' it keeps him away from home. I probably will not get back for Xmas but soon after—unless I fly back from Geneva—I'll let you know as soon as possible. I'm waiting to hear from my American manager, what dates they have for me there.

To Sir Alan Lascelles
(Private Secretary to the King)

[November 25, 1951]
Stratford-on-Avon

I cannot refrain from writing to thank you for arranging my visit to the Palace last Friday, for the presentation of the Insignia of the C.B.E. by the King.

I was so happy to be received by Her Majesty the Queen, and of course surprised and so deeply honoured when I learned that His Majesty wanted to hand me the Insignia himself! I found it quite impossible to find words to express my feelings, and I beg you to convey to the King my profound gratitude for this precious gift, the symbol of such a high honour. Its significance is unique, and many sided at the same time, for as an American I feel the tribute to my country and the recognition that I am a small link in the chain that binds England and America, and as an actress, I feel the tribute to my profession, and the place I am proud to hold in the affection of the public in Great Britain, and in many cities and towns throughout the Commonwealth and Empire.

May I ask you, if possible, to tell His Majesty of the deep emotion and gratitude I felt in receiving the honour from his hands, and that I shall cherish forever the moments with him and Her Majesty, and the realization of their most generous kindness in receiving me.

The Times, *London, 19 December, 1951 Reported:*

HONOUR FOR MISS
RUTH DRAPER

Award Presented By
The King

Miss Ruth Draper, the American actress, was recently awarded the honorary C.B.E. and received the badge of the order at the hands of the King when she visited Buckingham Palace to see the Queen. It is very rarely that the King personally confers an honorary decoration below the rank of Knight or Dame, and the fact that honorary awards, unlike awards to British subjects, are not officially published in the *Court Circular* accounts for Miss Draper's distinction not having been recorded in the Press.

In an article headed SPECIAL AFFECTION, The Times' *dramatic critic wrote:*

The conferment of this order will give pleasure to playgoers in this country, who have held Miss Ruth Draper in special affection for more than 30 years. Her art has often been imitated, but the artist remained inimitable; the characters with which she peopled the empty stage were as much her own as the characters of a classic novel. The lady opening the bazaar, the spoiled wife in the motorcar, the eager copyist in a Florentine church, the girl from South Carolina who by applying precisely the same method of beguilement to three partners at a dance encouraged each to think that he had made a unique conquest—all had the perennial freshness of finished art.

Yet this country is in area a mere province of the vast territory which she has conquered. Her work has been acclaimed from end to end of the British Commonwealth; indeed, to find a parallel for the familiarity of her art in many lands one must turn from the theatre to the cinema and to the ubiquitous appearance of Charlie Chaplin in the days of the silent film. Miss Draper has appeared in all the great cities of South Africa, Australia, New Zealand, India and Canada. Paris, Berlin, Rome, Florence, Vienna, Warsaw, Stockholm, Copenhagen—in each of these capitals she has taken her stand on an otherwise empty stage and presented characters in their quiddity without departing from the canvas of tolerant comedy.

To Dorothea Draper
(Mrs. Henry James)

[December 23, 1951]
Hôtel Vendôme
[Paris]

I got here on Friday a.m. and have a sweet suite—so could have Bill as my guest and he seemed delighted to come. The room is full of parcels, cards, ribbon and paper, books and toys, and looks just as a room should at Xmas! Very cosy.

After Christmas Dinner at the American Embassy in Paris, Ruth Draper was off in a Cunard Queen *on the 30th of December for four months at home.*

To Bernard Berenson

May 31 [1952]
155 Cranmer Court
Chelsea
London S.W.3

Dearest B.B.

I have thought often of my brief but lovely hour with you at I Tatti, and have wanted to write and say how glad I was to have had even that brief glimpse to remind me of all you give to us who are privileged to be in your magic circle. I hated to see you suffering with that miserable infection and I do hope that the soft sea air has cleared up the inflammation. I hope that darling Amey has arrived to cheer you too—do give her my dearest love if she is with you now, and to Nicky too. She looked so well, and so beautiful, and as ever dear and welcoming. I read Luisa's book with keen interest and pleasure, and am so glad she gave it to me.

I am enclosing one of my reviews. They were all splendid and I am playing at the Criterion Theatre, to packed houses again! I have an enchanting little flat, and am so happy to be in London again, loving it as always. I've seen beautiful reproductions of some of the Ravenna Mosaics and the public is flocking, and thrilled. The darling Hands arrived yesterday, and I hope to see them soon. I plan to go to Cambridge on the 5th to see the Judge get his Degree.

I made good use of my short visit in Florence for as well as seeing you—I saw Signora Rosselli, Reggie Temple, and Salvemini, the Leonardo drawings,—and the Uffizi! I flew over the Alps on Saturday afternoon and spent a peaceful night and day near the Hague with the Loudons, and arrived slightly breathless on Sunday night in London.

My dear love to you and to Nicky—and may your stay in Ischia be restful and salubrious!

Your devoted Ruth

To Dorothea Draper
(Mrs. Henry James)

June 7 [1952]
155 Cranmer Court
Chelsea, S.W.3

I am sending under separate cover the program and citation at Cambridge [Judge Hand's honorary degree]. The Latin read most beautifully—really recited—by a great scholar, sounded like the most living and lyrical language; it was thrilling to try and follow, and easier to understand than reading the text, so descriptive of the meaning was his voice and manner—delicate, subtle and charming, deep and rich, and full of significance in a curious way. It's all simpler than the Harvard Commencement, far less impressive in scale, because only nine Honor Degrees are given—in a beautiful old room—no music—and friends, wives, etc. filling the rest of the room and gallery, Mr. Butler, Chancellor of the Exchequer, made the *most* beautiful speech at the luncheon, and Lord Tedder (Air Marshall) who is the Chancellor of Cambridge, only appearing on such an occasion (and not a scholar). It was a lovely day. I motor'd down, and brought the Hands home with me. It was all impressive and interesting, and they loved the Braggs—my friends—and I was so proud of L.H. and Dr. Compton, the other American, both so fine looking, and such great figures. Yesterday [we] lunched at the Zoo with an old barrister friend of C.C.B. [Charles C. Burlingham].

To Dorothea Draper
(Mrs. Henry James)

[June 29, 1952]

I'm going to [———] to-night to meet the Italian Ambasador and his wife—for cocktails—then going to Verdi's "Requiem" with Arthur and Ethel Salter, and back for a bite of supper with them. I've had a heavenly quiet a.m. in my darling flat—packing and tidying, so I'll be free to-morrow. I slept late, and had a fine rest. I was *terribly* sad to stop last night, to a crowded house, and I made a little farewell speech.

Princess Alice and Tom Goff and the Earl [of Athlone] and two other "fitting" friends came to tea on Wednesday and it was a great success. I had lovely flowers, and a delicious cake and scones, and they laughed a lot and enjoyed themselves. I also had a little luncheon— I've had several—and all went well. I move to Ellen Parks' on Tuesday but go away at once to Letty Benson for one night and Benefit at Cheltenham, Irene Gater for one night and Benefit at Oxford, Fermoys for one night and Benefit at King's Lynn; London one night and big party at Jamie Hamilton's. That day I'm having a film test, which will be exciting, and painful I'm afraid because it's terribly hot! To-morrow I "televise" which will also be exciting, and very painful in the heat I fear.

I must take a snooze now after a delicious little lunch of cold Kedgeree and salad, cake and wine (*iced*).

To Dorothea Draper
(Mrs. Henry James)

[January 25, 1953]
Flat 11, 39 Hyde Park Gate
London, S.W.7

Nancy [Astor] asked me for [next] weekend but I feel it will be an effort staying with her at Sandwich so I prefer to remain here as it's just before my opening on Monday—and with her I'll have to talk (or rather listen!) so much. But I'm also tempted by the sea and fresh air.

I'm told there is a slump in the theatre and I am rather worried about the prospects of my 'season'! I think my manager, who owns the Globe, was *very* glad to put me in to keep it open. We'll see—but I'll be surprised if it's a success. I can't see why anyone ever wants to go out at night in this weather! They are certainly a hardy and stoical race.

To Dorothea Draper
(Mrs. Henry James)

Friday [January 31, 1953]
39 Hyde Park Gate
London, S.W.7

I wish my handwriting were better—it's always so uneven; some words come out nicely but it's so curiously immature, semi-copybook and changes with different pens. Yours is *always* distinguished.

I've had a full day; last fittings on my theatre dress, to see my manager, to rehearse the music for the Spanish sketch on the Haymarket stage. I'm doing it on my first night in order to give *something some* of the poor critics have not seen! I only gave it years ago and I'm hoping they've forgotten it and will think it new!

I lunched with Thelma Cazalet who was an M.P. for years and now runs a flower shop—with flowers and plants from her own greenhouse—tho' she's very intelligent! Victor Gazalet's sister.

To Dorothea Draper
(Mrs. Henry James)

February 4 [1953]
39 Hyde Park Gate
London, S.W.7

Thanks so much for your cable. I'm sorry you were worried—the great storm did not affect London—apart from a rather windy cold day. But the horror and the misery and tragedy of the coast dwellers, and worse even in poor Holland, is devastating and keeps one so distressed, and feeling so silly and selfish, going about one's material way—warm and cosy and well fed, and not helping at all. I only have one shrunken pair of bloomers to give away! I'd already given my tweed suit and blue dress away, so my wardrobe will yield nothing more! Money of course, but I envy the people who are able to help with more. It is incredibly awful—the pictures in the papers are terrible. Poor brave Holland—I know the Island of Walcheren—so miraculously reconstructed after having been flooded by the British to chase out the Germans—re-dyked and drained and green again, and now under the sea once more. I wish we'd do a swift and generous act, and take in those splendid Dutch farmers and families to start a new life under safer conditions, for it will be months and years before the spoiled land is reclaimed. And I wish we'd give them at once the Marshall Aid money they've recently declined, for emergency aid. That Irish Sea disaster was too hideous—the night after Peggy and John Wakehurst returned to their new post after ten days holiday here. And plane crashes—and ships burning, and lost in the storms— It's been an awful month. As I write the sun is pouring into my room, and onto this paper!

Friday I'm lunching with Arthur Salter and the head of B.B.C. Arthur is terribly concerned about my not recording my work, and annoyed with Korda, and insists on making further efforts to get it done. The trouble is I can't take on anything more now, even if it is offered to me.

I had a *superb* opening! Packed house, cheers and yells of laughter, masses of flowers and messages. Business is slow, however and I am not expecting much! There is so much sickness—a wave of economy—great depression because of these awful disasters, and many people (as can) going away seeking health and sunlight. But I'm delighted to be at work again, and I'm having every care, I promise you. Fred comes to fetch me at 6:45 and he has a stoneware hot-water bottle in the car (I nearly wept, I was so touched the first night). I have a small meal at 6, and hot milk at 10:15 when I get home. The sweet maid waits for me, and I have a lovely breakfast in bed, write and read the papers, and go for a walk before lunch, or do errands, and rest most of the afternoon. So don't worry about me! I' taking vitamins, and took some sunlight when I felt the dark, grim, foggy days were penetrating body and soul—it's wonderfully helpful I think—anyway it stirs the imagination, and I pretend I'm on the hot beach in Iselsboro' lookingit the blue bay and Islands, and my skin gets rosy and sunburned and I'm sure it's salubrious! One definitely needs more little 'aids to energy' in this climate, frequent little extra meals. So far, no germ has got me. My new velvet dress seems very nice, graceful and simple (Worth) and I have a new crepe for the Spring, a new "Clerical grey" jersey and a red coat, which I haven't worn yet and am a little afraid of!

The Globe has my name in the biggest electrical lights, below the dome of the building, on Shaftesbury Avenue, and you see it from the Circus [Piccadilly] and it makes me laugh every night. It's always done at that theatre—it's a nice warm theatre, with fine acoustics. I tried a hearing aid, and didn't find it any good! Only *increases* the sound, but doesn't clarify the words. I also tried old Lady Hambleden's ear trumpet, and liked it better!

I enclose Kathleen [Ferrier]'s notice, opening in Orfeo last night. I went to the Dress Rehearsal all Monday morning. Her voice is sublime, and her looks so beautiful. She suffers terrible lameness, she says, from rheumatism in her hips, but those who know the hideous fear that hangs over her are deeply anxious it may be something worse. She is superbly courageous, and her voice is more rich and beautiful than ever—and heart breaking too. What lovely serene classic music—it seemed to transcend the agony in the world and make the thought of the Elysian Fields really comforting!

At this time Kathleen Ferrier was just 41. Born in a Lancashire village, daughter of a school-master, she was nurtured in the musical environment of the area and of her home, for both her parents sang in the Halle choir. After giving up school at 15, she worked at the Post Office switchboard to earn money for music lessons, and at the Carlisle Festival in 1937 began to win singing contests which led in two years to a B.B.C. contract and serious coaching. With a natural dignity of style and extraordinary purity of voice, she was to become one of the great contraltos of her time. Having made her London debut at one of Myra Hess's lunchtime concerts early in 1943, she quickly went on to a brilliant career, singing the Handel Messiah *in Westminster Abbey with the young Peter Pears, at Glyndebourne, and in Amsterdam. Her great triumphs were in Mahler's* Kindertoten Lieder *and* Das Lied von der Erde *under Bruno Walter, and Orfeo in the Gluck* Orfeo and Eurydice.

With her great love of music and special interest in young talent, Ruth Draper responded quickly to Kathleen Ferrier's delightful personality—they became mutually appreciative friends, with Ruth welcoming her third concert tour to the United States in December 1949 with "a wonderful party" in New York. By 1951 Kathleen Ferrier already was ill and had had an operation for cancer. With radio therapy and several hospital stays, she courageously carried on. Awarded a C.B.E. in the 1953 New Year's Honors, she was unable to attend the investiture, for she had collapsed after the second of four scheduled appearances as Orfeo early in February. Carried from the stage after the final curtain, she returned to hospital.

To Dorothea Draper
(Mrs. Henry James)

[February 21, 1953]
39 Hyde Park Gate
London, S.W.7

Yesterday was a lovely bright sunny day. I walked thro' the Park to 14 Prince's Gate and watched the three coaches (closed landaus I suppose you'd call them) arrive to take Winthrop [Aldrich, U.S. Ambassador] to the Queen. It was great fun. Harriet [Mrs. Aldrich] was taking photos of the carriages and spectators and W. getting in! I stopped in to see her, and she followed fifteen minutes later to have an audience herself. She looked *lovely*—very smartly and appropriately dressed in a very becoming hat and fur cape, and she looked so happy and gay. The secretaries and servants were about, and it was a lovely picture. The outriders and old coachmen in long scarlet coats and three capes, the carriages and harness sparkling, trappings and brasses, and shining windows, and beautiful horses! The house looked lovely, full of Spring flowers, and Harriet said everything was perfect—same staff and everything running smoothly. I could see H's warmth and humor and geniality has won their hearts. I'm sure she'll be wonderful. I telephoned last night and she said they'd had a lovely time—the Queen was enchanting—and they talked about her family. The Queen has just made this new arrangement for Ambassadors' wives to follow on the meeting with the Ambassadors—and all the Embassy staff—they didn't use to be introduced the same day. H. is lunching with me on the 3rd and I'm trying to plan a pleasant group—only six.

To Dorothea Draper
(Mrs. Henry James)

Sunday [February 22, 1953]
39 Hyde Park Gate
London, S.W. 7

Mrs. [Belinda Norman] Butler was so interested in your letter and memory of your visit to her aunt and uncle in Ireland [and] was so interested you were Mrs. Henry James because she's a James enthusiast—knew that her grandmother was his friend and [that] you and Harry knew her aunt Mrs. Fuller. It's all very pleasant. I did have the privilege of meeting the old Lady Ritchie, with Mrs. Yates Thompson, and Mother was with the party when we all went to Cambridge [in 1909] to the Darwin Centenary! I have never forgotten her. She had a big garden hat in a bandbox in the train going down and returning.

I went to see Kathleen Ferrier this morning; she's in the hospital taking daily radio therapy. It's a terrifying outlook, but she is responding well, and her general health is fine, and her voice superb, but she had to cancel two of the four Orpheus performances and lots of concerts. She hopes to be at work again at Easter time. They 'call it' arthritis—but it's not—but one tries to keep the public from knowing. I got her a lovely wrapper, shetland jacket, and shawl and bed cover, and she looked too beautiful—with flowers everywhere and she's cheerful and sanguine and calm in her own mind. Perhaps it can be arrested—it was in her back, and that's stopped, now in her hip, and it's improved already.

To Dorothea Draper
(Mrs. Henry James)

March 3 [1953]
39 Hyde Park Gate
London, S.W.7

My lunch party was a *great* success! Harriet [Aldrich], Sylvia, Ruth Fermoy, Claudia Ottley and Dr. Jane de Jongh—a delightful Dutch lady. Everybody liked everybody, the food was good, the room was flooded with sun, and *full* of flowers!

I had a marvellous day on Sunday—Fred motor'd me to Winchester. I lunched with the Gaters in the lovely Warden's Lodging looking over the Cathedral and old city walls, and a trout stream tearing thro' the garden; then I gave a show in a most beautiful building before about 600 boys—such glowing happy looking youths—eager and gay and they laughed so spontaneously and applauded loudly with powerful young hands. Such intelligent responsive adorable young. The Lord Chancellor and Lady Symonds, he a former Warden, were at lunch, also the Head Master and his wife. After the show there was a tea party with the Prefects and Scholars and some masters and head boys, and then Chapel. A *lovely* choir, and you know the sound that 600 boys 'yelling' hymns in a lofty chapel makes! It is stirring to one's heart and mind. Everything is so beautifully done—so simple, orderly, ancient and serene, and one gets the feeling that education is fundamentally character building after all (profound observation!).

To Dorothea Draper
(Mrs. Henry James)

[March 14, 1953]
London

[Written on the back of a letter from Constant Huntington thanking R.D. for providing seats for Jacob Epstein, the sculptor, and urging, in the face of her displeasure, that she have Epstein do a bust of her. He calls her "an angel, even if rather a cross one!"]

He asked me for tickets at my last performance. I *was* a little cross as the house is sold out—and I had to pay for the three tickets for the Epsteins! I told C. had they really wanted to see me they could have come during many other seasons! Sir Alec Martin, the head of Christie's, is also eager for Epstein to do a head of me. I wouldn't think of it—I *hate* his work anyway—C. is a sweet soul, and I think his letter is charming. I felt a little cross and showed it I guess.

Well, I've reached my saddest day—the end of my season. I'm sorry, as always, to leave—for I'm playing to splendid houses—it's always that way. The fall of the curtain is a poignant moment and I shall have to make a speech which I hate, too!

On the 15th of March Queen Mary's Lady in Waiting, Lady Cynthia Colville, wrote to Ruth: "Queen Mary was so much touched by your charming thought for her and bids me thank you very warmly for the superb lilac which gives Her Majesty much pleasure. I showed Queen Mary your letter and I am to say what happy memories Her Majesty has of you and the immense enjoyment you gave her on every occasion when she saw you. Queen Mary is very sorry that during your time here this year she has not been able to go to the Theatre to see you."

Queen Mary died on the 24th of March, 1953.

To Dorothea Draper
(Mrs. Henry James)

[March 16, 1953]
Royal Hibernian Hotel
Dublin

I 'open' to-night at the 'Gaiety', and I'm sure I shall enjoy my fortnight here. No 'contacts' yet, and it's lovely not having any telephones or mail here *yet*! It will probably start to-morrow. I shall spend a silent and restful day! Yesterday—my secretary and my dear old 'dresser' Ada came in the morning and Peter Lubbock came for lunch, and then I went to the great Mexican Exhibition at the Tate, a *remarkable* show! Then Jelly d'Aranyi came for tea, and drove with me to the Airport—with Fred as always to see me off!

Winthrop and Harriet came on Saturday night and sent me a great bouquet, and were so nice coming back afterward. Epstein the great sculptor came down too, so I presented him and his wife, and Maurice and Ruth Fermoy were there in my room too, so it was quite gay. The house was full, and I got a rousing farewell and had to make a short speech but I didn't have the thrilling response as I did on Thursday night, for instance, when the atmosphere was absolutely *charged* with deep emotion and gay laughter. I look forward to a riotous Irish welcome to-night!

I'll write again when my Irish life begins! I know few people here and forget their names anyway—so I must wait and see who remembers me!

To Dorothea Draper
(Mrs. Henry James)

[March 20, 1953]
[Dublin]

I enclose nice letter from Iris [Origo]—amazing that such a brilliant person should have such a miserable script—but I've noticed it before—hope you can read it! I thought the Greek actress [Paxinou] so beautiful—what a triumph! I wish I could hear her—that beautiful voice—it bears out my theory that voice and rhythm and cadence are enough—and the ridiculous success of my tirade in "The Actress" is an example. Nice letter from Sybil Thorndike—I sent her *Charlotte's Web* and *King Solomon's Ring*—my two favourite books of last year—*Period Piece* a third! Wasn't it adorable? I'm now reading *A Pattern of Islands* another marvel—and you'll love it too.

I am thinking of Corinne so much, and wonder if she'll live on there alone, or if John will want to carry on the farm. What problems come up when a person like Joe dies, leaving the perfected work of years—that a son may not be desirous of carrying on? Corinne's children and grandchildren mean everything to her, but I don't think it will be enough for her to just await their occasional visits, and to live for that reason in the big house.

I had a delightful luncheon yesterday at the Kildare Street Club with a witty and charming Irishman named Terence White, and his wife, and a chemistry Professor. The men were delightful and *so* funny and urbane and Irish—the wife gentle and sweet and silent—the talk was marvellous, and I laughed a lot over Mr. White's description of his visit to U.S. He met Freddie James in Dublin and was charmed, and loved what he saw of New England and Boston. He said one grand lady in Boston, on being introduced said: "So you're Irish! My cook is Irish, and my butler is Irish, and my maid is Irish"! to which he replied: "Well, I'm sure we'll all get along very well"! He wouldn't tell me who it was—very Boston attempt at 'affability', I thought!

I must get on with my writing and then go to the museum and a walk.

Marvellous audiences; the whole town is coming, rich and poor, and it's great fun. I have pleasant dates for Sunday and the weather is lovely.

To Dorothea Draper
(Mrs. Henry James)

[March 30, 1953]
Glenarm Castle
Glenarm, Antrim
Northern Ireland

Your letter praising me for frequent letters came at the end of nearly a week of silence and I felt quite unworthy! My last week in Dublin I had very pleasant engagements in the mornings, which cut short my long "quiet times" (not Buchman's kind) for writing; for I have to be up by eleven, so I fell away from good intentions!

I came here yesterday afternoon and am enjoying the great beauty of this place, my beloved Lady Antrim's old home—and where Angus [McDonnell] grew up. The dowager Lady Antrim, who is a sister of Dame Meriel Talbot and an old friend of Paul Phipps is here too. I knew her first with her husband in 1911—he was an angel, Lord Dunluce—called Ducie always, even after he was Lord Antrim. His son is the present Earl—his wife Angela very charming, and his boy Dunluce just going to Oxford, a girl of fourteen at school, and a six-year old Hector, who is here. I never saw a more romantic and beautiful place; looking right across the sea to Scotland, from whence the McDonnells came in the 13th century. A great castle on a cliff was abandoned, or burned in the 17th century and this house was built. I'm looking up a glen down which runs the "arm" to the sea, close by. I see green fields and cattle, stone walls, cultivated hillsides, beautiful trees, and daffodils in the grass, and the garden wall. I'm waiting for breakfast—it's terribly cold but I have on lots of wool; my, but these people are stoical— there is *no heat* in the house, huge fires, where we sit, and the rest of the rooms and the halls like ice. Portraits, books, Aubusson rugs and lovely things from the past.

I hated to leave Dublin—such marvellous audiences. Open in Belfast to-night.

A maisonette apartment, without stairs, and opening on a large yard, was found for Kathleen Ferrier in Hamilton Terrace, where Ruth Draper, knowing of Kathleen's love for the garden she had to leave at her former house, sent, as a surprise gift, a firm of gardeners to plant and care for a large garden. In April Kathleen wrote, "Bless you, dearest Ruth—you couldn't possibly have given me a lovelier present—it is with me all the time, and my pride and joy."

Kathleen Ferrier was to die on the 8th of October, 1953.

To Dorothea Draper
(Mrs. Henry James)

Monday [April 6, 1953]
Birmingham

I'm resting before my first night's show here! Just had a big tea—I have a lovely room and bath—no flowers yet—and no sun—it's 6:30. I flew from Belfast to London yesterday, and went to Ellen's at 39 for the night. It was lovely to see her again, and have a delicious dinner and quiet night in the nice spare-room! She was out when I came, so I went to see Kathleen Ferrier and stayed for tea. She's just moved into a charming new house with a garden—She was lovely, and John Gielgud and Jamie and Yvonne Hamilton (great friends of the Hands) were there. Ireland was *wonderful*! Dublin audiences *so* much fun—so gay and welcoming, and packed every night; and Belfast in a way more wonderful, for I'd not been for twenty-one years! People were turned away—they *flocked,* and were rapt, and so responsive and I wish I'd been able to stay longer.

Now it's Tuesday morning, and I had a nice long sleep after cheese, biscuits and Guinness stout, and woke to a lovely bright day and breakfast of bacon and tomatoes and delicious coffee (for a change!) and the enclosed fine review—which please keep. I'm going to lunch with the David Cadburys—(friends of Harriet's) a very interesting family—Chocolate wealth—Quakers—wonderful citizens. I know another brother and his wife, with whom I flew the length of Africa in '34, and I'm lunching with them on Thursday. To-morrow I have a matinee. There's a very nice art gallery here, and I know the Director, and several agreeable people, so I'll not want for pleasant contacts, and there's a very good shop for children's clothes, and I long to get some things for the little Draper girls, if they have their sizes.

To Penelope Draper
(younger daughter of Dr. George Draper)

April 14, 1953
Sheffield

Darling Penny,

I just must extract a little news from you—a little testimony of your continuing affection, a little laugh and cozy confidence, a few choice observations on the Universe—life—the Soul, and the weather! How is Art, Music, the dance, the culture of Cleveland, the male sex—the boarding house inmates, your mother's visit and re-action to the "ambience"? *Do* write! *I love you* and *admire* you—*long for your well-being and happiness, Soul's progress and fortune!*

All goes well with me *except* Time! It's too speedy and there's too little left to suit my liking for this life and work, friends and travel, and I've not even begun to learn what it's all about. I mean *life* and *opportunity* and our waste of both! Who said: More brains oh *God*! I've been so careless with the little I have!

I'm now going to have a large tea—then drive to the theatre—make them laugh—come back to eat and sleep. A dizzy round! I've had a lovely winter in spite of the bitter cold—wonderful audiences—hard work—a lovely flat. Ireland was marvellous and after these grim Midland Towns I have Oxford and Cambridge to end up with—and those adorable youths!

Wish you were with me for a good laugh. Greetings to your housemates. Look about for wider horizons. How's the exchequer? How's the family— the various members? Can't you get to Islesboro?

Dear love, Aunt R.

To Dorothea Draper
(Mrs. Henry James)

[May 6, 1953]
[Cambridge, England]

I had *such* a heavenly week in Oxford. On Saturday I lunched with Isaiah Berlin, in his rooms at All Soul's. He is *so* brilliant so charming, and the most amazing human being—of any, and all ages—of a depth of wisdom, a light touch, wit and humor, and a warm sensitive heart. A really incredible combination—a new, and *old* friend. On Friday I lunched with Gilbert Murray, and one would almost like to kneel at his feet. His great gentleness and goodness, and all that Greece had given to the world seems to be contained in his vast knowledge, his clear and clean and lofty mind; at 87, frail, but ardent still with shy and courtly manners, modest and unassuming, and working hard still at his broadcasting, translating; and active, too, taking buses to and fro'. Then on Sunday morning, a cloudless sunny day, I went to Worcester College gardens, just to see the blossoms and flowers and ducks in the pond, and boys lolling on the grass with books under the great trees; then to the University Press to see my old friend John Johnson—the late Printer to the University (one of the line since the 14th century) one of the quaintest characters I've ever known and most delightful; then to see David Cecil, and his darling wife (Desmond McC's daughter) and their little girl of six and boy of eleven—who's to be his uncle, Lord Salisbury's, page at the Coronation. Of course David is one of the most rare and quaint and distinguished young men to be found anywhere—*such* brains—*such* race—such sensitivity, but a darling person and Professor of Literature at the University, and now working on the latter part of Melbourne's Life.

Lovely opening last night—with lots of friends. Lunching with the Braggs to-day, (He's the Head of the Cavendish Laboratory) Lord Rutherford's (who discovered the atom) successor. Alice, his wife, has been Mayor of Cambridge, and is a Magistrate, a lovely person, you'd love them both—he knows Conant of course, and all the big scientists. To-morrow I'm lunching with Harry Hollond, a Don at Trinity. I enclose his letter. The room [in Nevill's Court, built c. 1612, and originally occupied by Thomas Nevile, Master of Trinity 1593–1615] is a dream—all panelled—it was Gaillard [Lapsley]'s—and the food will be super, I hope for crème brûlee—the great 'specialty' of Cambridge—the colleges are rivals in its perfection, and Jesus claims to have the best! I used to have it there with Quiller-Couch, looking on a glorious tree, that was planted by some famous youth, who had picked up some acorns at Thermopylae, and who found them in the pocket of an old tweed coat years afterward and put them in a hole on the lawn. I must try and remember to ask again who it was? [Oriental Plane tree planted 1802 by Edward Daniel Clarke, the first mineralogist ever appointed in Cambridge] The weather is lovely—blossoms in their glory, and I have a huge bunch of cowslips, forget-me-nots, wall flowers, tulips, lilac and what-nots in my window. I must get up— I could spend every morning writing letters.

Bob Littell wants to do what he calls a "Portrait" of me for the *Reader's Digest*. I refused. Don't you hate those things? He wants to talk to me for "hours", "perhaps days", he says, one of those awful 'interviews' to pick my brains and memory. The same sort of stuff I give to newspapers—only more of it. I hate publicity—it's only a sham sort of literature, pre-digested by someone else for 'ready reading'. Hope you think I was right?! He's a dear person, and writes well—but it's going over the same old 'line' that has been done *so* often, and *so* boringly—why should I 'talk' about myself? My work is what counts, and appears still to give pleasure—that is all I care about. Anyway I said 'no'!

I shall be in London next week—seeing friends, and plays, and galleries, and packing away things to be sent directly to the ship. I shall travel light on the continent. My plans are still a bit vague—whether to go to Paris first or direct to Nice by air, and on to Lerici, to Percy Lubbock's. I'm looking forward to that.

To Dorothea Draper
(Mrs. Henry James)

[May 9, 1953]
Cambridge

Too beautiful for words here; and, oh, the boys—in their sloppy gowns—so young and beautiful—with books, hurrying along on bicycles or on foot—in punts—lying under trees; the magic precious heritage of scholars creates such an atmosphere of hope and faith in values we cling to. Lists of names of the fallen, crosses and monuments remind us how futile our efforts are, but youth and books and beauty go on forever in spite of losses. I'm off to the Fitzwilliam to see, as on each visit, Keats' manuscript of "Ode to a Nightingale". It makes me cry and fills me with such awe—like what a devout person feels in a church.

To Dorothea Draper
(Mrs. Henry James)

[May 17, 1953]
[London]

Thanks for your good letters—I've had excellent care—a wonderful man in Bath whose father was Queen Mary's dentist, and who also cared for the royal jaws. Of course I'm sorry now that I didn't plan to stay [for the Coronation]! Excitement grows and it's all thrilling. The young Queen is a wonder, and I don't see how she can sustain the burden of her job and the love showered upon her.

My heart is heavy over lovely Kathleen. Her beauty and goodness and marvellous voice all to be sacrificed to this evil thing. She's so brave and keeps cheerful—and one only hopes for a miracle. They continue to try and hide the truth but all who love her know.

To Charles C. Burlingham

June 11 [1953]
Florence

My very dear and wonderful C.C.B.

I loved your letter—every word of it—and was happy to know you thought of me! Last night I dined with our favorite Professor [Salvemini] and spoke of you, and read to-gether a letter from Roberto . . . I am so sad you had to go through with that dreadful accident, and I do hope the pain has gone by now. The Professor seems older and frailer, and he is afraid of getting ill again; he says "he has become a coward" and fears to come to America, lest he be a burden to his friends. He had so hoped to come, and me to have him, but perhaps it is best to remain here, and go to a quiet mountain resort with friends—and write more books—his favorite pastime!

I've had a wonderful winter of my favorite pastime, also work—if a different kind!

I stayed for the Coronation which was incredibly beautiful, moving and exciting. I spent three days on the bay of Lerici thinking of Shelley and his boat and his genius. Now I'm in this city of beauty, and go on to Siena and Rome for brief days—but to see good friends in the historic and overwhelming setting where ordinary lives go on! I fly to Amsterdam—then Paris, and sail the 30th of June on "La Liberté." If you're still in town July 6th I'll run in, but I hope you'll be cool in your lovely summer home, and the peace of shade trees and sweet smells.

Much love—Ruth

When she took over the Empire Theatre from the Lunts in New York in 1947, Ruth Draper also took over their stage manager, Charles Bowden. There had been little or no advance work and the beginning was dismal, but gradually the audiences improved and Bowden's professional technique in lighting strengthened the dramatic quality of the performances over what had, in earlier years, been acceptable. A year later, with Richard Barr, Charles Bowden became her manager. He had been reluctant to do so because he felt a strong promotional campaign was essential which probably would raise production costs to $15,000–an amount his new partnership could not undertake. Ruth Draper's response was unhesitating: "I don't want anyone, ever, to gamble on me. I will write you a cheque for $15,000 and when I have got it back from the box-office we will divide 50/50 from then on." The $15,000 was made up within three weeks; she played a total of six weeks in New York, Mr. Bowden insisting that his share be limited to one-third. In touring the large cities, Bowden and Barr sent a promotion man in advance and the audiences began to grow.

The nearly prohibitive costs of playing in legitimate theatres ate up her profits (the Union requiring that she take on a company manager, a stage manager, six or eight stage hands, and ushers, in addition to theatre rent and advertising). The concert circuit was far more profitable without advertising, Union regulations, or theatre costs, and having a subscription or college audience booked in advance. Her theatre image was of over-riding importance to her, however, although Peat had managed her on the concert tour basis in the smaller American cities.

To her delight a youthful audience began to develop. High-school and junior high-school students came in droves, the younger children with their mothers (many long-time fans) at Saturday matinees. She was intensely interested to find that a generation that had grown up passively viewing television could—to their mutual amazement—participate imaginatively in her character dramas. And when Katharine Hepburn brought five young friends, Ruth Draper was thrilled: "I'm bridging the gap to the young people." It is ironic that a wholly new audience was filling the theatres at the end of her career.

She thought of retirement—thought that probably she ought to retire, for she was now in her seventieth year. Her closing performance in New York at the Vanderbilt Theatre on March 13, 1954, was announced as her "Fare-well." It was a brilliant performance and after the final curtain she made a short, tense speech. The House stood to cheer, calling out "No—No!" She knew in her heart she really did not mean it, and it was the Theatre itself that bowed out that night—the seats were being removed as she left the stage-door!

However, the encouragement to continue was compelling: Maurice Chevalier told her she had been his inspiration from the beginning of his international work; Fred Keating said she always had been his inspiration for perfection in the creation of illusion—in pure magic. One admirer, who had not seen her since his student days, wrote: "You clearly have the secret of perennial youth! Here am I, with three grown-up children, and grey hair, a senior in my profession, and there you are just the same as thirty-two years ago."

She frequently expressed a horror of growing old, of mental incapacity, for she had seen friends, her own brother, sister, and sister-in-law go through months—even years—of sad decline. Yet she could not imagine life without her work—and wandering—it was her very breath of life—her happiness—her vital spark. She could not bring herself to give it up.

To Grace Martin
(Mrs. David Terry Martin)

March 21 [1954]
66 East 79th Street
New York

I am sending you the enclosed [cheque] with so much love—to use for extras for your trip to Italy, and wherever else you go this Spring. I am so happy for you and Terry to be taking this trip, to which you've looked forward so long, and that I can have some share in increasing the pleasure, and beauty, and memories that will last you all your life, makes me glad. Take a car now and then—and don't walk your feet off and deny yourself too many little comforts. Everything is always more expensive than you think it will be, and this little additional fund is for the 'margin', and extras, and a sense of added security. I love you, and respect you and admire you so much—your faithful enthusiasm for all that is fine and lovely in the world. You deserve the best, and it's not often one finds people so worthy. So get an extra folder of Express cheques, and think of me happy—when you use them.

My seven weeks have been marvellous—and this week is jammed every time! Wish you were here to share my triumphs—I sent you a parcel of all reviews—as I thought you'd enjoy reading them.

I sail the 31st Queen Mary—care of Morgan & Co. 14 Place Vendôme.

To Grace Martin
(Mrs. David Terry Martin)

April 3 [1954]
66 East 79th Street
New York

I *didn't* sail! I got an awful cold—really bad—sinus, and chest, and couldn't have struggled to Halifax! (Queen Mary sailed from there!) So Sicily is off! Don't know if I'll make Italy at all—as it's possible (if I *ever* get well!!) that I may do a film for T.V. My young managers are looking into it all—I loathe the commercialism of it all—but the *only* way I can ever get *any* record of my work for the future, is to do a film. T.V. *alone* has money, and alone will buy film for T.V.! Anyway it's being looked into.

I'll probably be here when you come thro'! Let me know where you'll be staying. I suppose I will get well someday! I'm so mad—all the happiness and beauty of my season is bleached out! I *was so* well—never better. I got this two weeks after I'd stopped, and then had so many social engagements I just couldn't take care of myself.

To Dorothea Draper
(Mrs. Henry James)

[June 11, 1954]
16 Montpelier Walk
London, S.W.7

[An] unforgettable and heartwarming [day]. It was cool and grey, but with lovely flashes of sun. The Professor and Mrs. Trevelyan and her nurse and I left the house about 10:50. After meeting the Vice Chancellor (who runs the show) and the other graduands, as we are called, we processed slowly to the Senate House, a beautiful 18th century building where the ceremony takes place. It was packed with people, but I didn't see, or look for anyone I knew. It's all very solemn and slow—no music—we took our places and the Orator speaks in *Latin*; so beautifully spoken and phrased that one almost understands. By turn we each approached the Chancellor in his superb robes—the Latin rolls out as one faces the Orator, and listens. Then the latter takes one's right hand and places it in the Chancellor's hand, and he also speaks in Latin, just a short phrase, I think it must have been what our University-Presidents say, ending up with the names of the Trinity! Then one sits down again, on the Dais next the Chancellor. There was great applause when I rose—but of course my back was turned to the crowd. We all walked out and went in procession thro' the streets to Magdalene College where the luncheon was held. The sun was shining and people along the streets snapped cameras. No formal photograph was taken—for which I was sorry—but if anything appears in the papers I'll send it. The luncheon was delightful—*wonderful* food and wine and the food all prepared in the college kitchen. The chef is running as a Labor member on the City Council. Surely this is the greatest democracy! Can you imagine a cook at home running for a political seat? The Chancellor's speech was fine and Lord Tedder's (late Air Marshal); Lord Salisbury spoke for the eight Honorary graduates, a beautiful speech. I left hurriedly (but it was all over) sorry as I was to go and not see friends and chat about it all. I ran thro' the enchanting garden, into the Master's House and left my scarlet robe and velvet hat, and dashed into the waiting car. In it was my fur cape, hat, gloves, purse, and luggage, and I got ready for the next show!

Two hours of fast driving got me to the Abbey at 4:55, just in time to join the British Committee and the Aldriches. About two hundred people were seated on the Poets' Corner, an impressive showing, I thought. Lady Crewe and I sat in the centre; the Sitwells, Harold Nicolson, and other members of the Committee. Winthrop, the Dean, Dr. Masefield, and clerics on the side. The Laureate's speech, too long but moving and fine; then Winthrop—excellent, speaking on behalf of the Keats-Shelley Association of America, but he made one awful 'gaffe'. At the end he quoted that sublime line from "Adonais"—"He has become (sic: "is") a portion of that loveliness that once he made more lovely" and said "this might have also been said of John Keats." I, thinking he was going to say "also have been said of Shelley himself," or "might be paraphrased" to "they have become" etc. gasped with horror! I hope it escaped the notice of others. Winthrop was reading his speech, so it couldn't have been a slip—whether a secretary wrote it, or he himself, one will never know! But it was nice and fitting that he and Harriet were there and saw how real is the love for the poets still.

Then I came home (after a cocktail party at Lady Crewe's, and seeing many friends). My house is a gem—full of wonderful Regency furniture, and lovely things, and a *paragon* of a maid. A perfect dinner with the most shining silver was spread for my delight. Nancy and Evan Fraser-Campbell came in later for a chat. Bill [Carter] arrived about 10—having had a wonderful day in Cambridge, and being asked to the lovely luncheon and also given a choice seat in the Senate House. Now, I've had my breakfast, and am sitting up in a tiny four-post bed like a Princess—papers, letters strewn about.

Ruth Draper was most generous to any charity or cause that excited her sympathy. She would give benefit performances, and often she gave from her own funds, but never would she take on sustained active leadership—she was not in one place long enough, she was far too busy, her abilities lay in other directions. Immediately after the war, however, she received an appeal that spoke to her heart: the house of John Keats in the Piazza di Spagna, in Rome, and the graves of Keats and Shelley in the Protestant Cemetery there, had been under the care of the Keats-Shelley Memorial Association since 1901. There had been active committees in Rome, in England, and in America, but the work, necessarily, had lapsed during the war. Her own love of Shelley was strong, and had been greatly reinforced by the de Bosis' love of Shelley – the translations and Lauro's Shelleyan intellect. In reading of Shelley's life, she had said: "as always I am deeply moved—his character is so like Lauro's."

In the spring of 1946, while playing at the Apollo Theatre in London, a young R.A.F. officer, Neville Rogers, visited her to ask her help in reviving interest in the Association in the United States. The House and graves had been neglected during the war but now the Library was again in use and much visited by the officers and men of both the British and American armies. Upon her return to New York Ruth Draper had sought the help of Arthur Houghton and, since then, the American Committee had grown and provided a Journal, the micro-filming of valuable material in the Library; and contributed toward the plaque in Westminster Abbey. She had been elected President of the Committee but referred to herself as a "ghost president," giving full credit to the other officers and the members.

To Dorothea Draper
(Mrs. Henry James)

[June 15, 1954]
16 Montpelier Walk
London, S.W.7

I've done it again—it's all incredible. Dear Fred drove me to the [Duke of York's] theatre, Merica and Maude had all in perfect readiness—sixteen bunches of beautiful flowers were spread all over the chairs, tables and sofa in my dressing room—telegrams and letters piled on the table—a lovely public welcomed me and the kind critics again gave me praise! I went to a party at Irene Ravensdale's afterward for Arthur [Rubinstein], who had played at Festival Hall, and we spoke with feeling of the early days forty-one years ago, when in Edith Grove after supper I would get up and amuse them, as they relaxed after the wonderful music—such memories! Here we were again—performing in different halls on the same night. He's not been in England for years—I never quite understood why?

At last the sun is shining. I am as always overwhelmed with letters to write—even with Lorna Carew's help. Barbara, Robert and Sir Ernest Pooley—an adorable old and mutual friend of ours—are coming to lunch. I have someone every day. My maid is perfect, and a lovely cook. I dined with the Salters Sunday, and they were there last night at the Theatre and sent flowers too. The account of Churchill's Installation in Windsor is so thrilling—lovely pictures—I might have gone to see the procession—and longed to—a friend offered a ticket, but I felt I shouldn't get tired before my first night.

The days are flying, already I dread the end of my brief season. Ellen will help me with Anne [Draper] and Rosemary's girl, same age, will too. I hope I can give her twelve happy days here. Then I plan to fly to Paris the 12th for four days and then to Rome—Florence and Venice running into Amey. Bill Carter will be in Venice, and will motor us thro' Switzerland back to Paris from whence we'll fly August 2. It sounds crazy, but I think it's better than nothing for Anne, don't you? Of course I'd love to stay here and go to Scotland, but I also want to see Salvemini, and going to Italy it is foolish not to have a glimpse of the three cities.

Enclose nice letter from G. M. Trevelyan. Really that day was something! Such a rare mixture of tradition and form and easy casual human behavior, kindness and consideration. Simon [Phipps] is a darling—he came to tea at the Trevelyans' and I walked back to his rooms along the lovely "Backs" and home, stopping in at King's Chapel and hearing the choir by candlelight, *so* lovely.

To Alice Draper
(Mrs. Edward C. Carter)

[June 29, 1954]
16 Montpelier Walk
London, S.W.7

I know too many people!

I must go rest a bit before my show. A friend from Wellington N.Z. came for tea. The Bishop of Pretoria wants me to lunch. Old friends of Paul and Muriel turn up. Jane [de Glehn?] has been here two days. James came for supper. Elliots and Braggs [Sir Lawrence and Lady] and my Stillwater, Oklahoma friends are coming for lunch tomorrow. The house is *so* adorable I never want to leave it. The maid, a jolly good cook—such lovely silver, china, flowers, Aubusson rugs—everything exquisite—linen sheets and huge towels—never want to leave!

Will you do something about this nice boy if you can? He is the son of Renzo Rendi, who died of cancer a few years after he was released from prison. The mother is a wonderful woman who has brought up three fine boys—all intelligent, serious, fine students, and eager helpful sons. Her letter will explain his coming and as I'm not home and can do nothing, perhaps if you are in town off and on, you'd get in touch with him. I'd be grateful.

To Dorothea Draper
(Mrs. Henry James)

July 27 [1954]
Bolzano, Italy

This will be my last word from this country! We have had a lovely time, of course too short—but heavenly—hot in the mornings, lovely breeze in the afternoons and cool nights. [In Venice] we had rooms with balcony, top floor of the Grand and gazed at Santa Maria della Salute as *we* gazed with the boys in '27—and I, often, since. Anne really got excited in Venice and adored it, and her young musical Italian beau added greatly, of course, to her enjoyment! Olivia Kammerer and her seven lovely girls turned up, and we all went to Torcello on the last night, including Bill and Anne's young man; it was quite wonderful—sunset, stars—delicious dinner in a pergola and garden full of roses and pansies and a fountain—the old church apricot colored in the evening light—the mosaics glowing in the dark old cathedral, beautifully lit. Venice just as beautiful and radiant and mysterious and fascinating at 69 as at 17—and plus all the memories, more so. Bill in fine form—glorious drive yesterday, and tea with Nannina Fossi in her mountain summer home—Bolzano (was Bolzen—remember when we were here with Mother and Emma J. and Bertha White and the children?) for the night. All go to St. Moritz to-day. We shall go on to Geneva to-morrow and take the train to Paris, as Anne wants to see G. and buy a watch for her mother, and shall be in Paris one or two days before we fly on the 4th T.W.A.

Gazing over the Grand Canal and Santa Maria della Salute from their hotel balcony, Ruth said, over her shoulder, to Anne: "You'll think of this—when you're on your honeymoon in Asbury Park, New Jersey!"

This was the last of the "grand tours" for nieces and nephews. The beauty and experience of the Old World, with its riches, meant so much to her that sharing it with them, she felt, must inevitably enrich their lives; and she took infinite pains to give them a good time.

To Grace Martin
(Mrs. David Terry Martin)

October 14 [1954]
Jefferson Hotel
Iowa City, Iowa

Here I am, on the road again—the atmosphere so familiar in these hotels, a splendid audience of young at the awful college auditorium, and a large group all "majoring in speech" to meet me afterward—when I was so tired,—just eager to 'look' and ask impossible questions. I am going to refuse to do that anymore—I love the young, but I just can't give interviews and "pose" for college paper photos, after spending all my energy on the stage, and only longing for milk and crackers and bed! They only offer coffee and cookies and keep me standing—it's torture, to be stared at and shake hands with clammy young hands—what good does it do them anyway!! It's been hot working.

I fly home to-day and have quite a rest period tho' I don't find New York very restful. I've just finished *Melbourne*—a masterpiece. If you haven't got it—I'll send it to you. Tell me. I've also read Helen Keller's Life and found it absorbing—really she is the greatest woman and the greatest phenomenon that ever lived, and I don't think people realize it enough. There isn't enough time in these times to be deeply moved over anything or anybody. Her achievement is just incredible and Annie Sullivan's likewise.

To Grace Martin
(Mrs. David Terry Martin)

November 2 [1954]
The O. Henry Hotel
Greensboro, North Carolina

I dined on Sunday at [Sir Pierson] Dixon's with the Queen Mother (where she's staying) and she is lovelier than ever. What a woman! A radiance of spirit shines in her face and whole personality. A perfect mother for a Queen!

I'm performing at Salem College to-night—twenty-five miles from here and flying home to-morrow for the English-Speaking Union ($25.00 a plate) dinner to the Queen Mother! I thought it worth the price to wear (for the first, and probably *only* time) my order of the C.B.E.!—as one can only wear it on occasions where "decorations" are requested.

My young theatre managers are trying to get me a theatre at Xmas holiday season—and then on tour for about six weeks. All uncertain yet. I've no particular news—glad Election Day is over—I always doubt if it makes any difference who is elected—everybody is a mixture of good and bad, in politics mostly bad!

To Dorothea Draper
(Mrs. Henry James)

December 1 [1954]
Wooster, Ohio

I wish you could have seen the plate of food I got at a luncheon given for me (recently): about nine lettuce leaves were arranged around, and overflowing a plate, in one nestled potato salad made with that vile bottled mayonnaise; in one a pickled peach; in another two kinds of cheese and two Crax; another a chunk of banana; another a chunk of orange jello with lots of fruit in it; another a stuffed egg; another a pear with green grapes; and another a half peach with red grapes; wedges of tomato filled the gaps; another had a beet red object which I think was a pickled crabapple; and nestled in the center was a small second joint, very tough, of fried chicken, buried under French fried potatoes once hot! There were twelve people, and we each got a plate—and most of the plates went out as full as they came in—the beds of lettuce were so lush! This dish was followed by balls of orange sherbert and, of course, large cups of coffee were filled from the beginning. The Inn was charming. It's a famous place and they were doing their best for me, but I longed for a chop and a baked potato. I have a three-hour trip to Tiffin to-morrow, but a nice long afternoon to rest.

I travelled nearly twelve hours yesterday but in a lovely train thro' lovely country, and I enjoyed it, and got to bed by 8:30 here, and I have a lovely room on the campus. I must now get ready for my show—an easy program—I'll send you a post-card from Tiffin—my birthday town! [December 2nd—70th birthday] I love this funny life—never feel sorry for me "on the road"!

To Grace Martin
(Mrs. David Terry Martin)

[December 7, 1954]
Hotel Van Orman
Fort Wayne, Indiana

I am sitting in the warm and airless and belamped lobby of this hotel, waiting for my train at 5:27 to New York. I motor'd over with two kind ladies from Portland (Indiana) this morning. It is such a beautiful clear day that I was tempted to fly from here (tho' I have my R.R. ticket and space and it's always a bother to change), so, when I got to this hotel I found the T.W.A. office in the lobby, and asked if there was a plane? Yes—but they wouldn't take my cheque (tho' stamped with my name and Chase Bank) nor would the Fort Wayne National Bank opposite. Of course I should have my Social Security number and other official identification with me—but it amused me that my very genteel looks—purse, bags, address book, visiting card, all with my name, and the list of my contracts to play in six towns were all of no avail! I said to the timid young man in the deluxe marble bank "I should think you could trust your intuition that a person was decent"; he seemed a little embarrassed, and I said I was sorry not to have a happier impression of Indiana! I only had $25. and I needed $45. As a matter of fact I don't mind. I like the old train and the beds are so comfortable and I have that wonderful book *The Reason Why* to read. Do you want it? It gives a grim and horrible picture of the British in the 18th and 19th centuries—so cruel—mean—and inhuman toward the common soldier. It came out in the wonderful Florence Nightingale book—but this is worse!

I also have written several letters, and outlined my program for a three-weeks season at Xmas. I open at the Bijou on December 26 and have asked Paul to join me on the program. It may give him a break at last—and I think our joint show presents a unique and interesting combination. I do hope it will be a success for his sake (not to say my own!) for it's always a risk, and rather terrifying to re-open on Broadway, after my success (which I called "Farewell") last year! I hope to go to Boston for a week on January 17th—then Washington for a week—then Chicago for two weeks. I turned seventy the other day, and the prospect of such a strenuous season alarms me slightly I must confess—but you know how I love working; and I do want to re-visit those cities after years of absence—before I stop! I know you'll wish me well!

To Neilla Warren

January 2, 1955
66 East 79th Street
New York, N.Y.

How did you know that <u>painful</u> date?! *Many* thanks just the same for your kind good wishes! I appreciate them, and send mine in return, for this New Year—and many more! You have been a "faithful fan" for so long and I hope perhaps you will look in and see my nephew dance in our current season.

With all good wishes, I am always, Yours sincerely,

Ruth Draper

So, after her fall tour, she was back again, supporting her nephew Paul in his return to New York where there was one threat to picket him—but it remained only a threat. They played, sharing the program at the Bijou, for three weeks—to mid-January—earning a pittance. She had slowed down to the extent of taking a hotel room near the theatre where she rested between matinee and evening performances—instead of returning to 66 East 79th Street for those few hours. But then she was off again—on the road: "My tour was fun, for I love to work, but financially not worthwhile. So glad Paul was a success." She could not face a life without her work—her reason of being.

In London in 1950 Ruth Draper recorded for Decca, with Joyce Grenfell accompanying her as "audience," for she needed someone to play to. But she was not happy with the result and remained reluctant to make further recordings, feeling the visual aspect of her work very important to the whole. Finally, however, when she was 70, and on the plea that her work not be lost entirely, Charles Bowden, with the help of Arthur Rubinstein, arranged for her to record for RCA in New York.

During 1954 and 1955 she had nine recording sessions. Her managers, Charles Bowden and Richard Barr, were present, as well as a former stage manager, Barnet Owens. At first she was disturbed by the stationary microphone, by the lack of an audience, by her inhibitions regarding the medium. Mr. Bowden suggested that she try a "warm-up session," forgetting the technical ambience. A warm-up session was not something Ruth Draper ever needed, and she had barely begun when those in the control room knew all was well and threw the switch. She was tricked once but not again, and the other sessions went well with a row of microphones to give her more mobility. She would say: "Is that really good enough? Let me try again"; and, after one or two additional recordings, "There—I'm sick of that—put it all together and let me hear it." Of the twenty-one sketches recorded, eleven were issued with her approval but the perfectionist in her was not entirely satisfied—as always, she depreciated herself.

In these sessions she had no props or shawls, only occasionally using the scarf she wore, as an aid in her accustomed gestures. The technical crew found "absolutely no difficulty in working with her—she was delightful, charming, thoroughly *professional." Was she interested in the technical process? Not* really! *The RCA Producer in charge of the recording sessions, Richard Mohr, remembers thinking: "She was so tiny—and was a thousand people! I was most of all impressed by her quality of such a great lady—and also a great artist—one does not often find this combination."*

When asked if she was amenable to suggestions, her manager, Charles Bowden, replied: "She was considerate—*she would think it over carefully, and if she did not agree she always proved to be right in the long run."*

To Stark Young

January 24 [1955]
[New York]

Dearest Stark,

I was so touched and pleased to have your lovely card, and all your comments on my work. You are one of my oldest critics and friends and I love knowing that you find me still on the upgrade. One should go on growing, in one sense, in spite of age, and I'm lucky to have been spared submersion so long. I do *hope* I'll know when to stop! I'm so glad you like 'Maine' [*On a Porch in a Maine Coast Village*]. I adore that old girl—and must restrain my inclination to talk on and on!

I tried the different head covering, but somehow it changed the type to bind my head in color, and I cling to the soft lace, but I will try and cover more successfully the grey hair [as young Italian Girl?].

I was *so* impressed by your painting—and long to see more! What fun it must be to develop a new form of expression. When I return, let's meet and talk, and let me see more of your work. Happy New Year and love to Wales, and thanks so much for coming to my show and for writing me. Paul was happy to have your message too.

Yours ever,
Ruth

To Dorothy Draper
Mrs. Henry James

Jan. 29 [1955]
Chilton Club
152 Commonwealth Avenue
Boston

To-day I had a lovely call on the Curtis girls. My, they're adorable, and the house likewise. I find I love the past and respectability more and more—and they're *such fun*! I nearly died laughing when Miss Harriot [Curtis] imitated her mother calling them all to breakfast as children. She yelled on an up-key—"Breakfast!—breakfast! Billy Fanny Ellie Stevey, Bella Harry Fraser Jimmy,—Harriot and Margaret, Breakfast!" It had a wonderful rhythm—4 names—then 4 more—then 2—ending with an upstroke on a high note!—it went very fast on the names—slow on Breakfast! Please keep this—I don't want to forget the sequence of names. How I love that old house—they used to slide down the stairs on leaves from the dining room table!

Then to Lily Norton's—very different type, but the same cosy secure past warms one; then to Mr. Howe in Louisburg Square and he sent you his regards or something—his poem this year is lovely and so moving. My luncheon with Esther, Sue, and Juliet was *lovely*; I wouldn't have picked the combination but it proved most happy and there was no other time. We nearly died laughing over tales of our youth and old customs, etc., and Sue said very intelligent things about education—which we discussed. Lots of other people I knew were there and we had a lovely time.

The "Curtis girls" lived on Upper Mt. Vernon Street and were known as "the Mighty Maidens"; they were daughters of a distinguished officer of the

*Union Army in the Civil War and his wife, Harriot Appleton, half-sister to
Henry Wadsworth Longfellow. Elinor married the painter Charles Hopkin-
son; Harriot was for a time Dean of Women at Hampton Institute in Virginia and devoted her life to Negro rights; all were involved in "causes";
Margaret smoked a pipe. They were hearty, forthright, and without doubt a
match for their five brothers.*

*About this time Ruth wrote to Dorothea of someone recently met on
tour: "[She] comes from Boston; it always amuses me to meet people from
Boston who are not our Boston—Amurican accent—you'd never recognize
the type as from Boston! We are snobs, no denying it, but I'm so grateful for
the Boston we know and love!"*

*On this trip to Boston Ruth Draper's managers arranged a Press party in
a suite at the Ritz—tea at one end, a bar at the other. She was at her most
gently charming best. Chatting with Eleanor Hughes, she said: "You are a
critic? ... Then you will review my show tonight? ... Well, then, why don't
you put down that drink and have a nice cup of tea?"*

Somehow, the bar had fewer patrons, after that!

To Grace Martin
(Mrs. David Terry Martin)

February 8 [1955]
Ambassador Hotel
Chicago

I enclose a Boston and a Chicago review—they've been fabulous
everywhere. Washington was wonderful and best financially; Boston and
Chicago both slow in starting the week—but building to capacity by the
end. After eight or ten years absence I should have stayed longer everywhere
to give a chance to build up. There is great competition everywhere (not
Washington) and even with superb reviews [the] public does not run, but
waits and then scrambles to get in! I'll make a *little* money but not much!
Paul and I took in $33,000. in the three weeks, and netted about $1000.!
Seems out of proportion. Paid jobs pay better, but *I far prefer* a real stage, a
real theatre public with people paying for their seats because they *want* to
come, not because they belong to a "course", or get it free. But the Unions,
and the Theatre rentals and publicity costs are *so* high. I thought seven
weeks steady work would be enough for me, and feared I might be tired—
but I'm not, and am so reluctant to stop! I may do a movie in March, so
perhaps I'll need a few weeks to get ready—probably some new costumes,
and cutting of my pieces to make them suitable for screen. I'll let you know
how the plan progresses.

To Bernard Berenson

[July 27, 1955]
Balcarres,
Colinsburgh, Fife
[with Lord and Lady
Crawford and Balcarres]

Dearest B.B.

I feel I must write you from this heavenly place, and David and Mary both send you their love, with mine, as we talk of you, and Italy and I Tatti and mutual friends! The pictures, and books—and all the beauty in the house, and the roses, and trees, and view, and the general atmosphere of peace and beauty without—fill me with emotion and thankfulness, and I wish I might stay on and on, and drink more deeply of such blessings; I had planned to do Recordings all this week in London—but I cancelled 3 days with the Victor Studios, in order to give myself the rest and inspiration of being here, after closing my season in Edinburgh on Saturday.

I return to London tonight and next week prepare to make a Film of the "Church in Italy" and the "Three Generations" and the "Debutante" for T.V. I am dreading it, but feel I must at least try the experiment. If it turns out well, it may be done at cinemas and I would prefer that, as I hate T.V. I expect to fly home August 10th and and go to my island in Maine. I think of you and Nicky now at Vallombrosa and envy the friends who are enjoying it with you. I recall so well the vast and lovely view of the great valley and hills, as one sits at tea-time in the "arbor"—restoring one's soul in pleasant talk.

It is a joy to be here, too. I know you love David as I do; he is a rare person—and I had a wonderful hour with him and his books yesterday. The pictures that you know so well, all seem so happy in this house, with luscious colors of old brocades, old gilt, sunlight and flowers all about them, and the reverence and affection of generations pervading the atmosphere. Scotland is having a long stretch of divinely beautiful weather and the air is full of sweetness.

My love to dear Nicky, and much to you—Amey and her 2 small and active great-nephews are now in Holland, and her journey here was a great success. I marvel at her courage and energy—but it has all been a great success. The Judge and Frances [Hand] gave up their plan to come to England, and I am sure regretted it.

Always your devoted Ruth

As it had been in the previous four years, the call of the road still was heard by Ruth Draper: although the margin of profit was discouraging; although any platform but a stage was hateful; although the gatherings, seat-

ed or standing, were an incomprehensible infliction—"Why must women
organize for culture and enjoyment, and exclude men?"—yet something in
her still responded: in her need for variety, in her ability to rise above the
drab hotels and hazards of travel; in her warmth and joy at seeing again old
friends "en route"; in her ability to find interest in new faces and scenes—a
dinner of 400 professional women was almost more than she could bear,
after a night of travel and a platform performance to follow, yet she greatly
liked and admired—even enjoyed—the two Mid-western women of inde-
pendent careers and accomplishment who sat either side of her.

So it was that after Islesboro she set forth in the Autumn: Toronto (again
visiting at Cruikston Park), Detroit, Cleveland, and, right after the New
Year, Baltimore, Chicago jointly with Paul Draper, and a round of univer-
sities.

To Grace Martin
(Mrs. David Terry Martin)

10:30 a.m., Tuesday, April 3 [1956]
At the Hairdresser's
New York

I always write you from odd addresses—often on the eve of departure!
Well, I'm off at 6—flying T.W.A. to Rome! I always feel squeamish and solemn as I set forth on these journeys, and wonder why I pursue my strange
destiny of wandering—when I have such a pleasant nest? But I know that,
always, I have a more aware sense of happiness when I'm on the road, and
working! I have a few jobs, alas, only a few, over there, but at least it gives
me a purpose—which makes the great journey worth while. I shall give two
Benefits in Rome and two in Florence, and make a lot of money for a good
cause; then on to Paris where I hope to arrange a few shows; then Holland
where I have some already booked; then Vienna, where dates are not yet
fixed, but where I expect to play in early June at the same beautiful little
theatre where I played in 1928! "Theater in der Josefstadt," an 18th century
gem! Then I shall go to England—to work, I hope, for a few weeks.

I thought of you this morning, when I took some left-over honey to my
brother, and another friend who is poor, and loves and needs it in her diet.
So always you and I pass on good things we give each other! What fun it is?
Several friends of mine have so enjoyed Sydney's book. I wrote him recently
to tell him; the report of him you sent was saddening—poor old weary soul.
My dear brother lives on—so tragically—his life so useless from having
been so active and useful. I saw poor Osbert Sitwell the other day, shaking
to pieces with that cruel Parkinson's disease. He comes over here hoping to
find some new cure, and seeking distraction, I suppose.

To Dorothea Draper
(Mrs. Henry James)

[April 6, 1956]
La Rufola, Capo di Sorrento
Italy

I'm sitting up in a huge antique bed with a lama [sic] rug over me, between the finest linen sheets I ever felt, looking out over olives and oranges to a wild stormy sea, wind howling and rain beating against the windows. I've just washed in cold water and am waiting for my 'café-laté'! I came down yesterday afternoon with Marchesa Benzoni—daughter of the grand old lady, Signora Ruffino, who owns the Villa. Her husband was the great friend of Professor Salvemini and, after his death, Salvemini, who frequently visited here, stayed on. It is a perfect place for him to end his days.

Now I've had my delicious breakfast, and suddenly rain is stopped, gale abated, and a pale sun is struggling thro' a broken sky—so all is promising. My breakfast, on a huge silver tray and sparkling coffee and milk pots, was so good, brought by a 'Concetta' with a face of calm beauty to remember; an angel of a woman, wife of the gardener, mother of the waitress, and devoted friend of the family. She looks after the Professor and is one of those strong serene Italians with a smile that warms the heart. The Professor is pretty well but can only work three instead of eight hours a day, which he finds very hard! But he reads and writes the rest of the time!

I had a lovely luncheon with Iris [Origo] and the girls, two ladies who are arranging the Benefit, and all was settled quickly. The house is a dream of beauty—such colors and taste, and lovely painted walls in the rooms and a garden. I went there once before when the old Duchess of Sermonetta lived there, but Iris has made it too beautiful. She leaves for London to-day but will be back before my show. She is more wonderful than ever and was pleased to have your message and asked affectionately for you. The girls are lovely, and my, these Italian children work! They study all afternoon, and of course school all a.m. Benedetta plays the piano beautifully but can't decide whether to be an archeologist or pianist Iris told me. They both speak four languages and are studying Greek and Latin, reading the Classics, Philosophy etc. How *do* they do it? And *such* lovely manners—sweet unspoiled natural girls. Antonio was at La Foce as the crops have suffered in the bitter winter weather.

The flight was wonderful, tho' we were delayed by head-winds and three hours late, but coming into Rome in the golden light of the late afternoon was too beautiful. Irene met me in a friend's beautiful car, and I found the Hotel so comfortable, and after a bath and dinner went early to bed. I telephoned several friends, went for a walk, and Iris fetched me at 12:30. I shall stay here till Monday a.m. and go to Naples for one night in order to have a good day at the Museum, meet Mina on Tuesday and leave that night for Palermo. I intend to get the Professor to tell me *all* about Sicilian history in the next few days! I'm reading "Garibaldi and the Thousand", and another book on legends and very early history.

I left my costume bag and hat box at the "Hotel de la Ville" where I return the 22nd so you can address me there for that week. I don't yet know where I shall be staying in Florence, so address 'American Express' there up to May 5th; then Paris—Hotel Bourgogne, Place du Palais Bourbon—or Morgan & Co. from then on will be the safest—tell anyone who asks.

I must now write Nannina and B.B. and then get up and put on my warmest clothes; it's now raining and blowing again and I'd like to lie under my lama [*sic*] rug forever! But it will surely be warm downstairs; the old lady is lovely, but very frail, and the house is kept pretty hot for her and the Professor. I have a stove in my room, but didn't let Concetta light it as bed is so warm. I make everybody laugh at my Italian, which in a way sounds like the real thing, and is confusing, being full of mistakes and wrong words. How I regret never having been *made* to *work* at anything! Darling Barie tried hard to make me apply myself to lessons, when she helped me as a child, but never succeeded.

Salvemini remained at Sorrento with Signora Ruffino, whose husband had sheltered him after his arrest and trial by the Fascists in 1925. Already weakened by influenza, the news of Ruth's death was to be a great and chilling shock—for two days he could not speak of it, then in writing Neville Rogers he would speak only of her "unifying influence among her friends." Following this blow was to be the loss of another close friend, Arturo Toscanini, who long had refused to conduct in any Fascist country. Salvemini failed steadily until his death on September 6, 1957, at the age of 84.

On the outskirts of Florence, in the Trespiano Cemetery, there is a special quadrangle surrounded by cypresses; here Salvemini lies buried with the Rosselli brothers, Carlo and Nello, who had been assassinated in France in the summer of 1937. Both active anti-Fascists, Carlo had made a spectacular escape from political prison on the Isle of Lipari in 1929.

Off the Corso in Florence there is now a small "Piazza Salvemini," not far from the avenue formerly named "Viale Re Umberto" but after the war changed to "Viale Fratelli Rosselli."

Over the years, Ruth kept in touch with the Rosselli family.

To Dorothea Draper
(Mrs. Henry James)

Thursday [May 10, 1956]
Milan, Italy

I'm here just for the day to see the Brera, Poldi-Pezzoli and Ambrosiana, and leave for Paris to-night by train. I left Florence yesterday at 5:30,— Cesari Vivante met me at the train here, and took me to dinner at his flat. He and his wife are perfectly charming, both very beautiful to look at, and both with the *most* lovely speaking voices I've ever heard. I went with Anne to their wedding two years ago [in Lugano]. I hated to leave Florence, it was lovely—lovelier than ever. I managed to see many of the familiar and beautiful things, and some new ones. The trip to La Verna was wonderful, on a perfect day. I never took a meal alone—for people were so kind. I'll give you a list for it may amuse you, and it will save me space and time! You always want to know who my 'friends' are:—

Monday, 30th (April) —arrive 3:30. Performance in the evening.

Tuesday 1st (May)	Lunch Marion Kaftal; Tea George Posts.—Dined with Reggie Temple's old servant's daughter, a dressmaker and dear person who lived on with him after her mother, who had served him for forty years, died.
Wednesday	Lunched Biba Coster. Tea Nannina. *Dine B.B.*
Thursday	Big luncheon at Conte and Contessa Rucellai's (the old lady's eldest son's wife) in the lovely palace. Reception at the Lyceum Club—lots of ladies. Dine Maria Roselli.
Friday	A drink at Contessa Medici's and Signora Gigliuci's. *Lunch B.B.* Tea with my old cook Maria and dine with Nannina.
Saturday	Lunch Adrienne (Fachiri) d'Aranyi. Tea Giangio and Teresa Rucellai. Cocktails Lady Dick Lauder—big party—Dine Lorenzo Emo—nephew of Gladys Huntington—very nice party.
Sunday	*To Siena* for the day—lunch with Vivantes. Dine Marion Kaftal and Opera—'Traviata'
Monday	*La Verna* for the day with Nannina Fossi and Miss de Roebeck (a great student of St. Francis)
Tuesday	Lunch Contessa Serristori—a wonderful old lady in a wonderful palace. Kaftals were there and other agreeable people. Tea old Contessa Rucellai. *Dine B.B.*
Wednesday	Sight-seeing and errands—lunch Maria Roselli.

In between meals I saw: Santa Trinita, a Pontormo show at Palazzo Strozzi, Santa Maria Novella, The Bargello, The Badia, Uffizi, Pitti, Santa Croce, San Marco, San Miniato, Michael Angelo's house, The Duomo and Baptistry, visited the graves of two friends to leave flowers, drove in the Cascine with old Countess Medici to see the fountain where Shelley is said to have written the "Ode to the West Wind"!

To see a Progressive School with Nannina; to see a Boy's Home with Biba, for which I gave part of my profits; ordered and fitted lovely shoes at Ferragamo's; bought two round table cloths and odds and ends, and a new kind of Espresso coffee pot; wandered thro' the enchanting streets; wrote many post cards and a few letters; washed my clothes; rested—ate—talked fluent and *atrocious* Italian and had a wonderful ten days.

I'm sure you're laughing, horrified and breathless—but I'm very well! Wish I didn't have such heavy luggage, I'm going by train to Paris, as 'overweight' on a plane is so costly. Lovely weather now. I'm off to see the pictures—had a good sleep and breakfast—and look forward to a pleasant day. Hope you're feeling well and that spring has come at last. I'm thrilled to think of your new car and coat. My love to everyone in Boston. This is such a boring letter—lists are tiresome to read, but I thought you'd get a coup d'oeil of my busy life and be amused.

To Bernard Berenson

> Sunday [May 13, 1956]
> Hotel Bourgogne
> Place du Palais Bourbon
> Paris

Dearest B.B.

I must tell you again how happy I was to see you, to be with you and Nicky in that serene and beautiful room; to sit beside you again, and feel the same wisdom and wit, caustic and kindly in turn, the same faithful and generous friendship and welcome, and the affection and understanding, unchanged. My ten days in Florence were lovely indeed, and the three visits to I Tatti the high-lights! I had a wonderful time in my brief stop-over at Milan. The Brera bowled me over! (The new installations and arrangement of the pictures made me wish that Francis Taylor had seen it before he bought so much brocade for the Metropolitan!) I saw again with delight, things I'd not seen since I was 18, and the Mantegnas and Piero della Francesca and many others gave me great joy and wonder. What treasures in Milan, so often scorned as just a great commercial city! I went to the Poldi Pezzoli and the Castello (also marvellously re-arranged with such skill and taste), and to Sant' Ambrogio—so my day was crammed with beauty. Now Paris— radiant in sunshine and flowering trees, and I'm off to Fontainebleau for the day.

I saw an enchanting exhibition of Italian pictures from Provincial museums, at the Orangerie—such lovely things one would not expect to find in places like Cherbourg, Dijon, Strasbourg, Lyon and Aix-en-Provence (you, of course, would—). The French are wonderful the way they plan these exhibitions for the "ignorentsia" and the place was jammed, so I'll be going again.

I send you my grateful and loving thoughts dear B.B. and I hope you will not let yourself be fatigued with too many devoted friends. I am happy that I could give you a little pleasure with my sketch, and make you laugh at Daniel Webster's remark about the Pacific! Much love always, and to Nicky—

Your devoted Ruth

To Charles C. Burlingham

May 28 [1956]
The Hague

Dearest C.C.B.

My journey has gone very happily, and I've had lovely weather every where, and kept very well, and enjoyed every moment since I flew away on April 3rd! I had six delightful days at Sorrento, and saw the dear Professor [Salvemini]—very happily established in a lovely villa, in a garden by the sea, with dear and devoted friends, and an Italian—like your angel, Nora—to attend to all his needs. I don't think he could be more perfectly cared for—and students and old friends come every day to visit him, and discuss their lives, and studies, and bring him news. Some travel from far—and he does not feel cut off from life and action. He writes and reads, and has a routine of work and rest.

On the 11th of April my friend Mina Rand joined me and we had ten wonderful days in Sicily. It is an amazing country—unique in the vivid impression of a great and colorful past, which is imprinted in the faces of the vigorous people; and the Greek Temples, the Byzantine mosaics, Norman churches, and Spanish Baroque architecture, give constant evidence, as one drives thro' the country ablaze with flowers and spring blossoms—austere mountains and cultivated fields! Ancient legends from the Greek and Roman and Mediaeval times are painted on the carts, and of course the Madonna is not forgotten.

After that I had a week in Rome—and gave two very successful Benefits for District nurses. I saw a lot of people there and had a gay and delightful time mixed with sight-seeing, and gasps of wonder at the fantastic beauty and the awful encroachment of modern buildings into the rich sanctuary of history. Then I had ten days in Florence—so gentle and so completely Renaissance at every turn—so does its message still possess the place, even tho' there too, of course, modern taste and needs have been imposed, and clash with the old—but have not yet spoiled the beauty. I saw many beloved places and pictures and many friends, and was sorry to leave. I spent one day in Milan; there are marvellous pictures there and a church that I love, Sant'Ambrogio, badly injured by bombs but beautifully repaired. Then Paris—ten crowded days—a lovely peaceful Sunday at Fontainebleau with Dean and Anne Jay, and another at Vézelay, one of the greatest Romanesque buildings in the world—and the site is unique—on the top of a small hill, with old houses clambering up in close formation to the summit where amid flowering and enormous chestnut trees, the great church stands looking down over the surrounding plain. The country was a dream of beauty. Chestnuts and fruit trees and hawthorn in full bloom. Carpets of lily of the valley in the woods; and in the fields, white cows, white sheep, white ducks and geese; lovely little villages—and *such* delicious food in the restaurants, gay with checked table cloths and flowers. France is radiant with charm, beauty, and a continuity of habit and taste that are disarming when one reads and hears of the tragic political trouble she's always disturbed by, and the awful fact of continuous little wars, and threat of more—as the African problem remains—taking her young men—and with no solution in view. It's awfully sad. Now I'm in Holland and I love the country, such order and cleanliness and industry and well-being has a calming and salubrious effect. Everyone who has nervous prostration, and suffers from high blood pressure, and all the effects of 'tension' should come to Holland! There's something healing about the very features of the land, the wideness of the skies, the greenness of the fields cut thro' by the quiet canals, the perfection of the gardens and the little houses with shining windows that look so well kept and happy. Even pigs are pink and clean, grazing at will in the meadows beside the cows and sheep and baby lambs, not kept in muddy pens as one generally thinks of pigs!

To Dorothea Draper
(Mrs. Henry James)

[June 5, 1956]
Hotel Kummer
Vienna

Heavenly weather here. Dined at the Embassy last night—very smart people—some English and Americans I knew—all young. They made me recite. I suppose in real life I'm so 'unprofessional' in looks and in manners, that they think they can ask me without compunction! It probably will help bring people to my show on Sunday, so may be of profit—anyway, it gave pleasure! Some very pretty dresses—but that diplomatic world is very lightweight. We have a *beautiful* Embassy and lovely grounds—near Schön-brunn Palace—very grand. [Llewellyn] Thompson is the Ambassador. Mrs. T. is very sweet—comes from Boston, pretty, capable, well-dressed, gay and young.

I'm in a nice clean new hotel—couldn't get in to the Bristol which I stayed in on my first visit, and was sorry. Going to the play to-night. I had to give up Fidelio to go to the Embassy—a real sacrifice—but I felt meeting people might help my show! There's *so* much going on—I don't think it was wise to come at the Festival time. My name is on the lamp-posts with lists of other things in music, theatre and opera, but I'm afraid (as I knew) one show won't be much use. They'll want more, and I really don't want to stay longer. I expect to fly to London on the 12th and am negotiating for a flat. I must get up and go and see the Museums—lots to see—I know no one here and a companion would be nice. It's quite warm—my clothes are very adequate and I'll not bother with getting anything till I get to dear old Lon-don. I *adored* my Holland ten days—such nice people—and such happy times—and, oh, so lovely and clean and full of flowers. Earle [Balch] drove me to Schiphol for a delicious lunch and saw me off.

I had dinner my last night with two enchanting women—one, one of the *most* beautiful women I ever saw—Mme. de With—a friend of the Bliss's—long in the diplomatic world—now a widow about sixty-eight; and one who did Red Cross nursing all thro' the war, Baroness Pallandt—a charming and thrilling person—nursed also in Suez, when the wounded were coming there from Java. My, what these people have seen and done in the war—and the agony of the 'occupations', which we can't conceive - - - The revival everywhere is *so* impressive—the will to live, and the joy in freedom is moving.

To Dorothea Draper
(Mrs. Henry James)

June 6 [1956]
Vienna

With my usual luck I've got a flat, and I hear it's charming! I asked Ethel Salter, who lives near, to look in and she tells me it's awfully nice—so I took it, and fly over on the 12th. I tried to go to Figaro to-night but couldn't get a seat, so I'm home in bed busily writing letters. I had a lovely drive in the Wienerwald this morning with a retired Diplomat I knew in Copenhag-en—an awfully nice American who comes from Worcester! And I went this afternoon to the Albertina, and held Dürer's lovely drawings in my hands—a great thrill—it's an amazing and beautiful place. I then did a Radio talk in German! I made them write the answers to the questions—

fearing my grammar was too imperfect! Of course it sounded fine (because we all have a perfectly good accent!) Viennese is the nicest sounding German.

My show is at 11 a.m. Sunday. Doubt if it's any good because the new management hasn't done much advertising, and there is *so* much going on! I'm driving out on Sunday afternoon to see old Colloredo Mannsfeld. He was so kind to me here twenty-eight years ago and I liked him so much.

To Dorothy Draper
(Mrs. Henry James)

June 10, 1956
Vienna

Groessten erfolg Herzlichte Guresse an alle

To Dorothea Draper
(Mrs. Henry James)

[June 11, 1956]
Vienna

Did you laugh at my cable in German?—it amused me to send it, and I hope it came while the party was still on at 'Greenleaves'—I thought I remembered that the Carters were coming for the 10th week-end. Well, my matinee is over and was a *huge* success! Contrary to expectations it was packed, with "the best audience in Vienna" I was told. Mostly Austrian too, tho' some British and American. Now, of course, what I anticipated, is happening—I could have given many more shows, but it is too late. They could promise me nothing, and I didn't want to stay on with no certain work, just on the chance. It is a pity, but nothing to be done. Your cable has *just* come, and I'm so glad to know mine reached you at a propitious moment! What luck!

I must get up now. Frau Thimig-Reinhardt is coming to fetch me, to pick up my things at the theatre, and to go and see Beethoven's and Schubert's houses. I'm lunching at the Embassy. Gladys Széchényi's niece is picking me up there for a drive at 2:45. An old fan, Dr. Schmidt, is coming at 5 to take me to tea. I'm going to a Mozart quartet concert and dining at Sacher's with a party afterward. I have beautiful roses from the British Embassy secretary and his wife—old London acquaintances. It's a lovely day, and I'm in a glow of wonder over a performance of *Don Carlos* at the Burg Theatre last night. *Never* have I seen such *acting—such a production—such lighting—taste, costumes, voices,* and diction! It was breath-takingly beautiful, indescribably perfect. The old Burg Theatre (like the Comédie Française) burned out in the war—superbly done over—the most splendid and superb place I ever imagined. I was carried away. Everything at home seems so tawdry, shallow, inelegant, and without dignity and taste. The work at the Opera and State Theatre here is something unequalled—and we could never achieve it. I'll try and remember things to tell you. The Strauss Opera was magnificent beyond words. We came out to a downpour of rain,—after one hour waiting for taxis—two nice American ladies dropped me at home. I must run— I'm meeting my supper friends at Beethoven's statue. Such a nice rendez-vous—what?

To Dorothea Draper
(Mrs. Henry James)

[Wednesday] July 4 [1956]
16´Burton Court
Chelsea, S.W.3

My first night went wonderfully—the theatre is *perfection* for me, and so central! My flat is a dream and bursting with flowers—I got about twelve bouquets, three plants, and some smaller offerings—a 'superb one' from Laurence Olivier and Vivien Leigh. Lovely audiences so far, and fine reviews—how *can* they keep it up! I have two shows to-day and am waiting for lunch. I got back from a happy week in Dublin on Sunday and had supper that night with Ethel and Arthur Salter. Monday I had Mary Erdman, Lady Linlithgow and Peter Lubbock to lunch. Yesterday Marion Rawson and John Rosselli (by the way he´is arriving [next] Saturday about noon by air from Manchester and is going straight to 66 East 79th). If it's easy for you, to call him, and perhaps ask him for a night, it would be lovely for him, and for me, and I think for you—because he's a rare and intelligent young man—on the staff of the 'Guardian', and knows a lot, and is very sensitive and wise and a dear fellow.

To Dorothea Draper
(Mrs. Henry James)

[July 22, 1956]
[London]

Thanks for your letter about this awful complication of the cook's demands! I suppose I'm cornered! I *must* have a cook—so tell Johnson unless she found a paragon in her search to tell the firm I'll agree to her last wages plus $25. more;—i.e. $5. more a week. I did tell Bridget I'd offer that.

(Then I realized I'd only *meant* $5. more a month, and had made a mistake; I must abide by my first offer.) I'll write Bridget or cable to delay her going with the others. I'll pay them all as from August 1st.

The dates you mention for your visit will be O.K. *any time,* you're welcome and for as long as you'll stay. I'm going to take Ba's room for mine this year—I love it, and feel close to her there, and that gives me three fine big spare-rooms. It will be so lovely to see you again and talk quietly under your trees.

I'm off to lunch with Kathleen's sister, to see Kew Gardens, and visit my old friend Sir Sydney Cockerell, who lives near by. Other friends coming to supper.

Sorry as I am to stop—I'm really ready to—it's been a *marvellous* season—but August is not ever so good—and one feels like a holiday when it comes, somehow! The pattern of my life repeats itself in a pull both ways—always—

To Dorothea Draper
(Mrs. Henry James)

Tuesday p.m. [July 31, 1956]
London

My last night was a triumph—cheers and a speech and about ten curtains—packed house—a sad farewell but I hope I'll be here again!

Ruth Draper played at the St. James Theatre from July 2nd through the 28th—six evenings and two matinees each week. Nearly every year since 1920 she had had a London season of 4 to 12 weeks.

Her final performance in England was on Thursday, August 2nd, before the women prisoners at Holloway. To a friend, who was carrying her shawls, she said: "They are looking very old and shabby, but when I die I hope my coffin will be covered with them. They have been my faithful friends."

The next day she visited the National Gallery and, on Saturday, the British Museum. Ellen Parks came for lunch and Fred drove her to the airport for the 6:30 BOAC flight to New York, where she was met by Roberto Bolaffio. After two days with family she left for Islesboro.

In reviewing the detail of her engagement diary, it is evident that during this summer she saw nearly all the friends she most cared about, and eagerly—almost compulsively—revisited all the "beloved places" in each city, the museums, the galleries, at a time when she might well have taken a more leisurely pace.

To William Adams Delano

Tuesday [August 14, 1956]
Dark Harbor

I confess to a great ache for London—the St. James Theatre and my hard work with its enormous reward each night. I had *such* a lovely time!

It is beautiful here and gay, I believe—but I rarely leave the place—and go to bed at 9—happily all my household likes to retire early so no one has to struggle to keep awake to be polite!

I can't bear the thought that one must now read about the conventions for weeks, and that with all the trouble in the world that our political scene takes primary importance! No one talks of anything but Suez in England—everyone asked me what *we* were going to do! As if *I* knew! I only know I can't bear Nixon—or Dulles—and can't think who I'll vote for? but November is far off!

To William Adams Delano

[September 13, 1956]
Dark Harbor

My brief holiday is nearly over—tho' I always feel my life is all holiday—interspersed with work which I enjoy enormously, so that it doesn't seem like work—if work is the opposite of holiday!

At Islesboro Ruth filled the house with family and with old friends she loved; she drove about the island to see the Islesboro people she had known since childhood; she gave her annual benefit for the church; quietly she touched again all points of contact with her youth, with sixty years of deep happiness and memories–Islesboro was part of the very fabric of her being. But she did not join the scramble to the beach, saying only that she "felt odd, in the early mornings"; she did not swim so often in the icy waters; she decided to sell her little sailboat as she no longer had the strength to handle it alone–and in telling her niece Penelope of this, while wafting gently across the harbor on a "blue" day, she added, in a most curious tone of voice, "Isn't it a shame that one has to die—and leave all this."

In the spring when thinking about her trip to Sicily and working in Vienna, she had remarked, "It takes lots of energy to plan it, but I hope it will come off." This was planning of a kind that she had done without breaking stride for so many years—and now, as usually before, with the help of an agent. Although it had been slightly evident the previous year, this summer her writing was noticeably less sure and her once faultless spelling was frequently careless.

All the same she set off on tour in October—Ohio, Illinois, Oklahoma (with Grace Martin joining her in Tulsa for a day), Chicago, South Carolina, Pennsylvania, Baltimore, and so home to New York in December.

On the 11th she went for some publicity photographs to a new young photographer who had never seen her act, knew nothing of this elderly Ruth Draper, less of Miss Draper. It was a tiring session of several hours, for his "direction" ran counter to all her sensibilities. Finally he gave up; she took a shawl and instantly, before his astonished gaze, became a girl of 16. In all the more than eighty "shots" she appeared alarmingly tired and old—her eyes hurt and baffled. She was exhausted.

But that evening she attended the bridal dinner of Eva Rubinstein and performed for the party—appearing quite her ageless, vital self. On the drive to the wedding the next day, Arthur Rubinstein could speak only of Ruth—her genius, her youth, her joy.

Just two weeks later, on Christmas night, she opened a four-week season at the Playhouse Theatre, east of Broadway on 48th Street. This year she did not give her usual Christmas party, and the preceding day had told her dentist that she was so tired she did not know how she could perform. Each evening that week she scheduled the same program:A Children's Party; In a Railway Station on the Western Plains; Three Women and Mr. Clifford; A Scottish Immigrant at Ellis Island. On Wednesday and Saturday there were matinees; she dreaded the two performances. The opening went well and she hoped to overcome her fatigue with the stimulation of enthusiastic audiences full of young people. At the mid-week matinee she told Gerald O'Brien, her stage manager, that she was tired and would have to drop The Railway Station on the Western Plains *as it was too exhausting; since Lauro's death it had been emotionally almost unendurable for her.*

At the Saturday matinee she mixed the sequence of happenings in one of her dramas, although it was not evident to the audience. However, the satirical, amusing sketch At an Art Exhibition in Boston, *substituted for the* Railway Station, *ran about four minutes longer than usual and Gerald O'Brien noticed that some entirely new characters were evoked and new incidents brought into it. When Ruth Draper came off she seemed dazed and said to O'Brien, "I just went blank—and kept on talking. I never did that before." Obviously she was disturbed.*

That Saturday night, the 29th, in her last character, Lesley MacGregor, the Highland lass at Ellis Island come to marry her young man after three years' separation, she finally sees him in the crowd and rushes off, stage right, her face radiant, eager, certain of happiness, calling out, "Sandy, my Sandy—I'm here!"

The ovation was long, the packed house standing to cheer and applaud a superb performance. She was content. She asked to be driven to see the Christmas lights and, arriving home, ate her supper and went to bed. At eleven thirty the next morning her maid found her—apparently sleeping quietly. She had died peacefully in the early hours.

Epilogue

Ruth Draper stands alone, solitary—perfect—

Lord Balfour

The great lights over the theatre marquee, spelling out, simply, RUTH DRAPER, remained up, unlit, until after her funeral.

In England the shock and grief was deep and poignant—somehow she had belonged to them. In America, where a new generation had just discovered her, disbelief overlay the sadness, for even to her old friends she seemed ageless. For days the newspapers of both countries carried Editorials and Letters that attempted to express what she had meant to their writers and to the Theatre. Responsive always, her friendships had been at many levels, differently oriented, in a variety of idiom, but ever warm, generous, compassionate, and gay. A letter Olin Downes wrote her in 1930 sums up what most deeply could be said of her genius, even twenty-six years later, for her power deepened and matured, was honed and tempered, and to the very last was in no slightest way diminished.

> I received the highest and the rarest inspiration from your performances this evening. Everything that I personally desire to find in dramatic art— and indeed in all art— I found there, and came away with a new realization of the variety and depth and poignancy of human experience.
>
> One's prayers in this life really don't go entirely unanswered. I am thinking now of standing with a friend in Paris one early sunny morning looking over the roofs of the city from his apartment which was far up in the Montmartre Hill—Charpentier calls it "the sacred hill"—and I turned to my friend and said, "If God would give me one wish, it would be to know all that the human hearts under all these rooftops had known in the last twenty-four hours." Tonight, in a very great extent you answered that wish, and appeased in a large measure that desire which I think torments most of us as we face the inevitable limitations of our lives, to know a little more of the experience of which the greater measure must always elude us. And this, accomplished by you in terms of such perfect, sincere, and gracious art, makes me very happy. It furthermore means a great deal to discover someone of your sensibility and spirit, and someone whom these gifts have not destroyed as they do so many. With them I feel you have built your citadel, which, consequently, is a strong one, not only for you, but for everyone who comes into touch with such a noble and true and human art. In a great many years I have not had such happiness and such reassurance that the treasures of life are worth so much more than its burdens and its pains.

As announced in *The Court Circular*, a Memorial Service (organized by John Phipps, Anne Holmes, and Joyce Grenfell) was held in London on January 10th at St. Martin's in the Fields, Trafalgar Square. Lord Brand and John C. Phipps read the Lessons; William Carter represented the Draper family. As in New York the church was crowded to the doors with Ruth's friends from both her worlds, social and Theatre, in which she filled so great a place.

In New York on January 2nd, her casket lay at the head of the long aisle of Grace Church, surrounded by her family and the friends of a lifetime. Her nephews, Paul Draper and John Carter, Thomas Phipps, and Gerald O'Brien, Charles Bowden and Richard Barr, her managers, acted as ushers. The Episcopal Service was read by the Rector and in the Chancel Lillian and Carol Fuchs played Mozart on unaccompanied viola and violin. There was no choir but, at the end, the Bach Passacaglia in C Minor was played on the organ as Ruth Draper was borne head-high above the congregation, slowly down the crowded church, her worn shawls, crowned with white roses, deeply draping her casket: the rose silk of the Actress at the head, "Lesley MacGregor's" plaid, the black wool of the Dalmatian Peasant, and the brown fringed wool of Three Generations with the black lace of the young Italian girl covering the foot. Alice and Dorothea walked close behind, followed by the rest of her family and closest friends. "It was so like Ruth," a friend wrote, "dignity and drama, simplicity and sophistication."

At Dark Harbor, by her wish, Ruth's ashes were scattered over the sea— her place of peace and spiritual joy—over deep waters such as those into which Icarus had fallen.

Inseparably associated in her mind with Dark Harbor and sunset over the Camden Hills, one poem from her cherished collection had held, above all others, great meaning for her:

> A late lark twitters from the quiet skies:
> And from the west,
> Where the sun, his day's work ended,
> Lingers as in content,
> There falls on the old, gray city
> An influence luminous and serene,
> A shining peace.
>
> The smoke ascends
> In a rosy-and-golden haze. The spires
> Shine and are changed. In the valley
> Shadows rise. The lark sings on. The sun,
> Closing his benediction,
> Sinks, and the darkening air
> Thrills with a sense of the triumphing night—
> Night with her train of stars
> And her great gift of sleep.
>
> So be my passing!
> My task accomplish'd and the long day done,
> My wages taken, and in my heart
> Some late lark singing,
> Let me be gather'd to the quiet West,
> The sundown splendid and serene,
> Death.

William Ernest Henley
Margaritæ Sorori

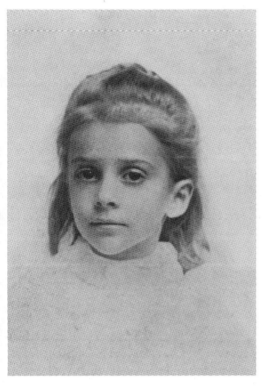

Ruth Draper, 1893.

A sketch made in 1896. (*Courtesy of The New-York Historical Society, New York City*)

Breakfast at Isleboro, mid-1950s; Ruth Draper (left) with Aileen Tone.

Ruth Draper, about 1930.
(Photo by Vandamm)

Ruth Draper in 1938.

Ruth Draper's dressing room
at Brighton, England, 1951,
showing her assortment of
hats and shawls.

Lauro de Bosis. *(Courtesy of The Oxford University Press, New York, and Faber and Faber, London)*

The Scotch Immigrant. Charcoal drawing by John Singer Sargent, 1914. *(Theatre and Music Collection, Museum of the City of New York)*

The Dalmatian Peasant.
(Photo by Muray)

As the Italian woman in the final
episode of A Church in Italy. (Photo by
Vandamm)

Charcoal drawing of the same
character by John Singer Sargent, 1914. (Theatre and
Music Collection, Museum of
the City of New York)

On a Porch in a Maine Coast Village.

At a Children's Party. (Photos by Trude Fleischmann. Theatre and Music Collection, Museum of the City of New York)

Doctors and Diets. (Photo by Trude Fleischmann)

Opening a Bazaar. (Photo by Muray)

Bibliography

Barnes, Eric Woollencott. *The Man Who Lived Twice.* Charles Scribner's Sons, New York, 1956. Biography of Edward B. Sheldon.

de Bosis, Lauro (Editor). *The Golden Book of Italian Poetry.* Oxford University Press, London, 1933. Foreword by G. M. Trevelyan.

de Bosis, Lauro. *Icaro.* Oxford University Press, London and New York, 1933. In the original Italian with English translation by Ruth Draper. Preface by Gilbert Murray.

de Bosis, Lauro. *Icare,* published by Claude Aveline, Paris, 1933. French verse translation by Ferdinand Herold. Foreword (in French) by Romain Rolland. Privately printed—1000 copies.

de Bosis, Lauro. *The Story of My Death.* Faber & Faber, Ltd. London, 1934; Oxford University Press, New York, 1934. Written in French by de Bosis the night before his flight over Rome.

de Bosis, Lauro. *La Storia della mia morte e ultimi scritti.* Published by Francesco de Silva, Turin, 1948. Edited with Introduction by Gaetano Salvemini. Italian translation of de Bosis' *Story of My Death* and of five letters to Ruth Draper and letters to Salvemini.

Draper, Muriel. *Music at Midnight.* Harper & Brothers, New York, 1929. By the wife of Paul Draper, telling of their life in Florence and London between 1906 and 1914, and of "the Edith Grove days."

Grenfell, Joyce. *Joyce Grenfell Requests the Pleasure.* Macmillan London Limited, London, 1976; St. Martin's Press, New York, 1977. Autobiography. Biographical chapters on Paul Phipps (J. G.'s father), Mrs. W. W. Phipps, and Ruth Draper.

Hoffman, Malvina. *Heads and Tales.* Charles Scribner's Sons, New York, 1936. *Yesterday Is Tomorrow,* Crown Publishers, New York, 1965. References to family relationship with Drapers.

Italy To-day. Booklets put out by Friends of Italian Freedom, edited by Mrs. V. M. Crawford. Published by Hendersons, London, 1931. 2nd Series: Nos. 11 and 12 (Nov.–Dec. 1931) *Lauro de Bosis.* Nos. 9 and 10 (May 1931) *The Case of Vinciguerra and Rendi.*

James, Henry, edited by Leon Edel. *The Complete Plays of Henry James.* J. B. Lippincott & Co., New York, 1949. Contains the monologue written in 1913 for Ruth Draper, an account of the circumstances, and quotes H. J.'s letter to R.D.

Lugné-Poe, Aurélién-François. *Dernière Pirouette.* Editions Sagittaire, Paris, 1946. Tells of R.D.'s first visit to the Théâtre de l'Œuvre and of her acting there.

Nitti, Francesco Fausto. *Escape.* G. P. Putnam's Sons, New York, 1930. Arrests and escape of Carlo Rosselli, F. F. Nitti, and Emilio Lussu from political prison on the Isle of Lipari.

Origo, Iris. "Ruth Draper and her Company of Characters." *The Cornhill* (Magazine), No. 1014, Winter 1957/58. Published by John Murray, London. Reprinted in *The Atlantic* (Magazine), Boston, October 1958.

———. *A Few Portraits.* John Murray, London. Planned publication 1979. Contains articles on R.D., de Bosis, Salvemini, and Berenson.

Rogers, Neville. "The Art of Ruth Draper." *The Ohio Review* (Winter 1978). Personal reminiscences about R. D., and a description of her recital before Mussolini.

Rubinstein, Arthur. *My Young Years.* Alfred A. Knopf, New York, 1973. Tells of his friendship with Paul Draper and of "Edith Grove" evenings with R.D. performing.

Ruff, Loren K. *Edward Sheldon.* Boston: Twayne Publishing Co., 1978. A newly researched biography of the playwright.

Vivante, Arturo. *The French Girls of Killini.* Little, Brown, Boston, 1967. Originally published in *The New Yorker* (Magazine), v.d. Short stories by a nephew of Lauro de Bosis; some refer to L. de B. and some refer to A. V.'s internment in Canada.

Wilson, James Harrison. *The Life of Charles A. Dana.* Harper & Bros., New York, 1907.

Zabel, Morton Dauwen. *The Art of Ruth Draper.* Doubleday & Co., Inc., New York, 1960; Oxford University Press, London, 1960. Contains text of thirty-seven of R.D.'s best-known monologues, well illustrated; also memoir of R.D.

Discography

All recordings issued by Spoken Arts.

779 (H-C)—*The Art of Ruth Draper* (Volume I)
The Italian Lesson
Three Generations in a Court of Domestic Relations
The Scottish Immigrant

798 (H-C)—*The Art of Ruth Draper* (Volume II)
In a Church in Italy
An English House Party

799 (H-C)—*The Art of Ruth Draper* (Volume III)
A Southern Girl at a Dance
On a Porch in a Maine Coast Village
The Children's Party

800 (H-C)—*The Art of Ruth Draper* (Volume IV)
Three Women and Mr. Clifford

805 (H-C)—*The Art of Ruth Draper* (Volume V)
Doctor and Diets
The Actress

Ruth Draper's Monologues

An alphabetical list of the best-known monologues, showing time on stage, approximate date of first performance, the number of characters played by Ruth Draper in each sketch, as well as the number she evoked on stage with her to whom she spoke or brought into the action. An asterisk preceding the title indicates those monologues available on Spoken Arts recordings (see Discography). It should be noted that there were, over the years, superficial variations in some titles.

In these 36 monologues Ruth Draper portrayed 53 different characters and evoked a total of 310 upon the stage with her.

*The Actress   (19 min.)
1st performed: before 1920
Characters: portrayed, 1; evoked, 11.
Speaks in English, French and a simulated mid-European language, possibly Polish. Polish friends told R.D. that some of the words were "actually rude." Into the drawing-room of her apartment in a Paris hotel strides a middle-aged actress, famous, consciously theatrical in manner, gesture, and temperament. Although fatigued, she welcomes with feigned delight a succession of visitors: a rich, fat, elderly American visitor, who leaves her his car and chauffeur; a young poet at her feet, who writes for her an unsatisfactory play; her manager; her leading man (on the telephone); at the end a group of twenty. She speaks to five of these individually.

At an Art Exhibition in Boston   (15 min.)
1st performed: early 1920s
Characters: portrayed, 1; evoked, 5.
A woman from a Boston suburb with her little niece, cousin Kate, and a friend visit an exhibition of paintings. She comments on the pictures, finds likenesses to friends—prefers pictures with a story.

A Board of Managers Meeting
1st performed: before 1920
Characters: portrayed, 1; evoked, 11.
A busy New York lady arrives late for a meeting of the Board of a Day Nursery. The other members have already assembled in her drawing-room. Confusion, chatter, and arbitrary decisions. She rushes off to her children's dancing class.

A Charwoman   (5 min.)
1st performed: before 1913
Characters: portrayed, 1; evoked, 3.
A charwoman in a New York office building—early morning. In a strong Irish-American brogue she chats with another charwoman, discussing their families and working conditions. She tells of her young son who has just been killed in fighting a fire.

*A Children's Party   (20 min.)
1st performed: 1922
Characters: portrayed, 1; evoked, 18.
A young mother brings her four small children to their first real party—a Children's Christmas Party. It is a crowded, excited roomful of children and their mothers. Her constant frenzy over her children's behavior and their response alternates with a forced delight, interspersed with fleeting moments of gossip.

Christmas Eve on the Embankment at Night (4 min.)
1st performed: before 1920
Characters: portrayed, 1; evoked, 4.
A young woman of the London streets, threadbare, cold, and worn, about to go into the river, talks with two "old boozers," finds a baby under a bench; a gentleman gives her money. Exit singing, "Hark, the Herald Angels Sing."

*In a Church in Italy (30 min.)
Described: Marple letter, July 24, 1925
1st performed: 1925
Characters: portrayed, 6; evoked, 20.
A church in Italy. The characters enter and exit left and right.
    1. An English woman in hat and smock sits painting. She chats with a fellow artist.
    2. A bent old Italian crone, shawl over her head, begs of various tourists, pleading age, poverty, "cinque bambini." "Tante grazie"—is refused: "che brutta gente!"
    3. An American tourist—long grey coat, flat hat, umbrella, and a red Baedeker from which she reads aloud, compelling her friends to listen.
    4. A lovely young Italian girl eagerly rushes into the church, seeking her young man. With a black shawl over her shoulders and a lace scarf on her head, she carries a red rose with which she plays alluringly. She whispers of her love, of the difficulties of meeting, and arranges a rendezvous for the evening, crosses herself before the Madonna—the gesture ending in a blown kiss—and lightly runs off.
    5. A German tourist—tall, gaunt, with metal-framed spectacles, green loden cape, and Bavarian felt hat, cane, and many bundles on strings—guides her party to look at the Madonna. "Einmal war der Kaiser hier—und Goethe auch." They exit in search of Munchener Bier, protesting, "Macaroni, macaroni, macaroni!"
    6. A mature Italian peasant woman with a long black shawl over her head enters quietly, gazes sorrowfully at the Madonna, crosses herself, and sinks to her knees in an agony of prayer, eyes closed. Gradually her expression changes to one of peace and as she opens her hands the curtain slowly descends.

A Class in Greek Poise (12 min.)
1st performed: before 1920
Characters: portrayed, 1; evoked, 5.
A tall woman with a Mid-Western voice leads her class of four over-weight ladies toward the poise of figures on a Greek frieze.

A Cocktail Party (12 min.)
1st performed: c. 1950
Characters: portrayed, 1; evoked, 25.
A middle-aged New York society woman, smart, chatty, greets various friends as she twists and turns her way through the crowded room, constantly shifting her handbag, martini glass, and hors d'oeuvres.

In County Kerry (15 min.)
1st performed: 1920

Characters: portrayed, 1; evoked, 3.
(Based on an actual incident) An old Irish peasant woman invites two American women (R.D. and Harriet Marple) to take shelter in her cottage from a shower. She speaks of her daughters in Boston, Massachusetts, U.S.A., of her pig, a "creature bewitched," and of her son, who was killed at Gallipoli. She tells how she suddenly knew, on the day of his death, that he had been killed and how, after weeks of weeping, he appeared to her as she prayed, and he said, "Give over weeping, now, Mother, or me wounds will never heal." She stands in her doorway, seeing off the Americans on their bicycles, then suddenly exits, shouting, "That pig—he's out again—the creature!"

At the Court of Philip IV
1st performed: 1921
Characters: portrayed, 1 at 3 ages; evoked, 7.
This is the only monologue in which R.D. wore a full costume (see p. 41) and the only one based on a historical incident. The scene is a court ball at the Royal Palace in Madrid in the seventeenth century. A lady of the Court speaks with other guests in French, English, Spanish, and Italian, and dances a stately Minuet. She asks the advice of a friend: the King had come to her window the previous night and had been seen and lashed by her husband. They would now be banished. She is advised to ask Olivares, the Conde Duque, to intercede with the King. Olivares promises to do so—at his own price.

A Dalmatian Peasant in the Hall of a New York Hospital (12 min.)
1st performed: before 1920
Characters: portrayed, 1; evoked, 4.
A young Dalmatian peasant woman, only four months in the city, desperately anxious and bewildered, goes to a hospital to find her husband. She holds a newspaper clipping telling of his being hurt in a street accident. She carries a baby under her shawl and leads a four-year-old boy by the hand. She talks with another woman also waiting in the hall, and then is told her husband has been transferred to Bellevue Hospital—she leaves to find him. She speaks a broken, heavily accented English and a simulated Slavic tongue.

A Debutante at a Dance (10 min.)
1st performed: before 1913
Characters: portrayed; 1; evoked, 3.
A young debutante enters, laughing, over-eager, self-conscious, constantly twisting and playing with her handkerchief. She sits with her partner between dances; a witless, deeply serious discussion of life and society. She interrupts herself to greet two friends.

*Doctors and Diets (19 min.)
Described: letter to Marple, July 24, 1925
1st performed: Berne, August 12, 1925
Characters: portrayed, 1 at 3 ages; evoked, 7 (1 at 3 ages).
Mrs. Grimmer, with her three guests, works her way through a crowded restaurant—"the best in town"—only to find that all are on diets: "One cold boiled

turnip. One bunch of raw carrots, washed, green left on. The juice of eleven lemons, no water, no sugar. Three chocolate eclairs." They discuss diets, doctors, symptoms, and gossip.

*At an English House Party (25 min.)
1st performed: before 1920
Characters: portrayed, 4; evoked, 10.
The drawing-room of an English country house; ten weekend guests are to arrive. The hostess is tall, assured, worldly; she speaks of each expected guest, all of whom join the group but only three of whom are portrayed: Little Rhoda, her niece, 18, from a country parsonage, gentle, shy, excited, tells of events at home. "I've never been anywhere, before this." Lady Vivian, tall, supercilious, very bored, thinks only of horses and hunting. Flora, an American from Virginia, outgoing, warm, enthusiastic; each man is asked to sit next her at dinner, so he can tell her——! All leave to dress for dinner and Flora is alone with the catch of the house party—Sir John Herter—who invited himself. They have just become engaged.

A French Dressmaker (in French and accented English) (6 min.)
1st performed: before 1913
Characters: portrayed, 1; evoked, 7.
A Parisian couturière receives two American ladies, a mother and daughter, wishing to order dresses for the younger. All is hurry, tension, busyness, one voice and manner for the customers, a very different one for her assistants.

Five Imaginary Folk-Songs (12 min.)
Described: Letter to Marple, September 10, 1922
1st performed: Cambridge, October 1922
Characters: portrayed, 5.
A *Slovak Lullaby*, *A Swedish Polka*, and *An Arabian Beggar's Chant* remained in the repertoire. *A Cossack Lament* and *A Corsican Love Song* were dropped after a few years. Bits of costume were put on over her basic dress, and changed on stage, each characterization a national vignette; the language was simulated and, like the tunes, entirely imaginary. At the time these songs took form, R.D. had not been in any of the countries, and was much amused in later years, when she visited them, to find how accurate her imagining and ear had been. Her Swedish was based on the English spoken by Swedish people in America.

The German Governess (8 min.)
1st performed: before 1913
Characters: portrayed, 1; evoked, 10.
Thin, elderly, worn, and frayed—with instant dripping sniffles. "Say nicely, 'Guten Morgen, Fraulein.'" (Sometimes the audience responded.) Ten children—German grammar quite beyond them. Garters are snapped, guinea-pigs in the shirt-front.

Glasses (15 min.)
Described: letter to Merica, April 16, 1945
1st performed: 1945
Characters: portrayed, 1; evoked, 7.

An elderly lady with spectacles pushed on top of her head—many pairs, continually lost and found. A friend comes to call, and five young grandchildren are in and out.

*The Italian Lesson (28 min.)
1st performed: c. 1926
Characters: portrayed, 1; evoked, 12.
Busy, energetic New York society woman, wearing a peignoir and seated on a chaise longue, is having her Italian lesson. With Signorina, she starts Dante: "Nel mezzo—del cammin—di—nostra—vita—" She never gets much further along; telephone calls, three young children, a baby in the wastebasket, a new puppy to be named Dante, dinner-party orders to the cook, a manicurist, a seamstress, and, finally, secretary and maid to pick up all the pieces—and off in several directions, scattering goodwill, good works and benevolence—and romance.

Love in the Balkans (5 min.)
1st performed: c. 1922
Characters: portrayed, 1; evoked, 1.
There is no manuscript of this drama. A woman has an altercation with her husband, who has discovered her with her lover in the forest, and stabs him. It was performed in a simulated Slavic language. There was no need for recognizable words for the meaning of the sounds was unmistakable.

A Miner's Wife (14 min.)
Described: letter to Marple, December 14, 1929
1st performed: 1929
Characters: portrayed, 1; evoked, 14.
Early morning in the kitchen of a Scottish miner's very poor cottage. The wife is struggling with Donald, her husband, and upbraids him—his money goes in drinking and wenching while his "bairns" are without shoes or enough food. She sends him off to work—"Ye needn't come back, for all I care." The children go off to school. Mrs. McTavish stops in to visit and while they are talking the siren blows at the mine, where there has been an explosion. They rush off.

Late that night at the pit-head the wives wait for news of the men trapped. Her husband is brought up—dead. She screams, "Donald—I didn't mean what I said this morning—"

Opening a Bazaar (25 min.)
Described: letter to Marple, May 25, 1929
1st performed: 1929
Characters: portrayed, 1; evoked, 27; and various groups
The lady of the Manor—perhaps titled—walks onto the terrace of her country house to greet the village people—her friends and neighbors—and to open the annual bazaar. It is a perfect English summer day for the large gathering on the lawn. She wears a very large beflowered hat, feather boa, and many pearl necklaces; she carries a lace parasol, a beaded bag, and a tortoiseshell lorgnette through which she looks and with which she gestures, points, and emphasizes. She has presence, great dignity, and a cultivated English voice, warm with benevolent concern. She reads telegrams of good wishes from the Duchess, from the dear Dean, and from her son in India. She lavishly patronizes the stalls: gilded bulrushes, fancy potholders, the fan-

ciest cakes, *all* the cream buns. She speaks with each of the six Boy Scouts, admiring their new uniforms; she urges old Mr. Drew, in his wheelchair, to use the sunlamp she sent him; she greets Buckle, for fifty years groom and coachman, who has known, taught to ride, and brought up four generations of her family. She exits for tea—often someone in the audience reminding her of the imaginary bouquet left on a chair. This is a period piece—a classic. It was said at the time that the old dear was, to many, mother, aunt, or grandmother—everyone's Lady of the Manor.

*On a Porch in a Maine Coast Village (18 min.)
1st performed: before 1913
Characters: portrayed; 1; evoked, 3.
An old "Down-East" country woman sits on her porch in the late afternoon and talks (separately) with two women friends who pass on the road. She tells of her son, her grandfather, and other relations and comments on the summer visitors. Her elderly husband is inside the house, being "poorly" with rheumatism—she speaks loudly to him occasionally.

At a Railway Station on the Western Plains (25 min.)
1st performed: Cambridge, England, November 17, 1920
Characters: portrayed, 1; evoked, 24.
The scene is the railway station of a small prairie town. It is snowing as the night-shift attendant at the waiting-room lunch counter comes to take over. She feeds the crews from the snow plow and from Number Nine, then washes and binds up Danny's injured hand. Word comes of a train wreck with many people killed and the injured being sent to this town—no hospital—only a doctor. Her fiancé, Jerry, is the engineer of the wrecked train. She alerts and organizes the whole village to provide care and shelter. The seriously injured are brought in. Jerry enters, unharmed.

Le Retour de L'Aveugle (in French) (10 min.)
1st performed: c. 1921
Characters: portrayed, 1; evoked, 4.
The time is at the end of World War I. A French woman on the terrace of her house tells her three young children that their father is coming home from the hospital, totally blind, and asks their help in keeping him a participant in their lives. He arrives and she leads him to the terrace—these first moments are tense and anguished.

The Return (22 min.)
Described: tried out at Mildred Graves' in October 1942
1st performed: probably 1943
Characters: portrayed, 2; evoked, 11.
Captain Drew, captured at Dunkirk, is about to return to England after five years as a Prisoner of War. Mrs. Drew had let their cottage to tenants while she was nursing at a London hospital. Now Mrs. Drew comes to see the cottage and consults Mrs. Hancock, the village postmistress, about cleaning up the dirt and disorder left by the tenants. Suddenly comes word that Captain Drew has been flown to England and she rushes for the London train.

To surprise the Drews, all the villagers have pitched in to clean and polish—they worked all night—and the next afternoon Mrs. Hancock supervises the finishing touches and the setting out of tea. Others arrive with jam, cake, scones, flowers. They light the fire and candles, draw the curtains, and steal quietly out the kitchen door as the Drews with their small son come in at the front.

*A Scottish Immigrant at Ellis Island (8 min.)
1st performed: before 1913
Characters: portrayed, 1; evoked, 13.
Lesley MacGregor arrives in America to marry her Sandy, who preceded her by three years and now has a farm and has sent for her. In a strong Highland accent she bids good-bye to her ship-board friends. She sees Sandy in the crowd and rushes off calling to him, "My Sandy—I'm here!"

Showing the Garden (10 min.)
1st performed: before 1920
Characters: portrayed, 1; evoked, 3.
A middle-aged, middle-class English woman takes a visitor, Mrs. Guffer, around her garden, stopping at each bed of flowers to extol and explain, although the garden "doesn't *compare* to what it was last year." Her *Glubjullas* never came up at all, the *Funnifelosis* will not bloom for a week, and the *Dampfobias* are not doing well. But she is thankful for *Punnyfunkums,* just over, and *Seccalikums* just coming up. They consult about creating a *vista*, and exit for tea.

*A Southern Girl at a Dance (9 min.)
1st performed: before 1920
Characters: portrayed, 1; evoked, 4.
A Southern girl charms three men, introduced by her hostess, and postpones her departure for home day by day as plans are suggested for further meetings. Her conversational approach is identical in each case: "I wasn't going to leave this party until I'd met *you*. . . ."

At a Telephone Switchboard (6 min.)
1st performed: Cambridge, England, October 1922
Characters: portrayed, 1; evoked, 10.
A hot summer morning in about 1920–22 at the plug-type switchboard of a public telephone office in New York City. The operator, probably from the Bronx, is cheery but obviously troubled. She continually works the plugs and switches putting through calls for the customers, but keeps up a running conversation with her colleague and, by phone, with her sister at home where her brother is seriously ill. She rushes off when he becomes worse.

Three Breakfasts (30 min.)
1st performed: before 1920
Characters: portrayed, 1 at 3 ages; evoked, 7 (1 at 3 ages).
   1. Eager young bride in a suburb—her first breakfast with her husband in their first home.
   2. Fifteen years later they breakfast in a city house; she is bored, cool—both are annoyed and ill-tempered. He is being laughed at for taking a young girl out dancing, and she has her own romance.

3. Forty years later they breakfast in their farmhouse with six grandchildren at the table. The atmosphere is mellow and warm as they remember the events of a long and happy marriage—completing the events of the two earlier scenes.

(All three breakfasts are served by "Mary.")

*Three Generations in a Court of Domestic Relations (22 min.)

1st performed: before 1920
Characters: portrayed, 3; evoked, 2.

A bent old Jewish grandmother with a brown-fringed shawl over her head tells the Judge that Rosie, her granddaughter, should not marry and go West but stay home and support her mother and grandmother. She sits down.

With the shawl dropped to her shoulders and wrapped under her paralyzed arm, Rosie's mother also protests to the Judge. She sits down.

Rosie, shawl discarded, springs from the chair—a 20-year-old New York stenographer. She tells of the prospects in the West and the old people's home she has found. Told by the Judge to bring her young man, she exits with the two elderly women.

*Three Women and Mr. Clifford (50 min.)

1st performed: 1929
Characters: portrayed, 3; evoked, 6.

This is a three-part drama in which Mr. Clifford, a successful New York businessman, is vividly present but seen through the eyes of the three women who play the major roles in his life: *Miss Nichols*, his personal secretary in his Wall Street office, who takes care of the daily events—his business and personal arrangements and gifts for his children, his wife's birthday present, Mrs. Clifford's domestic and social appointments for her day in town, and deals with the demands of his family—particularly Mrs. Clifford.

Mrs. Clifford returns in the motor with Mr. Clifford from the theatre.

Mrs. Mallory, who loves and understands him, sits on the arm of his chair.

Woven through all three sketches are the events of the two days, the children's scrapes and accomplishments—all seen from the three different points of view.

Vive la France!—1916 (in French) (15 min.)

1st performed: before 1920
Characters: portrayed, 1; evoked, 8.

In a village near Verdun, in the second year of the war, a young French peasant comes to meet her husband's regiment returning from combat. She wears a white peasant cap, black dress, and shawl and carries a small baby wrapped in another shawl. She speaks to the baby, quieting it, and speaks to neighbors, to the Curé. A group of soldiers come by—one of them tells her that her husband has been killed in a charge. She is stunned, sobs, sees the flag, and as she holds out the baby cries out: "Oh! V'là le drapeau! Vive la France! Vive la France!"

Ruth Draper makes significant references to the performance of this "sketch" in letters to Marple July 9, 1920, and to M. Draper, June 23, 1922.

Vive la France!—1940 (in French) (15 min.)

1st performed: 1941

Characters: portrayed, 1; evoked, 4.

The coast of Brittany in the Fall of 1940. A Frenchman is escaping from German-occupied France to join the Free-French forces in England. His wife, with a black shawl held tightly about her head and shoulders, comes cautiously to the beach to see him off. Her mother-in-law accompanies her. They talk of the dangers, of the clothes and other things she has packed for him. Two other men come to await the boat. Her husband bids good-bye to his mother, to her, and the boat leaves. As she warily leaves the beach the sound of R.A.F. bombers is heard overhead flying toward Germany. She waves her shawl and her arms, crying out: "Allez-y! Bonne chance, les gars! Vive la France!!"

R.D. makes interesting references to this drama in letters to A. Draper, March 16, 1946, and D. Draper, April 6, 1946.

The quiet tension in each of these dramas built to a breaking point. There were some in the audience who remained convinced that they heard the R.A.F. planes—a sound-effect. There was no sound-effect.

Occasionally R.D. performed these two dramas in tandem.

Other character sketches for which no MSS exist; most were very early—all before 1920:

Adopting a Child
An Afternoon Call
An Advanced Course—Introduction to the Study of Soul Culture
Dressing for Dinner
A Fashionable Wedding
A Jewish Tailor (the only male role—taken from an actual character)
A New York Factory Girl (1919)
A Philadelphian Visiting
A Quiet Morning in Bed (1910)
A Runabout Drive
A Seamstress (1903)

Index

Dorothy Warren, A fifth-generation New Yorker, graduated from Miss Spence's School in 1925 and grew up with many associations in Ruth Draper's world. After working in business and on various charitable projects, she has devoted her retirement to photography and biography.